THE SPANISH WELFARE STATE IN
EUROPEAN CONTEXT

To Flora and Marina
To Nicolás and Laura

Horas sibi serenas

The Spanish Welfare State in European Context

Edited by

ANA MARTA GUILLÉN
University of Oviedo, Spain

and

MARGARITA LEÓN
Universitat Autònoma de Barcelona, Spain

LONDON AND NEW YORK

First published 2011 by Ashgate Publishing

2 Park Square, Milton Park, Abingdon, Oxon OX14 4RN
711 Third Avenue, New York, NY 10017, USA

Routledge is an imprint of the Taylor & Francis Group, an informa business

First issued in paperback 2016

British Library Cataloguing in Publication Data
The Spanish welfare state in European context.
  1. Welfare state--Spain. 2. Spain--Social policy.
  3. Spain--Politics and government--1975-1982. 4. Spain--
  Politics and government--1982-
  I. Ana M. (Ana Marta) II. León, Margarita.
  361.6'1'0946-dc22

Library of Congress Cataloging-in-Publication Data
The Spanish welfare state in European context / [edited] by Ana Marta Guillén & Margarita León.
    p. cm.
  Includes bibliographical references and index.
  ISBN 978-1-4094-0293-0 (hbk.) -- ISBN 978-1-4094-0294-7 (ebook)
  1. Welfare state--Spain. 2. Spain--Social policy. 3.
Spain--Economic policy. I. Guillén, Ana M. (Ana Marta) II. León, Margarita.
  HN583.5.S65 2011
  330.946--dc23

2011017904

ISBN 13: 978-1-4094-0293-0 (hbk)
ISBN 13: 978-1-138-26815-9 (pbk)

Contents

List of Figures

List of Tables

Notes on Contributors

Ayala, Luis, Professor of Economics, Universidad Rey Juan Carlos I.

Calzada, Inés, Research Fellow 'Juan de la Cierva', Institute of Public Goods and Policies (IPP-CSIC), Spanish National Research Council.

Chuliá, Elisa, Associate Professor of Political Science, Universidad Nacional de Educación a Distancia (UNED).

Del Pino, Eloisa, Senior Research Fellow, Institute of Public Goods and Policies (IPP-CSIC), Spanish National Research Council.

Gallego, Raquel, Associate Professor, Department of Political Science and Public Law, University Autónoma of Barcelona.

Guillén, Ana M., Professor of Sociology, Universidad de Oviedo.

Ibáñez, Zyab, Freelance Researcher based in Barcelona.

Laparra, Miguel, Associate Professor of Sociology, University of Navarra.

León, Margarita, Senior Research Fellow, Institute of Government and Public Policies (IGOP), University Autónoma of Barcelona.

Molina, Oscar, QUIT, Lecturer in Sociology, University Autónoma of Barcelona.

Montagut, Teresa, Lecturer in Sociology, University of Barcelona.

Moreno, Luís, Research Professor, Institute of Public Goods and Policies (IPP) Spanish National Research Council (CSIC).

Rodríguez Cabrero, Gregorio, Professor of Applied Economics, University of Alcalá.

Salido, Olga, Señor Lecturer in Sociology, Universidad Complutense de Madrid.

Sarasa, Sebastián, Senior Lecturer in Sociology, Department of Political and Social Sciences, University Pompeu Fabra, Barcelona.

Serrano Pascual, Amparo, Senior Lecturer in the Faculty of Social Sciences, Universidad Complutense de Madrid.

Subirats, Joan, Professor of Political Science and Senior Researcher at IGOP.

Acknowledgements

We are grateful to the Spanish Ministry of Science and Innovation for the funding provided by the Subprograma de Acciones Complementarias (MICINN-09-CSO2009-07821-E).

List of Abbreviations

AACC	Autonomous Communities
AES	Social and Economic Agreement 1984
ANE	National Employment Agreement 1981
CCOO	Worker's Commissions
CEOE	Confederation of Spanish Employers
CEPYME	Spanish Confederation of Small and Medium Business
CES	Socio-economic Council
CIS	Centre for Sociological Research
CSIC	Spanish National Research Council
ECHP	European Community Household Panel
ECS	Living Conditions Survey
EMU	European Monetary Union
EPA	Spanish Labour Force Survey
EPF	Family Budget Survey
EU	European Union
FT	Full Time Employment
GDP	Gross Domestic Product
ILO	International Labour Organization
IM	Women's Rights Institute
IMEN	National Employment Institute
IMSERSO	National Institute of Migration and Social Services
INE	National Institute of Statistics
INSALUD	National Health System
INSS	National Social Security Institute
IRPF	Personal Income Tax
MITIN	Ministry of Labour and Immigration
MTAS	Ministry of Labour and Social Affairs
NAP	National Action Plan
NGOs	Non-governmental Organizations
OECD	Organisation for Economic Co-operation and Development
PGE	General State Budget
PP	People's Party
PSOE	Spanish Socialist Party
PSP	Union Priorities Proposal
PT	Part-time Employment

SAAD	System of Autonomy and Dependency Care
UCD	Union of the Democratic Centre
UGT	General Union of Workers
WLB	Work–Life Balance

Chapter 1

Introduction

Ana M. Guillén and Margarita León

This volume aims to explore, from a comparative perspective, the evolution of the Spanish welfare state since Spain's transition to democracy in 1975. The book seeks to go beyond a case study and to situate Spain within the European Union (EU) and among other south European countries. While several volumes have been published in English on the Italian and the Greek welfare states, this is the first such study of the Spanish one. Given that Spain has the fifth-largest economy in the EU, such a gap needs to be filled. To be sure, the number of experts assessing the evolution of social policy in Spain and the number of articles and book chapters published in English on the Spanish welfare state have increased steadily since the 1990s. Yet the bulk of the research results tend to be published in Spanish. We hope, therefore, that this book will encourage and help scholars to include the Spanish case in their comparative research endeavours. We also believe that it will be useful for policymakers and social and political actors who seek information on Spain.

The authors who have collaborated in this volume are all members of the recently constituted ESPAnet-Spain (Red Española de Política Social, REPS), a national network affiliated to the European Social Policy Analysis Network (ESPAnet). The creation of, and the activities developed by, REPS can be considered the catalyst of this book. The authors are all well-known researchers in Spain and internationally in their areas of expertise. ESPAnet-Spain has already celebrated two annual meetings, in 2009 and 2010. Membership has increased rapidly, to over 500 academics and representatives of the policy community at the beginning of 2011. The book has also profited from financial support provided by the Spanish Ministry of Science and Innovation (CSO2009–07821–E).

At the time of writing (early 2011), Spain has been a stable democracy for over three decades. It therefore already has a substantially long tradition of democratic reform of social policies. This, in turn, enables longitudinal analyses that identify, among various reform episodes, those that initiated long-term trajectories of reform. It also helps us to distinguish real reform achievements from shortcomings that are yet to be tackled and resolved, especially in the face of the economic crisis that began in 2008. The present volume thus appears at an interesting point in time.

Spain's welfare state was consolidated after those of most west European countries. Together with the other south European countries, Spain followed an 'atypical trajectory of change' (Gunther et al. 1995) framed fundamentally by a late (mid-1970s) transition to democracy (with the exception of Italy) and a rapid process of modernization. Spain and indeed also Italy, Portugal and Greece were seen as 'unique' in comparative social policy and welfare research to the extent that their welfare systems were, compared with the more advanced ones in western Europe, in their adolescence if not infancy (Leibfried 1993).[1] Welfare arrangements in the four south European countries were also supported by distinctive political, cultural and socio-economic traits. Labels such as the 'southern model', the 'Latin rim', or the 'Mediterranean periphery' were designed precisely to classify these countries in a different category from the three well-established welfare regime types. However, given the intense modernization and Europeanization of Spanish social policy,[2] questions arise as the extent to which the Spanish welfare system can still be considered peripheral to west European welfare states. Furthermore, as argued below, the characterization of the southern model itself is still a subject of much controversy.

A Note on the Southern Model of Welfare

Ever since the main traits of the southern model of welfare were first identified (Ferrera 1996), many southern experts on social policy have tended to accept it without discussion. Later analyses of the evolution of southern welfare states carried out by Ferrera (2000, 2007), among others, also constitute very salient and influential pieces of research. However, and contrarily, Esping-Andersen (1999) argues that the Italian and the Spanish welfare states, rather than constituting a different model, show similar traits to the conservative systems, such as Germany's, whose origin and development are in the Bismarckian tradition. The only difference is that the commitment to the male breadwinner/female carer model is both stronger and more pervasive in the south. For the Spanish case in particular, Guillén (2010) argues that the evolution of the Spanish welfare state may be explained and understood by reference to the fact that conservative regimes constitute a blend of status segmentation and familism (as defined by Esping-Andersen 1999: 81). In Spain, while intense corporatist traits were never present, the conservative-familist character has been more difficult to overcome. Weak corporatist arrangements greatly eased the paradigmatic reforms towards universalism in the health care and education domains in the 1980s and recalibration in the 1990s. In turn, the conservative-familist character has posed difficulties for major expansion of care and family policies and social assistance. Castles (1994, 1995), van Kersbergen (1995) and van Kersbergen and Manow

---

1   It should be noted, though, that Leibfried considers only social assistance policies. Also, modest safety nets have become much less modest since Leibfried published his analysis.

2   See, for example, Mangen (1996); Guillén and Matsaganis (2000); Moreno (2001); Guillén and Álvarez (2004); Rodríguez Cabrero (2004); Moreno and Palier (2005); Ferrera (2007); Guillén (2010).

(2009) defend the importance of cultural and religious traditions in the shaping of welfare states in general and of gender roles in particular. Katrougalos (1996) understands southern welfare states as less developed versions of the Bismarckian model. Hence, controversy persists.

We would like to introduce some further considerations of the southern model in this introductory chapter with the sole aim of inviting experts (from the south and any other geographical origin) to reflect on how we have collectively defined the model. Given that much more than a decade has elapsed since the 'birth' of the southern model, an assessment is overdue not just of the model itself but also of its usefulness for analysis, interpretation and explanation of what is happening in southern welfare states. The recent publication of a proposal to enlarge the southern grouping only makes the endeavour more pressing. Gal (2010) proposes to include Cyprus, Malta, Israel and Turkey in the same family of welfare states as Portugal, Spain, Italy and Greece (note that he talks about a 'family' of nations rather than a 'model').

To begin with, it seems to be necessary to cite a very long list of variables to characterize southern welfare states. Ferrera (1996) had already talked about the insider–outsider divide, the generational bias, universal health care combined with a perverse overlap of the public and private spheres of provision, soft/inefficient states and clientelism. He did not include, though, a consideration of potential differences affecting either social assistance or social care policies. Apparently, the enlargement of the southern 'family' of nations requires an even longer list of variables. For his characterization, Gal (2010: 285–9) cites lower levels of economic production, lower levels of social expenditure, a higher proportion of the population at risk of poverty, higher levels of inequality, delayed processes of industrialization and modernization, labour market rigidity and segmentation, larger shares of shadow economies, weakened structures of the unitary state, political systems prone to crisis, ineffective and politicized bureaucracies, path dependencies with lingering impacts, an absence of Protestantism, the presence of strong familism and different forms of clientelism and particularism.

This is in sharp contrast with the parsimony with which Esping-Andersen (1990) defined his three welfare regimes. The welfare regimes are each grounded on a common and lasting basic philosophy or principle, namely, a universal citizenship right of access in the social-democratic case, protection of workers and (through them) their dependants in the conservative-corporatist case, and the superiority in distribution of the market to the state in the liberal case. The fact that it is necessary to cite such a long list of variables to define the characteristics of the Mediterranean family makes one suspect its usefulness. The fact that Mediterranean countries score very differently on those variables makes one even more suspicious. The fact that no qualitative or quantitative comparative indicators of 'state weakness/softness' or of different modes of 'clientelism and particularism' have ever been developed to substantiate two of the most cited characteristics of Mediterranean welfare state makes one react against scholars who take it for granted that southern welfare states must score higher on these variables than traditional ones.

Scepticism is intensified when one examines further the list of variables cited to characterize the model and, especially, the 'extended family' of Mediterranean welfare states. In his concluding section, Gal (2010: 296) declares that 'A common modern history of late industrialization shows that authoritarian or colonial rule, and weak, ineffective states have contributed to similarities in the structuring of [Mediterranean countries'] welfare states and in their ability to achieve acceptable welfare outcomes'. However, other than levels of social expenditure, Gal fails to provide empirical evidence of the similarities in the institutional structure of the social protection systems, such as principles and levels of access, coverage and entitlements, packages of services provided, management procedures and governance issues. One also wonders how an 'acceptable welfare outcome' should be defined.

Furthermore, the list of variables seems to have been put together with the main aim of identifying all the aspects in which southern welfare states appear in a disadvantaged, negative light in comparison with other, supposedly more advanced, fully-fledged and richer, European welfare states. A model or definition of a family of nations is supposed to highlight the essence of a certain social agreement rather than to make a value judgement. The characterization of the southern family seems to invite one to think that southern welfare states have no right to decide on their own understanding of principles, but should rather become similar to the more advanced (liberal? social-democratic? continental?) ones. Finally, one can hardly deny that achievements in the expansion of social protection policies have been much larger than shortcomings during the last few decades, at least in Portugal, Spain, Italy and Greece. Temptations to resort to social-dumping or social-devaluation strategies have been absent in these countries. Hence, one wonders why it seems so important to focus only on shortcomings, while achievements tell us a story of which both southern countries and the EU should be proud of.

Our opinion is that traditional Mediterranean welfare states have undergone a rapid and deep transformation in recent decades in economic, social and political terms, including drastic path-breaking reforms. The result is a combination of principles in social protection, so that income maintenance has remained mostly occupational, health and education have been universalized, and social care services and social assistance are largely based on liberal principles. This result has been labelled a '*via media*' by Moreno (2001), a peculiar syncretic version of three principles à là Esping-Andersen. Such a transformation can hardly be assessed only in terms of 'everything is worse in the south'. Nor, in our view, is the transformation captured by the declared intention of Gal (2010) of superseding the existing definition of the Mediterranean model with a looser but more viable extended family of Mediterranean welfare states, defined in terms of religion, family and clientelism/particularism, an even more complex set of variables and overstretched and fuzzy arguments. For example, it is hard to accept, in the absence of empirical evidence, that a colonial past has the same effect as a dictatorship on the design of social policies, or that Catholic, Orthodox, Islamic and Jewish credos produce necessarily the same effect in terms of social protection institutions. Besides, it seems to be forgotten that welfare states are not built in national isolation. National cultural, historical, political and socio-economic inheritances are important, but the same can be applied to transnational interactions and interdependencies. It is our contention that Cyprus, Malta, Israel and Turkey can indeed be included in the Mediterranean family (along with other countries) but only provided that the 'family' is properly defined, that is, based on a parsimonious set of *common* and *stable* principles.

The argument defended above is of importance not only to rethinking the southern model/family of nations, but also to developing new typologies for other geographical areas. The aim of this book is not to reassess the Mediterranean model, but the state of the art in this respect should be taken into account when one reads the different chapters. Given pervasive controversy about the southern model, we have chosen to leave the contributors to this volume free to adhere to whatever understanding of it they find useful or to place Spain openly in the European context, regardless of models and families of nations. In other words, when making comparisons, this book is not necessarily grounded on an understanding of the Spanish case as representative of the southern model/family of welfare states.

Before turning to the plan of the book, we wish to remind readers that the transformation of the Spanish welfare state since the mid-1970s can only be called spectacular. At that moment in time, Spain constituted a clear example of an underdeveloped version of the Bismarckian model. Nowadays, the Spanish welfare state counts on a highly redistributive system of retirement pensions (based on low occupational segmentation), a non-contributory invalidity and retirement system and a private tier. Health care and compulsory education are of a universal social-democratic character. Also, care for dependants has recently become a universal right. However, access to social assistance remains means-tested and underdeveloped for the needs of the population, which is also the case with family protection and care policies, despite substantial efforts to expand them. Finally, the Spanish welfare state is very largely decentralized to its 17 regions or Autonomous Communities (*Comunidades Autónomas* in Spanish terms).

Plan of the Book

This volume is divided into three parts. The first part deals with broad issues and trends in the evolution of the Spanish welfare state. The second is devoted to an analysis of the interplay among levels of governance, social dialogue, the welfare mix, and public opinion and support for social policies. The third and final part deals with the assessment of key challenges for the Spanish welfare state. We have chosen to avoid arranging the analysis solely by policy sector, as is traditionally done, since such an approach is easier to find in articles and book chapters published in English. Also, research questions become more interesting when they are framed in a different and more encompassing way, not necessarily limited to the evolution of a particular policy domain.

Key to this study is the question of how different (or similar) the Spanish welfare state has become to other welfare states: that is, which features (if any) of welfare development and welfare change in Spain are distinctive? Our commitment to studying the evolution of welfare policies across time and space leads us to mainstream throughout the book the impact of the current economic downturn, to the extent, obviously, that data on the impact of the crisis are already available. After over a decade of intense and rapid economic growth, shockingly high unemployment and the collapse of real estate and construction industries are forcing a revision of the growth model. The chapters of this book comprehensively take into account the way in which the economic downturn is imposing restrictions for further developments of social policy and/or offering new opportunities for a paradigmatic shift.

The first part of this volume (which, as already noted, is devoted to the analysis of broad tendencies) comprises Chapters 2, 3 and 4. The authors explore the evolution of the welfare state in Spain from the democratic transition to the present in terms of the consolidation of social protection policies. They also pay attention to the process of Europeanization, which we believe has been a major force in shaping the direction of welfare reform in recent decades. The final chapter of this first part is devoted to gender equality. Since the transition to democracy, new legislation on gender equality has brought enormous change to established patriarchal and familistic conceptions of welfare and social participation. While still lagging behind many European countries in key indicators such as female employment and the gender pay gap, Spain now has some of the most advanced legislation regarding gender equality.

In Chapter 2, Gregorio Rodríguez Cabrero analyses the consolidation of the Spanish welfare state (1975–2010) and frames the issues tackled in the remainder of the volume. The chapter defines the institutional nature of the Spanish welfare state as a specific case among the Mediterranean countries of Europe, from the initiation of the transition to democracy in 1975 to the current economic crisis. The consolidation of the Spanish welfare state and its growing Europeanization are analysed on three levels. The chapter first looks at the historical coincidence, from 1975 onwards, of three different processes, namely, the late development of reform of social protection, the acceleration of social and economic change and the consolidation of political democracy. Such processes have resulted in the development of a set of relatively contradictory social policies: a wide universalization of services (health care and education), a selective but growing privatization of social care services, a precarious labour market and poorly articulated social assistance. The chapter then considers the most relevant present challenges for Spanish social policy, with reference to health care, pensions, social exclusion, gender equality and long-term care. The chapter finally pays special attention to the problems raised by a rapidly ageing population, the integration of immigrants, and the persistence of high rates of relative poverty despite the recent period of sustained economic growth. The devolution of powers in most areas of welfare provision, the influence of globalization and the indirect institutional imprint of the European social model (ESM) are three important factors that shape responses to these challenges.

The process of Europeanization and 'catching up' is further analysed by Luis Moreno and Amparo Serrano in Chapter 3, by focusing on employment policies. After a period of international isolation during the rule of General Franco (1939–75), Spain's full participation in the process of Europeanization brought about profound social transformation. Membership of the European Economic Community (later the European Union) also brought increasing incentives for Spain to achieve 'real' economic convergence. The process of Europeanization has had a great impact on Spain's welfare development. The chapter analyses some of the potentialities and limitations of the Europeanization of the social dimension promoted by the ESM, as it has related to the growth of social policymaking in Spain since the transition to democracy.

In Chapter 4, Margarita León explores the quest for gender equality. Since the inauguration of contemporary democracy in 1975, Spain has witnessed a sea change in the framing of gender equality as a political issue. After decades of gender blindness in policymaking, the presence of women in politics and the volume and depth of legislative changes as no-turning-back steps towards enacting the principle of equal opportunities have placed Spain among the European countries with the most pro-gender equality legislation. In Chapter 4 it is argued that the process of Europeanization has been key in this rapid process of transformation both formally (through the transposition of European directives) and informally (through the policy learning route of best practices). However, and despite comprehensive legal changes and positive action measures, Spain continues to score badly on key indicators of gender discrimination. On the one hand, a strongly dualistic labour market with scarce flexicurity mechanisms puts women at a disadvantaged position in terms of access to and quality of employment. On the other hand, the familistic features of the Spanish welfare state, which gives women the main responsibility for caring, have changed surprisingly little after so much 'political noise' on this issue over the years. Well-intentioned legislative innovations in the terrain of gender equality are seen as a necessary albeit not sufficient condition to achieve real equal opportunities between men and women. The future remains quite open as to the capacity of these formal policy changes to deliver their intended effects.

In the second part of this volume, attention is turned to governance issues, such as collective bargaining, levels of government, the welfare mix and public support for social policies. First, the links between social pacts and negotiated welfare and social protection reforms are studied. In a context of greater economic deregulation, social dialogue in Spain has increased levels of coordination and centralization of collective bargaining. Contrary to current trends in many European countries, however, one can detect recent examples of social policy reform legislated outside the social dialogue framework. Also in this part of the book, authors analyse the evolution of the Spanish welfare state on one very important front: decentralization and levels of government. The division of responsibilities in welfare delivery among central, regional and local governments, envisaged by the 1978 democratic Constitution and enhanced by the European principle of subsidiarity, has created new opportunities for policy experimentation but has also posed threats to territorial solidarity. The replacement of the national health system in 2002 by regional and autonomous systems of health care provision is probably the most prominent example of devolution. The new law on long-term care, the so-called *ley de dependencia*, is another good example of the difficulties of building a national system in policy areas where the central state has a very limited capacity for action.

The increasing participation of the market and the third sector in welfare provision is a common trend in the most advanced welfare states. Hence, this part of the book looks at developments in the welfare mix and the increasing visibility of non-governmental organizations in welfare delivery backed by strong public-sector funding. Finally, the second part of the book assesses public opinion and public debates regarding current expressions of the Spanish welfare state. Analysing one international data set and one national data set, the corresponding chapter gauges the evolution of public support for welfare provision since the 1990s.

In Chapter 5, Oscar Molina argues that policy consensus has played a crucial role in the development and transformation of the Spanish welfare state. Many of the reforms introduced since the transition to democracy have been preceded by negotiations among social partners and the government. Nonetheless, the patterns of negotiation as well as its impact on social policy and welfare state development have changed significantly over the decades. In the years immediately following the transition to democracy, welfare issues became subject to tripartite consensus as part of the political exchange underlying social pacts. Welfare programmes and income policy were negotiated within the same package deal, and very often social policy became the currency for achieving wage moderation. More recently, we have witnessed a change in this pattern whereby welfare issues are now negotiated separately. This is occurring precisely when in most other Continental European countries there is an increasing awareness of the need to link industrial relations to social policy in order to offset the negative effects of welfare state retrenchment.

The classic form of conceptualizing the evolution of social policies was based on two clear distinctions: first, the distinction between the public and private spheres and, second, within the public sphere, the asymmetrical distribution of political responsibilities between different levels of government, with the absolute supremacy of the nation-state. In Spain, as in other countries, both distinctions have been subject to a process of redefinition. On the one hand, there is a new dialectic between public and private regulations (market but also social, communitarian and informal) competing for the same areas of influence and configuration of social policies. Citizenship demands spaces for involvement and engagement of a new type, both in the definition of problems and policies and in the management of programmes and services. And these spaces have different configurations in each of the 17 Spanish autonomous communities. On the other hand, the quasi-monopoly of the nation-state collapses and is transformed into a complex institutional framework on multiple levels, with new territorial balances in favour, often, of supra-national or intra-national levels. Spain has been fully subject to both tendencies. In Chapter 6, Raquel Gallego and Joan Subirats analyse the current situation of regional welfare regimes in Spain, a reality that represents a multi-level, territorially organized system of governance of social policies, which operates within a framework of pluralist and interactive public, market, social and community regulations.

Just as in other European democracies, a new mode of social provision has emerged in recent decades in Spain with elements of privatization on the one hand and the increasing visibility of non-profit organizations on the other. The most significant of these changes can be seen in health and social services. In Chapter 7, Maite Montagut assesses the changes within each of these areas, which have their own logic. In the national health system, the introduction of quasi-markets – and signs of privatization as well – have been justified as promoting greater efficiency in services delivery. By contrast, in the realm of social services the welfare mix implies greater cooperation between non-profit organizations and public – often local – authorities. The chapter explores this new landscape of public–private mix in welfare provision, stressing a number of explanatory factors: the impact of EU guidelines on this issue, the effect of globalization on national policies, and cultural and social changes that allow for a greater complexity in the welfare mix.

The second part of this volume closes with Chapter 8, by Inés Calzada and Eloísa del Pino. In most Western countries, for decades, there was not the slightest doubt that any attempt at welfare state retrenchment would always be unpopular. However, in recent years a change in public attitudes has been detected over the intensity and scope of public spending on welfare. Some studies have found changes in support for public welfare when there is uncertainty about the future viability of public services – for instance, pensions. It has also been shown that public opinion may change due to perceptions of the deterioration or chronic inefficiency of public welfare services. It has also been suggested that new cleavages caused by changes in the economic, social or cultural spheres may intensify the existing social divisions – for example, unemployed citizens versus immigrants – and as a result alter the basic social consensus about who deserves social protection. Chapter 8 aims to analyse the evolution of attitudes towards the welfare state in Spain since the 1990s, and situates Spanish attitudes in the broader European context.

The third and final part of the book addresses what we consider to be the five main challenges facing the Spanish welfare state in the twenty-first century. First, the Spanish economy generated massive employment growth from the mid-1990s to the advent of the economic crisis in 2008, mainly due to a steady increase of the participation of women in the labour market. However, much of this growth has been in flexible and unprotected employment. In Spain the share of temporary contracts in total employment is the highest among EU countries. Furthermore, the country also has one of the highest proportions of unskilled service workers in Europe (Bernardi and Garrido 2008). One important challenge for the Spanish labour market is how to combine flexibility with security in employment. Hence, this part of the book examines the need to adapt social and employment policies to a rapidly changing labour market. Furthermore, it focuses on the specific features of female employment and the evolution of policies for the reconciliation of work and family life. Central and regional governments have in recent years promoted new measures and legislative initiatives in labour law and social policy to deal with the work–family conflict. These are important in terms of recognition and political visibility, although still minor in relation to the existing needs of large sections of the population (León 2007).

Another important challenge that the Spanish welfare state is currently facing is how to coordinate immigration policies with existing welfare services. In a very short period of time Spain has shifted from being country of emigration to a country of immigration. The immigrant population has increased from 1 per cent of the total population in 1999 to about 10 per cent in 2010. Although Spain had one of the lowest participation rates of foreigners in the total labour force at the beginning of the 1990s, it now has one of the highest in Europe. This has clear implications for welfare services. The rising influx of immigrants over a short period of time has put pressure on welfare services, health and education in particular, especially in geographical areas with the highest concentrations of immigrants. A much less explored aspect of immigration is the contribution of foreign workers towards welfare provision, whether formally or informally, especially in areas of care where supply does not match demand.

Finally, this third part of the book focuses on problems linked to an ageing population, which, in the context of a clear deficit in the provision of services and the aforementioned increase in female participation in the labour market, becomes an important challenge for current reforms of the welfare state architecture. Yet another crucial challenge for the Spanish welfare state is the persistent high levels of relative poverty. Rapid economic and employment growth over a decade has not been matched by a decrease in levels of social inequality. An open question that is also addressed is how the economic recession is affecting poverty and social inequality. Last but not least, the evolution and reform of the pension system are considered.

Chapter 9, by Zyab Ibáñez, opens with an overview of levels of part-time employment in Spain from a comparative perspective and in relation to other labour market indicators. The main policies and regulations affecting part-time employment are analysed, together with an assessment of the views of the main social actors – employers and employees' organizations – on part-time employment. The chapter looks at the social and institutional factors that explain low levels of part-time employment in Spain. It is argued that although the current literature on part-time employment in the Spanish labour market overwhelmingly agrees that high percentages of temporary contracts and other forms of precarious employment reduce opportunities for stable part-time employment, little attention has so far been paid to how institutionally constrained access to part-time employment actually is. These difficulties in finding good part-time jobs are more striking in the public sector, where the government's and trade unions' express concern with the promotion of normalized part-time employment could have materialized in greater incentives to make part-time employment contracts an easy and attractive option. Nevertheless, recent measures and legislative initiatives in labour law and social policy to promote work–life balance and access to part-time employment as an early retirement arrangement may mark the start of a different approach.

Increasing women's labour force participation can be considered one of the most relevant social changes of recent decades. As Olga Salido argues in Chapter 10, this general tendency has been especially marked in Spain. Although still lagging behind the European average, the female rate of employment has risen rapidly since the turn of the twenty-first century (by 50 per cent in the period 1999–2007). This has also given rise to a deep readjustment of the welfare model that characterizes Spain, where women have traditionally assumed the main responsibilities for caring tasks. In a scenario of low fertility and increasing ageing of the population, the conflict between work and family life has come to the forefront of public debate. Both regional and national levels of government have recently implemented several measures to deal with the problem, although in some cases a gender-biased orientation is maintained, which helps to reinforce more than to break the old sexual division of roles. In Spain, as in most southern welfares states, most of the traditional measures have a fiscal character (in the form of tax deductions on personal income) while social services are still underdeveloped. The peculiar territorial configuration of the country introduces an additional factor of complexity in the articulation of the final result. The chapter reviews these recent developments in work–family balance, highlighting their flaws and showing possible paths of future improvement.

As noted above, Spain has experienced an intensification of international migration flows since the mid-1990s, reaching a very relevant position as one of the main destinations within the OECD countries during the first decade of twenty-first century. In Chapter 11, Miguel Laparra argues that the emerging migratory model has important consequences for the Spanish welfare and employment regime. This model displays very specific characteristics: the intensity of (partly) irregular immigration flows (a net annual migration rate higher than 1 per cent of the population); the type of migration (more labour migration for low-qualified jobs than for family reunion or asylum) and migrants' performance in the labour market (higher employment rates than for the host society). Foreign-born workers have contributed to the substantial economic growth in the twenty-first century, including their financial support for Social Security and welfare programmes. The rapid increase of immigrants in Spain also poses an important challenge for the welfare state, since the public services, especially in education, health, social services, training and housing, need to expand and adapt. In its concluding section, this chapter tentatively addresses possible changes in this new migratory model due to the current economic climate.

The purpose of Chapter 12, by Sebastià Sarasa, is to analyse recent initiatives in the field of long-term care undertaken by the Spanish central government. Put forward as the 'fourth pillar' of the welfare state, the new law on long-term care approved by the Spanish Parliament in December 2006 was meant to put an end to a long-standing tradition of means-tested social services by offering universal eligibility criteria to those in need of long-term care. The chapter examines these recent developments, taking equity and efficiency issues into consideration. Adopting an international perspective, the study first shows how the needs of care, family burdens and formal resources are distributed in Spain among gender and social strata. Second, it reveals options that the Spanish welfare state could have chosen in order to cope with trade-offs such as the one between rationalising public expenditure and increasing women's employment, or that between equity and citizens' free choice. Such options are derived from nations representing different welfare regimes in Europe. The author also analyses some of the major problems in the implementation of the new long-term care legislation and predicts the distortion of some relevant lawmakers' principles.

In Chapter 13, Luis Ayala reviews long-term trends in public policies to combat poverty and social exclusion in Spain. Over recent decades, the path taken to confront both problems has been to reinforce means-tested benefits through a progressive widening of the safety net. This has produced an important internal and territorial differentiation of the Spanish welfare state. The point of this policy was to manage the coverage of growing social needs with a relatively limited growth of public expenditure. This chapter analyses the main characteristics and results of this model. First, the long-term changes in poverty levels and patterns are assessed with the available micro data. Second, the most relevant shifts in the design of welfare policies in Spain are reviewed. In the third section, the chapter focuses narrowly on the results of the system in terms of poverty reduction and demographic groups at risk. The final section evaluates the main challenges faced by welfare policies in Spain designed to reduce poverty and promote social inclusion.

The chapter authored by Elisa Chuliá (Chapter 14) considers the evolution and recent reforms of the pension system. Since its origins in the 1960s, the Spanish Social Security pension system has undergone a significant expansion by virtue of its maturation as well as of public policies geared towards improving coverage. All governments and political parties have been reluctant to cut contributory benefits – the major pillar of the Spanish welfare state – despite recurrent warnings by experts and international organizations of the worsening financial prospects of the pension system due to rapid population ageing and structural impediments in the labour market to job creation. The symbol of such reluctance is the Toledo Pact, a parliamentary all-party agreement on pensions approved in 1996. Originally designed to promote incremental pension reform, the Pact has functioned since its inception as an institutional brake on change, first and foremost because of the unwillingness of any party to initiate debate, to put forward reform proposals or to be publicly blamed for welfare cuts. In the context of deep economic recession and the subsequent loss of confidence of international markets and European governments in Spain's financial solvency, at the beginning of 2011 the Socialist government was driven to approve a major reform proposal postponing the retirement age to 67 and expanding the contributory period for calculating benefits. To avoid blame for this 'forced reform' the minority government of Rodríguez Zapatero did not spare efforts to obtain the backing of trade unions and employers' associations as well as of political parties.

Finally, the concluding chapter by the editors seeks to round off the contents of the book by summarizing and integrating the research included in this volume.

References

Bernardi, F. and Garrido, L. 2008. Is there a New Service Proletariat? Post-industrial Employment Growth and Social Inequality in Spain. *European Sociological Review*, 24(3), 299–313.

Castles, F.G. 1994. On Religion and Public Policy: Does Catholicism make a Difference? *European Journal of Political Research*, 25(1), 12–40.

Castles, F.G. 1995. Welfare State Development in Southern Europe, *West European Politics*, 18(2), 291–313.

Esping-Andersen, G. 1990. *The Three Worlds of Welfare Capitalism*. Cambridge: Polity Press.

Esping-Andersen, G. 1999. *Social Foundations of Postindustrial Economies*. Oxford: Oxford University Press.

Ferrera, M. 1996. The Southern Model of Welfare in Social Europe. *Journal of European Social Policy*, 6(1), 17–37.

Ferrera, M. 2000. Reconstructing the Welfare State in Southern Europe, in *Survival of the European Welfare State*, edited by S. Kuhle. London: Routledge, 167–81.

Ferrera, M. 2007. *Democratization and Social Policy in Southern Europe: From Expansion to 'Recalibration'* (rev. edn). Geneva: United Nations Research Institute for Social Development.

Gal, J. 2010. Is there an Extended Family of Mediterranean Welfare States? *Journal of European Social Policy*, 20(4), 283–300.

Guillén, A.M. 2010. Defrosting the Spanish Welfare State: The Weight of Conservative Components, in *A Long Good-bye to Bismarck: The Politics of Welfare Reforms in Continental Welfare States*, edited by B. Palier. Amsterdam: Amsterdam University Press, 183–206.

Guillén, A.M. and Alvarez, S. 2004. The EU's Impact on the Spanish Welfare State: The Role of Cognitive Europeanization. *Journal of European Social Policy*, 14(3), 285–99.

Guillén, A.M. and Matsaganis, M. 2000. Testing the 'Social Dumping' Hypothesis in Southern Europe: Welfare Policies in Greece and Spain during the Last Twenty Years. *Journal of European Social Policy*, 10(2), 120–45.

Gunther, R., Diamandouros, P.N. and Puhle, H.J. (eds) 1995. *The Politics of Democratic Consolidation: Southern Europe in Comparative Perspective*. Baltimore and London: Johns Hopkins University Press.

Katrougalos, G. 1996. The South European Welfare Model: The Greek Welfare State in Search of an Identity. *Journal of European Social Policy*, 6(1), 39–60.

Leibfried, S. 1993. Towards a European Welfare State? On Integrating Poverty Regimes into the European Community, in *New Perspectives on the Welfare State in Europe*, edited by C. Jones. London and New York: Routledge, 133–56.

León, M. 2007. Speeding Up or Holding Back? Institutional Factors in the Development of Childcare Provision in Spain. *European Societies*, 9(3), 315–37.

Mangen, S. 1996. The Europeanization of Spanish Social Policy. *Social Policy and Administration*, 30(4), 305–23.

Moreno, L. 2001. Spain, a *Via Media* of Welfare Development, in *Welfare States Under Pressure*, edited by P. Taylor-Gooby. London: Sage, 100–122.

Moreno, L. and Palier, B. 2005. The Europeanization of Welfare: Paradigm Shifts and Social Policy Reforms, in *Ideas and Welfare State Reform in Western Europe*, edited by P. Taylor-Gooby. Basingstoke: Palgrave Macmillan, 145–75.

Rodríguez Cabrero, G. 2004. *El Estado del Bienestar en España: Debates, Desarrollo y Retos*. Madrid: Fundamentos.

Van Kersbergen, K. 1995. *Social Capitalism*. London: Routledge.

Van Kersbergen, K. 2009. *Religion, Class Coalitions and Welfare States*. Cambridge: Cambridge University Press.

PART I
Evolution/Tendencies

Chapter 2

The Consolidation of the
Spanish Welfare State (1975–2010)

Gregorio Rodríguez Cabrero

Introduction

This chapter analyses the consolidation of the welfare state in Spain from 1975, when Spain's political transition to democracy began, to 2010, when the economic and financial crisis reached its peak. The main thesis is that the consolidation of the Spanish welfare state was caused by four driving forces of change: *the establishment of political democracy*, *the social-democratization* of a significant range of social policies (education and health in the 1980s), the increasing *decentralization* of social policies and, finally, the growing *Europeanization* of social policies ever since Spain acceded to the European Union (EU) on 1 January 1986.

These driving forces of institutional change have generated a peculiar welfare state that combines a number of models (Bismarckian, social democratic and social assistance). As a consequence, the social impact of the welfare state has been uneven; services and economic benefits have been expanded or universalized in parallel with high rates of relative poverty, low levels of protection, severe labour market rigidities and, recently, the emergence of certain centrifugal tensions in the management of social policies. This has taken place against a backdrop of profound institutional restructuring and social spending restraint, which have prevailed in Spain since the 1992 crisis[1] and have been reinforced by the Maastricht strategy and the growing ideological and political influence of neoliberal views of social policy.

In such a context, new social risks (Taylor-Gooby 2004; Bonoli 2005) facing Spanish society, notably an ageing population, immigration and social exclusion, are imposing strains on the welfare state, which the economic and financial crisis, together with the inexorable pressure of neoliberal ideology, appear to be leading in the direction of greater spending restraint, extended privatization of management, and higher degrees of social inequalities and territorial differences in social policy. In a nutshell, the present century has opened on a welfare state which is *expanding* into new fields of social protection (long-term care and social

---

1   The 1992 economic crisis was motivated by a strong fall of the building sector. Unemployment increased to a maximum of 24.2 per cent in 1994.

exclusion policies) at the same time as it is being *limited* by the restricted growth of social spending and the selective recourse to the market.

The Rationales of the Expansion, Consolidation and Restructuring of the Spanish Welfare State (1975–2008)

The project to modernize Spanish capitalism between 1960 and 1975 called for the functional development of a Bismarckian-type social protection system that would guarantee the reproduction of the industrial working class and enable it to participate in mass consumption. As a result, between 1963 (the year of the first Social Security Act)[2] and 1972 (when the first attempt was made to streamline and rationalize social security) a peculiar system of social security was implemented whose low level of protection and partial cover of the population not only laid the foundations of a kind of authoritarian welfare state (Rodríguez Cabrero 2004), but also, from 1977, formed the core of the democratic welfare state. In other words, the foundations of the Spanish welfare state were laid not in the political transition to democracy (1975–8) but in the capitalist modernization that took place in 1960–75, the last years of the reign of General Francisco Franco.

The development, consolidation and social and political impact of the Spanish welfare state can be explained by reference to two types of rationale (see Table 2.1). First, there is the *socio-economic* rationale: this refers to the *needs* or *interests* that the Spanish welfare state caters for, and the way the needs of capital are reconciled with those of the public (Gough 2000). In this connection the Spanish model combines three distinct logics: the Bismarckian (labour market), the social-democratic (social rights) and the liberal social assistance (control and social integration). During 1975–2010 these three logics have interacted more or less smoothly in accordance with Spain's incorporation in the global economic system, with social conflicts and demands, and with the different social policies of successive governments.

One interpretation of the complex nature of the Spanish welfare state (Guillén 2010) is that in essence it still observes the Bismarckian underlying principle (Comín Comín 1996, 2008). This would account for a good number of the labour conflicts and general strikes in Spain during the period. For its part, the social-democratic logic was predominant under the socialist governments of the 1980s and early 1990s, during which time education, health and the pension system were universalized, and personal social services began to be modernized. As for the liberal social assistance logic, it has been increasingly important since the 1990s, resulting in a complex and incomplete system of minimum income programmes (*rentas mínimas*) at both the national level (through social security) and the level of the 17 Spanish regions (*Comunidades Autónomas*). As well, the selective

---

2   The *Social Security Act* set up the grounds for the expansion and future development of the national social security system.

outsourcing of the management of social, educational and health services has been progressively extended.

The pivotal role of social security and the extension of social assistance have in practice reinforced the crucial role of employment as the key to social legitimacy and access to welfare benefits and services. This fact affects the pension system and unemployment protection (both of which are financed by social security contributions) and, to a much lesser degree, general taxation. At the same time, a consensus has emerged that citizens, *qua citizens*, enjoy the right to education, health, a social security pension and long-term care, and that these services should be financed from general taxation.

Second, the *institutional* or *political* rationale is important in so far as it conditions the particular ways in which social needs are satisfied and economic and political interests are catered for (Moreno 2009). A noteworthy aspect of this rationale is the strength of path dependency or the impact of the aforementioned combination of models, with its deep roots in the social security system. More significant are three new institutional developments that affect the way the Spanish welfare state is designed, how political decisions relating to it are made, and how it is managed. These developments are the intense process of decentralization, the growing Europeanization of social policies, and the rationalization and restructuring of the Spanish welfare state. These three processes are subject to in-depth analysis in subsequent chapters of this volume. In what follows, attention is briefly paid to how Europeanization, decentralization and processes of rationalization and restructuring have together contributed to consolidating the Spanish welfare state.

As may be seen from Table 2.1, the European dimension (Moreno and Palier 2005) has had repercussions on the consolidated universalization of essential services and, indirectly, on the development of a minimum income scheme, ways of managing and rationalizing the welfare state and, to at least the same degree, the assumption to the ideology and practice of activation and flexicurity policies (Serrano Pascual 2004). The Spanish system has made its own the European logic of an investing and active welfare state that combines a concern for social protection and social cohesion with employment activation and job flexibility – and that largely means acknowledging the need for the continuous restructuring of the welfare state.

Decentralization is the second institutional factor of relevance to any analysis of the Spanish welfare state. Since the 1980s, health, educational and social services have been extensively decentralized. Only the public pensions and unemployment systems remain centralized as parts of the social security system. This decentralization has meant bringing service delivery close to citizens as well as innovations in the design, production and management of services, which have facilitated learning and improvement. At the same time, decentralization has generated growing territorial imbalances as a result of political tensions at the national and the regional levels and differences in the resources available.

Finally, rationalization and cost containment (Navarro 2000; Álvarez and Guillén 2004) are two institutional factors exerting a growing influence on the development of the Spanish welfare state politically (as a source of social conflict), economically (through the encroachment of private interests at the heart of the welfare state), socially (through the consolidation of far-reaching universalization, albeit with a low level of protection) and, above all, ideologically (through the spread of the view that citizens must assume greater personal responsibility for individual risks in a context of growing uncertainty about the sustainability of the welfare state).

This overlapping of two rationales has produced a welfare state which historically has adopted a sort of middle way or *via media* (Sarasa and Moreno 1995; Moreno 2001; Mangen 2001) that goes beyond Esping-Andersen's seminal classification (1990) and comprises a hybrid where the tension between the demands of the labour market and those of citizens, conditioned as it is by Europeanization and neoliberal globalization, issues in a complex welfare system (Ferrera 1995; Arts and Gelissen 2002).

Stages, Institutional Processes and Social Policies in the Spanish Welfare State

In order better to explain the nature and dynamics of the rationales that form the backbone of the Spanish welfare state, this section analyses the stages in its recent history, the role of the social actors, and the most significant social policies. Table 2.2 summarizes this process of change.

Four stages may be distinguished in the development of the Spanish welfare state between 1975 and 2010: *expansion* (1975–85); *consolidation* (1986–95); *Europeanization* (1996–2005); and *recalibration* (2006–2010), a stage combining containment with expansion.

The Expansion of Social Policy Programmes, 1975–85

Most studies of Spanish social policy do not dwell on this period since they view the 1990s as the key period of social reform. In many ways, this view is ideologically freighted since it leans towards a social-democratic explanation of the development of the Spanish welfare state without taking into account other factors that had a crucial institutional impact on the evolution of social policies, whether political (the political transition), social (emerging social claims) or economic (economic crisis and industrial restructuring).

The decade 1975–85 witnessed a sharp rise in social spending on social security benefits (pensions and unemployment benefits) and a rapid widening of health cover to the point of universality. With the Moncloa Pact of 1977, the political parties gave their full support not only to political democracy but also to the enlargement of the welfare state. In fact, the three-year period between

Table 2.1 Rationales of the socio-economic and institutional development of the Spanish welfare state and their realization in social policies

Institutional rationale / Socio-economic rationale	Decentralization	Europeanization	Rationalization/cost
Bismarckian	Employment services Programmes promoting employment and training	Pension system reform: Toledo Pact of 1995, renewed in 2003 Labour market reforms of 1994, 2002 and 2010	Act 26/1985: Rationalization of Structure and Protective Action of Social Security System Act 24/1997: Consolidation and Rationalization of Social Security System Act 43/2006: Enhancement of Growth and Employment Act 40/2007: Measures concerning Social Security
Social democratic	Social service legislation in Autonomous Communities Management of education and health	Education Act 1985 General Education System Act 1990 General Health Act 1986 Non-contributory Benefits and Pensions Act 1990	RDL 3/1989: Additional measures of a social nature Act 39/2006: Promotion of Personal Autonomy and Care for Dependent Persons
Liberal social assistance	Minimum incomes Community plans for integrating non-EU immigrants	Active Insertion Income 2000 Social inclusion policies	Temporary job contracts since 1984 Private employment agencies since 1993 Growth of outsourcing in education, health system and personal social services Private pensions since 1987 Act 30/1995: Private insurance

Source: Authors' elaboration.

1976 and 1978 witnessed the greatest-ever growth in social expenditure in Spain. Moreover, the universal social rights built into the Constitution of 1978 generated expectations in this regard, as did the general economic crisis of 1979, which marked the end of the late-Francoist model of growth. Finally, the transformation of the industrial sector (shipbuilding, iron and steel, textiles) which began in 1979 and reached its peak under the socialist government of 1983–5 meant a significant rise in the social budget.

Thus it is that a Bismarckian model of the welfare state came into being and was consolidated, albeit more by chance than design.

The Consolidation of the Spanish Welfare State, 1986–95

This period of socialist governments is the high point in the expansion of a social-democratic model of a welfare state based on subjective rights to health and education, financed through taxation and based on the central idea that universal services contribute to lessening inequalities and enhancing female access to the labour market (Rodríguez Cabrero 1993).

This period was not free of tensions and conflicts, since although the aforementioned reforms of health and education were carried out, the reform and rationalization of the pension system in 1985, which extended the contributing period from eight to 15 years and altered the way pensions were calculated, paved the way for the first general strike to occur in the new democracy in 1988. As a result of the strike, spending on pensions and unemployment rose sharply, the universalization of health cover was rushed through in January 1990 (following the lead of the Basque Country, which had done the same in 1989). Moreover, the Non-contributory Pensions and Benefits Act of 1990 was passed, which universalized the pensions system[3] and a system of benefits for dependent children, particularly those suffering from a disability.

During the same period, the regions set about transforming the remaining traditional social assistance programmes into modern personal social service systems. This burgeoning of the social services and the introduction of regional minimum income schemes on the pioneering Basque model of 1989 are landmarks in the modernization and extension of the social services. Means testing and the containment of public spending continued to mark the development of social services and assistance benefits (Laparra and Aguilar 1997; Ayala 2000; Arriba and Moreno 2005). The economic crisis of 1992–4 was so acute in terms of unemployment (which reached a peak of 24 per cent in 1994) that it made necessary a big increase in social spending in order to stave off possible social conflicts. The reform of eligibility for unemployment benefits and the reduction in levels of protection led to a second general strike in 1992, followed by a third

---

3   The new system guaranteed a pension to those unable to work for reasons of disability and to those above the age of 65 without means and who had not made the minimum contributions necessary to qualify for a contributory pension.

in 1994. Once again the labour market bore the brunt of reform and labour unrest. As a result, employment became more precarious while there was a drop in the extent and level of social protection. Budgetary pressures were also felt in the pension system, which nonetheless, unlike the labour market reform, received the backing of a broad consensus in the form of the so-called Toledo Pact signed in April 1995, which consolidated a model of ongoing, agreed reform of the pension system, a model that has survived to the present.

The Europeanization of Social Policy in Spain, 1996–2005

It is too much of a simplification to state that the Europeanization of social policy in Spain began in 1996 with the new government of the conservative Popular Party, given that in the preceding years such a process had already made itself felt in the length and breadth of labour market and pensions reforms and in the development of minimum income schemes. Since 1986, the European Social Fund and programmes of regional cohesion had already been assisting Spain's economic integration in the EU.

However, this 10-year period saw the coming to maturity of the cognitive (Guillén and Álvarez 2004) and applied (Jepsen and Serrano 2005) Europeanization of economic and social policies. The effects of the Maastricht Treaty, entry into the eurozone and the Lisbon Strategy of 2000 were landmark events for Spanish social policy making, which were influenced by the importance of activation, social cohesion, and the rationalization and recalibration of the welfare state. So much was this the case that it could be said that Spain's membership of the EU set the seal on the consolidation of the Spanish welfare state within a framework that embraced universal protection and ongoing rationalization.

Between 1996 and 2007 Spain enjoyed a period of economic growth thanks to low interest rates and the building boom, the latter ushering in the massive influx of immigrant workers to occupy jobs in construction, intensive agriculture, hotels and catering, and domestic service, as well as accelerating the entry of women into the labour market to the point where slightly more than 50 per cent were in gainful employment. Until it came to a halt in 2008, it was also a period of growth in which temporary employment accounted for almost a third of all jobs, the percentage of the in-work poor rose, relative poverty rates remained stable at around 19 per cent of all households and social inequalities increased (Gimeno Ullastres 2002; Ayala, Martínez and Sastre 2006; Ayala 2008; FOESSA 2008).

During the same period social spending was restrained while levels of protection were reduced, management was increasingly rationalized and moves were gradually made towards outsourcing social services. Thus, the widespread and intensive privatization of the corporate public sector came to be reflected in the arrival of selective privatization in the public welfare services.

While it is true that social pacts between government and unions remained effective throughout the period, social conflict was by no means absent: the general strike of June 2002 was a symptom of the failure of labour market reform.

Recalibration, 2006–2010

Taken as a whole, the latest stage in the development of Spanish social policy may be regarded as one of readjustment, leading to a certain consolidation of a blend of welfare and increasing influence of the market, containment at the state level, a growing third sector (Marbán and Rodríguez Cabrero 2008) and a family-based system still under the sway of traditional patterns of looking after children, non-emancipated young people and dependent elderly persons. Like other EU welfare states (Ferrera and Rhodes 2000; Taylor-Gooby 2004), the Spanish welfare state was beset by tensions between expansion and contraction, between a protecting state and an investing state, and between protection and activation.

The Spanish welfare state is having to face simultaneously ongoing processes of rationalization and containment in the health service (private management of hospitals, cuts in pharmaceutical expenditure) and in social security (control of invalidity pensions, the battle against unemployment benefit fraud), as well as new forms of welfare state expansion into such areas as family-life balance and long-term care. Equally important in recent years has been the progressive transformation, in legislation by the regions, of social welfare services into more universal ones (Vilá 2010). Thus, the Spanish welfare state is facing a new period of recalibration of the institutions that have been built since the 1980s.

Since spring 2008, the severe impact of the economic and financial crisis in Spain has meant the growth of social spending on unemployment. This, together with measures to stimulate the economy, has increased the public budget deficit to 11.5 per cent of GDP. In the year of this writing, 2011, the intensity of the crisis has led to the implementation of measures of economic restraint that directly affect social spending and have halted the extension of social services and long-term care. At the same time, far-reaching reforms of the labour market and the public pension system are awaiting approval.

By way of summary, the Spanish welfare state may tentatively be described as a model with the following defining features. First, it is still heavily dependent (a) on social security (the Bismarckian model) to centralize and manage the needs of a markedly dual labour market with high unemployment and (b) on the management of a redistributive pension scheme. It is this situation that lies behind the bulk of the tensions and conflicts in the Spanish welfare state. To be more precise, the reforms of the labour market (Summer 2010) and the pension system (Autumn 2010) are the greatest bones of contention in Spain's social policy. Second, the Spanish welfare state has created a universal system of education and health services that are not directly linked to labour market participation, a system which is increasingly being extended to cover social services. Tax-financed, managed by the regional authorities, and accepted as legitimate by the public (Arriba, Calzada and Del Pino 2006), these services form the core of the system of social rights that ties in most closely with the social-democratic conception of the welfare state. Finally, the transformation of the traditional, fragmentary social assistance branch has entailed uneven development, since the extension of social rights in the areas of personal social services and minimum incomes has been accompanied by the growing liberalization of conditions of employment and eligibility for unemployment benefits, although the 'flexicurity' model is still a possibility only in a particular integrated and stable sector of the Spanish labour market (see Chapters 5 and 9 in this volume).

As of 2010, the Spanish welfare state may be said to have preserved its basic historical features (Adelantado 2000; Adelantado and Calderón 2005), to have become consolidated as a medium-sized mixed welfare state with social spending levels below the EU-15 mean (Muñoz del Bustillo 2000; Navarro 2005, 2007, 2009; González Temprano 2003), to enjoy widespread public opinion support and approval (Tezanos and Díaz Moreno 2006; Arriba, Calzada and Del Pino 2006), and to combine Bismarckian, social-democratic and extended social assistance rationales. In the context of neoliberal globalization and an EU under the strain of enormous competition, it is a model confronted by the underlying – sometimes open – conflict between (a) the social needs generated by the new social risks associated with an ageing population and new forms of social and labour exclusion and (b) new interest groups which call for the opening up of the welfare state to the private sector and the increased individualization of social risks.

Until recently, the development of the Spanish welfare state was the result of consensus based on social dialogue as far as social benefits and welfare services were concerned. But the Spanish welfare state was also a site of intense social and political conflict as far as reforms of the labour market and, to a lesser degree, of the pension system were concerned.

Reforms and the Social Impact of the Spanish Welfare State

As made plain above, any analysis and assessment of the reforms and impact of social policies in Spain needs to distinguish between policies of a Bismarckian nature (pensions, unemployment protection), those of a social-democratic kind (health, education, long-term care, work-family balance), and those inspired by a welfare philosophy (minimum income, inclusion programmes). As some of these policies are reviewed elsewhere in this book in more detail, here we set out merely the institutional framework, the orientation and the overall impact of some of the most notable policies in the three strands of social protection.

*Reforms in the Bismarckian Strand: The Ongoing Reform of the
Pension System and Containment/Expansion of Unemployment Benefits*

Ongoing, Agreed Reform of the Public Pension System   There can be no doubt that the most important reforms – those with the most political content, of the greatest social consequence, and the most contested – have to do with the Bismarckian strand of social protection. Since the 1980s, and just as in other EU countries (Pailer and Martin 2008), reforms have been permanent and in line with the logic

Table 2.2 Stages, development processes and impacts of the Spanish welfare state

Stages	Economic and social frame	Institutional context	Policies applied	Key social impacts
Expansion (1975–85)	Economic crisis and industrial restructuring Constitutional and social rights	Fiscal Reform Moncloa Pact 1977 1st General Strike 1985	Extension of unemployment cover Rise in spending on pensions	Improved standard of living for unemployed and pensioners with high rates of relative poverty
Consolidation (1986–95)	Economic growth and employment crisis of 1992	Membership of EU 2nd General Strike 1988 3rd General Strike 1992 4th General Strike 1994 Toledo Pact of 1995 regarding pension system	Universalization of health system and pensions Welfare benefit system Regional Minimum Income schemes	Reduction of inequality and extreme poverty rates
Europeanization (1996–2005)	Economic growth and entry into eurozone Rising immigration	Consolidation of Social Dialogue 5th General Strike 2002	Rationalization and efficiency of social spending Opening to private management Work–family balance policies 1999 Non-discrimination of Disabled Persons Act 2003	Universalization of low levels of protection Increased income inequalities Health and social service cover extended to illegal immigrants
Recalibration (2006–2010)	End of economic growth Economic and financial crisis Rising unemployment	Extension of Social Dialogue, which breaks down in 2010	Rationalization of social spending Flexible retirement Inclusion and activation policies Expansion of social protection for long-term care Effective Equality between Men and Women Act 2007	Universalization of long-term care Advances in gender equality Stagnation of relative poverty rates

Source: Authors' elaboration.

of Europeanization (financial sustainability, rationalization and the creation of mixed systems). The economic and financial crisis has thrust such reforms once more to the centre of political and ideological debate. In Spain, the reform of the public pension system has been permanent and attended by low levels of social conflict; the reform of the labour market and unemployment benefits has, by contrast, gradually led to open conflict.

In April 1995 the political parties approved the so-called Toledo Pact with a view to guaranteeing the future viability of the public pension system. This pact, a veritable model of political consensus, aims to offer long-term guarantees to that system through the following 'trickling' reforms:

- Reinforcing levels of contribution by increasing the number of contributing years, approximating rates of contribution to real salaries, and calculating pensions on the basis of a working life. The idea is to shore up the principle of capitalization within a traditional redistributive system with three main props: social assistance, contributions and privatization. In other words, financial sustainability is assured by reforms similar to those implemented in other EU pension schemes, with individual effort and capitalization at the centre of political debate.
- Reforms that separate sources of funding: levies to finance contributory levels and taxes to finance social assistance programmes and to increase the purchasing power of the lowest pensions. The pursuit of this goal through the application from 2000 of the 1997 Consolidation and Rationalization of Social Security Act has yet to be fully achieved given the inability of the state to guarantee minimum income top-ups – affecting almost 40 per cent of those in receipt of contributory pensions – through taxation.
- Encouraging private pension complements by means of collective and individual pensions plans. Now more than 20 years old, this pillar is still of negligible importance in Spain, accounting for little more than 4 per cent of GDP.

In short, the system of permanent reform has attempted at one and the same time to reconcile the financial sustainability of the pay-as-you-go system, to bolster its contributory nature and to promote private pension schemes (Ramos and Del Pino 2009) by means of institutional arrangements and in a context of a growing contributing working population between 1995 and 2007. In fact, gradual reform (Rodríguez Cabrero 2005; Arza 2009), based on social dialogue, has marked the way the management of the pension system, finding its justification in the high degree of public sensitivity towards any reform of the system and massive support for the pay-as-you-go system. But although slow, the reforms are beginning to bear fruit. For some (unions, public opinion) they have required adaptation, for others (the banking sector and insurance companies) only minimal change. The current economic and financial crisis has opened the door to a new reform in the making which, stemming from Act 40/2007 (Concerning Measures in the Field of Social

Security), has a marked orientation towards prolonging the working life and new ways of calculating pensions and the rate of replacing wages with pensions.

The renewal of the Toledo Pact in October 2003 offered a favourable assessment of its evolution, underscored its initial goals and introduced the commitment to developing a system of social protection for dependency. All these issues were the subject of debate, social agreements and legislation between 1995 and 2007.

According to current official projections, from 2021 the impact of an ageing population will force root and branch reform, a matter on which the positions of the different social actors diverge radically. Financial groups and insurance companies advocate the creation of a private system of capitalization that whittles down the public pension system to social assistance. However, everything seems to point to a more complex reform that will partially preserve the pay-as-you-go system while significantly reinforcing the principle of capitalization, prolonging the working life and decreasing rates of replacement. More particularly, the 2006 agreement between government, business organizations and unions in relation to the social security system, which became law in 2007 (Act 40/2007), gives its backing to the contributory nature of the system and aims to continue along the path of ongoing agreed reform even if there is no hard and fast agreement on the depth and rhythm of the reforms required given that the long-term interests and strategies of the social actors differ so widely.

Unemployment Benefits: Between Reform and Conflict In relation to access, contracts and unemployment benefit, the Spanish labour market has since the 1980s been a source of labour conflict and a target for reform given high unemployment rates (with rare periods of rates below 10 per cent of the active population), segmentation (30 per cent of workers with precarious contracts), and the historical difficulties surrounding the reconciliation of flexibility with social security.

Between 1980 and 2010 phases of extending protective action (1984–92; 2004–2009) have been followed by phases of severe restriction or retrenchment (1980–84; 1992–4), others of spending containment and rationalization (1994–2004) and yet others of social spending expansion (2005–2009). The overall historical trend has been one of combining social spending restraint for the unemployed – harsher eligibility requirements, reduction in duration and level of protection of contributory benefits, extension of assistance benefits to those who have exhausted their contributory benefits but have particular personal or family situations – with the progressive encouragement of activation. Incentivizing job search and raising the profile of occupational training have been part and parcel of the protection offered to the unemployed since the second half of the 1990s. In other words, passive policies have been gradually combined with active ones, thus making manifest the growing Europeanization of labour market policymaking and the exigencies of economic and financial convergence.

But taken as a whole, the explanation of the 'slow trickle' (Ramos and Del Pino 2009) of unemployment protection reform is more than a mere matter of the requirements of financial belt-tightening (1992–3) or of European activation

(2000–8). The strikes and conflicts of 1992, 1994 and 2002 were symptoms of the contradictions inherent in the labour market, with unemployment rates in times of crisis of more than 20 per cent (24 per cent in 1993: Toharia, Garrido and Muro 1994). Temporary and precarious contracts, the subordination of women and young people and a high rate of in-work poverty (Gutiérrez and Guillén 2007; European Foundation 2009) – that is to say, the increasingly dual nature of the Spanish labour market, together with the influence of neoliberalism – have brought about growing contradictions between a Bismarckian labour market and more flexible versions with or without systems of low-level social protection, as with the case of the submerged labour market (agriculture, hotel and catering, domestic service).

Up until 2009, the consolidation of Social Dialogue between government, unions and employers' organizations between 1996 and 2008 had made it possible to combine restraint in unemployment spending (in a context of economic growth) with activation policies, extending social protection to groups in precarious situations (in-and-out of work workers with permanent contracts,[4] the over-45s) and to the self-employed (from 2009), and encouraging permanent contracts; yet the rate of precariousness did not fall until the 2008 crisis decimated the ranks of workers with non-permanent contracts.

However, tension and conflict are part of the course in the history of the Spanish labour market and pension reform. Symptomatic of contradictory views and praxis regarding the labour market at both institutional and social levels, they will probably continue to exist in the wake of the breakdown of Social Dialogue over the labour market reform proposed by the government in June 2010 that ended with a call for a general strike by unions in September 2010.

Reforms of the Social Rights of Citizens: The Rationalization of the
Health System and the Expansion of Long-term Care

Social policies of a universal nature such as those regarding health and long-term care need to be analysed jointly for two reasons: on the one hand, in Spain as in other EU countries the development of long-term care has been facilitated not only by social demand, changes in the system of informal care, and the entry of career-women into the labour market, but also by the need for and the real possibility of cost rationalization and containment in the health system.

The current Spanish health system was created under the General Health Act of 1986. It provides universal cover, it is financed through general taxation and its management is decentralized. Since the act was passed, the health system has undergone profound changes (Guillén and Cabiedes 1997; Arza 2009; Moreno Fuentes 2009) such as the completion of its universalization, the transfer of responsibilities for health matters to the regional authorities, guaranteed funding

---

4   These are seasonal dependent employees mainly employed in the touristic and agricultural sectors.

against a backdrop of profound changes in social demand and public spending restraint, and progress in coordination and health-care quality.

Changes in social demand arising from, for example, the ageing of the population, the extension of health cover to non-EU migrants and the expectations of better health care quality that accompany improved standards of living have together led to strains in the public funding of the health system, which, as a result, has been subjected to constant spending restraint and management rationalization.

On the supply side, various process of change need to be highlighted such as the stagnation of public health spending at around 5.4 per cent of GDP (Navarro 2009) between 1998 and 2007, in contrast to the general trend of moderate growth in neighbouring countries. This stagnation has stimulated the growth of private spending on health, which in turn has enjoyed the backing of tax incentives. Thus, from 77 per cent of total spending on health in 1992, public health expenditure has fallen to 72 per cent in recent years (Navarro 2009). As a result, and notwithstanding the principle of universal cover, problems of efficiency have been exacerbated by that stagnation of public expenditure, excessive spending on pharmaceutical products, waiting lists, and imbalances of supply among the regions.

In this context of consolidation in terms of cover but shortcomings in accessibility and quality, recent years have seen a spate of reforms aimed at improving the system's efficiency, internal coordination and care quality, as well as guaranteeing its financial sustainability.

The Cohesion and Quality Act passed in 2003 strengthened each region's responsibility for health and guaranteed citizens equal health care by means of such reforms as the drawing up of a directory of health services and their expansion to include social care, palliative care and mental health care; the creation of the Institute of Health Information; the introduction of plans for quality and audit programmes; support for citizen participation (the Board of Social Participation);[5] and the creation of a Health Service Cohesion Fund[6] in order to ensure health-care equality across the nation. The magnitude of the act's ambition was not matched by the scale of its development – one need only mention the fact that social healthcare and long-term care benefits have not yet come into existence.

More attention has been paid to the problems associated with financial sustainability, starting with the reform of the health service finance under Act 21/2001. The financing of the health service is part of the general financing system of the regions. The health budget is recalculated on the basis of the proportion of each region's over-65 population and its degree of isolation.[7] Between 2002 and

---

5   The Board of Social Participation is made up of social actors' organizations as representatives of consumers' 'voice' but it does not exercise political decision-making power.

6   The Health Service Cohesion Fund aims mainly to decrease differences in health care services among the communities.

7   The Canary Islands and the Balearic Islands enjoy special financial privileges because of their isolation.

2004 the central government guaranteed financial self-sufficiency, while a new tax on petrol was introduced to top up regional finance. Additional finance was created in line with each region's relative income and the population covered.

The result has been mixed because, even if health cover has been expanded alongside new health services and a relative improvement of the quality of the care provided, the health system nonetheless remains hidebound by a major resource deficit. The current economic crisis together with rising social demand and the increase in the mean real cost of the care given has only accentuated the problems of sustainability. As a result the health system is now at a crossroads: financial sustainability is at the forefront of a debate that is ushering in not only greater spending restraint but also forms of rationalization, the possibility of mechanisms of copayment and, in some communities, the selective privatization of hospital network management.

As for the development of long-term care provision, this was approved in December 2006 and is a clear example of the expansion of the Spanish welfare state in response to the new social risks associated with the ageing population and new disabilities, in a context of deep changes in the traditional system of informal care (Bond and Rodríguez Cabrero 2007). It is also a way of alleviating the cost to the health system of the chronically ill and of giving an indirect boost to Spain's social services, while at the same time helping to generate employment. As well, the new law is a means of encouraging female carers to enter the labour market and to reconcile, where necessary, formal employment with informal care.

The new legislation is part of the European social model's general tendency to encourage long-term care policies (Pavolini and Ranci 2008; Rodríguez Cabrero 2009), which, in many ways alter the conventional logic of universal services in so far as universalization is combined with greater individual responsibility (through copayment of part of the cost) and family responsibility (through the recognition of time devoted to informal care, the cost of which is only partly covered by social benefits).

Three years after the start-up of the System of Autonomy and Dependency Care (*Sistema de Autonomía y Atención a la Dependencia*, or SAAD), an institutional assessment was to be conducted in 2010 designed to remedy any shortcomings. In brief, the key aspects of the assessment of the new system have to do with three issues (see Chapter 12 of this volume for a more detailed analysis). First, legislation aimed at providing services has in practice produced a system in which the majority of recipients (58 per cent according to 2010 data, IMSERSO 2010) receive cash benefits instead of services. Problems related to costs and management, the persistence of the culture of informal care, and the weak incentives for many female carers to occupy poorly qualified jobs are some of the reasons for this clear preference for cash benefits. Second, SAAD is run jointly by central government and the regional governments through the Regional Board within a framework of a system of responsibilities that requires institutional cooperation and trust if it is to function effectively. However, there are relative deficits of both prerequisites, and this has resulted in noticeably different rates of development, styles of management and results among the 17 regions, all of which have partly eroded the national cohesion essential to the new system. Third, the sustainability of the system, financed as it is through taxation, copayment and corporate contributions, has been subjected to the twofold pressure of rising costs and the impact of the crisis. Although long-term care has, since September 2009, become one of the essential services to citizens, the financial strain that its costs generate is leading to a deceleration in its application (due, in theory, to be completed in 2015) and to social spending restraint (Montserrat Codorniu 2009).

Thus, as a consequence of institutional failings and the impact of the economic and financial crisis, long-term care – a new branch of social protection – has been prematurely subjected to cost containment and rationalization.

Reform of Social Assistance: The Fragmented System of
Minimum Income Schemes

The development of minimum income schemes in the Autonomous Communities since 1989 (Laparra and Aguilar 1997), the incomplete construction of a last-resort social protection safety net (Arriba and Moreno 2005; Laparra and Eransus 2008) and Spain's involvement in the EU's national social protection and inclusion plans are all facets of a policy that nevertheless occupies a secondary position in relation to social policies as a whole. The gradual Europeanization of the minimum income system has not come to fruition as a coherent and coordinated system with enhanced protective efficacy (Ferrera 2005).

In connection with the minimum income system, three aspects need to be taken into account that have to do with its institutional structure, social nature and protective efficacy.

Institutionally, the Spanish system intervenes in two ways: through contributions to social security and through social assistance programmes, whether directly managed (contributory pensions and unemployment benefits) or jointly managed with the regions (non-contributory pensions). In addition, the regions manage their own regional minimum income schemes (*rentas mínimas de inserción*). This dual system is not only bedevilled with problems of coordination but has to date hindered the creation of an integrated system.

As a *social protection* measure, the minimum income in Spain varies in value according to the recipient's position in the labour market (Arriba and Guinea 2008). As beneficiaries move away from the labour market, so their right to protection diminishes while qualifications for access to a minimum income increase and the activation requisites are tightened.

Finally, it can be affirmed that the greater is the relation to the contributory level, the greater is the protective intensity and, more particularly, the closer it is to the minimum wage, the lower is the protective intensity: 60 per cent of the minimum wage in unemployment protection, 55 per cent in social assistance benefits and between 40 per cent and 85 per cent in regional minimum incomes (Arriba and Guinea 2008). This explains why the extension of flexicurity in Spain is difficult to implement given the limited level of protection (generally below the relative poverty line). As a result, in 2007 practically all welfare benefits were below the relative poverty threshold other than the contributory pension for severe invalidity, which benefits from a complement for informal carers. According to the Living Conditions Survey of 2008 (INE 2009) (the most recent available survey as of August 2010, its data relate to 2007), minimum incomes reproduce a hierarchy of poverty which is a clear reflection of the individual beneficiary's original position in the labour market. Noteworthy is the high degree of female uptake of welfare benefits, which demonstrates women's subordinate position in the labour market: in 2007, the percentage of women among recipients of the non-contributory unemployment subsidy was 60 per cent. If we consider all non-contributory benefits as a whole (which mainly include old-age and unemployment), women are 80 per cent of the recipients. Furthermore, almost 70 per cent of the regional minimum income schemes are women.

Briefly, Spain's minimum income system offers wide but incomplete cover, is fragmentary in accordance with position in the labour market, provides unequal levels of protection and imposes greater activation requirements at lower levels of benefit.

Conclusion: Summarizing the Social Impact of the Spanish Welfare State and its Rationales of Development

Since the 1970s Spain has witnessed the consolidation of a welfare state which is a hybrid of models: a Bismarckian system in a continual process of restructuring and adaptation to labour markets; a system of universal cover which materializes social rights that are not directly related to recipients' positions in the labour market; and a social assistance branch which has tended to expand on the employment front (with minimum income schemes) and among groups in precarious and vulnerable situations (the elderly, the disabled, non-EU migrants).

The Spanish welfare state is a system in which institutional logics – decentralization, Europeanization and rationalization – have built systems of protection that have been progressively oriented towards the activation of citizens, to the consideration of social expenditure as an investment, and to a better fit with the capitalist market in terms of provision and management. These three conditions have meant spending restraint, diminished levels of protection, the rationalization of management, and new ways of expanding social rights.

The consequence of the processes of restraint, rationalization and expansion between 1996 and 2007 was the stagnation of spending on social protection at around 20–21 per cent of GDP, while the mean cost per inhabitant in units of purchasing parity was 74 per cent and 85 per cent of the mean EU-15 and EU-27 costs respectively. This stagnation has been reflected in the persistence of relative poverty rates since 1995 (20 per cent compared with 16 per cent and 17 per cent for the EU-15 and the EU-27 respectively), while the rates are higher among groups under the age of 16 (24 per cent compared with 19 per cent for the EU-15) or over 65 (28 per cent compared with 20 per cent for the EU-15). Spain's mean spending in terms of GDP and in units of purchasing power is lower than in the EU-27 on family, accommodation or subsidized housing, old age and disability; only expenditure on unemployment is comparable. This partly explains why the system of social protection is no longer able to make effective changes to labour market conditions or to foster flexicurity mechanisms. The precarious employment of almost one-third of the working population, the low levels of benefits for dependent children, and the culture of the traditional family continue to hamper protective efficacy and gender equality within the Spanish Welfare State.

That said, protection has expanded to cover dependent and disabled persons, progress has been made in terms of equal rights, new developments have been introduced in the system of personal social services, relative improvements have been made in health, and some advance have been made in relation to minimum incomes – all of this in line with the Europeanization of social policy. But for all that, the overall trend has been one of extended cover unaccompanied by a level of protection that might reduce current rates of poverty and social and labour exclusion.

In view of all this, we may tentatively conclude that it is the Bismarckian strand that dominates the system as a whole; that is to say, what position in the labour market still counts for more than citizenship, need or exclusion. The expansion of social citizenship and the extension and coordination of welfare require new institutional and financial commitments which would appear to be anathema at a time when the requirements of a capitalist market are calling the tune, particularly so in a period of crisis like that which began in 2008. This is not to say that path dependency has prevailed in the Spanish case; quite the contrary: the intensity of change has outstripped institutional inertia in relation to the modernization of the social security system, the expansion of social rights in the fields of health, education and social services, and even the moderate reform of the welfare system. These are doubtless profound changes, but nonetheless limited because of the dual nature of the labour market and factors such as decentralization and the variability of political conditions, all of which have engendered an unbalanced and insufficient development of the Spanish Welfare State.

The ageing population, the integration of immigrants (12 per cent of the Spanish population in 2009), the new social risks associated with disability, female integration in the labour market, and changes in the structure and functions of the family require further changes to the welfare state (Esping-Andersen et al. 2002). The problem lies in uncertainty about which combination of socio-economic and institutional logics will predominate in the years to come. The economic and financial crisis that began in 2008 seems to be leading to the supremacy of some combination of Bismarckanism with rationalization and containment, as opposed to alternative combinations based on the logics of social democracy and decentralization; but that does not mean that these logics will cease to play important roles in processes of reform. But it will not be solely economic and financial factors that have the last word regarding any such combination of socio-economic and institutional rationales; political and institutional factors will also have a say. So a new path to recalibration is opening in Spain. Sometimes latent, sometimes open in the form of general strikes, conflict over social reform will be a key player, even if mediated by the Europeanization of social policy and the different forms of social policy retrenchment, containment and rationalization.

Without doubt, in the next few years the Spanish welfare state will be subject to ongoing tension between social policies of adaptation to the global market – flexible labour markets, rationalization and containment of social expenditure, selective privatization of public service management, and the strengthening of individual and family responsibility in the face of social risks – and the legitimacy of, and public support for, welfare states that are basic to the daily lives of the citizens and social integration, in the form of universal health care, long-term care, minimum income schemes, and so on. If Europeanization is an essential factor in any account of the recent development of the Spanish Welfare State, no less so are the specific political and ideological contradictions that give it its specific institutional form.

References

Adelantado, J. (ed.) 2000. *Cambios en el Estado de Bienestar*. Barcelona: Icaria.

Adelantado, J. and Calderón, E. 2005. Globalización y Estados de Bienestar: ¿respuestas semejantes a problemas parecidos? *Cuadernos de Relaciones Laborales*, 2, 15–44.

Álvarez, S. and Guillén, A. 2004. The OECD and the Reformulation of Spanish Social Policy: A Combined Search for Expansion and Rationalization, in *The OECD and European Welfare States*, edited by K. Armingeon and M. Beleyer. Cheltenham: Edward Elgar, 183–96.

Arriba, A., Calzada, I. and Del Pino, E. 2006. *Las Actitudes de los Españoles hacia el Estado de Bienestar (1985–2005)*. Madrid: CIS.

Arriba, A. and Guinea, D. 2008. Protección social, pobreza y exclusión social: el papel de los mecanismos de protección de rentas, in *VI Informe FOESSA*. Madrid: FOESSA, 325–47.

Arriba, A. and Moreno, L. 2005. Spain: Poverty, Social Exclusión and Safety Nets, in *Welfare State Reform in Southern Europe: Fighting Poverty and Social Exclusión in Italy, Spain, Portugal and Greece*, edited by M. Ferrera. Oxford: Routledge, 141–203.

Arts, W. and Gelissen, J. 2002. Three Worlds of Welfare Capitalism or More? A State-of-the-art Report. *Journal of European Social Policy*, 12(2), 137–58.

Arza, C. 2009. El sistema español de pensiones en el contexto europeo: estructura institucional, reformas e impactos sociales, in *La Situación Social de España*, edited by V. Navarro. Madrid: Biblioteca Nueva, 163–212.

Ayala, L. 2000. *Las Rentas Mínimas en la Reestructuración de los Estados de Bienestar*. Madrid: CES.

Ayala, L. 2008. *Desigualdad, Pobreza y Privación*. Madrid: FOESSA.

Ayala, L., Martínez López, R. and Sastre García, M. 2006. *Familia, Infancia y Privación Social*. Madrid: FOESSA.

Bond, J. and Rodríguez Cabrero, G. 2007. Health and Dependency in Later Life, in *Ageing and Society*, edited by J. Bond and S. Peace. London: Sage, 113–41.

Bonoli, G. 2005. The Politics of the New Social Policies: Providing Coverage Against New Social Risks in Mature Welfare. *Policy & Politics*, 33(3), 431–49.

Comín Comín, F. 1996. Las formas históricas del Estado de Bienestar: el caso español, in *Dilemas del Estado del Bienestar*. Madrid: Fundación Argentaria-Visor, 29–58.

Comín Comín, F. 2008. La protección social en la democracia (1977–2008), in *Solidaridad, Seguridad, Bienestar. Cien años de Protección Social en España*, edited by S. Castillo. Madrid: Ministerio de Trabajo e Inmigración, 161–99.

Esping-Andersen, G. 1990. *The Three Worlds of Welfare Capitalism*. Cambridge: Polity.

Esping-Andersen, G., Gallie, D., Hemerick, A. and Miles, J. 2002. *Why We Need a New Welfare State*. Oxford: Oxford University Press.

European Foundation for the Improvement of Living and Working Conditions. 2009. *Working Poor in Europe*. Dublin: European Foundation for the Improvement and Working Conditions.

Ferrera, M. 1995. Los Estados del Bienestar del Sur en la Europa Social, in *El Estado de Bienestar en la Europa del Sur*, edited by S. Sarasa and L. Moreno. Madrid: CSIC, 85–112.

Ferrera, M. (ed.) 2005. *Welfare State Reform in Southern Europe: Fighting Poverty and Social Exclusión in Italy, Spain and Greece*. London: Routledge.

Ferrera, M. and Rhodes, M. (eds) 2000. *Recasting European Welfare Status*. London: Frank Cass.

FOESSA. 2008. *VI Informe sobre exclusión y desarrollo social en España*. Madrid: FOESSA.

Gimeno Ullastres, J. 2002. Tendencias en la desigualdad de la renta, in *Clase, Estatus y Poder en las Sociedades Emergentes*, edited by J.F. Tezanos. Madrid: Editorial Sistema, 43–84.

González Temprano, A. (ed.) 2003. *La consolidación del Estado de Bienestar en España*. Madrid: CES.

Gough, I. 1979. *The Political Economy of the Welfare State*. London: Macmillan.

Gough, I. 2000. *Global Capital, Human Needs and Social Policies*. New York: Palgrave.

Guillén, A.M. 2010. Desfrosting the Spanish Welfare State: The Weight of Conservative Components, in *A Long Good Bye to Bismarck: The Politics of Welfare Reform in Continental Europe*, edited by B. Palier. Amsterdam: Amsterdam University Press, 183–206.

Guillén, A.M. and Álvarez, S. 2004. The EU's Impact on the Spanish Welfare State: Europeanization on Paper? *Journal of European Social Policy*, 14(3), 285–99.

Guillén, A.M. and Cabiedes, L. 1997. Towards a National Health Service in Spain: The Search for Equity and Efficiency. *Journal of European Social Policy*, 7(4), 319–36.

Gutiérrez, R. and Guillén, A. 2007. *Protecting the Working Poor in Spain: A Comparative Overview* (5th International Research Conference on Social Security, March).

IMSERSO. 2010. *Estadística de Dependencia*. Madrid: IMSERSO.

INE. 2009. *Encuesta de Condiciones de Vida*. Madrid: INE.

Jepsen, M. and Serrano Pascual, A. 2005. The European Social Model: An Exercise in Deconstruction. *Journal of European Social Policy*, 15(3), 231–45.

Laparra, M. and Aguilar, M. 1997. Social Exclusion and Minimum Income Programmes in Spain, in *Southern European Welfare States: Between Crisis and Reform*, edited by M. Rhodes. London: Cass, 87–114.

Laparra, M. and Pérez Eransus, B. 2008. *Exclusión Social en España*. Madrid: FOESSA.

Mangen, S.P. 2001. *Spanish Society after Franco. Regime Transition and the Welfare State*. New York: Palgrave.

Marbán, V. and Rodríguez Cabrero, G. 2008. Panoramic View of the Social Third Sector in Spain: Environment, Social Research and Challenges. *Revista Española Tercer Sector*, 9, 13–39.

Montserrat Codorniu, J. 2009. Evolución y perspectivas de la financiación del sistema para la autonomía y atención a la dependencia. *Documentación Administrativa* n° 276/277.

Moreno, L. 2001. Spain, a *Via Media* of Welfare Development, in *Welfare States under Pressure*, edited by P. Taylor-Gooby. London: Sage, 100–122.

Moreno, L. (ed.) 2009. *Reformas de las Políticas de Bienestar en España*. Madrid: Siglo XXI.

Moreno, L. and Palier, B. 2005. The Europeanization of Welfare: Paradigm Shifts and Social Policy Reforms, in *Ideas and Welfare State Reform in Western Europe*, edited by P. Taylor-Gooby. New York: Palgrave Macmillan, 145–75.

Moreno Fuentes, F.J. 2009. Del sistema sanitario de la Seguridad Social al sistema nacional de salud descentralizado, in *Reformas de las Políticas de Bienestar en España*, edited by L. Moreno. Madrid: Siglo XXI, 101–35.

Muñoz del Bustillo, R. (ed.) 2000. *El Estado de Bienestar en el Cambio de Siglo*. Madrid: Alianza.

Navarro, V. 2000. *Globalización Económica, Poder Político y Estado de Bienestar*. Barcelona: Ariel.

Navarro, V. 2005. *La situación Social en España I*. Madrid: Biblioteca Nueva.

Navarro, V. (ed.) 2007. *La situación Social de España*. Madrid: Biblioteca Nueva.

Navarro, V. (ed.) 2009. *La situación Social de España*. Madrid: Biblioteca Nueva.

Pailer, B. and Martin, C. 2008. *Reforming the Bismarckian Welfare State*. Oxford: Blackwell.

Pavolini, E. and Ranci, C. 2008. Restructuring the Welfare State: Reforms in Long-term Care in Western European Countries. *Journal of European Social Policy*, 18(3), 246–59.

Ramos, J.A. and Del Pino, E. 2009. Un análisis político del cambio en el sistema de pensiones en España, in *Reformas de las Políticas de Bienestar en España*, edited by L. Moreno. Madrid: Siglo XXI, 67–100.

Rodríguez Cabrero, G. 1993. La política social en España: 1980–1992, in *V Informe FOESSA*. Madrid: FOESSA, 1443–94.

Rodríguez Cabrero, G. 2004. *El Estado de Bienestar en España*. Madrid: Fundamentos.

Rodríguez Cabrero, G. 2005. La reforma permanente del sistema público de pensiones, in *Actores Sociales y Reformas del Bienestar*, edited by G. Rodríguez Cabrero et al. Madrid: CSIC, 27–52.

Rodríguez Cabrero, G. 2009. El desarrollo de la política social de promoción de la autonomía y atención a las personas en situación de dependencia en España (2007–2009). *Revista Gestión y Análisis de Políticas Públicas*, 2/2009, 33–57.

Sarasa, S. and Moreno, L. 1995. *El Estado de Bienestar en la Europa del Sur*. Madrid: CSIC/MAS.

Serrano Pascual, A. 2004. Activation Regimes in Europe: A Clustering Exercise, in *Reshaping Welfare States and Activation Regimes in Europe*, edited by A. Serrano Pascual and L. Magnusson. Brussels: Peter Lang, 275–316.

Taylor-Gooby, P. 2004. (ed.) *New Risks, New Welfare: The Transformation of the European Welfare State*. Oxford: Oxford University Press.

Tezanos, J.F. and Díaz Moreno, V. 2006. *Tendencias Sociales 1995–2006. Once Años de Cambios*. Madrid: Sistema.

Toharia, L., Garrido, L. and Muro, J. 1994. La evolución del empleo y el paro en España, in *V Informe FOESSA*. Madrid: FOESSA, 315–42.

Vilá, A. 2010. *Tendencias de la Nueva Legislación de los Servicios Sociales*. Madrid: EAPN.

Chapter 3
Europeanization and Spanish Welfare: The Case of Employment Policy

Luis Moreno and Amparo Serrano

Introduction

Europeanization processes are polymorphic and vary greatly from country to country. In Spain, the study of Europeanization processes is particularly important. After many decades of international isolation and ideological and economic autarchy, which led the Spanish people to believe that complete modernity was unattainable, becoming a fully fledged European country was viewed as a necessary condition for political and institutional modernization. In contemporary times, Europe has been perceived as everything that Spain was not. It was the 'point of arrival' the country needed to aim for. Europe became a 'master symbol' (Turner 1997), together with the semiotic meanings of 'civilization' and 'modernization'. This Europeanization of Spain has been a many-sided process, and the purpose of this chapter is to describe some of its dimensions, focusing mainly on employment policies designed, and eventually carried out, during recent decades. These policies have had important consequences for Spain's welfare arrangements.

Spain's model of social protection and risk institutionalization has changed considerably since the 1980s, largely as a result of the influence of economic and symbolic processes of EU integration. In this regard, as discussed in the first section below, there are two reasons why the development of social and employment policies should not be detached from the Europeanization process itself. First, Europe has been an essential benchmark as it is synonymous with 'good practices'. Second, various social and economic actors have used the appeal to Europe as a symbol of modernity and progress. Consequently, reference to Europe has been an important rhetorical resource in the hands of civil society to demand social justice or economic prosperity.

There are two sides to this Europeanization of Spain's social and employment policies, as explained in the second section. On the one hand, it involves the establishment of European entities and modes of governance, which goes hand in hand with the political production and construction of shared aims and objectives (the European social model); nevertheless, resources vary among the member states involved (Moreno and Serrano-Pascual 2009). On the other hand, it implies a process of convergence around social outcomes (employment rate, work activity, gender equality, and so on) and economic outcomes (single currency or budget austerity).

The third section in this chapter focuses on the specific case of employment policies in Spain, within the Europeanization process. Based on Surel's (2000) analytical distinction between three elements forming a paradigm of public intervention (normative principles and social beliefs concerning the nature of the problem, modes of action and mobilized instruments), we have focused on three dimensions of the Europeanization process in Spain. The first is cognitive Europeanization, or convergence at the level of the *doxa* – or conventional wisdom – about unemployment and social exclusion. A set of concepts (flexicurity, employability, activation, gender mainstreaming or active ageing, for example) disseminated by EU institutions come to form vertebrae in the political discourse (and in many cases the scientific discourse) of the national member states and structure ways of discussing and conceptualizing unemployment at the national level. Furthermore, these notions become strategic resources in the hands of civil society. In the battle of ideas and concepts characterizing the European arena (Serrano-Pascual 2009), such notions can be used to provide institutional and policy actors, social representatives and grass-roots organizations with symbolic hegemony and politic legitimacy.

A second dimension of this Europeanization process is the definition of the procedures adopted by public authorities to attain these objectives. Inspired by the new ethos of company management,[1] European institutions, rather than imposing a definition of specific objectives, set general procedures and aims in order, first, to encourage ongoing learning and, second, to incorporate the various points of view of member states and stakeholders. Such a principle of regulation has evolved into a model of multi-level governance, which accommodates diversity on the basis of procedures such as those concerning the participation of actors and organized interests. A good illustration within the so-called high-level groups ('expertocracy') is the growing interaction between the academic world (mainly economists) and the political sector (representatives of civil society, mainly political brokers and social mediators).

Third, European institutions have wielded a huge amount of influence in the dissemination of a series of indicators considered legitimate to measure the 'social performances' of employment policies. This instrument of Europeanization has encouraged the implementation of measures and comparative statistics so as to enable the Spanish people to look at themselves in the 'European mirror'. The mismatch between, for instance, the rates of social expenditure or employment in Spain and the average figures in the EU has been highlighted and, accordingly, made problematic.

---

1   Expressed as a: '… community of self-improvement dedicated to making Europe into a sort of social and economic "centre of excellence", [with] decentralization, granting spaces of autonomy, [and mutually] vigilante' (Walters and Haahr 2005: 19).

A central argument in this chapter is that Europeanization has been particularly meaningful given the Spanish historical context. It has involved incorporating objectives, indicators and procedures defined by European institutions. There has also been a tendency to look to Europe in order to legitimize or delegitimize certain policies or political proposals. In analysing Europeanization, we focus not only on the socio-cognitive influence of the concepts, methodologies and indicators disseminated by European institutions, but also on the role played by the coalitions of actors and institutions and on how social actors mobilize and instrumentalize cognitive and normative frameworks in policymaking. An important aspect of the Europeanization process that has attracted little attention relates to social actors' strategic 'use' of Europe so as to legitimize their positions and to gain a hegemonic or influential position in the policy or political debates. Reference to Europe is an important authoritative recourse to attain symbolic gains. Indeed, European institutions are provided with an often incontestable *linguistic authority*. Political battles can thus be understood as struggles for representations and classifications among actors who strive to name problems (Bourdieu 1992). There are often 'hegemonic voices' that have previously modified the frame of reference of *nameable* things. They are the result of a fragile balance of asymmetrical forces of influence and power among those actors. The recourse to Europe has consequently veered in different directions. For instance, it has justified policies of expenditure austerity after the 2008 economic crisis, and has allowed for greater participation on the part of the social partners in policymaking and equal opportunity measures.

The Process of Europeanization

Europeanization refers to the process of institutional system-building among EU member states as well as the practice of framing shared problems and assumptions, and the diffusion of procedures and policy paradigms. The unfolding of structures of governance at a supranational European level has been taking place through interactions among actors and policy networks whose operations have traditionally been confined to national arenas. As a supra-state political community the European Union is a compound of policy processes, and Europeanization implies that national, regional and local policies are to be partly shaped by considerations that go beyond the centrality of the member states. However, multi-level governance in Europe is often criticized for not being deployed in a centralized and vertical fashion.

Europeanization relates to economic, political and social domains in countries sharing a heritage and embracing egalitarian values of democracy and human rights. Nevertheless, the concept is far from precise. It is polysemic and subject to various degrees of understanding and interpretation. Europeanization is rather a dynamic idea expressed in the erosion of state sovereignty and the gradual development of common institutions in Europe (for example, the Schengen

Agreement, the Court of Justice and the euro)[2] on the one hand, and the dissemination of policy paradigms, enhancement of social learning and collective mobilization on the other.

The constitution of a United States of Europe is not the inevitable outcome of the process of Europeanization. The neo-functionalist school of thought has generally adopted the view that universal progress requires integration, which is equated with cultural assimilation and single-identity formation, along the lines of the American 'melting pot'. Often this approach is coupled with the view that 'command-and-control' policy provision is essential for securing organized solidarity and the maintenance of redistributive welfare. Pluralists envisage that European rules can be achieved and successfully accommodated only by taking into account both history and cultural diversity within the mosaic of the peoples in the Old Continent. The principles of democratic accountability and territorial subsidiarity are crucial to the idea of pluralistic Europe.

Despite the diversity of institutional forms and manifestations of the European social model, an 'umbrella' conception of it can be defined as one based upon a project of collective solidarity and as the result of contemporary patterns of social conflict and cooperation in the Old Continent. During the twentieth century the rise of the welfare state, a European 'invention', allowed provision for the basic needs of citizens through income security, health care, housing and education. There is a widespread belief that a distinct European social model provides a collective unity and identity to most EU countries, in contrast to other systems where individual re-commodification or 'social dumping' are distinctive tenets of welfare provision (in the US and South Asia, respectively). As a common strategic goal, the European social model aims at securing sustainable economic growth together with the preservation of social cohesion (Scharpf 2002; Adnett and Hardy 2005; Jepsen and Serrano-Pascual 2005; Giddens 2006; Moreno and Serrano-Pascual 2009).

In the preservation of social cohesion with social and economic policies, a variety of aspects and emphases is evident. For the European Confederation of Trade Unions, for instance, the concept of social cohesion implies an improvement in the living conditions of all citizens based upon full employment, decent jobs, equal opportunities, welfare protection, social inclusion and citizens' participation (ETUC 2005). For employers aligned with 'flexicurity', cohesion would translate into a combination of easier – and cheaper – labour redundancies, generous public benefits for the unemployed and active labour market policies (EuroActiv 2005). The Assembly of European Regions points to gender equality and the universal access to social benefits and services based on inter-territorial solidarity (AER 2005). There are also discordant voices on the plausibility of a comprehensive

---

2   Cowles, Caporaso and Risse (2001: 3) claim that Europeanization is characterized by 'the emergence and development at the European level of distinct structures of governance', that is, of political, legal, and social institutions associated with political problem solving that 'formalize interactions among the actors, and of policy networks specializing in the creation of authoritative European rules'.

model that could work well in some member states but could be dysfunctional and counterproductive in others (Munchau 2005).[3]

Arguably, the EU and its member states are facing a manageable process of adjustment, which is in need of pragmatic rather than grandiose solutions. According to this view, welfare reform should be carried out by member states on their own, as the influence of the European Union in the construction of a 'Social Europe' is considered as necessarily limited (Rhodes 2006).

There is wide agreement on the desirability of establishing 'floors' or 'safety nets' of legal rights and material resources to enable citizens to participate actively in society. This is regarded as a common primary concern of the European countries. Viewed from below, however, European social policies appear much more diverse, as a kaleidoscope of sediments and peculiarities, although sharing a common perspective on the coverage of social risks and the promotion of social citizenship (Flora 1993; Ferrera 1996; Scharpf 2002).

European welfare states are in a process of convergence concerning, among other indicators, income inequality, public expenditure and social protection expenditure (see Table 3.1). Gini coefficients and the risk of poverty have been reduced slightly, while expenditures have risen in absolute terms (Adelantado and Calderón 2006; see also Chapter 13). The politics of the so-called welfare retrenchment have in fact translated into a generalized concern for cost containment, which manifests itself in: (*a*) a hardening of the criteria of access to and eligibility for welfare entitlements in Continental Europe; (*b*) a reduction of about 10 per cent in the generous welfare benefits provided by Nordic welfare states; and (*c*) a transfer of responsibilities from the public sector to the profit-making private sector in the British welfare state (as with pensions) (Moreno and Palier 2005). In all three instances, approaches to reform have been – at least partially – path-dependent on the ideas, institutions and interests upon which the welfare states were first built and later developed (Kuhnle 2000; Pierson 2001; Taylor-Gooby 2001).[4]

---

3   Given the ongoing global economic changes, some observers maintain that the European model is unsustainable in the medium or long term, that tax levels deter not only investment but also job creation. They point out that, for instance, employees without children pay half of their salaries in payroll taxes and social security contributions in Belgium and Germany, while their counterparts in New Zealand pay little more that 20 per cent, and those in countries such as Mexico and South Korea pay even less (Shackleton 2006).

4   The various programmes of 'recasting' and 'recalibration' reflect a paramount concern for making viable the economic (fiscal) sustainability of welfare spending in EU countries (accounting for some 60 per cent of total public expenditures). Main threats to such sustainability are: (*a*) increased internationalization of national economies; (*b*) the higher relative costs of producing human services and social care ('Baumol's disease'); (*c*) the 'greying' of the population; (*d*) slower productivity growth in the private sector; (*e*) persistent unemployment and low employment rates; and (*f*) disincentive effects produced by the welfare state itself, including moral hazard (Lindbeck 2006).

Table 3.1   Social expenditure as percentage of GDP (EU-15), 1990–2005

	1990	1995	1998	2002	2005
Continental Europe	29.6	30.1	28.8	29.3	29.5
Nordic countries	28.1	32.1	30.1	28.8	28.2
Southern Europe	18.0	22.2	23.7	24.6	24.1
United Kingdom	24.3	27.7	26.8	27.6	26.8
Average EU-15	N.A.	27.7	27.1	27.4	27.8

Notes: Unweighted averages.
Continental Europe: Austria, Belgium, France, Germany, The Netherlands; **Nordic countries**: Denmark, Finland, Norway, Sweden; **Southern Europe**: Greece, Italy, Portugal, Spain.
Source: Eurostat.

In the case of Spain, critics have pointed out that economic convergence has been carried out to the detriment of social convergence (Navarro 2007). A result of this has been a late and limited institutionalization of the *Etat-providence*, as compared with the situation in other European welfare states (Rodríguez Cabrero 2008). On the other hand, societal changes in recent decades are in line with those taking place in other central European countries. In particular, developments in Spain in recent years show how the emergence of gender and family issues in the political arena generates pressure for major changes in its Mediterranean-type of welfare mix (Moreno 2004; León 2005; see also Chapters 4, 10 and 12 in this volume).

Europe: A Metaphor and a Challenge

A cruel Civil War (1936–9), which was the tragic prelude to the Second World War (1939–45), left Spain outside mainstream developments in democratic Europe until the late 1970s. The dictatorship of General Franco (1939–75) fought liberal democracy and human rights, the very pillars on which the EEC/EU was built. For many Spanish democrats, Europe was not only a metaphor of civilization and modernity but an aspiration of 'normality' beyond tawdry and despotic practices. Francoism was a case of 'exceptionalism' in one of the core historical countries of the Old Continent. In no little measure, Franco's dictatorship had built itself against a background of disdain towards Europe.

After 1975, the transition towards democracy in Spain was strongly legitimized by a widespread desire to return to mother Europe and to repudiate the anti-European sentiment of 'let them invent!'[5] Such an aspiration involved the formidable challenge of making up for the lost time. Since its accession to the EEC/EU in 1986, Spain's economic growth has accelerated in order to catch up with the main European economies (see Table 3.2). There is no evidence to support the 'social dumping' explanation for this achievement (Guillén and Matsaganis 2000). If anything, Spain offers a good example of 'leapfrogging', or a very compressed transition from pre-industrial to post-industrial socio-economic structures (Ferrera 2007). Table 3.2 illustrates the Spanish economy's catching up with the European economy generally.[6] Spain has thus passed from semi-peripheral to core status within the international economic order, and has deployed in the process a 'mixed market economy' variant of the 'coordinated mixed economy' version of contemporary capitalism (Hall and Soskice 2001).

Table 3.2   Spain's economic catch-up drive (EU-15), 1945–2008

1945	1960	1985	2008*
49.5	57.2	69.8	94.1

Note: Figures are per capita income (in PPP) as a percentage of the European mean.
* Estimate for the EU-15. The corresponding figure for EU-27 was 102.6 per cent.
Source: Moreno (2004), Eurostat.

The development of social policy in Spain can be understood only in the context of the historical background prior to the transition to democracy in 1975–8 (see Chapter 2). This peaceful, reformist democratic transition was made possible by the articulation of highly consensual politics among representatives of political parties and social partners. These accepted that the reform process had to take into account the previous institutional framework. Thus, the consolidation of Spain's welfare state had to evolve from the institutions and social protection policies developed mainly during late Francoism, which had developed a system

---

5   This sentence was expressed by the Spanish philosopher Miguel de Unamuno in a long-standing dispute with his colleague, José Ortega y Gasset, on the issue of the 'Europeanization of Spain' (or the Hispanization of Europe). European 'practicality' was to be confronted with Spanish 'spirituality'. Since then the expression has often been used to criticize the lack of scientific interest in Spain.

6   Per capita GDP in purchasing power parity (PPP) or purchasing power standards (PPS) is commonly used to compare countries' average income and economic growth. We are aware that this is a problematic indicator, but it can serve the purpose of illustrating the long-term process of Spain's economic catching up with the rest of Europe.

of social insurance along the lines of other Bismarckian contributory systems in Continental Europe.

Already in the early 1990s, Spain's welfare development appeared as a *via media* that incorporated elements of the three worlds of welfare capitalism (Moreno and Sarasa 1992). Since then, while Spain's macroeconomic policies have become more liberal, social policy-making has followed a pattern of generalization – and even universalization – of welfare entitlements and provision, and has moved away from the Bismarckian principle of income maintenance.[7] However, together with an extension of social entitlements, the protective intensity and the generosity of benefits have fallen below those of other advanced systems of social protection in Europe. Likewise, the family continues to play a major role in providing well-being and resources (for example, in housing and micro-solidarity) to a large part of the population (Moreno and Rodríguez Cabrero 2007).

Consensual party politics shaped Spain's main political developments after the death of Franco in 1975. Since the 1980s the two main governmental parties (the social-democratic PSOE, in power during 1982–96 and since 2004, and the conservative PP, in office power 1996–2004), and their parliamentary allies (mainly the Basque, Catalan, Galician, Canarian nationalists and, intermittingly, the ex-Communist United Left), have come together and have articulated patterns of *diálogo social* (a corporatist type of social dialogue), along with the Employers' Confederation (CEOE) and the main trade unions (UGT and CCOO) (see Chapter 5). This general climate of consensus has been highly effective in legitimizing the process of welfare-state development since Franco. Europe has continued to be viewed as an embodiment of all of that Spain was not during the dictatorship. As a 'master symbol' (Turner 1997), Europe has been regarded by most of Spain's social actors as the realization of 'civilization' and 'modernization'. Europe has frequently been invoked so that symbolic rewards could be obtained without major contestation.

The EU's Input into Spanish Welfare

In recent decades, the EU's national economic policies have abandoned the view that the Keynesian welfare state was set to to implement social policies that favoured growth and internal demand. The new economic paradigm, along the lines of a Schumpetarian workfare state, which proclaims market freedom as essential to economic success, is aimed at strengthening the competitiveness of national economies and subordinating welfare policy to the demands of flexibility (Jessop 1994). Most governments defended these changes and policy reforms as necessary to meet the criteria set down in the 1992 Maastricht Treaty for national

---

7   This shift is manifest in a less actuarial-based pension system and in the gradual completion of a 'safety net' of non-contributory schemes of income support (Arriba and Moreno 2005; Sarasa 2007).

membership of the European Monetary Union. In this way, EU political, social and economic dynamics became a part of domestic political discourse and public policies in the field of the welfare state, making it evident that the process of welfare state reform was, at least partially, Europeanized (Scharpf 1996).

All things considered, the role of the EU in inducing changes in social policy has grown very significantly. It has functioned alongside the ambivalent process of the diminishing sovereignty of the EU's member states in both *de jure* (legal authority) and *de facto* (sovereign capacity) terms. Such a decline of state sovereignty runs in parallel with the requirements imposed by the Court of Justice and the European Commission for the consolidation of EU's 'open' internal market and the so-called four freedoms (the free movement of capital, goods, services and workers). As a consequence, national social policies have become increasingly embedded in a framework of 'hard' and 'soft' EU dispositions. Arguably, the European welfare states have been transformed into *semi*-sovereign entities with a pro-market bias and are increasingly shaped by the rulings of the European Court (Leibfried and Pierson 1995; Pierson 1996).

Indeed, the impact of Europeanization on the Spanish welfare system has been deep and intense.[8] This chapter focuses on the area of employment and labour policies. As a quasi-Bismarckian country, Spain's social provision is closely linked to the labour status of claimants and beneficiaries. At the European level most EU nationals have traditionally been treated more as workers and less as citizens entitled to social rights (Moreno and Palier 2005). In recent decades, policies aimed at coordinating employment and social policies at the European level – by means of the Open Method of Co-ordination – have attempted to offer perspectives for reconciling the dichotomies between economic and social issues. We feel that this is a key area of observation to assess the impact of Europeanization on the general orientation of social protection in Spain.

For the purposes of our analyses, three main dimensions of the process of Europeanization should be identified: (*a*) the power to disseminate a *doxa*, or common belief, structured in terms of a set of concepts (flexicurity, employability, activation, gender mainstreaming or active ageing, to name a few), which come to form vertebrae in the political discourse and in many cases the scientific discourse of the national member states; (*b*) techniques of policy implementation, which have inspired the procedures adopted by member state governments in order to achieve the aforementioned aims; and (*c*) the establishment of indicators by reference to which governmental intervention is assessed and justified.

In analysing the orientation of public policies, the role played by actors' networks and advocacy coalitions can be singled out as paramount (Jobert and Muller 1987; Sabatier 1998; Surel 2000). Indeed, a key element in actors'

---

8   Additional instruments of Europeanization, such as the Open Method of Co-ordination and 'hard' legislation of directives and the Structural and Cohesion Funds, have already been examined by the authors (Moreno and Serrano Pascual 2007). They should be approached from a different analytical perspective.

strategies has been the utilization of the 'master symbol' of Europe to legitimize their interests and frames. With the acceptance of EU's 'linguistic authority', political actors have waged the battle of ideas in order to conceptualize problems and to make their representations on the issues of debate prevail. As a result, the concepts that the European institutions have greatly contributed to 'name and frame' (Lakoff 2007) are to be regarded as strategic resources that the actors can use to shape the political agenda.

Normative Frames

The incorporation of key concepts and proposals of the EU's institutions (such as that of activation) into Spain's political debate has turned a system of beliefs into assumptions, such as: (*a*) the alleged disincentive effect of 'passive' social protection policies, and (*b*) the proposals that the unemployed should become 'active' in order to avoid social exclusion. A certain epistemological consensus has emerged among academics and policymakers. As in other EU member states, the fight against unemployment was to be replaced by a fight against the low employment rates (Salais 2006). The trend in Spain to take on board the tenets of activation (individualization, employment-centred schemes, or contractual insertion) was reinforced in the employment reform of 2002 (Law 45/2002). With the transformation of the political concept of security, unemployment protection was conceived more in line with employees' own self-insurance and responsibility. Accordingly, the emphasis on activation as a 'solution' to the problem of unemployment superseded the effectiveness of the 'traditional' programmes of unemployment protection.

The Spanish Employment Law of 2003 (56/2003) put forward a new vision of 'employability' linked to the promotion of individual opportunities to '... articulate itineraries of personalized service to job seekers'. With the internalization of these normative views, the new interpretative framework aimed at establishing a linear causality between unemployment and tax revenue, the unemployment rate and economic growth, and unemployment benefits and the activity rate.

Although EU institutions did not *sensu stricto* invent terms such as 'activation' or 'employability', they have been very effective in promoting them and are responsible for coining them in the public debate on the strategies of intervention to fight unemployment (Moreno and Serrano Pascual 2007; Serrano Pascual 2007). In any case, this cognitive Europeanization is far from being a simple and unilateral process by which problems and interventions are to be deployed vertically. As in other areas of public policy-making and provision, the selection of the 'problems' requiring political action is the result of a process articulated ideologically by several social actors (Salais, Baverez and Reynaud 1986; Muller 1990; Topalov 1994; Jorgensen 2002).

The capacity of EU institutions to respond to the voice and influence of certain actors is another important, though often neglected, area of analysis. Some researchers call into question the real impact of the European Employment

Strategy (EES) because the new orientations have reinforced long-term traditions such as labour activation in the cases of Anglo-Saxon and Nordic member states (Jacobsson 2004). However, this strategy has also had an impact on countries traditionally 'alien' to these policy proposals and with different historical traditions, such as Spain. A brief analysis of the debate on labour activation and flexibility in Spain after the transition is highly illustrative in this discussion.

Since the 1980s both PSOE and PP governments have made appeals to EU guidelines in order to propose labour reforms in tune with the economic situation in Europe (Serrano et al. 2010). They have often used the 'blame-avoidance' device of regarding the high unemployment rates as a result of the 'rigidity' of Spanish employment legislation. The Spanish trade unions have with considerable success mobilized citizens against this metonymical appropriation of the concept of 'labour market' by its juridical regulation (in the general strikes of 1984, 1988, 1992, 1994 and 2002).

In 1984 labour standards favouring fixed-term employment were implemented. The government claimed that the 'modernizing' European context required '... more flexible and realistic criteria ... to bring the Spanish situation into line with that of other Western economies ...' (Law 32/1984). As a result, the 'fine-tuning' of Spain's labour legislation to the patterns of other EU member states was considered the key reform in overcoming endogenous difficulties (see Chapter 9).

With the economic crisis of the early 1990s, a renewed controversy broke out over the need to reform Spanish employment legislation, focusing on the fulfilment of the Maastricht criteria for the single European market. The emphasis was again placed on the 'excessive' regulation of the Spanish labour market in comparison with European standards. At the end of the 1990s, the OECD strongly advised Spain to cut employment benefits and to favour a 'make-work-pay' strategy to encourage the unemployed to seek and accept job offers (Espina 2007). EU institutions – in particular General Directorate II in charge of economic and financial affairs – continued to insist on making recommendations about 'activation' and 'motivation' of the unemployed with the publication of the White Paper on Growth, Competitiveness and Employment (European Commission 1993).

The labour reform of 2002 coincided with a new drive from EU institutions to encourage member states to comply with the promotion of active labour market policies, the propagation of an entrepreneurial spirit, the flexibilization of labour relations, and adaptation to new scenarios in the global economic order (see Chapter 4). Not surprisingly, the introductory statement of the Spanish Employment Law (56/2003) reads: '... globalization and the process of European integration [with] the coordination of EU policies make it imperative to Spain ...' Thus, the European Union appeared to champion and lead these changes, whereas the member states were happy to accept a secondary role and to intensify their 'blame avoidance' devices (Guillén and Álvarez 2004).

These examples show how 'Europe' has acted as an undisputed moral authority in Spain's path to modernization. In those areas where there was already a broad cross-sectional consensus among the actors, the EES reinforced the new policy proposals, despite the lack of a tradition of labour activation in Spain. Acting as 'master symbol', Europe, as the European Union, has strived since the 1980s with a high degree of legitimacy to shape Spain's political agenda. It has fully exercised its authority in a country with a recent history of despotic and anti-European ideas embodied in Francoism.

Resources: Procedures and Rules

The EU's regulatory capabilities go beyond the harmonization of ideas, representations and political aims (López Santana 2006; Palier 2006). European institutions have also been very influential in the procedures that realize such notions and proposals. The mode of European governance based upon decentralization and the involvement of stakeholders in policy elaboration and design has had a considerable impact on Spain's 'State of Autonomies'.[9]

One instance of the influence of Europeanization on member states' policy-making has been the increasing participation of epistemological communities (academics, scholars and think tanks) or 'high-level' groups made up of social scientists – primarily economists – advising EU entities of various types.[10] Spain has followed the same pattern. The symbolic efficacy of the language diffused by European institutions is firmly based on the self-referential appeal to the 'expertocracy' and the scientific community as the main producers of ideas and political constructs that are of an 'exclusively' technical nature and, consequently, apparently 'neutral' (Serrano Pascual 2009).

Such epistemological communities can also perform a role as 'policy brokers'. They can act as privileged mediators in the production and diffusion of cognitive and normative frames (Muller 1990; Surel 2000). With the increasing sophistication and complex articulation of the instruments of public action, the codes of access to the process of policy elaboration and decision-making are 'validated', not infrequently, by the assent of scientists and experts.

Illustrating the growing role played by think tanks in Spain was the confrontation in the spring of 2009 between economists analysing the effect of the economic crisis on the Spanish labour market. An economists' group (the G-100) claimed that the introduction of 'flexibilization' measures was a necessary reform in Spain's labour relations.[11] Claims made by this informal network of economists

---

9   Spain can be regarded as a 'federation in disguise' composed of 17 regional *Comunidades Autonomas* (Autonomous Communities), and with a high degree of self-rule as compared with other nominally 'federal' countries (Moreno 2001).

10   In November 2004, for instance, the High Level Group chaired by former Dutch Prime Minister Wim Kok issued the High Level Group report (2004).

11   This proposal was put forward by a group of economics researchers affiliated to various universities. It was first signed by 100 economists from various Spanish and foreign universities and research centres, and presented in April 2009. In spring and summer 2010

were widely amplified by large sections of Spain's media favourable to both flexibility in and deregulation of the labour market in Spain. An alternative forum of 700 experts in labour relations (mainly, economists, lawyers and sociologists) offered a distinct view. Their representations and prescriptions presented a symbolic matrix that referred to earlier debates on the alleged 'regulatory disease'. The G-100 insisted that the main evidence for their views emerged from comparing Spain's unemployment rate with that of the eurozone as a whole. As the authority of such analyses is usually based upon the unquestioned legitimacy of 'rational and apolitical science', the debates between these networks were centred on the very definition of and monopoly claims to 'scientificity' and, thus, the appropriation of the associated prestige and credibility.[12]

The standard institutional rituals (international credentials, number of articles published in Anglo-Saxon indexed journals, citations, or academic positions) set the tone and the level of competence of the participants in these 'battles of ideas', providing them with 'indisputable' scientific authority. As a consequence, it often happens that the debate is not on a confrontation of ideas but on the scientific legitimacy of the contenders. At the time of writing these lines, the G-100 continues to put forward their diagnostics and presses ahead on a way of changing the Spanish socio-economic model.

Indicators: Benchmarking and Policy Priorities

A third dimension of the European process refers to the adoption of indicators and monitoring methodologies put forward by the EU's institutions. One of the key procedures of EU regulation is 'benchmarking', or the identification of a group of indicators for measuring the *outcomes* and performance of public policy provision. The diachronic (over time) and synchronic (between countries) statistical comparison of benchmarking indicators has been an important instrument of social standardization. Certainly, the utilization of 'objective' indicators cannot be regarded as a neutral and technical exercise because it incorporates political elements.[13] Such an exercise has allowed the diffusion of new statistical categories

---

it was widely publicized by the media, which dubbed it the 'Manifesto of the 100'. The 100 have continued to play a significant role in influencing public opinion after the recent political debate on labour reform, with the ongoing appearance in the press of public declarations by this group (see *Manifiesto G-100: Propuesta para la reactivación laboral en España*, http://www.crisis09.es/propuesta/).

12   In what was labelled the 'economists' war' by the press, the group of 100 prepared a study in which they defended the intellectual authority of the opinions they expressed by reference to their academic credentials. They referred to the number of their articles published in scientific journals collected by the Institute for Scientific Information (ISI), and to the number of citations in these same journals, all of them on social science (Social Science Citation Index, SSCI), to prestigious and well-known awards, to their international influence as a result of articles published by foreign scientific journals, and so forth.

13   For a review of the EU's 'normalization' on policy indicators, see Salais (2006).

– for instance, regarding employment rates – that set alternative classification rationales to previous data – for example, on unemployment rates. The purpose is to compare the results achieved by all the member states and to encourage a common approach to problems. However, statistical indicators often reduce a multiplicity of dimensions into a single one that over determines the scope for action.

In fact, indicators not only are an instrument of technical monitoring of the evolution of unemployment, but may contribute to producing it by giving a representation of what unemployment is about. Labour market and unemployment statistics often construct the social phenomena they measure. Harmonized statistical categories induce the exposure of certain problems by providing public agencies, such as Eurostat, with data. This statistical office of the European Union has enormously increased its influence and political ascendancy in recent decades.

If a concept such as 'activation' generates an ample semantic field that induces a vision of unemployment, a statistical category generally implies an analytical and political materialization of the problem (Gómez 2005). The use of charts and comparative tables and figures shapes both cognitive 'ways and means' and political (de)mobilization. Accordingly, the incorporation of a certain set of indicators, such as female or old-age employment rates, make it possible to 'make visible' representations of problems which could have remained low down on the political agenda. As a consequence, the apparently technical exercise of measuring and comparing labour market trends may become an incentive for member states to be aware of their weaknesses and to learn how to 'problematize' and how to 'problematize' them in the public discourse. In this line of argument, the unemployment category which has traditionally been a central focus of public and governmental action has lost its relevance vis-à-vis the employment category. It has also favoured an individualized approach to tackle 'activation'. Activity and employment rates have become the main indicators of the member states' labour 'health'.[14]

Benchmarking has contributed to the production of a European interpretive framework for social and labour policies. Three main changes can be identified as resulting from such statistical monitoring in Spain: (*a*) the substitution of the unemployment rate by activity and employment rates as the crucial variable for the analysis of labour markets; (*b*) the incorporation of a gender perspective in the statistical indicators, which has facilitated the 'deconstruction' of previous political assumptions; and (*c*) the use of cross-variable statistics on binary comparisons. In debates on social exclusion and unemployment attempts have been made to establish linear causal relationships between unemployment and national taxation, between the unemployment rate and economic growth, or between unemployment benefits and activity rates.

---

14   This hegemony of the rate of activity and employment as an indicator of the 'good health of the Spanish labour market' is being nevertheless reformulated by the severe financial and economic recession Spanish society is experiencing, with the resurrection of the rate of unemployment as a key indicator.

As in other European member states, an important process in the Europeanization of Spain's public policies is noticeable, namely, the adoption of norms of intervention, interpretive frameworks and representations of problems formulated at EU level. Thus, the European dimension has become a strategic locus where challenges, issues and proposals are conceptualized and where the approaches to dealing them with are also defined.

Conclusion

Europe as an 'aspiration' and a 'master symbol' has played a role of the foremost importance in the development of welfare in democratic Spain since the 1980s. This chapter has scrutinized the Europeanization of Spanish social policies in the particular field of employment and the labour market. Three domains in the area of employment policies have been discussed: normative frames, resources (procedures) and indicators. 'Activation' has been relentlessly promoted by European institutions since the 1990s as the main goal to be achieved. In the Nordic and Anglo-Saxon countries there has been a long-standing tradition of policy intervention in the labour market. Spain has been induced by EU institutions to follow a similar path of internalizing activation, employability, equal opportunities or 'flexicurity' as cornerstones for overcoming the endemic 'disease' of unemployment.

The Europeanization of Spain's social policies has been also reflected in those techniques of policy implementation – by both Social-democratic (PSOE) and Conservative (PP) Governments – that are designed to achieve the aims agreed by the member states (for example, in the Lisbon Agenda). Likewise, European governance based upon decentralization and the involvement of stakeholders in policy elaboration and design has had a considerable impact in Spain's federal-like 'State of Autonomies'. Spain has also followed the pattern of EU influence on member states' policymaking by allowing the increasing participation of academics, experts and think tanks.

Benchmarking by identifying groups of indicators that justify and assess the social performance of public policies by measuring their *outcomes* has been greatly encouraged by EU institutions. The role of Eurostat, as the statistical office providing 'reliable' and 'objective' data, has been crucial as well. As has happened in other European countries, in Spain indicators not only have been an instrument of technical monitoring but have also contributed to constructing the social phenomena they measure from a position of 'neutrality'.

Spanish social policy will continue to be shaped by the process of Europeanization. This should come as no surprise in a country with an 'optimistic' view on the future of Europe.[15] The drive to catch up with the rest of the central

---

15   According to figures published in Eurobarometer (2009) three out of four Spaniards felt optimistic about the future of the European Union, which compared with an

European member states and to become a 'normal' European country is still powerful. Such a desire is shared by a large majority of Spaniards, who retain their aspiration to forget – or ignore – Franco's dictatorship of 1939–75 for good.[16]

References

Adelantado, J. and Calderón Cuevas, E. 2006. Globalization and the Welfare State: The Same Strategies for Similar Problems? *Journal of European Social Policy*, 16(4), 374–86.

Adnett, N. and Hardy, S. 2005. *The European Social Model: Modernisation or Evolution?* Cheltenham: Edward Elgar.

AER (Assembly of European Regions). 2005. *The European Social Model Must be Grounded in Diversity.* [Online] Available at: www.a-e-r.org/en/news/2005/2005101301.html [Accessed: 1 November 2010].

Arriba, A. and Moreno, L. 2005. Spain: Poverty, Social Exclusion and Safety Nets, in *Welfare State Reform in Southern Europe. Fighting Poverty and Social Exclusion in Italy, Spain, Portugal and Greece*, edited by M. Ferrera. London: Routledge, 141–203.

Bourdieu, P. 1992. *Language and Symbolic Power*. Cambridge, MA: Harvard University Press.

Cowles, M.G., Caporaso, J. and Risse, T. (eds) 2001. *Transforming Europe: Europeanisation and Domestic Change*. Ithaca, NY: Cornell University Press.

Espina, A. 2007. Estado de bienestar, democracia y pactos sociales en España: las políticas de empleo, desempleo y mercado de trabajo, in *Modernización y Estado de Bienestar en España*. Madrid: Fundación Carolina, 279–312.

ETUC (European Trade Union Confederation). 2005. *What is the "European Social Model" or "Social Europe"?* [Online] Available at: http://www.etuc.org/a/111 [Accessed: 12 January 2010].

European Commission. 1993. *Growth, Competitiveness, and Employment. The Challenges and Ways Forward into the 21st Century*. Brussels, COM (93) 700 final (05.12.1993).

---

average of two out of three Europeans in the whole EU-27. Among the six countries with the largest populations in EU-27, Spain was the most 'optimistic' with 75 per cent, followed by Poland (74 per cent), Italy (69 per cent), Germany (68 per cent), France (58 per cent) and United Kingdom (50 per cent).

16   The authors are grateful for comments and inputs made by the editors of this volume. Luis Moreno acknowledges the support provided by the international projects 'Welfare Attitudes in a Changing Europe' (WAE, European Science Foundation), and 'New Social Risks, Economic Crisis and Mediterranean Welfare' (Spanish Ministry of Education, PR2010-0095). Amparo Serrano Pascual is also grateful for the use of the findings of the research project, 'Qualitative evaluation of activation policies: the limits of the active and the passive' (Spanish Education and Science Ministry Project (SEJ2007–64604)).

EuroActiv 2005. *Hans Skov Christensen, Director General of the Federation of Danish Industry*. [Online] Available at: http://www.euractiv.com/en/socialeurope/hans-skov-christensen-director-general-federation-danish-industry/article-146400 [Accessed: 12 January 2010].

Eurobarometer. No. 72, Autumn. [Online] Available at: Public Opinion Analysis – Standard Eurobarometer, http://ec.europa.eu/public_opinion/archives/eb/eb72/eb72_en.htm [Accessed: 12 January 2010].

Ferrera, M. 1996. *A New Social Contract? The Four Social Europes: Between Universalism and Selectivity*. EUI Working Paper RSC 96/36. Florence: European University Institute.

Ferrera, M. 2007. *Democratization and Social Policy in Southern Europe. From Expansion to "Recalibration"*. Geneva: United Nations Research Institute for Social Development (UNISRID).

Flora, P. 1993. The National Welfare States and European Integration, in *Social Exchange and Welfare Development*, edited by Luis Moreno. Madrid: CSIC, 11–22.

Giddens, A. 2006. Debating the Social Model. Thoughts and Suggestions, in *The Hampton Court Agenda: A Social Model for Europe*. London: Policy Network, 95–150.

Gómez, M. 2005. Dos formas distintas de investigar el problema del paro en los albores de la encuesta social. El juicio público frente a la taxonomía. *Empiria*, 9, 115–41.

Guillén, A.M. and Álvarez, S. 2004. The EU's Impact on the Spanish Welfare State: The Role of Cognitive Europeanisation. *Journal of European Social Policy*, 14(3), 285–99.

Guillén, A.M. and Matsaganis, M. 2000. Testing the 'Social Dumping' Hypothesis in Southern Europe: Welfare Policies in Greece and Spain during the Last 20 Years. *Journal of European Social Policy*, 10(2), 120–45.

Hall, P. and Soskice, D. 2001. An Introduction to Varieties of Capitalism, in *Varieties of Capitalism. The Institutional Foundations of Comparative Advantage*, edited by P. Hall and D. Soskice. Oxford: Oxford University Press, 1–68.

High Level Group (Kok Report). 2004. *Facing the Challenge. The Lisbon Strategy for Growth and Employment*. Office for Official Publications of the European Communities, Luxembourg). [Online] Available at: http://www.vitae.ac.uk/cms/files/Facing-the-challenge-wim-kok-November-2004.pdf [Accessed: 12 January 2010].

Jacobsson, K. 2004. A European Politics for Employability: The Political Discourse on Employability of the EU and the OECD, in *Learning to be Employable. New Agendas on Work, Responsibility and Learning in a Globalising World*, edited by C. Garsten and K. Jacobsson. Houndmills: Palgrave, 42–62.

Jepsen, M. and Serrano Pascual, A. 2005. The European Social Model: An Exercise in Deconstruction. *Journal of European Social Policy*, 15(3), 231–45.

Jessop, B. 1994. The Transition to post-Fordism and the Schumpeterian Workfare State, in *Towards a Post-Fordist Welfare State?*, edited by R. Burrows and B. Loader. London: Routledge, 13–37.

Jobert, B. and Muller, P. 1987. *L'État en action. Politiques publiques et corporatismes*. Paris: PUF.

Jorgensen, H. 2002. *Consensus, Cooperation and Conflict*. Cheltenham: Edward Elgar.

Kuhnle, S. (ed.) 2000. *Survival of the European Welfare State*. London: Routledge.

Lakoff, G. 2007. *No Pienses en un Elefante*. Madrid: Universidad Complutense.

Leibfried, S. and Pierson, P. (eds) 1995. *European Social Policy between Fragmentation and Integration*. Washington, DC: Brookings Institution.

León, M. 2005. Welfare State Regimes and the Social Organisation of Labour: Childcare Arrangements and the Work/Family Balance Dilemma. *Sociological Review*, 53(2), 204–18.

Lindbeck, A. 2006. Sustainable Social Spending. *International Tax and Public Finance*, 13(4), 303–24.

López Santana, M. 2006. The Domestic Implications of European Soft Law: Framing and Transmitting Change in Employment Policy. *Journal of European Public Policy*, 13(4), 481–99.

Moreno, L. 2001. *The Federalization of Spain*. London: Frank Cass/Routledge.

Moreno, L. 2004. Spain's Transition to New Welfare: A Farewell to Superwomen, in *New Risks, New Welfare: The Transformation of the European Welfare State*, edited by P. Taylor-Gooby. Oxford: Oxford University Press, 133–57.

Moreno, L. and Palier, B. 2005. The Europeanization of Welfare: Paradigm Shifts and Social Policy Reforms, in *Ideas and Welfare State Reform in Western Europe*, edited by P. Taylor-Gooby. Houndmills: Palgrave Macmillan, 145–75.

Moreno, L. and Rodríguez Cabrero, G. 2007. Política social y estado del bienestar, in *Sociología en España*, edited by M. Pérez-Yruela. Madrid: Centro de Investigaciones Sociológicas/Federación Española de Sociología, 645–66.

Moreno, L. and Sarasa, S. 1992. *The Spanish "Via Media" to the Development of the Welfare State*. [Online] Available at: http://www.ipp.csic.es/doctrab1/dt-9213e.pdf [Accessed: 12 January 2010].

Moreno, L. and Serrano Pascual, A. 2007. Europeización del bienestar y activación. *Política y Sociedad*, 44(2), 31–44.

Moreno, L. and Serrano Pascual, A. 2009. Modelo Social Europeo y políticas sociales: una evaluación formativa institucional. *Gestión y Análisis de Políticas Públicas*, 2, 11–32.

Muller, P. 1990. *Les Politiques Publiques*. Paris: Presses Universitaires de France.

Munchau, W. 2005. Why Social Models are Irrelevant. *Financial Times*, 24 October, 13.

Navarro, V. (ed.) 2007. *La situación Social en España II*. Madrid: Editorial Biblioteca Nueva.

Palier, B. 2006. *The Europeanisation of Welfare Reforms*. [Online] Available at: http://www.hks.harvard.edu/inequality/Summer/Summer06/papers/Palier.pdf [Accessed: 12 January 2010].

Pierson, P. 1996. The Path to European Integration. *Comparative Political Studies*, 29(2), 123–63.

Pierson, P. 2001. Coping with Permanent Austerity: Welfare State Restructuring in Affluent Democracies, in *The New Politics of the Welfare State*, edited by P. Pierson. Oxford: Oxford University Press, 410–56.

Rhodes, M. 2006. *The Future of Europe: Renewing the Project*. [Online] Available at: http://www.ippr.org.uk [Accessed: 12 January 2010].

Rodríguez Cabrero, G. 2008. L'État – providence espagnol: pérennité, transformation et défis. *Travail et Emploi*, 115, 95–111.

Sabatier, P. 1998. The Advocacy Coalition Framework: Revisions and Relevance for Europe. *Journal of European Public Policy*, 5(1), 98–139.

Salais, R. 2006. Reforming the European Social Model and the Politics of Indicators: From the Unemployment Rate to the Employment Rate in the European Employment Strategy, in *Unwrapping the European Social Model*, edited by M. Jepsen and A. Serrano Pascual. Bristol: Polity Press, 189–212.

Salais, R., Baverez, N. and Reynaud, B. 1986. *L'invention du Chômage: Histoire et transformations d'une catégorie en France des années 1980 aux années 1980*. París: Presses Universitaires de France.

Sarasa, S. 2007. Pensiones de jubilación en España: reformas recientes y algunas consecuencias sobre el riesgo de pobreza, *Política y Sociedad*, 44(2), 87–99.

Scharpf, F. 1996. Negative and Positive Integration in the Political Economy of European Welfare States, in *Governance in the European Union*, edited by G. Marks et al. London: Sage, 15–39.

Scharpf, F. 2002. The European Social Model: Coping with the Challenges of Diversity. *Journal of Common Market Studies*, 40(1), 649–69.

Serrano Pascual, A. 2007. Reshaping Welfare States: Activation Regimes in Europe, in *Reshaping Welfare States and Activation Regimes in Europe*, edited by A. Serrano-Pascual and L. Magnusson. Brussels: P.I.E. Peter Lang, 11–35.

Serrano Pascual, A. 2009. The Battle of Ideas in the European Field: The Combat to Defeat Unemployment and the Struggle to Give it a Name. *Transfer*, 15(1), 5–71.

Serrano Pascual, A., Artiaga, A., Fernández, C., Martín, P. and Tovar, J.F. 2010. *Protección y Flexiguridad: la Modernización de los Servicios Públicos de Empleo*. Report of the research project FIPROS 2008/35. Madrid: Spanish Ministry of Labour and Immigration.

Shackleton, L. 2006. *The European Social Model: Past its Sell-by Date?* Madrid: Fundación Rafael del Pino. [Online] Available at: www.fundacionrafaeldelpino. es/9 [Accessed: 1 November 2010].

Shotter, J. 1984. *Social Accountability and Selfhood*. Oxford: Basic Blackwell.

Surel, Y. 2000. The Role of Cognitive and Normative Frames in Policy-making. *Journal of European Public Policy*, 7(4), 495–512.

Taylor-Gooby, P. (ed.) 2001. *Welfare States under Pressure*. Thousand Oaks, CA: Sage.

Topalov, C. 1994. *La Naissance du Chômeur 1880–1910.* Paris: Albin Michel.

Turner, V. 1997. *The Forest of Symbols: Aspects of Ndembu Ritual.* Ithaca, NY: Cornell University Press.

Walters, W. and Haahr, J.H. 2005. *Governing Europe. Discourse, Governmentality and European Integration.* New York: Routledge Advances in European Politics.

Chapter 4

The Quest for Gender Equality

Margarita León

Introduction

In recent years Spain has been politically praised for its commitment to gender equality. In the general elections of 2008, the re-elected Spanish Prime Minister, Rodríguez Zapatero, formed the first European government with more women than men. This parity government followed the recently introduced law on gender equality (2007), which, among other things, set up the 40 per cent rule of political representation, which forbids political parties that contest national or local elections from fielding more than 60 per cent of their candidates from one sex. Women already make up over 36 per cent of the deputies in Spanish Parliament, one of the highest percentages of female representation in Europe. The 2007 legislation was preceded by two other innovative gender equality laws: the new law on domestic violence introduced in 2004 and the legislation on gay marriage approved in 2005 against the opposition of the Conservative Party (*Partido Popular – PP*) and the Catholic Church. In the welfare field, the so-called *Ley de Dependencia* introduced in 2006 guaranteed for the first time in Spanish history the universal right of dependent individuals to long-term care, the provision of universal pre-school education, and several other new measures designed to reconcile work and family life. In so doing it has challenged, at least at the prescriptive level, the strong familistic assumptions underlying the Spanish welfare state.

The merit of these legal and political changes cannot be underestimated in a country where not long ago women's rights were subordinate in law to those of men. However, after more than three decades of strenuous efforts to remove discriminatory practices against women in the legal, political and social realms, the question that remains is the extent to which these changes have had an impact on the *de facto* equality between men and women. Do these pioneering laws mirror comparable social changes? We can say Spain has done well in the 'politics of presence' (Phillips 1996), with participation understood as a fundamental political value in democracy, but can we also demonstrate progress towards substantive equality? As several chapters of this volume show, the labour market participation of women on a more or less equal footing with that of men still is an unfulfilled and remote goal. In contrast to the majority of European Union (EU) Member States, and despite the aforementioned policy innovations, in Spain successive governments have failed to counteract strong gender imbalances in the labour market, especially in relation to access to employment, unemployment, and the high degree of temporality that affect both genders but especially women. Likewise, in Spain as in the other south European countries, the costs of having children fall disproportionately on women's shoulders, with little state support. Despite the threat of a rapidly ageing population, vividly present in public debates, labour market and social policies have been unable to reverse the tendency of fertility rates to fall.

This chapter examines the evolution of gender equality on the social and political agenda since Spain's transition to democracy until today, paying special attention to how gender equality has been framed at the macro-institutional level. While the quest for gender equality has followed its own internal dynamics, the impact of the EU on this process is also assessed. It is argued in this chapter that, although Spain has clearly been a latecomer in gender equality legislation, given the political evolution of the country, it can now be considered a front-runner among EU countries. What is still lacking, however, are implementation procedures with the potential to tackle inequalities between men and women in the labour market and effective state involvement in caregiving. It is also claimed that the impact of some of the most recent pro-gender equality measures has been weakened by the current economic climate, which has prompted severe cuts in public spending.

Gender (In)equality in Pre-Democratic Spain

Gender equality played a very limited role in the origins of the Spanish welfare state, for two main reasons. First, the Bismarckian rationale (see Chapter 2) of the initial development of social insurance in Spain during Franco's dictatorship practically excluded women from access to social benefits if it were not via a dependency status of some sort. Second, the ideal of a traditional family model based on the male breadwinner functioned as an indispensable complement to these initial rudimentary forms of social provision. Especially during the first two decades of the Franco regime, family programmes were a central part of the system of social provision. In fact, they were a complementary source of income for many workers (Valiente 1996). Designed to stimulate population growth, family policies were not, as Valiente argued, a hidden or implicit policy but a recurrent theme in the rhetoric and propaganda of the regime (1996: 102). The profile of policies for women and the family under Franco was ideologically defined and encouraged by the powerful Catholic Church and the Falange, a pro-Franco political organization.

Other measures were adopted to constrain women's activities outside the home and the institution of marriage itself. The right of divorce, introduced during the Second Republic,[1] was abolished in law, and responsibility for family law was

---

1   The Second Republic (1931–6) introduced fundamental changes in the legal treatment of women and the family. The Republic took away power from the Church, and

restored to the Church. Equality between legitimate and illegitimate children was removed, adultery and the use of contraception were prohibited, and the rights of women outside and within marriage were severely restricted (Cousins 1995). From 1938 married women had to obtain permission from their husbands to work outside the home.

During the 1960s, although Spain was still under the Francoist dictatorship, several circumstances created the basis for the development of the 'authoritarian welfare state', as Rodríguez Cabrero (1989) termed it. Economic autarchy was progressively abandoned, and the country began a process of international economic integration. Economic growth triggered significant processes with a clear impact on everyday life. Massive migration from rural to urban areas generated rapid urbanization, which ultimately triggered changes in traditional social and cultural patterns, such as secularization processes. One of the most important changes that took place during the 1960s was the transformation of family life and sexual patterns. Female labour force participation in Spain, although still well below the levels of other European countries, started to rise, and after 1964 the birth rate started its downward curve. Thus, although political change did not come until the late 1970s, the behaviour and attitudes of the majority of citizens had already transformed the Spanish family. Family benefits became obsolescent from the beginning of the 1960s. They were rarely updated, which meant that, with the impact of inflation, their real value diminished considerably. Moreover, due to the new socio-demographic patterns of Spanish society, certain programmes, such as those aimed at supporting large families, were no longer effective. However, the formalization of equal rights between men and women had to wait until the first democratic constitution was adopted in 1978.

The First Steps: Tackling Formal Discrimination Against Women

The 1978 Constitution became the legal framework for the modern welfare state by providing explicitly for social rights such as the universal rights to housing, education, health and pensions. It brought about formal equality, eliminating remnants of unequal treatment between men and women within marriage as well as that of children born out of wedlock. Article 14 of the 1978 Constitution establishes equality between men and women, while Article 9.2 leaves the door open for the adoption of positive action to combat discrimination on the grounds of sex, age, ethnicity or religion. Notwithstanding, key issues of women's rights were not incorporated to the final document. The Constitution makes no reference to the rights to birth control (although contraception was made legal in 1978) or

---

the new Republican Constitution introduced new laws that favoured gender equality, such as the female suffrage, divorce by consent, and the reformed abortion law. However, these projects were unfinished when the Civil War (1936–9) suddenly broke out, and they were abandoned as soon as Franco came to power.

abortion, two important demands of the feminist movement. These issues were an important source of confrontation between left and right; and, given the consensus character of the transition to democracy, they were issues of the kind that had to be set aside.[2] A few years after the Bill of Rights was drawn up, the centre-right government of the Union of the Democratic Centre (UCD) introduced equal pay legislation (1980), divorce by consent (1981) and equal rights of men and women within marriage and of children born out of wedlock (1981) (Cousins 1995). The last two pieces of legislation, especially that legalizing divorce, were the tip of the iceberg which ultimately provoked a profound breach between Adolfo Suárez, the Prime Minister, and the head of the Spanish Catholic Church (*El País* 1981).

With the first victory of the Socialist Party (PSOE) with an absolute majority in 1982, the gender equality agenda would progress. The 'institutionalization' of the feminist movement, or 'state feminism' as it has been called in other countries with similar experiences, was formalized in 1983 with the creation of the *Instituto de la Mujer* (IM, Women's Rights Institute). The first period of the IM was characterized by demands for immediate action against highly visible discrimination. It is evident that the historical legacy greatly conditioned the activities of the IM, at least during these early years. The IM was laying the groundwork for future action: '(...) we needed to build the structure of the house before we could walk in'.[3] During the first Equal Opportunities Plan (PIOM 1988–90) efforts were made to set up databases to analyse discrimination, to train professionals and technicians, and to develop strategies and procedures of action. One of the important achievements of the plan was the creation of an administrative culture around gender equality by setting up similar governmental bodies at regional and local levels. The plan was also important in rectifying basic deficiencies such as the establishment throughout the country of refuges for battered women, counselling services to report sexual discrimination, and women's rights campaigns. In general, the IM generated awareness of and publicity about women's rights issues.

This public consultation body became from the start a fundamental nexus between the European and national levels, especially in the transposition of EU directives (Guillén et al. 2010). Moreover, European equality policies served to legitimize the actions and demands of the IM. In this sense, Spain's accession to the EU in 1986 contributed towards the greater political visibility of gender issues: 'we would frequently travel to Brussels and bring ideas back. We used

---

2   The sharp political and social tensions of the 1960s and 1970s prevented the emergence of common ground among feminists of different political and social backgrounds. As several authors have pointed out, the independence of the Spanish feminist movement during the early democratic years was deeply compromised by the more general political conflict between left and right (San José 1986; Astelarra 1992; Threlfall 1996).

3   Interview with Martínez Ten, head of the IM from 1988 to 1991, Madrid, 19 February 2000.

Europe as a reference, as a learning experience'.[4] In the area of employment and welfare policies, all interventions promoting gender equality channelled through the IM centred on equal opportunities at work and the universalization of basic social rights, such as to health, education and access to the public pensions system. One of the first victories of the feminist movement, also with the IM playing an important role (Valiente 2000), was the abortion law approved in 1985. It made abortion legal under three circumstances only: up to 22 weeks of pregnancy in cases of foetal malformation; up to 12 weeks of pregnancy in cases of (reported) rape; and at any time when the physical or mental health of the pregnant woman was considered to be at risk. The law was viewed as a mixed blessing by feminist groups, who lobbied for free abortion and blamed the government for succumbing to pressure from Church-led anti-abortion activists. In practice, however, private clinics have been carrying out free abortion, taking refuge in the third circumstance (the health of the pregnant woman)[5] without ever having been persecuted. Feminist groups who were pushing for a revision of the law claimed that, although the law was very permissively applied, it discriminated heavily against women from low-income groups who could not afford to have abortion at private clinics.[6] As it will be described below, although the revision of the law was on the agenda of the Socialist Party since it was first approved in 1985, it took its time to be implemented. The new law that would frame women's right to abortion was finally approved in 2010.

Notable improvements were also made during the 1980s in the application of the anti-discriminatory principle in labour law. Gender equality benefited from the social-democratic tendency of this period (see Chapter 2), when basic social rights, such as those to education and health care, as mentioned above, became generalized to the whole population. The first Equal Opportunities Plan focused on the promotion of positive action programmes to eliminate sexual discrimination in the workplace, to facilitate women's access to paid employment and to encourage legal changes.[7] This Equal Opportunities Plan gave priority to the correct transposition of the 1992 EU directive on the health and safety of pregnant workers and women who were breastfeeding. Therefore, Spanish gender equality policies

---

4   Interview with Purificación Gutiérrez, head of the IM from 1991 to 1993. Madrid, 19 February 2000.

5   In 1999, 97 per cent of the abortions were performed under this third clause (Ministry of Health 2009).

6   In 2009, 98 per cent of all legal abortions were performed in private clinics (Ministry of Health 2009).

7   The first PIOM promoted within the National Plan for Professional Formation (FIP) programmes of positive action to combat sexual discrimination in the workplace. The programmes were developed under agreements between the Ministry of Labour and Social Security, the Ministry of Social Affairs, the Institute for Employment (INE) and the IM. The IM also developed employment and occupational programmes supported by the European Social Fund.

put forward during this period are a clear example of European integration soon after Spain joined the EU (see Chapter 3).

However, women's access to the labour market during the 1980s was hampered by the need for economic restructuring and the dynamics of the political economy. The paradox is that while the Socialist Party came to power with an open commitment to gender equality, the actual economic and social reforms that were enacted during this period, compromised to a large extent by very high unemployment rates, had a damaging effect on the opportunities of non-core group of workers such as the youth and women to access both the labour market and the social protection system. In this context of major economic restructuring, the social protection system acted as a safety net to cushion possible social conflicts. Early retirement, unemployment and invalidity benefits significantly increased GDP expenditure during this period. Consequently, restrictive reforms introduced in the second half of the 1980s were designed principally to contain costs. The 1985 reform of the social security system tightened the links between eligibility for social insurance and the employment record.[8] Some observers held the IM responsible for the lack of progress on women's everyday lives. The radical feminist movement accused 'femocrats' (female members of the Socialist Party holding positions of power, such as IM directors) for imposing a top-down view of the gender problem and being blind to its social-class dimension (Astelarra 1992).

In conclusion, the change in gender roles was one of the most prominent signs of the 'catching up' effect of Spanish society with neighbouring European countries, and the implementation of gender equality law was a clear example of top-down learning from European institutions. The 1980s also signified major progress in women's access to education. However, the segmentation of the labour market, together with an income-maintenance social protection system and the marginal role of safety net mechanisms, imposed severe restrictions on women's economic independence during the 1980s. Just as in other south European countries, expanding social programmes in times of economic recessions and under neoliberal macroeconomic and labour market policies proved a hard yardstick to meet. Finally, while efforts were made to tackle formal discrimination against women, more needed to be done to actually improve the conditions of women across social strata.

---

8   The 1985 reform increased the minimum qualifying period of contributions for retirement benefit from 10 to 15 years. This five-year increase in the time threshold, together with the lack of crediting mechanisms to compensate for spells outside employment (except for maternity leave and the first year of voluntary leave, which have both counted towards the contribution record since 1989), damaged the prospects of women, who tend to have shorter and more fragmented careers (León 2002).

The 1990s: The 'Family' Regained

The Second Equal Opportunities Plan (PIOM 1993–5), while continuing to pay attention to the labour market,[9] took a wider view than the first Plan in considering for the first time the impact of the 'double burden' on women's employment. It is this second Plan that finally acknowledged the importance of a work–family balance and the need to increase childcare services for children under school age (Guillén et al. 2010: 127).

The 1990s were also important in terms of compliance with EU directives. The 1994 reform (*Ley 42/1994 de 30 de Diciembre*) was a transposition of the European directive on pregnant workers and women who were breastfeeding (Council Directive 92/85/EEC).[10] Up until this point, maternity leave was included within the contingency of employment injuries and occupational incapacity. The major policy change to be implemented was to treat pregnant workers and workers who had recently given birth as subject to a different risk from sick leave. The 1994 reform also increased the period of the allowance (from 14 weeks in 1989 to 16 in 1994) and the amount of the benefit (from 75 per cent of the salary in 1989 to 100 per cent in 1994). Access to maternity benefits was also improved, by reducing the minimum period of entitlement to the benefit from one year to 180 days and by relieving employers of the financial costs of maternity leave. All these changes made maternity leave in Spain one of the most generous in Europe. However, at the beginning of the 1990s maternity and family protection measures more broadly conceived were still completely lacking. Given the framing of family programmes as undesired territory for the left, childcare was best channelled through the educational 'needs' of children under compulsory school age. The new legal framework for the regulation of the national education system LOGSE 1990 included, for the first time, the education of children under the age of six within the national education system. This new normative paved the way for a progressive increase in the schooling rates of children aged under six, with practically 100 per cent coverage rates for children aged from three to the compulsory age (León 2007: 324).

The victory of the centre-right People's Party (PP) in 1996 was the first step towards the introduction of family issues into the political debate (Salido and Moreno 2009). The newly elected People's Party was never very keen on gender

---

9   During this second PIOM the Workers Articles of Association were modified in Article 28. The concept of 'equal job' was substituted for that of 'job of equal value', referring to equal salary. The change was implemented in the 1994 labour market reform. The European programme NOW (New Opportunities for Women) was introduced to develop positive actions within enterprises and training courses in non-discriminatory practices for members and representatives of the unions in enterprises.

10   Directive 92/85/EEC of 19 October 1992 on the introduction of measures to encourage improvements in the safety and health at work of pregnant workers and workers who have recently given birth or are breastfeeding.

equality measures such as positive action. Contrary to what happened under the previous Socialist governments, right-wing women would distance themselves from the feminist movement while at the same time supporting equal opportunities for men and women. During this period the IM lost much of its prominence but, albeit less proactive in campaigning for women's rights, the first centre-right government since the beginning of democracy was ready to modernize and reframe family policy as an essential part of contemporary Spain. Following the European Employment Strategy's guidelines and recommendations, most measures adopted by the government of Prime Minister José María Aznar were geared towards facilitating and protecting the participation of women, and especially young mothers, in the labour market through a better work–family balance. The *Law on the Reconciliation between Family and Working Life* approved in 1999 openly recognized the need to support families and working mothers. In practical terms, the 1999 law continued to comply with the 1992 EU directive on pregnant workers and the parental leave directive (Council Directive 96/34/C). It introduced changes in the Bill of Workers Rights (*Estatuto de los Trabajadores*) in relation to leave arising from maternity, paternity and care of dependent relatives. The law gives breastfeeding mothers the right to working breaks. Adoptive mothers are given the same rights with regard to maternity leave. The law also introduced the right to working-time flexibility for employees with caring responsibilities (León and Millns 2007). Thanks to this new provision and those introduced by previous governments, Spain now conforms *de jure* to EC standards of maternity leave.

The re-elected centre-right PP government of 2000–2004 continued its commitment to help families. The National Plan for Family Support (*Plan de apoyo integral a las familias 2001–2004*), approved in 2000, sought, among other goals, to promote women's entry into the labour market. The two most important measures adopted during that time, and still in force today, were the tax breaks worth 100 Euros per month for all working mothers with children under three years of age (Law 46/2002) and the subsidies to firms employing women for social security contributions (RD 3/2003) (Ministry of Employment and Social Affairs 2010). As is made clear in Chapter 10 of this volume, the PP governments were criticized, especially by the main opposition party, for not comprehensively tackling the problem of gender inequality. Still, in retrospect a clear success of the two Aznar governments was their capacity to reformulate a policy domain that had been left unattended since the transition to democracy. Clear evidence of the popularity of some of the family-friendly measures (tax breaks and employment-related child benefits) introduced by the PP governments is provided by their continuation by the succeeding Socialist governments. In the labour market area, female participation in the labour market experienced a sharp increase from the mid-1990s until the end of the economic expansion in 2008. Much of the employment growth that occurred during this period consisted of female employment, which contributed towards narrowing the gap in relation to the EU average. Nevertheless, the increase in the quantity of jobs was achieved largely at the expense of their quality. Very high percentages of short-term employment contracts, together with very low levels of secure part-time employment (Ibáñez 2007), limited the genuine opportunities of working women to achieve the desired balance between their family and working lives.

The 2000s: Gender Equality Legislation in Turbulent Times

The years immediately preceding the outbreak of the economic crisis in 2008 have quite an impressive record for pro-gender equality legislation and political action in Spain. However, as is shown in this section, just a few years later the imperatives of controlling public spending overshadowed the 'progressive spirit' of Zapatero's Socialist governments (2004–2008, 2008–). The Prime Minister has been accused, even from within his own party, of compromising social spending when the hurricane of global recession was already engulfing Spain.

The formation in April 2004 of the first gender-parity government in Spanish history was the first big gesture confirming Zapatero's commitment to feminism. The new government comprised eight male and nine female ministers. Of these appointments, perhaps the most controversial, attracting considerable media attention, was that of Carmen Chacón, a then pregnant woman, to the Ministry of Defence. Parity was sustained in Zapatero's second government after his re-election in 2008. On this occasion, a further political gesture confirming Zapatero's engagement with gender equality was the creation of a new Ministry for Equality headed by Bibiana Aido, a young woman who was largely unknown in either political or feminist circles. The creation of this new ministry, and the minister herself, were subjected to crude criticisms, especially from the right-wing media. Nevertheless, the gesture on this occasion did not last long. Just two years after its creation, the Ministry for Equality was abolished and the minister lost her job when the first 'anti-crisis cabinet' was formed. The ministry was downgraded and headed by a Secretary of State (*Secretaria de Igualdad*).

During the period from 2004 to 2010 the following noteworthy acts came into force directly or indirectly addressing gender equality:

1. The law against domestic violence of 2004 (*Ley Orgánica 1/2004 de 28 de diciembre, de medidas de protección integral contra la violencia de género*).
2. The law on same-sex marriage of 2005 (*Ley 13/2005 de 1 de julio, por la que se modifica el Código Civil en materia de derecho a contraer matrimonio*).
3. The law on long-term care of 2006 (*Act 39/2006, of 14th December, on the Promotion of Personal Autonomy and Care for Dependent Persons*).
4. The Equality Act of 2007 (*Ley organica 3/2007 de 22 marzo para la igualdad efectiva de mujeres y hombres*).

5. The new abortion law of 2010 (*Ley Orgánica 2/2010, de 3 de marzo, de salud sexual y reproductiva y de la interrupción voluntaria del embarazo*).

In the following, details are provided of all five new laws.

1. Fulfilling an electoral promise, the government, which commanded a majority in the parliament, passed the law against domestic violence in 2004. This new Act was passed supported by an unusual consensus across the political spectrum on the need for this first piece of legislation on domestic violence. The main objective of the new Act was to mainstream the problem of domestic violence across all governmental units. It introduced measures of positive action for victims of domestic violence in the workplace (right to time off work and right to unemployment benefits in the event of interruption of employment). It established special units in the police and *Guardia Civil* as well as special courts exclusively dedicated to domestic violence cases. The new Act also increased jail sentences for the perpetrators while creating programmes for their social rehabilitation. The law aimed at preventing domestic violence through coordination between education and health authorities. A one-term course on 'education for equality and against gender violence' was made compulsory in secondary education. The law also envisaged the creation of special units within health centres on the prevention of domestic violence. Although the number of deaths from domestic violence has not decreased since the law came into force, there is undeniably greater social awareness of the problem.

2. The law on same-sex marriage approved in 2005 amended the Civil Code to allow gay and lesbian couples to marry, divorce and adopt children. It also gave homosexual couples the same rights as heterosexual ones in relation to inheritance, tax benefits and pension entitlements. This new norm was seen as constitutional to the extent that the Bill of Rights does not define 'family' in terms of heterosexual marriage, so allowing for a broader interpretation (Platero 2007: 330). As Platero (2007: 331) remarks, this national law was preceded by same-sex partnership laws enacted in 12 different autonomous regions, starting with Catalonia in 1998. This second piece of legislation was, as one would expect, much more controversial than the aforementioned law against domestic violence, which attracted widespread support. The law was criticized by the Church, which saw it as an attack on the institution of marriage. The centre-right People's Party appealed against it in the Constitutional Court.[11] The initiative was also crudely attacked by the most reactionary sectors of the media. Still, different surveys revealed widespread support across Spanish society for equal marital rights for same-sex couples. According to the survey undertaken by the Centre of Sociological Research (CIS 2004: 9) some months before the law was passed, 66.2 per cent of Spaniards were in favour of legalizing same-sex marriage. On the issue of adoption rights for same-sex couples, 48.2 per cent of respondents strongly agreed (21.9 per cent) or

---

11   At the time of writing this line, the Constitutional Court has not yet resolved the case.

agreed (26.3 per cent) with the statement 'homosexual couples should have the same rights to adopt children as heterosexual ones' (CIS 2004: 9).

3. The first Spanish law on long-term care, or the 'Dependency Law', as it is generally known, was approved by parliament in December 2006, in order to rectify the historical absence of institutional support for dependent individuals (Rodríguez Cabrero 2005, 2006). Until February 2010 over half a million people assessed as eligible for long-term care under the new system were receiving some kind of benefit. The law is ambitiously aimed at people of all ages who need help to perform everyday activities. In practice, however, the new system is primarily geared towards those aged 65 years or more. Women benefit from the creation of this new system on three different fronts. First, given their longer life expectancy, the majority of beneficiaries (67 per cent) are women (SAAD/IMSERSO 2010). Elderly women are one of the groups at greatest risk of poverty, and therefore this new initiative should alleviate the conditions of a particularly vulnerable group. Second, the overwhelming majority of carers are women. They, too, form a vulnerable social group inasmuch as they perform around-the-clock unpaid caring and do not receive any regular financial compensation for their work (IMSERSO 2004). The majority of these informal carers (most of them in the 45–65 age group) have never participated in the labour market, which leaves them with no entitlements to the old-age pension (they are eligible only for the widows' benefit and means-tested non-contributory benefits). The new long-term care system envisages a cash allowance for informal carers designed ultimately to partially compensate them financially for the hitherto unpaid care work these women do at home.[12] Third, if implemented correctly, the new long-term system would create job opportunities for women by expanding the public social services sector.

The greatest merit of this new Act, then, is that it gives political recognition to an outstanding feature of the Spanish welfare state: it formally acknowledges the role that the family, and particularly women inside the family, play in providing care and support for the elderly and other dependants. However, the actual implementation of the new system has been riddled with difficulties, as explained at length in Chapters 12 of this volume. Insufficient and unclear financing, tensions between different levels of government and lack of a realistic assessment of available resources have translated into a weak transposition. While it is too early to evaluate the success of a system that will not be in full swing until 2015, in the few years since the approval of the law care has remained unprofessional and largely outside the scope of public regulation. This is viewed negatively by those, especially trade unions but also employers involved in the sector, who asked for greater public and private investment in the social services, not just to meet the demand for care but also to foster the growth of employment, particularly female

---

12 Interview with director of IMSERSO, Pilar Rodríguez and Jesús Norberto Fernández. Madrid, 20 April 2009.

employment. There are also concerns about the quality of the care provided and the adequacy of efforts by non-professionals to attend to certain care and medical needs in the home. Furthermore, and as shown by Sarasa and Billingsley (2008), when non-family care has to be purchased on the market because of insufficient formal provision, access is highly unequal across social strata.

4. The national Equality Law approved in 2007 is perhaps the most ambitious intervention in the field of gender equality. Preceded by other equality laws already in place in several autonomous regions, this new law attempts to mainstream gender across all governmental units. Three main areas of intervention are employment, improvements in maternity, paternity and parental leave, and gender-balanced representation on the executive boards of firms and in political parties. In terms of employment, the law complies with European directives concerning equality between men and women, such as Directive 2002/73/CE which deals with the principle of equal treatment between men and women in access to employment, training and working conditions. It also subsumes Directive 2004/113/CE, which establishes the principle of equal treatment between men and women in access to goods and services. The Equality Act makes compulsory the negotiation of equality plans within the collective agreements of firms with more of 250 employees. Maternity leave is improved on several fronts, especially for the more vulnerable groups of women. The period of maternity leave can now be increased in exceptional circumstances, such as in the case of premature babies and babies who need to stay in hospital for a long period of time. The Act gives access to statutory maternity leave to specific groups of women, namely, women under 21 years of age, unemployed women, and women with no contributory record for claiming maternity benefit. The Equality Act recognizes paternity leave of 13 days, progressively increasing to four months by 2013. As for the parity principle, the Act makes it compulsory (the 40 per cent rule) for the executive boards of large firms (those with more than 250 employees) and for political parties fielding candidates in national or local elections.

Once again, however, implementing the Act has proved much more difficult than drafting it. The Equality Act has encountered three types of problems. First, things that seem right on paper do not work well in particular situations. This has been the case with equality plans in collective agreements, which do not seem to be happening due to the reluctance and lack of awareness of (mainly male) negotiators (Arroyo 2010). Second, the economic crisis, which the government did not foresee, imposes severe constraints on the funding of social programmes. This is the case with the paternity benefit that the Equality Act provides for; its implementation has been postponed until 'further notice'. Third, the absence of a political consensus on the content of the law brings into its survival beyond the relatively short duration of a single term of office. In this case, the Popular Party in June 2007 appealed recourse against the Equality Act's provision for electoral parity (*El Mundo* 2007). The PP considered that the obligation of all political parties to comply with the 40 per cent rule was a 'clear restriction of the freedom of political parties'.[13] The Constitutional High Court (*Tribunal Constitucional*), however, dismissed the appeal in January 2008 (*El País* 2008).

5. The last of Zapatero's electoral promises to be implemented is the new law on sexual and reproductive health approved by the Spanish Senate in 2010. This new norm relaxes restrictions on women's access to abortion. The law was approved with the votes of the Socialist Party and nationalist minority groups, against the opposition of the centre-right Popular Party and votes of individual members of other parties. The new law allows abortion under any circumstances up to 14 weeks' gestation and declares the procedure to be a woman's right. It also permits abortion up to 22 weeks in cases of foetal impairment or when two doctors certify that the pregnancy poses a serious threat to the woman's life or health. Spain's new law also requires that public policies related to health, education and social issues promote universal access to sexual and reproductive health services and programmes – including family planning services – and makes comprehensive sexual education mandatory in schools. Just as in 1985, the Socialist government and the Church clashed over abortion. Especially divisive was a provision allowing girls aged over 16 to have an abortion without parental consent.

What the Future Holds

Since it opened to contemporary democracy in 1975, Spain has witnessed a sea change in the framing of gender equality as a political issue. After decades of gender blindness in policymaking, the presence of women in politics and the volume and depth of legislative changes as no-turning-back steps towards enacting the principle of equal opportunities have placed Spain among the European countries with the most pro-gender equality legislation. It has been argued in this chapter that the process of Europeanization has been key in this rapid process of transformation, both formally (through the transposition of European directives) and informally (through learning best-practice policies). However, and despite comprehensive legal changes and positive action measures, Spain continues to score badly in key indicators of gender discrimination. On the one hand, a strongly dualistic labour market with few flexicurity mechanisms places women at a disadvantage in terms of access to and quality of employment. On the other hand, the 'familistic' features of the Spanish welfare state, which gives women the main responsibility for caring, have changed surprisingly little given the amount of 'political noise' about this issue on recent years. Well-intentioned legislative innovations in the field of

---

13   In regional and local elections in May 2007 all political parties were required to draw up lists of candidates of whom no more than 60 per cent could be of one sex. One all-woman list presented by the PP at a local election was disqualified because it did not comply with the law (*El País* 2008).

gender equality are seen as a necessary albeit not sufficient condition to achieve *real* equal opportunities between men and women.

Furthermore, as Lombardo and Bustelo (2010: 8) argue, gender inequality has occupied a clearly hegemonic position in the Spanish institutional framework, to the detriment of other kinds of inequalities, especially racial and ethnic. Thus, the country needs to do more to appraise intersectionality within understandings of gender equality (Bustelo 2009). This is so not only to comply with the most recent EU anti-discriminatory legislation, especially Council Directive 2000/43/EC of 29 June 'implementing the principle of equal treatment between persons irrespective or racial or ethnic origin', but also to respond to new social risks, especially after the massive influx of immigrants, many of them female, since the turn of the millennium. The situation of immigrant women in the largely informal care and service sector (León 2010), for instance, is a new phenomenon that demands a broader and more complex understanding of social inequalities based not only on gender but also on race and socio-economic position. Overall, the future remains quite open as to the capacity of the several 'windows of opportunity' described in this chapter to materialize in effective new policies.

References

Arroyo Romero-Salazar, L. 2010. Han asumido los agentes sociales la Ley de Igualdad a efectos de eliminar las discriminaciones con las medidas establecidas en los Convenios Colectivos?, in *¿Se Están Asumiendo en el Ámbito Laboral los Principios de la Ley de Igualdad?* Fundación Themis de Mujeres Juristas. Madrid: Fundación Themis, 15–44.

Astelarra, J. 1992. Women, Political Culture and Empowerment in Spain, in *Women Transforming Politics: Worldwide Strategies for Empowerment*, edited by J. Bustudzoemski. Indiana University Press, 41–50.

Bustelo, M. 2009. Spain: Intersectionality Faces a Strong Gender Norm. *International Journal of Feminist Politics*, 11(4), 530–46. [Online] Available at: http://www.informaworld.com/smpp/title~db=all~content=t713722173~tab=issueslist~branches=11-v11 [Accessed: 10 January 2011].

Bustelo, M. and Lombardo, E. (eds) 2007. *Políticas de Igualdad en España y en Europa: afinando la mirada*. Madrid: Cátedra.

CIS (Centre for Sociological Research). 2004. *Barómetro Junio 2004*. Estudio n. 2.568.

Cousins, C. 1995. Women and Social Policy in Spain: The Development of a Gendered Welfare Regime. *Journal of European Social Policy*, 5(3), 175–97.

El Mundo. 2007. El PP recurre ante el Constitucional las listas paritarias de la Ley de Igualdad. 25 June.

El País. 1981. Suárez: historia de una crisis más política que personal. 1 February.

El País. 2008. El Tribunal Constitucional avala la Ley de Igualdad que estableció las listas paritarias. 29 January.

Guillén, A.M., Moreno-Manzanaro, N. and González, S. 2010. Conciliación de la vida laboral y familiar en España. El impacto de las políticas de la Unión Europea. *Documentación Social*, 154, 119–38.

Ibáñez, Z. 2007. *Access to Non-vulnerable Part-time Employment in the Netherlands, Spain and the UK, with Special Reference to the School and Local Government Sectors*. Ph.D thesis. Florence: European University Institute.

León, M. 2002. The Individualisation of Social Rights: Hidden Familialistic Practices in Spanish Social Policy. *South European Society & Politics*, 7(3), 53–79.

León, M. 2007 Speeding Up or Holding Back? Institutional Factors in the Development of Childcare Provision in Spain. *European Societies*, 9(3), 315–37.

León, M. 2009. Gender Equality and the European Employment Strategy: The Work/Family Balance Debate. *Social Policy and Society*, 8(2), 197–209.

León, M. 2010. Migration and Care Work: The Domestic Sector Revisited. *Social Policy and Society*, 9(3), 409–18.

León, M. and Millns, S. 2007. Parental, Maternity and Paternity Leave: European Legal Constructions of Unpaid Care Giving. *Northern Ireland Legal Quarterly*, 58(3), 343–58.

Lombardo, E. and Bustelo, M. 2010. *The Political Treatment of Inequalities in Southern Europe: A Comparative Analysis of Italy, Portugal and Spain*. II Congress of REPS, Madrid, 30 September–1 October.

Ministry of Health (Ministerio de Sanidad, Política Social e Igualdad). 2009. *Salud Pública: Datos Estadísticos Interrupción Voluntaria del Embarazo*. [Online] Available at: http://www.msc.es [Accessed: 10 January 2011].

Phillips, A. 1996. Dealing with Difference: A Politics of Ideas, or a Politics of Presence, in *Democracy and Difference: Contesting the Boundaries of the Political*, edited by S. Benhabib. Princeton, NJ: Princeton University Press, 139–52.

Platero, R. 2007. Love and the State: Gay Marriage in Spain. *Feminist Legal Studies*, 15, 329–40.

Rodríguez Cabrero, G. 1989. La política social en España: realidades y tendencias, in *Crisis y Futuro del Estado de Bienestar*, edited by R. Muñoz del Bustillo. Madrid: Alianza Universidad, 183–205.

Rodríguez Cabrero, G. 2005. La protección social de las personas dependientes como desarrollo del Estado de Bienestar en España. *Panorama Social*, 2, 21–33.

Rodríguez Cabrero, G. 2006. La protección social a la dependencia en España en el marco del espacio social europeo. *Documentación Social*, 141, 23–44.

SAAD/IMSERSO 2008. *Estadísticas del Sistema para la Autonomía y la Atención a la Dependencia*. Situación a 2 de Noviembre de 2008. [Online] Available at: http://www.imsersomayores.csic.es [Accessed: 10 January 2011].

SAAD/IMSERSO 2009. *Estadísticas del Sistema para la Autonomía y la Atención a la Dependencia*. Situación a 1 Junio de 2009. [Online] Available at: http://www.imsersomayores.csic.es [Accessed: 10 January 2011].

SAAD/IMSERSO 2010. *Estadísticas del Sistema para la Autonomía y la Atención a la Dependencia.* Situación a 1 Junio de 2010. [Online] Available at: http://www.imsersomayores.csic.es [Accessed: 10 January 2011].

Salido, O. and Moreno, L. 2009. Familia y género, in *Reformas de las políticas del bienestar en España*, edited by L. Moreno. Madrid: Siglo XXI, 281–308.

San José, B. 1986. *Democracia e Igualdad de Derechos Laborales de la Mujer.* Madrid: IM, Ministerio de Cultura.

Sarasa, S. and Billingsley, S. 2008. Personal and Household Care Giving from Adult Children to Parents and Social Stratification, in *Families, Ageing and Social Policy*, edited by C. Saraceno. Cheltenham: Edward Elgar, 123–46.

Threlfall, M. (ed.) 1996. *Mapping the Women's Movement.* London and New York: Verso.

Valiente, C. 1996. El feminismo institucional en España: el Instituto de la Mujer 1983–1994. *Revista Internacional de Sociología*, 13, 163–204.

Valiente, C. 2000. Género y Ciudadanía: Los organismos de igualdad y el Estado de Bienestar en España, in *Ciudadanía y Democracia*, edited by M. Pérez Ledesma. Madrid: Pablo Iglesias, 199–229.

PART II
Levels of Governance, Social Dialogue, Welfare Mix and Public Debates

Chapter 5
Policy Concertation, Trade Unions and the Transformation of the Spanish Welfare State

Oscar Molina

Introduction

The development and consolidation of European welfare states has historically been closely linked to trade unions' organizational configuration, strength, and forms of representation, as well as to the presence of neo-corporatist patterns of interaction between trade unions and business organizations and governments (Wilensky 1976). Class-based power-resource approaches to welfare states assume that strong, centralized and encompassing trade unions, in conjunction with social democratic governments, explain why some countries have higher levels of social expenditure than others (Korpi 1978). Nonetheless, the importance of class conflict and neo-corporatist politics has been questioned by the literature on the new politics of welfare state reform (Pierson 1994, 1996). According to this literature, differences in welfare retrenchment paths triggered by post-industrial change and government budget deficits are explained by the resistance to change of new welfare clients in the face of the erosion of neo-corporatist structures and trade union weakness (Lash and Urry 1987; Schmitter 1989). Although Pierson's work has become the point of reference in explanations of retrenchment policies, the return since the early 1990s to social pacts and competitive corporatism in processes of welfare state reconfiguration (Rhodes 1998) introduced new elements to the interpretation of welfare adjustment. This return partly explains persisting varieties of welfare development and makes it necessary to examine more closely domestic factors shaping the preferences and attitudes of social partners with regard to welfare reform, as well as the form and degree of their participation in policymaking.

Because of its specific historical conditions, the Spanish case is of interest in testing the validity of different explanations of welfare state development, and more specifically in understanding the impact of neo-corporatist politics. Since 1978 policy concertation has also played a central role in the development and transformation of the Spanish welfare system. Concertation and social pacts lack some of the structural and institutional prerequisites theorized by neo-corporatist theory. Nevertheless, they have been crucial for political and economic transition.

They have had little impact upon the expansion of welfare programmes, with the likely exception of unemployment benefits and pensions; nonetheless, they have played a much more important role during the most recent phases of consolidation and rationalization. In fact, Spain has been presented as a champion in the literature on competitive corporatism or return to social pacts (Pérez 2000; Molina 2005; Royo 2002). After the breakdown of social dialogue and concertation in the late 1980s, concertation gained new momentum after 1996, and has remained a key factor in Spain's most recent period of economic expansion. However, the economic downturn since 2007 seems to have undermined the consensus that had characterized the relationships among social partners since the early 1990s.

This chapter explores the interaction between concertation and the transformation of the welfare state in Spain. Many of the reforms that have been implemented since 1980 have been preceded by negotiations among social partners and the government. This has been the case particularly for social protection programmes like pensions and unemployment benefits. Nonetheless, the priorities of actors regarding income (re)distribution and negotiation patterns have changed significantly during this period. In the years from the transition to democracy until 1987 trade unions were mostly worried about their organizational and institutional consolidation; and as a consequence, welfare issues were included in comprehensive social pacts as part of the political deal to guarantee wage moderation. The consequence was a significant fall in the wage share in the economy and only a moderate increase in social spending levels. The 1990s witnessed a change in this pattern whereby welfare issues moved to the top of the trade unions' agenda, coinciding with a shift towards narrower pacts. Even though this shift made it possible to adopt a more consensual approach to reform attempts, policy concertation still depends largely on the political preferences and needs of incumbent governments.

The analysis of social dialogue processes surrounding the main episodes of welfare state reform and more specifically unemployment benefits and pensions shows first of all how policies have been shaped not only by the forces of globalization or the government's ideology within a changing macroeconomic environment, but also by other domestic factors such as the social partners' demands and political and organizational capabilities. The blame avoidance and legitimizing character of policy concertation in a country where trade unions have an institutional role and mobilization capacity that far exceeds their membership base have certainly influenced the form and direction of the executive's reforms. However, this influence has been tamed by context-related and institutional or organizational factors.

The chapter is organized in three sections. The first section describes the evolution of concertation and social pacts from the early years of democracy up to the present. The second provides an interpretation of these developments in the light of existing theories exploring the relationship between concertation and welfare state development as well as the policymaking and institutional context.

The final section analyses the implications of the evolution of concertation for the transformation of the Spanish welfare state.

Social Pacts, Concertation and Welfare State Development

In order to analyse the impact of concertation and social dialogue in welfare state development, we have identified four main periods which partly overlap with existing classifications of welfare state development in Spain (Rodriguez Cabrero 2004). For each of these periods, we first explore the socio-economic and political context, and analyse the preferences and dynamics of the negotiations among the social partners, and end with a description of the main outcomes in terms of agreements reached and implications for welfare state development.

Social Pacts and the Expansion of a Democratic Welfare State (1978–1988)

After 1976, Spain entered into a transition period whose atmosphere was one of surprising calm and order. The spontaneous forms of organization and general mobilization against the regime that followed the death of Franco were progressively brought under control by the newly organized unions, as shown by the extraordinary increase in union membership density rates (Jordana 1996). The imperative to engage simultaneously in macroeconomic adjustment and political stabilization marked the pattern of policymaking interactions in those years. Executives needed to keep social conflict at low levels, while trade unions wanted to profit from their power of mobilization in order to win political recognition and organizational benefits. This strong strategic interdependence characterized the experience of concertation and social pacts in the early 1980s (Molina 2007).

The political and economic needs of Spain at that time were addressed through the Moncloa Pacts (1978), which put economic issues at the top of the policy agenda and proposed a strategy of consensus and social dialogue to accompany reforms. Trade unions and employers' organizations did participate very actively in the implementation of the guidelines for economic management contained in the Pacts. Incomes policies together with the expansion of social programmes and consolidation of the industrial relations system were the main targets of the social agreements in the 1979–86 period, which would lead some authors to claim the consolidation of social corporatism in Spain (Giner and Sevilla 1984). However, the organizational characteristics of the trade unions (which were weak and ideologically divided) and the employers were far from the neo-corporatist ideal type. The trade union movement that emerged during the transition was an attenuated duopoly of two large national confederations (UGT and CCOO), along with some small professional and/or regional confederations. The General Union of Workers (*Unión General de Trabajadores*, UGT) was historically the dominant union confederation and managed to reorganize abroad during the Franco dictatorship with the support of the International Confederation of Free

Trade Unions. During the 1960s some groups of workers opted to act within the limits of the law but at the margins of the Franco regime, thus creating what would be known as Workers' Committees. This strategy of militant 'entrismo' (entrism, i.e., a strategy consisting in the gradual extension of trade union members in companies), which faced strong opposition from the Franco government, would crystallize after Franco' death into Comisiones Obreras (CCOO, Workers' Commissions). The different ideological orientations persisted during the early years of the democracy, with the communist CCOO being more rooted at local or company level and endorsing a class ideology of industrial unionism and political confrontation, while UGT followed a more cooperative strategy of political action based on concertation and participation in social pacts.

On the employers' side, the Confederation of Spanish Employers (*Confederación Española de Organizaciones Empresariales*, CEOE) was created in 1977 and very rapidly monopolized employer representation. It nowadays has over 1,350,000 businesses affiliates, which cover around 95 per cent of the total number of employees in the economy. Initially, small- and medium-sized firms developed their own confederation, CEPYME, but it soon became integrated into CEOE although it retains a degree of autonomy. Even though CEOE has a relatively centralized structure, sectorial organizations have enjoyed greater power within the confederation. This representative monopoly favoured the process of concertation in the early years after the transition to democracy.

The first social pact was the 1981 National Employment Agreement (*Acuerdo Nacional sobre el Empleo*, ANE). It was initiated by the *Unión de Centro Democrático* (UCD) centre-right government some months after a failed *coup d'état* and its primary political objective was to maintain confidence in the young Spanish democracy as well as to combat the effects of the economic crisis. Even though all actors agreed on the social and political need to reach a social pact, CCOO showed some reluctance to participate in an agreement entailing a moderation of industrial action that would legitimize a harsh economic policy imposing significant costs on workers. In order to sort out these difficulties, the government made recourse to secret agreements or parallel pacts. These secret pacts contained a series of organizational and financial compensations that overcame trade unions opposition in some of the core issues of the pact. First of all, unions and employer organizations became part of the executive committees of the four specialized bodies that would manage social security, namely, the National Employment Institute (INEM), the National Social Security Institute (INSS), the National Health System (INSALUD) and the National Institute of Social Services (INSERSO). Moreover, the government increased old-age pensions by 10 per cent and augmented the coverage and duration of unemployment benefits. A 1.5 billion Spanish pesetas' fund was set up for extraordinary unemployment circumstances jointly managed by trade unions, employers and INEM.

In addition to some other bipartite union-employer inter-confederal collective bargaining agreements, the most important social pact in terms of its implications for welfare development in Spain was the 1984 Social and Economic Agreement

(*Acuerdo Económico y Social*, AES). The context of the negotiations for the 1984 social pact differed in two significant ways from that of the negotiation of the ANE: a Socialist government was elected in 1982, and fear of political instability largely disappeared as the new democratic institutions proved to be sufficiently strong to accommodate the diversity of political and social demands. As for the economy, even though the government had undertaken a major effort at industrial restructuring, industrial employment continued to fall strongly. Yet the first signs of economic recovery arrived in the middle of 1984. Government plans consisted of negotiating an agreement on wage moderation that would include other issues such as the reform of the social security system. Even though unions insisted on certain preconditions for negotiations (they would accept wage moderation only in exchange for a substantial increase in social spending and an extension in welfare entitlements, that is, the so-called social wage), both the UGT and the CCOO reacted positively to the government's announcement of talks, if only because they perceived it was a good opportunity to obtain further organizational concessions on top of the government's commitments on social spending. After a few meetings, the CCOO dropped out of negotiations as it judged that supporting the pact, and by extension the government's economic policy, 'had a delegitimizing impact upon our trade union'.[1]

Notwithstanding this setback, the government persisted with its objective of signing an agreement with the UGT and the CEOE in order to legitimize an economic policy of austerity that was imposing high costs on workers. Finally, a document was agreed consisting of an incomes policy, a declaration setting out guidelines for the negotiation of labour market reform and pension reform in the coming months. As well, a tripartite committee was set up to discuss the reform of social security. In order to gain the support of the UGT, the government made a series of organizational concessions to the trade unions, some of which were reflected in the 1985 law on trade union freedom. Most importantly, there were significant commitments regarding social spending; chapter one of the agreement contained some measures on unemployment protection and chapter five provided for a reduction in social contributions, an increase in smaller pensions as well as the establishment of a standing committee for social security reform. Finally, there were some general guidelines for pension reform consisting of the consolidation of the universal and contributory pillars as well as the extension of the non-contributory pillar. With hindsight, the analysis of the bargaining process shows how the government conceived the social pact as a purely legitimizing instrument, since only some months after the agreement was signed, and in the absence of consensus on pension reform, the government unilaterally passed law 26/1985 that was heavily contested by both the UGT and the CCOO as it restricted pension eligibility.

---

1   Interview with Salvador Bangueses, Head of Institutional Relations (Política Institucional), Madrid, 14 April 2005.

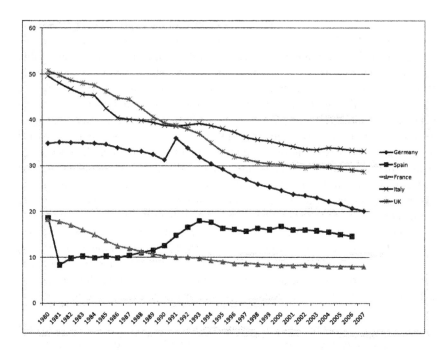

Figure 5.1   Adjusted wage share as a percentage of GDP, 1980–2009

Overall, social pacts in the 1980s did not have social protection as their major concern. Rather, industrial restructuring, macroeconomic stability, and wage increases in particular (Espina 2007) were the priorities of the Socialist government. Moreover, the trade unions in these years focused on the consolidation of their organizational structures and their institutionalization as socio-political actors. The political exchange underlying the social pacts signed in this period involved a trade-off between wage moderation and organizational and institutional benefits. The main contribution of the social pacts consisted in permitting the moderation of wage increases and, hence, a lower inflation rate. But, contrary to the traditional notion and practice of political exchange, this was not accompanied by a significant increase in social spending. As Figure 5.1 shows, social pacts were very effective in tackling high inflation fuelled by wage increases, but in a period of rapid productivity growth due to industrial restructuring they triggered a capital-biased income distribution. This redistribution and its effects on workers were only partly compensated by the extension of social programmes. As part of its economic policy based on fiscal austerity, the Socialist government's extension and universalization of social benefits and services in areas such as education, health and pensions did not contribute to closing the gap with the other major European economies (see Figure 5.2). The conflict that characterised the second half of the 1980s was motivated precisely by trade unions' perception that the costs incurred

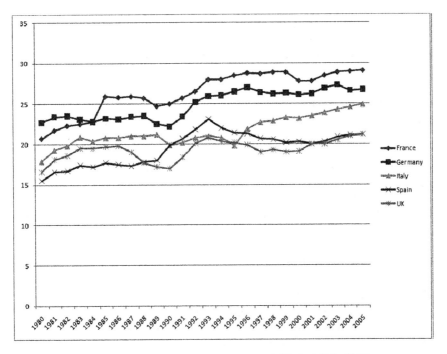

Figure 5.2   Social spending as a percentage of GDP, 1980–2005

by wage moderation far outweighed the social benefits. Nonetheless, some of the most important changes in the configuration of the Spanish welfare state in this period are not reflected in a purely quantitative assessment of social spending. This is the case with the decentralization to regional and local governments of some programmes and general services like education, health, housing and public employment.

Universalization Despite Conflict (1988–1995)

After the 1984 AES Social Pact, and having obtained an absolute majority in the 1986 elections, the government in 1987 launched a new proposal for a tripartite social pact around the economic policy and budget for 1988. Initial contacts between trade unions, government and employer organizations soon broke down as unions condemned the inclusion of wage moderation and the economic policy of austerity being followed by the Socialist government. However, unions' criticisms were directed not only against the substance of the government's plans but also against the process and format of the negotiations, which were to culminate in a broad social pact to be accepted or rejected as a whole. In the unions' views this form of negotiation was mostly aimed at achieving an ambitious social pact that would legitimize government policy. At the end of 1987 the government announced a package of labour market measures that were heavily contested by the trade unions and triggered the first general strike called by the two main confederations against the Socialist government's economic and labour market policies. The underlying cause of conflict was disagreement over social expenditure and the tightening of eligibility for unemployment and other benefits. The absence of a significant departure from the economic policy of austerity as demanded by the trade unions became an insurmountable obstacle to the success of the negotiations.

The political costs of conflict with trade unions and the impact of the 1988 general strike forced the government to undertake the so-called *giro social* (social turn) in its economic policy with the objective of regaining popular support from the left of the spectrum. Moreover, in a context of rapid growth it became more difficult to justify an austerity budget and restricting social expenditure. Following the general strike, the government agreed to initiate a new process of social dialogue, which took place, in line with the preference expressed by trade unions, on separate tables for each of the issues negotiated. By doing this, trade unions aimed to endow social dialogue with a less distributive and a more problem-solving character, as already outlined in the 1988 Union Priorities Proposal (*Propuesta Sindical Prioritaria*, PSP), a programmatic accord between the CCOO and the UGT over their strategies, proposals and priorities. As a result of both the government's social turn and the social dialogue with unions, a series of measures related to social protection were passed. Hence, Law 3/1989 extended the coverage of unemployment benefits to some particularly exposed groups, set minimum pensions at the level of the statutory minimum wage and increased the lowest pension benefits. This, together with Law 26/1990, led to the universalization of social protection by guaranteeing universal access to the public health system and the extension of pensions to individuals without accumulated contributory rights. Moreover, the third means-tested pillar was finally developed and implemented at both state and regional levels (Arriba and Pérez 2007).

The rapid catch-up process resulting from the social turn came to a sudden end with the change in economic conditions and the deep economic recession starting in 1992. The crisis was soon mirrored in skyrocketing unemployment (23 per cent in 1993) and a further increase in the budget deficit, which quite significantly worsened the political situation. The Socialist government thus intensified its search for consensus with the social partners in order to regain legitimacy, and proposed a social pact in 1992 and 1993. However, these attempts ended in failure because of disagreements about social protection, with unemployment benefits a particularly contested issue. The Socialist government in 1992 invited the trade unions and the employers to negotiate with it a 'Social Pact for Progress'.[2] Unions' opposition to both the government's and employers' proposals focused on wage moderation as the mechanism to restore the competitiveness of the Spanish economy. Moreover, the unions judged the government's commitments with respect to unemployment benefits to be clearly insufficient. But the unions also

---

2   Diario de Sesiones del Congreso de los Diputados, Pleno, n. 131, 19-9-1991.

disagreed with the idea of negotiating and signing one large encompassing pact. As negotiations failed, the government unilaterally passed a law modifying the conditions of eligibility for unemployment benefits (law 22/1992, the so-called *decretazo*). The unions responded by calling for another general strike.

The further deterioration of economic and political conditions in 1993 favoured new attempts to negotiate a social pact, but the negotiations failed again as the trade unions believed that the government's plans did not entail a substantial change in the economic policy that was hitting workers hard. Negotiations for a 'Social Pact for Employment' started on the basis of the general guidelines of economic policy contained in the 1994 draft Budget. The document presented for discussion consisted of: (*a*) a three-year incomes policy pact, (*b*) reform of social protection, (*c*) reform of the labour market and (*d*) measures to support the productive system.[3] Nonetheless, trade unions maintained their opposition to including wage moderation in a tripartite catch-all pact, as well as to any cut in social spending. As a consequence, the government was forced to unilaterally implement the reforms in the labour market and the welfare state. The immediate response of the trade unions was to call a one-day general strike on 27 January 1994.

Faced with a lack of social consensus for embracing reform of social security, the Socialist government looked for political support. The result of this search was the signing of the so-called Toledo Pact in 1995. This pact consisted in a series of measures to guarantee the sustainability of the pension system (for a more detailed analysis, see Chapter 2 in this volume). Among other things, this pact established a clear separation between the funding of contributory and universal benefits. Moreover, it established a reserve fund to ensure social benefits and services in times of crisis. Overall, this pact laid the foundations for the sustainability and development of the social security system in the following years.

Contrary to what happened in the previous period, the years 1988–95 were characterized by an absence of social pacts and high levels of conflict, as the 1988, 1992 and 1994 general strikes show. However, looking at Figure 5.2 we can observe a remarkable increase in social spending over this period. On the one hand, economic conditions improved significantly on the years following transition to democracy, hence permitting the government to relax its fiscal austerity. But equally important was the political context as the conflict with the trade unions translated into the electoral arena. Hence, the social turn implemented by the Socialist government between 1988 and 1991, notwithstanding the finance's minister opposition, had the ultimate goal of restoring a cooperative relationship with the trade unions in order to avoid competition from the left. As a consequence, social protection was universalized as the third pillar of the Spanish welfare state was extended significantly. The last few years of the Socialist government were nonetheless characterized by a return to open conflict as the government was forced to implement an economic and fiscal austerity programme to deal with the

---

3   *El País*, 4 September 1993.

effects of the economic downturn and to meet the Maastricht Treaty criteria for joining European Monetary Union (EMU).

The Renaissance of Social Dialogue and the Activation of
Rationalized Welfare Programmes (1996–2004)

The victory of the Popular Party (PP) Conservative government of Prime Minister José Aznar in 1996, together with the first signs of economic recovery, allowed tripartite policy concertation to gain new momentum. First, the recently appointed government demonstrated considerable apprehension about the reaction of the trade unions to its economic policy. Having in mind the experience of its socialist predecessors, the new government made notable efforts to maintain permanent dialogue with the trade unions and employers' organizations in order to gain legitimacy. At the same time, both the trade unions and the employer organizations believed that the change of government opened new and less costly windows of opportunities for concertation and participation in policymaking. One month after his election, the new prime minister held a meeting with representatives of the union confederations. As the unions remained firm in their rejection of a catch-all type of social pact, the social partners and the government decided to create seven thematic tables where negotiations would proceed separately. The first step of the new government regarding social protection consisted in the negotiation of mechanisms and forms to implement the reforms in the social security system outlined in the 1995 Toledo Pact. An agreement between the trade unions and the government on the Consolidation and Rationalization of Social Security was signed in October 1996 with the opposition of the employers' organization CEOE. The agreement was passed into a law (24/1997) that established a clear differentiation between the funding sources of contributory and non-contributory benefits as well as the indexation of pensions to annual price changes. Some months later, the Conservative government gave definitive momentum to the negotiation of labour-market and collective-bargaining reform, which was finally agreed in April 1997.

Just after being re-elected with an absolute majority in 2000, the Conservative government reiterated his intention to make dialogue with the social partners its priority over the coming four years of his mandate. Four issues figured at the top of the agenda: labour market reform, collective bargaining, the pension system and the reform of the unemployment benefit system.[4] The government's preference in holding social dialogue was for respecting the autonomy of the unions and the employers. However, the government was also interested in securing tripartite agreements that would further legitimize its actions. In this vein, the government initiated contacts to negotiate a labour market reform that was nonetheless fraught with difficulties. Trade unions in October 2000 presented the 'Common Proposal for Social Dialogue', focusing on employment creation and the reduction of temporary contracts. Similarly, the CEOE presented a document about Social

---

4   *El País*, 11 July 2000.

Dialogue whose main priorities were the reform of collective bargaining, a reduction of dismissal costs, greater flexibility in part-time contracts and a reduction of social charges paid by employers. Common to both proposals was the abandonment of any reference to social pacts and the preference for more flexible forms of social dialogue.

The success of this flexible strategy can be seen in the fact that, notwithstanding the raising of new obstacles to tripartite social dialogue because of the incumbent government's absolute majority, *bipartite* policy concertation has delivered agreements in many areas. The pension agreement signed in 2001 with only the CCOO on the union side, and the tripartite agreement on reform of collective bargaining in December of the same year, show that social dialogue can progress whenever negotiations are so framed that a failure in one area does not necessary entail a similar outcome in the others. As a matter of fact, bipartite agreements between unions and employers continued in spite of the conflict triggered by the 2002 unilateral reform of unemployment protection and other measures to boost employment which triggered a general strike the same year.

At a time when meeting the Maastricht fiscal deficit criteria became the goal of economic policy, the Conservative government assiduously sought the support of trade unions and employers. Population ageing, together with the need to consolidate some welfare programmes, to rationalize the system as a whole and to activate social protection, constituted a difficult environment in which to undertake reform. Notwithstanding these obstacles, policy concertation proved to be a valuable resource in the hands of Conservative governments in an increasingly competitive environment. On the basis of the Toledo Pact, social partners and the government made significant progress in guaranteeing the financial sustainability of the system. Nonetheless, developments during the second term of the Aznar government show how concertation in Spain is very often used instrumentally as a legitimizing device. As soon as the right-wing government attained an absolute majority, there was no longer any need to count upon the support of trade unions and employers' associations, and tripartite concertation weakened significantly.

The Consolidation of Social Dialogue and the Fourth Pillar of the Welfare State (2004–2009)

The continuity in the economic policy of the Socialist government elected in 2004 with that of its PP predecessors contrasts with its innovative agenda in civil and social rights (Kennedy 2007). The maintenance of high rates of GDP growth and employment creation provided a favourable context for engaging in an ambitious reform programme in areas of gender equality, civil rights, social protection and the labour market. From the outset, the government headed by Mr J.L. Rodríguez Zapatero showed a strong determination to negotiate and reach consensus on social policy and labour market issues. Hence, the protocol for social dialogue signed between the new Socialist government, trade unions and employers opened a new process with a particular focus on social protection. The new government did not exhibit any preference for the signing of tripartite social pacts. Instead, the protocol for social dialogue established a series of issues where negotiations would progress in parallel. The first important agreement in the field of social protection was the so-called *Ley de Dependencia* (39/2006) that was intended to provide assistance to those unable to care for themselves. This is probably one of the most important pieces of legislation regarding social rights in Spain since the return to democracy. Nonetheless, recent assessments of its implementation have highlighted the financial difficulties in implementing it (see Chapter 12 in this volume). Some other agreements and reforms were reached in these years in the context of the social dialogue opened in 2004; for example, law 40/2007 established new provisions for retirement at age 65 as well as disability and widowers' pensions.

The re-election of the Socialist Party in the 2008 elections coincided with the first symptoms of economic recession affecting the Spanish economy. The intensity and duration of the crisis have accordingly contributed to eroding the process of social dialogue. First, the trade unions and the employers did not renew the peak inter-confederal agreement on collective bargaining that had been signed on a yearly basis since 2002. Disagreements surfaced regarding the labour market reform proposal as negotiations broke down before the summer of 2009. New attempts in the later months of 2009 and early 2010 faced many difficulties because of trade union opposition to a government proposal to increase the pensionable age to 67. The rapid growth in social spending triggered by increasingly high unemployment together with an ad hoc extension of unemployment benefit duration added further elements of stress and uncertainty to the picture, and significantly reduced the Socialist government's room for manoeuvre in reaching agreement with the social partners. The package of measures adopted in May 2010 to reduce the budget deficit in future years, including a freeze on some pensions, cuts on public employees' salaries and reductions in some family programmes, reopened conflict between unions and government. Indeed, the labour market reform that the government enacted unilaterally in June 2010 led the trade unions to call a new general strike.

The Relationship between Concertation and Welfare State Development in Spain

As the previous section shows, there has been a clear evolution in the form as well as the substance of negotiations since the early 1980s. First, there has been a reduction in the number of issues negotiated. That is, a move from broad to narrow concertation. Second, and related to the previous point, the issues subject to either bipartite or tripartite concertation have also become more regulatory and less distributional. As the number of issues dealt with in the same negotiation process increases, so do the possibilities of profitable quid pro quos for the participants. Nonetheless, these exchanges are more likely to take a purely distributional form than when negotiations are limited to one or two policy issues. In such cases, consensus is reached following a more a problem-solving rather than a purely distributional logic. However, this does not mean there is no political exchange. As shown in the previous section, the multifaceted and often inter-temporal character of the exchange process underlying negotiations has allowed actors to deploy resources of very different kinds in order to reach agreements. Even though some of these reforms did not directly impinge upon welfare state programmes, the underlying quid pro quo had important indirect effects for future welfare development and social protection. Hence, the labour market strategy followed by the first Socialist government, consisting as it did in increasing flexibility at the margins of the labour market together with trade unions' defence of protected employees, had a very negative impact on some particularly vulnerable groups. The strong labour market segmentation produced by the 1984 reform, with a rapid increase in temporary employment affecting mostly the young, women and, more recently, immigrants, has placed new and increasing demands on the welfare state for protection against unemployment, low wages and so forth.

In light of the above, how does the Spanish experience fit within the existing body of research linking welfare states to the concerted action of social partners? Power-resource theory has provided the main framework for explaining cross-country diversity in social spending levels and welfare policies by emphasizing the strength of social democratic labour movements (Korpi 1974; Esping-Andersen 1985). The democratic class struggle or working class mobilization allowed workers and their representative organizations to play a critical role in expanding welfare states, and as a consequence provided an alternative explanation to the dominant logic of the industrialism paradigm (Kerr et al. 1960).

Neo-corporatism provided further insights in this direction by claiming that not only membership-based power but also the structure of interest intermediation contributed to explaining the superior macroeconomic performance and more developed welfare states in some countries, including higher levels of social protection, lower unemployment and inflation rates, and lower wage and income inequalities (Pontusson 2005). The alleged superiority of neo-corporatism to neo-liberalism as an economic system lay, among other things, in its capacity to combine socially sustainable (equitable) economic growth with high levels of social protection thanks to the encompassing nature and centralization of its organized interests (Pekkarinen, Pohjola and Rowthorn 1992). These organizational configurations delivered all their potential benefits when interacting with a social democratic government within a demand-oriented macroeconomic framework.

The relationship between neo-corporatist structures and spending levels has nonetheless been challenged since the late 1970s. First, the erosion of neo-corporatist structures and institutions as a result of the decentralization of collective bargaining and falling trade union membership levels led many authors to predict the death of neo-corporatism (Streeck and Schmitter 1991). Second, the extension of neo-liberal agendas and growing constraints on national governments arising from economic and financial internationalization made it increasingly difficult for governments to engage in the type of political exchange that sustained neo-corporatist politics. Together, these developments have put into question some of the claims of power-resource and neo-corporatist theories as they have diminished the impact of social partners on the restructuring and reconfiguration of welfare states and/or their capacity to avoid cuts in spending levels. At the same time, employer-centred approaches have developed and gained increasing relevance since the early 1990s. Swenson (1991, 2002) argues that power-resource approaches underscored the role of employers and employers' organizations in welfare state development. Building upon this insight, 'varieties of capitalism' literature has claimed the need to place the firm back at the centre of the analysis (Hall and Soskice 2001).

Even though some of the trends just mentioned have affected the development of welfare states and spending levels, most of the studies that predicted the end of neo-corporatism and by extension the deconstruction of welfare states and expenditure retrenchment failed to acknowledge that, while structures had certainly eroded (though not disappeared), practices and processes remained alive and well (Baccaro 2003). The implications of this distinction are important for understanding the effects of interest group politics in the recent processes of welfare state adjustment. Hence, while neo-corporatism as a system of interest representation ('neo-corporatism 1', see Lehmbruch and Schmitter 1982) relied upon the incentives provided by the organizational structures of trade unions and employer organizations in order to explain outcomes, neo-corporatism as a policymaking system ('neo-corporatism 2') focuses on the political exchange that underlies negotiations between governments and organized social interests (Pizzorno 1976; Molina and Rhodes 2002). This implies that, notwithstanding the erosion in organizational structures and resources, trade unions remain important political and institutional actors which can use resources of different kinds in negotiations with governments and employer organizations.

It follows from this analysis that the relationship between policy concertation and the welfare state is mediated by variables other than just the organizational characteristics of the social partners. These variables determine both the possibilities for exchange and consensus among the government and social partners and their attitudes. An illustration of this point is the power of trade unions in Spain. If we had to judge their agenda-setting power and capacity to influence the outcome of negotiations solely by reference to their membership, we would conclude that they are very weak, as Figure 5.3 suggests. However, in spite of their very low levels of density, the two main union confederations in Spain have managed to retain a significant social and political role thanks to the institutionalization of collective bargaining, their adaptation to the requirements and demands of the new industrial and economic context, and their unitary strategies of political action since the mid-1990s. Organizational indicators in this case provide little insight into the effective power of trade unions or the perceptions other actors have of it.

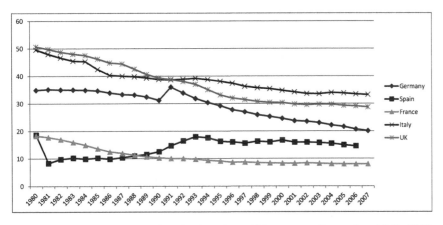

Figure 5.3   Trade Union density in selected European Countries, 1980–2007

Another aspect of the Spanish case that tells against a narrow focus on organizational characteristics is the role of the public sector. In a country like Spain, characterized by adversarial industrial relations amongst social partners, the state plays a critical mediating role both in the industrial relations sphere and also in the political arena. As pointed out by Oliet (2004: 94), what is distinctive of the Spanish experience is that the state 'engineered' the whole process of concertation, at least until the 1990s, because of the organizational fluidity and the adversarial style of industrial relations. This mediation has nonetheless varied with the colour of governments. Since its very beginning, the Spanish party system has been characterized by a bipolar equilibrium, and most often than not, strong governments. This stability has resulted from an electoral system that rewards large parties and penalizes small- or medium-sized ones. The legitimacy provided by the participation of social partners in the negotiation and drafting of policies has been of the utmost relevance in promoting some of the most important reforms of social protection. The importance of the public sector in the process of concertation is also magnified by the weak institutionalization of social dialogue and concertation in Spain, which makes it highly dependent on the political and economic context as well as state action. Indeed, the Spanish policymaking system for many years lacked a formal institution channelling tripartite social dialogue. Such a body was not created until 1992 (*Consejo Economico y Social*). In spite of governments' attempts to turn it into a privileged forum for negotiations among social partners, this institution has failed to institutionalize the process of social dialogue in Spain.

It is only when we incorporate these contextual and attitudinal elements into the analysis of concertation that we can explain the process of negotiation (including its form and substance) and its outcomes. These variables are particularly important in the case of Spain in explaining the changes that have occurred in the pattern and substance of negotiations.

Concluding Remarks

Policy concertation in Spain has followed an atypical pattern when compared with other western European countries. First, it gained momentum precisely when commentators throughout Europe were proclaiming the death of neo-corporatism. Second, contrary to the predictions of neo-corporatist theory, the decade of Socialist government between 1986 and 1996 was characterized by conflict with trade unions, as the 1988, 1992 and 1994 general strikes show. Finally, tripartite concertation re-emerged under the first term of the centre-right PP and has remained alive and well since then, with the exception of a short interval during its second term. The return to power of the Socialist Party in 2004 and its re-election in 2008 have confirmed that social dialogue remains in good shape in Spain, although the recent economic crisis that broke in 2008 seems to have revived old tensions among the social partners.

The Spanish case is nonetheless similar to other European experiences in that it is impossible to understand the transformation of welfare programmes without reference to the influence of tripartite and bipartite policy concertation. Governments of different persuasions have relied upon the social partners to negotiate their proposals, and whenever they have tried unilaterally to enact reforms in the social protection system they have encountered strong opposition from the trade unions, which have on some occasions managed to force the government to withdraw its proposed legislation. Given the lack of formal channels for concertation as well as the organizational characteristics of the trade unions, the political exchange underlying the negotiation process is the crucial dimension to examine in order to understand the success or failure of the negotiation process as well as its outcomes. The resources that social partners and the government can use in order to find a mutually beneficial quid pro quo include not only their capacity to deliver on the terms of their agreements but also intangible assets such as the capacity to legitimize them.

The characteristics of, as well as the possibilities for, a successful political exchange have nonetheless varied with the context as well as actors' preferences or priorities regarding both the substance and the process of negotiations. Hence, welfare policy featured only marginally in the tripartite social pacts of the early 1980s, as both the government and the trade unions had other economic and social priorities. Because of the high unemployment rates triggered by low growth levels and industrial restructuring, unemployment benefits became the main aspect of social protection dealt with in tripartite negotiations in those years. Nonetheless, the 1985 pension reform imposed unilaterally by the Socialist government represented a turning point in the relationship between the Socialist UGT trade union confederation and the government, and opened a period of conflict. Paradoxically, it was precisely during this period that welfare spending expanded as the Socialist government implemented a social turn in its economic policy in response to a favorable economic environment in order to alleviate tensions with the trade unions, the UGT in particular. Nonetheless, the pressures on social policy created by the economic crisis of 1991–3 as well as Maastricht public deficit-debt criteria largely limited the possibilities for political exchange, leading to new disagreements on the unemployment benefits scheme.

By contrast, policy concertation has played a more important and direct role in the consolidation and rationalization phases. More specifically, the role of the social partners in welfare policy has been enhanced by the implementation of the 1995 Toledo Pact, which has provided a new framework for recasting welfare programmes in general and the pension system in particular. At the same time as the trade unions reconsidered welfare policy as a priority, they also changed their preferences about the form of negotiations. This change has also had implications for welfare policy; the shift towards narrow, bipartite negotiations has contributed to the adoption of a more consensual and less purely distributional approach to policymaking in a favourable economic context. The downside of narrow bipartite concertation is that it potentially limits the possibilities of establishing positive complementarities across policy areas, and, in the context of European guidelines, to successfully activate social policy in order to make welfare work.

Overall, the Spanish case shows how the neo-corporatist arena remains important for explaining welfare state development. Even though the Spanish trade unions are weak in terms of membership, they nonetheless retain significant resources that they can use in the political exchange process underlying concertation. Apart from their historically strong mobilization capacity, which they can use as a threat in the negotiation process as well as in the electoral arena, they maintain a capacity over wage policy which in the context of EMU has become a major determinant of macroeconomic performance. More importantly, the gradual inclusion of social policy issues in collective bargaining processes is opening new spaces of action and influence for trade unions.

References

Arriba, A. and Pérez, B. 2007. La última red de protección social en España: prestaciones asistenciales y su activación. *Política y Sociedad*, 44(2), 115–33.

Baccaro, L. 2003. What is Alive and What is Dead in the Theory of Corporatism? *British Journal of Industrial Relations*, 41(4), 683–706.

Espina, A. 2007. La vuelta del 'hijo pródigo'. El Estado de Bienestar español en el camino hacia la Unión Económica y Monetaria. *Política y Sociedad*, 44(2), 45–67.

Esping-Andersen, G. 1985. *Politics Against Markets*. Princeton: Princeton University Press.

Giner, S. and Sevilla, J. 1984. Spain: From Corporatism to Corporatism, in *Southern Europe Transformed*, edited by A. Alla. London: Harper Row.

Hall, P. and Soskice, D. 2001. *Varieties of Capitalism: The Institutional Foundations of Comparative Advantage*. Oxford: Oxford University Press.

Jordana, J. 1996. Reconsidering Union Membership in Spain, 1977–1994: Halting Decline in a Context of Democratic Consolidation. *Industrial Relations Journal*, 27(3), 211–24.

Kennedy, P. 2007. Phoenix from the Ashes. The PSOE Government under Rodríguez Zapatero 2004–2007: A New Model for Social Democracy. *International Journal of Iberian Studies*, 20(3), 187–206.

Kerr, C., Dunlop, J., Harbison, F. and Myers, C. 1960. *Industrialism and Industrial Man*. New York: Oxford University Press.

Korpi, W. 1974. Conflict, Power and Relative Deprivation. *American Political Science Review*, 68, 1569–78.

Korpi, W. 1978. *The Working Class in Welfare Capitalism*. London: Routledge.

Lash, S. and Urry, J. 1987. *The End of Organized Capitalism*. Oxford: Polity Press.

Lehmbruch, G. and Schmitter, P. (eds) 1982. *Patterns of Corporatist Policy-making*. Beverly Hills: Sage.

Molina, O. 2005. Political Exchange and Bargaining Reform in Italy and Spain. *European Journal of Industrial Relations*, 11(1), 7–26.

Molina, O. 2007. Social Pacts in Spain. From Neo-corporatist Euphoria to Union Disenchantment, in *The Emergence and Evolution of Social Pacts*, edited by M. Rhodes et al. Country Papers, Report for the NEWGOV Project, reference 18a/D06.

Molina, O. and Rhodes, M. 2002. Corporatism: The Past, Present, and Future of a Concept. *Annual Review of Political Science*, 5, 305–31.

Oliet, A. 2004. *La Concertación Social en la Democracia Española: Crónica de un Difícil Intercambio*. Valencia: Tirant lo Blanch.

Pekkarinen, J., Pohjola, M. and Rowthorn, B. 1992. *Social Corporatism: A Superior Economic System?* Oxford: Clarendon.

Pérez, S. 2000. From De-centralization to Reorganization: The Resurgence of National-level Social Bargaining in Italy and Spain. *Comparative Politics*, 32(4), 437–58.

Pierson, P. 1994. *Dismantling the Welfare State? Reagan, Thatcher, and the Politics of Retrenchment*. Cambridge: Cambridge University Press.

Pierson, P. 1996. The New Politics of the Welfare State. *World Politics*, 48, 143–79.

Pizzorno, A. 1976. Scambio politico e identità collettiva nel conflitto di classe, in *Conflitti in Europa. Lotte di Classe, Sindicati e Stato dopo il 68*, edited by C. Crouch and A. Pizzorno. Milan: Etas Libri, 165–98.

Pontusson, J. 2005. Varieties and Commonalities of Capitalism, in *Varieties of Capitalism, Varieties of Approaches*, edited by D. Coates. New York: Palgrave, 163–88.

Rhodes, M. 1998. Globalization, Labor Markets and Welfare States: A Future of 'Competitive Corporatism'?, in *The Future of European Welfare: A New Social Contract*, edited by M. Rhodes and Y. Meny. London: Palgrave Macmillan, 178–203.

Rodriguez Cabrero, G. 2004. *El Estado de Bienestar en España: Debate, Desarrollo y Retos*. Madrid: Fundamentos.

Royo, S. 2002. *A New Century of Corporatism? Corporatism in Southern Europe. Spain and Portugal in Comparative Perspective*. Westport, CT: Praeger.

Schmitter, P. 1989. Corporatism is Dead! Long Live Corporatism! *Government and Opposition*, 24, 54–73.

Streeck, W. and Schmitter, P. 1991. From National Corporatism to Transnational Pluralism: Organized Interests in the Single European Market. *Politics and Society*, 19(2), 133–64.

Swenson, P. 1991. Bringing Capital Back In, or Social Democracy Reconsidered: Employer Power, Cross-class Alliances, and Centralization of Industrial Relations in Denmark and Sweden. *World Politics*, 43, 513–44.

Swenson, P. 2002. *Capitalists against Markets: The Making of Labor Markets and Welfare States in the United States and Sweden*. New York: Oxford University Press.

Wilensky, H. 1976. *The 'New Corporatism', Centralization and the Welfare State*. London: Sage.

Chapter 6
Regional Welfare Regimes and Multi-level Governance

Raquel Gallego and Joan Subirats

Political Devolution and the Spanish Welfare State

The political and administrative decentralization process that began in Spain with the transition to democracy at the end of the 1970s is unprecedented in extent and intensity in the history of the country. It has turned what was initially a unitary state into one of the most decentralized states in Europe. It is an attempt to resolve long-standing tensions between the political centre and peripheral nationalism that even contributed to the civil war of 1936–9. In the three decades or so since they were established, Spain's Autonomous Communities (AACC from now on) have gone on to control more than a third of total public spending (a share that can be explained by the budgetary preponderance of programmes providing health care, education and social services), to manage more than a million and half civil servants (with a large number of health workers and teachers) and to enact, and to try to enforce, more than three thousand of their own laws. All of this is being done through institutions led by two hundred regional ministers and presidents and more than a thousand parliamentarians, alongside a level of local government that has its own strong traditions and is represented by over 8,000 town halls and dozens of provincial councils distributed throughout Spain's territory.

When in 1977 discussions began in Spain about the future territorial distribution of power, the advantages and disadvantages of a general decentralization of political structures in a country with a long centralist tradition became part of the central debate on the process of democratic consolidation. For some commentators, then and now, centralization ensured certain economies of scale in some services, involved efficient coordination and management on externalities in each area, guaranteed greater homogeneity in the provision of public services, facilitated redistribution policies and brought greater efficiency to stabilization policies. For those who favoured decentralization, regional autonomy would reduce the bureaucratic burden, allow a certain competence among institutions that would result in better services for the public, and would make possible a certain amount of experimentation in that problems could be tackled differently in each region.

To these technical and functional aspects were added the more political aspects that particularly affected regions which had traditionally been uncomfortable with the central government regime and which, in defence of their different historical identities, preferred solutions that reflected the way they fitted into a new multinational and democratic Spain. On top of all this was Spain's process of integration into the European Community in the mid-1980s and its impact on the regional levels of government. Among other consequences, the AACC were presented with new opportunities for political, economic and social projection, occasionally outside the framework of the central state.

Spain's AACC were conceived constitutionally as exercising major responsibilities for welfare policies. The distribution of competences prescribed in the 1978 Constitution gives the Spanish regions full control over health, education and social services, in accordance with the basic legislation passed by the Spanish Parliament. But the Constitution establishes different degrees of responsibility among the regions. As mentioned before, the political system that emerged from the transition to democracy in Spain attempted, for the first time in the country's contemporary history, simultaneously to resolve the tensions between the central state and peripheral nationalisms, and to decentralize government. One option was to establish a political system that recognized the historical, cultural and political diversity of Spain at the end of the twentieth century ('champagne for the nationalities'), the option that was partially adopted in Spain in the 1930s. Another option was a decentralized but homogeneous system, without big differences among the new territorial powers ('coffee for everyone') (Borzël 2002). Eventually, a combination of the two options was adopted ('coffee with liqueurs' for some and 'straight coffee' for others). That is how the 1978 Spanish Constitution acquired the diversity and the asymmetry of the so-called 'autonomous system', but at the same time it did not close the door on the system's evolving into a level of self-government that was relatively similar for all regions.

So the AACC that would historically have approved Statutes of Autonomy (Catalonia, the Basque Country and Galicia), along with those that requested autonomy following a referendum (Andalusía), achieved the highest level of competencies from the start, while others obtained the same levels of power thanks to a transfer from the central state (the Canaries, Valencian region, Navarre). The other 10 AACC had to wait until 2001 to obtain levels of competencies similar to the pioneers in areas such as health and education. At present, the 17 AACC have the same competencies ceiling for their welfare policies, although it is obvious that they have used this power in different ways and with varying frequency.

The diversity and asymmetry of the current system of AACC in Spain, three decades after it was put in place, can be seen in many and varied ways. The regions are very different among themselves in terms of size, population and socio-economic situation. In many, languages other than Spanish are spoken, to varying degrees. In some of the regions there are significant differences in the prevailing civil laws, in such major areas as matrimonial rights and inheritance laws. Some regions, as a result of past legislation, enjoy a recognized fiscal autonomy that would have been impossible to establish in the other regions. The Statutes of Autonomy recognize different laws in some regions governing their institutional organization (the possibility of dissolution, holding elections at different times from other regions, and so on) or the management of their criminal justice systems. The regions have also used their powers of self-government very differently; and the public's perception of the identity and future of the AACC varies widely.

Given the weight of the AACC in welfare policies, it is not surprising that the debate on decentralization and equality is increasingly salient in Spanish politics. In Europe and elsewhere, the debate has intensified on the interrelation between decentralization and equity. If decentralization has tended to be interpreted as a process that can help improve the quality and responsiveness of welfare policies, for some it can also endanger equity because of the dynamics of differentiation and the generation of new inequalities that this entails. All this forms part of a process of reconsidering welfare policies themselves, along with their limitations and their inadequacies in relation to new productive, social and family realities. The tension between 'social citizenship' and the formulae of federal or decentralized power is nothing new. The promise of citizenship that can guarantee equal status to all members of a community, and equal access to social services and benefits throughout a territory (Marshall [1950] 1992), could come into conflict with the capacity for self-government implied by a real process of political decentralization (Banting 2006). The challenge is to strike a balance between equity and diversity (Watts 1999). Many studies have analysed how the existence of a central state has conditioned the territorial deployment and innovation of the welfare state: should the capacity for territorial differentiation be sacrificed for the sake of guaranteeing equity in the state as a whole? But we could also ask how far the existence of a devolution process has conditioned and modified the deployment of central state welfare policies: has the regulatory capacity of decentralized governments conditioned the welfare structure of the state as a whole?

After a 30-year decentralization process, Spain is still immersed in this debate. The discussion is about the threats that the continuation and intensification of the process of decentralization to AACC pose for the Spanish system as a whole, or, from another perspective, about how the future development of the AACC conditions the demands for social policies in the country as a whole. This discussion is particularly relevant when the central aim of all processes of decentralizing political decision-making is to increase the range of options available to those regions, so that they can meet as well as possible the specific demands of a given part of the territory. In Spain this is intensified by the ambition expressed in the Constitution to recognize and generate spaces of diversity (of different nationalities and regions) in relations between the citizens of each autonomous region, between different AACC, and between the regions and the whole that is represented by the state.

In this chapter we analyse the development of this issue, which is especially relevant in Spain, where the development of welfare policies has coincided historically with the process of political decentralization. This experience has not been shared by the European or Anglo-Saxon countries that have been analysed in more depth in the comparative literature. To this end, we rely on the results of a recently completed research project on decentralization and inequality in Spain, coordinated by Gallego and Subirats (2010).[1] We first analyse the extent to which the AACC have generated distinct welfare regimes. Due to space limitations, we centre the analysis on the options adopted for regional health and education policies, which are programmes that consume the largest budgets in the area of social policy. The analysis shows how the capacity for self-government has led the AACC to generate specific configurations of actors involved in the production of welfare, while a common structure of rights and social benefits has been maintained for the whole territory of the central state, as part of an overriding logic of interrelationship that has been driven more by the dynamic of multi-level government than by that of command and control. Over these years the basic social inequalities that traditionally existed between the territories has been reduced, while the capacity for diversification has encountered spaces to be developed beyond the core of shared policies. We then use the results of 17 focus groups (one for each region) conducted within the aforementioned study to review the predominant perceptions of the impacts of decentralization on social and territorial equity. As will be shown, despite acknowledgement of a global increase in welfare and equity since decentralization began, the general perception is of deep suspicion that possible negative future effects of devolution could reverse the achievements made so far. But all of this is still subject to further evolution that is hard to predict in such turbulent times as the present.

Self-government and Welfare Policies

The evolution of the welfare state in Spain has been, and still is, fully associated with the territorial distribution of power. The reason is that the Spanish map of welfare policies is the result of two simultaneous processes over an equal period of time since the transition to democracy: on the one hand, the gradual (and as yet unfinished) creation of a modern, European welfare state and, on the other, the still incomplete decentralization of state competences in key areas of service provision. In this situation, owing to the lack of institutional mechanisms of either shared government or horizontal coordination, the dynamics of multi-level government have been subject to predominantly bilateral negotiations between central and

    1   This research project was conducted from March 2008 to November 2009, thanks to finance from the Institut d'Estudis Autònomics (IEA) of the Catalan government. The research team comprised José Adelantado, Miguel Àngel Alegre, Eva Alfama, Pablo Barberà, Xènia Chela, Mariña Couceiro, Julio Couto, Marta Cruells, Raquel Gallego, Sheila Gonzàlez, Mariela Iglesias, Gabriela Monteiro, Clara Riba, and Joan Subirats. The work is in press by the IEA under the title Descentralització i desigualtat en l'estat de benestar: Evolució sòcio-estructural, percepcions i polítiques autonòmiques in 2010 (see Gallego and Subirats 2010).

regional governments. Hence the schedule of transfers to the AACC and the consequent configuration of regional levels of government with differentiated capacities for decision and implementation have conditioned the evolution of the welfare state itself.

Newly created regional governments have enjoyed during this time major capacities for formulating and implementing welfare policies within the framework of basic state regulations. However, these regulations have not always pre-dated the initiatives of some AACC. As a result, the processes of implementing imitated, learned or adapted public policies, from the point of view both of discourse and of actual policy options, have not followed a clear directional pattern. In some cases, the innovation has started with one or several AACC and has spread both to other regions and to the central state administration. In other cases, it has been the central government that has innovated by proposing directives on options and actions in certain sectors. In yet other cases, the central government and the regional governments have adopted the parameters indicated by the European Union or even other international bodies.

In this context, our interpretation of how each autonomous region has used its capacity for self-government will be conditioned by at least three factors: the starting conditions (which include the degree of public participation in the different areas of intervention), the time scale (derived from the means of access to autonomy and the capacity for innovation) and the regional government budget (which varies depending on its tax system). First, regions differed in their health and education services, as they did in their social and structural characteristics. This original situation has conditioned the viable political options for each regional government. Second, the current map of regional education and health policies that we project in this analysis is the accumulated result of different time scales in the AACC.[2] After transferring education and health to the regions, the central state has conserved its competences associated with basic legislation and the guarantee of common foundations for rights throughout the territory, while the regions have legislated within this framework and assumed the management of services. Finally, the differences between the per capita budgets of the autonomous regions derived from the model of finance for the regions, also condition our interpretation of how they have used their respective capacities for self-government.

---

2   The transfer of childcare (for children aged up to three years) and compulsory education (for children aged from 3 to 16 years old) took place in the early 1980s in the AA CC that accessed autonomy by the so-called fast track (Andalusia, the Canaries, Catalonia, the Valencian region, Galicia and the Basque Country), and in 1990 for Navarre. In the remaining regions the transfers took place between 1992 and 1999. Health policy was transferred according to the following schedule: Catalonia in 1981, Andalusia and the Basque Country in 1984, the Valencian region in 1987, Navarre and Galicia in 1990, the Canaries in 1994 and the remainder in 2001.

Bearing these caveats in mind, we analyse here the policy options of the AACC on education and health on the basis of three policy dimensions: first, the discursive or symbolic dimension, that is, the frameworks of discourse with respect to the recognition of rights and principles; second, the substantive dimension, that is, the extension or intensity of the coverage policy options define and offer in each sector; and third, the operative dimension, that is, the governance structures and management tools deployed in the provision of services.

Education

The education system in Spain maintains basic features that are common to all of the AACC and that guarantee the accreditation and general validity of qualifications and certificates. In recent years, basic state legislation has been actively modified and this had affected all levels of the education system. The regions have also enacted legislation on education issues, but this has mainly been in complementary aspects or in operational and management areas. The discursive frameworks existing in regional legislation have adopted the central values and elements that have structured state legislation. However, beyond compulsory education (or mainstream schooling), broader educational aspects have provided the ideal terrain for greater differentiation. Thus, equity, effective equality, compensation for inequalities, and inclusion are frequently invoked values, along with more or less explicit, or more or less conditioned, references to families' freedom of choice in selecting schools.[3] The notable discursive homogeneity contrasts with the greater differentiation, as observed earlier, in education areas beyond the hard core of school education. For example, the differences in intensity of coverage are greater in the regulation of childcare for children aged up to three years, lifelong learning – that is, adult education – and activities relating education with its environment. This latter aspect is the most recent addition to the education agenda, which explains the greater differentiation in this respect among regions.

The data on the education systems in the different autonomous regions highlight how the generally positive perception of the hard core of the education system (the period between ages 3 and 16) is based on evidence suggesting convergence in terms of general improvements (Gallego and Subirats 2010). Throughout the period analysed, neither the quality nor the extent or coverage of the public education system suffered any significant changes, although a small dip is observed in quality issues, mostly in relation to the authority of teachers over pupils. The empirical analysis of the education factors tells us that those

---

3   Whatever the case, it is worth observing that remarkable variations exist in the specific area of the assessment of the points that are used for prioritizing the access of pupils to schools for which there is excess demand, beyond the most common references associated with income levels.

regions that tend to have higher-quality[4] education systems are those where public education is a larger part of the total system. As for the relative position of each region with respect to the subjects analysed, there is one prominent group in terms of the quality of the system (Basque Country, Navarre, Asturias and Castile and Leon), and one prominent group in relation to public coverage (Extremadura, Castile-La Mancha, the Canaries and Andalusia). A cross-analysis of the variables shows that some regions respond well to quality and coverage criteria (Asturias, Cantabria and Navarre), and one group presents more problems in the combination of the two factors considered together (Castile and Leon, Andalusia, Castile-La Mancha and Aragon). Nevertheless, we should stress that convergence and balance prevail over the differences. The data collected show that the educational inequalities that existed at the start of the process have persisted, but with the very significant peculiarity that, thanks to decentralization, they have tended to diminish. There have been improvements in catering for diversity, and there have been improvements in terms of reducing inequalities.

If we refer to the discursive or symbolic dimension of education policy, two major issues are observed that have also marked the debate on education in Europe in recent years. These are the degree of longitudinal scope of regulated or compulsory education (excluding higher education) and the scope of the educational aspects of people's lives other than the aforementioned regulated periods. Logically, from the point of view of coverage of the right to education, which is protected by the Constitution, the former aspect is of key importance. The second, meanwhile, marks the capacity of the system to deal with the challenges of lifelong learning.

An analysis of the interpretive frameworks, which show the conceptual elements of education policies in Spain, reveals the current values associated with the right to education (conceptually associated with mainstream schooling or compulsory education): quality, equity, and the criteria for priority in access to schools where there is excess demand for places. In general, the differences are not particularly significant with respect to the specification of general regulatory values in the specific frameworks in each region. However, the differences are clearer with respect to the assessment criteria used to prioritize candidates for incorporation in schools where there is excess demand: some regions use income-based criteria, while for others the proximity factor carries more weight. So in general, there are few differences in the basic conceptual elements of education policies, while there is more divergence in the operative areas of guaranteeing access to the education system when there is excess demand.

However, with respect to education issues that fall outside compulsory education, the differences are more significant. Characterization of the pre-school

---

4   In this research the quality of the education system was measured on the basis of indicators referring to resources (number of pupils per teacher or per education unit) and results (percentages of pass and fail at each level, educational level of the population) (see Gallego and Subirats 2010).

period (up to three years old) oscillates between those regions that essentially see it as one further stage of the education process, and those that see it more as a mechanism for reconciling work and family life, while others add goals such as compensation for inequalities or combine two or three of the aforementioned conditions. We find the same diversity in the field of lifelong learning. Some regions consider this stage of education to be strictly academic, while others lean more towards careers-based aspects and/or its impact on enhancing the active share of the population. In this area of informal, non-school education, some regions have legislated more in light of the logic of educational compensation, while others express a more generalist vision of education.

If we focus on the substantive dimension of education policy, two aspects enable us to identify different options for the regions: the finance effort made by each region and the level of coverage of school places that they offer at each stage of education. Also, in this case the differentiation is maintained between what we have called the central stage of education (ages 3–16) and education outside that period (pre-school and lifelong learning). An analysis of the finance data shows differences in the efforts made per pupil, fluctuations that are notably influenced by different taxation systems in the cases of the Basque Country and Navarre and, less significantly, by differences between the other regions. Here we also note greater diversity in the efforts dedicated to non-compulsory education, such as pre-school education vocational training and lifelong learning. But these varying intensities do not appear to have occasioned any outstanding impacts on the degree or extension of the population coverage of any stage of education.

Finally, we focus on the operative dimension of education policies, that is, aspects associated with implementation including management instruments and the level of involvement of different agents in the provision of services. Here we have identified different trends in privatization and municipalization. Privatization means the degree of presence of the private sector in the existing school network, including public expenditure in the so-called *concertado* (state-subsidized) sector. Municipalization refers to the weight of local or municipal governments' financial effort as a share of the overall public expenditure of each autonomous region, understood to be an indicator of the degree and significance of local government involvement in educational affairs. Although they are not educational administrations in the basic sense, their involvement can lend more weight to community aspects, which are present in so many analyses of the quality of education systems.

As for the degree of privatization of education, we should first note that in Spain generally direct publicly provided education accounts for about 66 per cent of the total, state-subsidized education around 30 per cent, and the non-state-subsidized private sector provides around 3 per cent; this pattern has been a stable one for many years. These figures vary significantly among the autonomous regions (Subirats and Gallego 2010), but these differences, especially in respect of the weight of state-subsidized education, existed before the creation of the AACC themselves. Even so, the greatest variation is in the autonomous region of Madrid, with respect to the percentage of pupils in the non-state-subsidized private sector, which is four times higher than the all-Spain average for compulsory education and more than double that for non-compulsory secondary and higher education. But the differences in the degree of privatization increase outside mainstream school education (that is, in pre-school and lifelong learning), basically because in these areas state legislation has less presence and the weight of educational traditions in each territory is considerably lighter. In some regions we even find a total absence of public involvement in pre-school education. The degree of municipality involvement in education varies notably. The municipalities of the AACC of Catalonia and Navarre spend twice the Spanish average on education, while at the other extreme the municipalities of Extremadura do not spend even half the national average.

An integrated vision of the options for regional education policies reveals that the bulk of the AACC notably converge in all the aspects concerning compulsory and non-compulsory secondary education (ages 3–18) analysed, especially in conceptual and normative aspects, with some differences in financial effort (Basque Country, Navarre), the presence of non-state-subsidized private education (Madrid), and municipal participation (Catalonia, Navarre). However, in the aspects analysed concerning non-compulsory childcare (the pre-school range and lifelong education) the variations increase significantly, leading to more well-known diversity. The final result enables us to speak of a major coincidence in the stage of education considered basic and compulsory, and of diverse expressions and preferences in the other educational areas considered. The combination of a shared basic core and a diverse range of discretionary educational policies has led, on the one hand, to convergent results (OECD 2007) and, on the other, to future perspectives in which the differential elements could be more significant in the medium term, as the educational perspective of the strictly school-based stage is extended to a vision of lifelong learning.

To summarize these findings, Table 6.1 classifies the AACC according to the degree of differentiation or innovation they show in each of the three dimensions analysed for education policy. In *italics* are those regions that appear in more than two dimensions with either a 'High' or a 'Medium' degree of differentiation or innovation – namely, Catalonia, Madrid, Basque Country, Cantabria, Asturias, Canaries and La Rioja. This analysis reveals that these regions, which have been among the first to introduce innovations in education policy, have also tended to pursue differentiated policy options with respect to central government regulations.

Table 6.1   Degree of differentiation in regional education policies in Spain

Degree of differentiation/ innovation	Discursive/ symbolic dimension*	Substantive dimension**	Operative dimension***
High	*Catalonia* *Canaries* *Asturias* *Madrid* Extremadura	País Vasco Navarra *Cantabria* *Asturias* Galicia	*Catalonia* Navarre Balearics *Madrid* *Basque Country* *La Rioja* Castile and Leon
Medium	Galicia *Cantabria* *Basque Country* Aragon Rioja Castile-La Mancha Murcia	*Catalonia* *Madrid* Balearics Castile and Leon *La Rioja* Aragon	*Cantabria* *Canaries* Aragon Murcia Valencia Asturias
Low	Andalusia Balearics Navarre Valencia Castile and Leon	Extremadura Castile-La Mancha *Canaries* Valencia Andalusía Murcia	Andalusia Extremadura Galicia Castile-La Mancha

Notes: *To assess the degree of differentiation/innovation in the symbolic or discursive dimension of regional education policy, we have combined three indicators: the values attached in regional legislation (*a*) to pre-school education, (*b*) to lifelong adult education, and (*c*) to education 'beyond school'. For pre-school education, we have considered how many of the following purposes regions specify in their legislation: as a further stage of the education process, as an instrument that facilitates the reconciliation of home and work schedules, and as an instrument of compensation for inequalities. For adult education, we have considered how many of the following purposes regions specify in their legislation: as an instrument to access the education system, as an instrument for vocational training, or as an instrument for the development of active citizenship. For education 'beyond school', we have considered how many of the following purposes regions specify in their legislation: as an instrument of educational compensation, and as an instrument of generalist education. For each education stage, the more purposes regions specify, the higher their level of differentiation/innovation.

**For the assessment of the degree of differentiation/innovation in the substantive dimension of regional education policies, we have taken into account regional public expenditure per student including compulsory education (for 3–16 year olds), vocational training, and adult education.

***For the assessment of the degree of differentiation/innovation in the operative dimension of regional education policies, we have combined two indicators: the weight of indirect provision (that is subsidized private schools) and the weight of local government financing spent on education. 'Low' includes those autonomous regions where both

indicators have lower weights, 'High' those where both indicators have higher weights, and 'Medium' where the two indicators either have the average weight or have different weights.
Source: Authors' elaboration.

Health Care

The general principles that sustain the symbolic or discursive dimension of health care policy in the AACC are based on the promotion of health and the prevention of disease, the correction of territorial and social imbalances in public health care, and universal, free access in effective conditions of equality. These principles are endorsed in the Spanish Constitution, in basic state legislation, and also in autonomous regions' statutes of autonomy (quasi-constitutions) and laws. In this sense, there is a remarkably homogeneous symbolic dimension that has achieved a high level of legitimization and consensus in being positively evaluated by citizens (Gallego and Subirats 2010). Even so, the concretion of the most specific principles has been subject to differences between AACC, but only in emphasis. The principles are specified in basic state legislation (General Health Law of 1986 and Law on the Quality and Cohesion of the National Health System of 2003) and include: the rationalization of the system, the efficiency, efficacy and exploitation of resources, the promotion of the environment, training and research, the quality and evaluation of the system, participation and the rights and obligations of users. All of these principles, despite the differences in emphasis, were incorporated in the legal frameworks of the AACC.

In general, the time scale of the legal recognition of these specific principles by the AACC has been associated with the timetable for the transfer of competencies on this matter. However, the direction of their later diffusion has not always been from central government to the regional governments. For example, the principles of rationalization and of quality and evaluation were made explicit in regional regulations subordinate to the law and implemented through numerous actions in cases such as that of Catalonia, prior to the legal initiatives or other types of action undertaken at the central government level. In Catalonia, the creation of the Hospital Network for Public Utilization in 1985, the Plan for Hospital Reorganization in 1986, the regulations prescribing the terms of contracting with health suppliers, and the creation of the Medical Technology Assessment Agency are examples of how innovation in public policies and their governing principles can originate in one autonomous region and later be used as a reference by other regional governments or by central government.

The evolution of the discursive or symbolic dimension in health policy has also progressed in line with the recognition of rights. During the first stage, the Spanish Constitution (1978) and the General Health Law (1986) recognized rights associated with the conditions for treatment, participation and claims, health care benefits, private health services and information. In a second phase, which started in the late 1990s, the AACC took the initiative by recognizing rights related to health information, intimacy, patient autonomy, medical history, medical documentation and the option of a second opinion. Led by Catalonia, Navarre and Galicia, the regional laws for health care planning began dedicating sections to citizens' rights to health care; the Basque Country was the first region to recognize the right to participation, and all the other regions have finally included rights related to treatment conditions. In this second period, the directives of international bodies paved the way for the central government passing its Law on Patient Autonomy of 2002 and Law on the Quality and Cohesion of the National Health System of 2003, all after the initiative of the aforementioned regions. Most AACC have amended their laws in order to include aspects of these latter two central government laws, although some others have not introduced any significant modifications to their own regulations.

Finally, an important part of the symbolic dimension of health policy has varied in recent years: the inclusion of a new and specific section on rights in the statutes of autonomy of some regions. Since the 1990s, all the autonomous regions apart from the Basque Country have modified their statutes of autonomy. But in this process, a point of territorial differentiation can be detected: only five regions (Catalonia, Castile and Leon, Andalusia, Aragon and the Balearics) have included such a specific section on rights. Coincidentally, the statutes of these five regions were the last to be modified (all in 2006).

In terms of the substantive dimension of the health policies of the AACC, that is, the extent and intensity of their coverage, the first thing we observe is that there was a significant increase in the average expenditure by families on health care between 1998 and 2006: Asturias, Castile and Leon, Cantabria, the Basque Country, Castile-La Mancha, Navarre, Catalonia and Galicia are the regions where this increase has been the greatest; only in the Canaries has there been a decrease, and in Murcia it has remained stable. In 2006 four regions already had between 20 per cent and 25 per cent of their population with dual (public and private) health care coverage (the Balearics, Catalonia, Madrid and the Basque Country), and only three had less than 5 per cent of their population with dual coverage (the Canaries, Navarre and Extremadura). In the remainder between 5.4 per cent and 13.5 per cent of the population had mixed coverage.

In this context, we note that since 2000 the differences between autonomous regions' percentages of public expenditure devoted to health have diminished. On the other hand, although per capita public expenditure on health generally increased in the period 1999–2005, the differences between the individual AACC have also increased, as has public expenditure on health care as a percentage of their respective GDPs. However, stable differences have been maintained in terms of staff and centres per protected population. Whatever the case, in 2004 Spain spent 1,329 purchasing power units (PPU) per capita on health care, far below the

European average, both of the EU-15 (2,900 PPU) and of the EU-25 (1,600 PPU) (Navarro and Freixanet 2007).

In this evolution, differences have also been observed between the average annual growth rates of public expenditure on health per person in the different autonomous regions and the respective average annual population growth rates on the one hand, and the average annual ageing rates on the other. In other words, regions with comparatively more ageing and/or population growth have not always commensurately increased their health care expenditure per person.

The data also show positive developments in the great majority of AACC in the key indicators of resources per capita, for example in the number of health centres and health personnel per 10,000 inhabitants in primary care during the 2004–2007 period. With health centres, Galicia and, at some distance, Extremadura, Castile-La Mancha, Castile and Leon, Aragon and Navarre, are the best equipped, while Madrid, the Balearics, Valencia, Andalusia and Catalonia are the worst equipped. As for the ratio of healthcare personnel, Castile and Leon, Extremadura, Aragon, Castile-La Mancha and Navarre are the best placed, while La Rioja, the Balearics, the Basque Country, Murcia, the Canaries and Valencia are the worst placed.

However, the number of hospital beds per 1,000 inhabitants fell in all regions between 1996 and 2005. At the end of the period, the regions with the highest ratio were Catalonia, Aragon, Castile and Leon, the Canaries, Navarre and the Basque Country, and those with the lowest ratios were Valencia, Castile-La Mancha, Andalusia, Murcia and La Rioja. In this sense, the aggregate data show that, although the quality and provision of health care have increased without interruption since around 1990, the quality and provision of hospitals in particular have shown an opposite trend – so it is primary care that carries the greatest weight in this improvement.

With respect to substantive options, the regions display clear differences, but only in terms of public coverage of certain benefits that are complementary to basic and generic coverage. An analysis of the discourse of the 17 focus groups used in this research shows that are differences that the public can detect on the basis of personal experience, the exchange of information with other people, or the coverage of the topic in the media. Many interpret them to be indicators of inequalities, and some as indicators of the capacity for adaptation to different territorial needs and demands.[5]

---

5   Some examples are: neonatal screening (in which Galicia was a pioneer), the far more numerous sleep units in the Balearics, direct aid for coeliac patients in Castile-la Mancha, the treatment of smokers in La Rioja, the pioneering child mouth and dental care in Navarre and the Basque Country, higher birth benefits in the Basque Country, the pneumococcal vaccine in Madrid, free medicine and health products for newborn babies during their first year and sex change operations in Andalusia, and assistance for natural childbirth and a higher number of palliative care units and of specialists (in all areas) in Catalonia.

On this account the operative dimension of regional health policies has been highly conditioned by the degree of diversity among the regions on the provision side of health services at the start of the devolution process. Despite this, the model for the provision of health services has been developed on the basis of a gradual increase in the diversity of management methods (that is, as between direct and indirect provision). This has affected the legal nature of the health authority – whether autonomous body, public body of an institutional nature, or directorship general – as much as the legal nature of the suppliers (with the increasing presence of private or mixed public–private ownership) and the legal instruments suppliers use in relation with health authorities (agreement, contract, contract-programme, organizational integration and direct control). Even so, differentiation can be identified with respect to the model of provision among regions, and also with respect to the balance between the public sector and the private sector in the provision of services. In this sense, Castile-La Mancha, Extremadura, La Rioja and Navarre clearly display a preference for a public and integrated model (direct provision), while Catalonia, Valencia, the Balearics and Madrid tend to go for an indirect model of provision with a major dependence on provision by private suppliers. In Andalusia, Asturias, the Canaries, Castile and Leon, Galicia and the Basque Country we find a model involving indirect provision, but through eminently public suppliers.

In sum, we observe clear symbolic and discursive homogeneity in terms of the right to health and to universal, free and equitable access to health care services, which is reflected in the regulations enacted by the AACC and by the central state. This homogeneity is maintained in the 17 regional health systems, to the extent that all of them respond to directives for public coverage that are included in a basic offer of benefits that are the same for all citizens of all territories. The differences appear in the choices that the different regions have made in relation to complementary benefits, in response to the different specific demands and/or needs of their social realities. Similarly, and despite the increasing popularity of certain options since 2000, the operative scenarios that characterize the networks for the provision of services reflect the structural (economic and productive) realities of the health care sector that, in the main, were already in place before the regional governments were established.

To summarize the findings of this study, Table 6.2 classifies the AACC according to the degree of differentiation or innovation they show in each of the three dimensions analysed for health care policy. In *italics* are those regions that appear in more than two dimensions in either a 'High' or a 'Medium' degree of differentiation/innovation – namely, Catalonia, the Basque Country, Galicia, the Balearics, and Castilla León. This analysis reveals that those regions that have been among the first to introduce innovations in health policy have also tended to pursue differentiated policy options with respect to central government regulations.

Table 6.2   Degree of differentiation in regional health policies in Spain

Degree of differentiation/ Innovation	Discursive/ symbolic dimension*	Substantive dimension**	Operative dimension***
High	*Catalonia* Navarre *Basque Country* Galicia	Navarre Aragon *Castilla León* Extremadura	*Catalonia* Valencia *Balearics* Madrid
Medium	*Balearics* Valencia Aragon *Castilla León* Andalusia Cantabria	*Balearics* *Basque Country* *Catalonia* *Galicia* Cantabria La Rioja Asturias Canaries Castile-La Mancha	*Galicia* *Castilla León* *Basque Country* Canaries Andalusia Asturias
Low	La Rioja Madrid Asturias Canaries Murcia Castile-La Mancha Extremadura	Madrid Andalusia Valencia Murcia	Navarre Castile-La Mancha La Rioja Murcia Cantabria Extremadura Aragon

Notes: *To assess the degree of differentiation/innovation in the normative dimension of regional health policies, we have taken into account the pace and scope of legal acknowledgement of new health rights.

**To assess the degree of differentiation/innovation in the substantive dimension of regional health policies, we have combined three indicators: per capita public expenditure, per capita primary care resources (centres and personnel), and per capital hospital care resources (beds).

***To assess the degree of differentiation/innovation in the operative dimension of regional health policies, we have taken into account the weight of indirect provision within the publicly financed health system. 'Low' includes those regions where direct public provision is prevalent, 'Medium' those where indirect public provision is increasing, and 'High' those where both private and public indirect provision tends to prevail.

Source: Authors' elaboration.

Perceptions of the Devolution Process

Over the past 30 years, Spain has been the protagonist of the creation of a multi-level system of government that is not only one of the most decentralized in Europe but also historically unprecedented in Spain. Central government and administration coexist with 17 regional governments that were created *de novo*, and are now responsible for more than a third of government expenditure, and enjoy very substantial legislative and executive capacity. Nobody now questions their existence. What is at issue is how well these powerful and deeply rooted regional institutions manage to respond to public needs, whether they adequately manage their public resources and, at the same time, the extent to which they manage to represent and satisfy the demands for the recognition of diversity, which in some cases (historical nationalities) were based on the claims for autonomy at the end of the Franco dictatorship.

The AACC were created at the beginning of the democratic period in order to resolve or pacify the historical dispute between the nationalist periphery and the central administration (see Chapter 2). This new model of the state presented a more efficient, citizen-friendly and therefore more decentralized way of governing Spain. After this long period, and with a focus on social and welfare policies, the questions are: what assessment can we make of these years? How have the 17 regions used their capacities for self-government in these areas? Has decentralization helped to improve internal cohesion or have the differences between the AACC increased in relation to social benefits and rights? There is a substantial literature on the subject in Spain (Bosch and Duran 2005; Castells and Bosch 1999; Gallego, Gomà and Subirats 2003, 2005; Subirats and Gallego 2002; Vilalta 2007), which in general terms offers some answers to these questions. Among the 'coffee for everyone' and 'champagne for the nationalities' (Börzel 2002: 99), the new regional institutions had to be able, in the medium term, to improve their capacity to provide public services, bringing administration closer to the problems it addressed, while also favouring the common recognition of multiple identities.

Over these years, aside from the symbolic and identity-based components, which are more present in some regions than in others, the regions have become the privileged managers of a set of basic social rights and resource centres to be exploited by the most entrepreneurial sectors. The regions and, more specifically, their executive bodies and administrations have become veritable power nuclei in highly specific sectors, playing a determinant role in key areas of welfare. Nevertheless, the general perception is that the shortcomings are as significant in relation to decentralization as they are in relation to 'multi-nationality'.

Periodic opinion polls[6] show the strong legitimacy of the State of the Autonomies, and the full incorporation of the regional-territorial dimension in the political-institutional imaginary of the Spanish people. However, a constant tension persists between those who are concerned by the lack of 'closure' of the system of Autonomies[7] and perceive that devolution has not lessened the differences

---

6   See the link in English to the studies that are periodically conducted by the Centro de Investigaciones Sociológicas on this matter: http://www.cis.es/cis/opencms/EN/index. html.

7   The expression 'closure' of the system of Autonomies is used in the Spanish political and academic debate as a synonym for definitively fixing or agreeing a system for distributing the competences and defining the powers of the AACC. Nationalist forces on

between territories, and those who view the current devolved system as unable to sufficiently recognize the diversity of origins that exists in the country. This tension is especially evident when one examines such a sensitive issue as social benefits and rights across the regions.

Indeed, findings from our recent study (Gallego and Subirats 2010), suggest that although territorial inequalities in terms of welfare in Spain are thought to have been reduced since the transition to democracy, and the economy and welfare are believed to have developed very positively throughout the state, the future remains uncertain. It is admitted that decentralization has positively contributed to the capacity of the regional governments to make and to implement decisions, which enables them to adapt better to the distinct needs or demands of the territories. Nevertheless, and apart from the 'historical' AACC or those with a nationalist identity, it is often noted that devolution, which has so far been positive, could turn the other way and intensify territorial inequalities. Those who believe this outcome is possible cite the dynamics of bilateral pressure (state-region) that are perceived in the struggle for resources and in the lack of transparency that is understood to surround these dynamics. Regional self-government in Spain has been built without the shared government mechanisms for joint planning and decision-making that some federal states possess. So, since there is a lack of institutionalized venues for territorial representation that could allow autonomous regions to participate in the configuration of central state policy, Regions have developed bilateral strategies (Grau 2000, 2010). However, beyond global considerations of the evolution of the welfare state, there is often no consistency between public perceptions of the main problems that are observed on a social and cultural level in the AACC (in health, education, social exclusion) and the data available on the provision and operation of the corresponding services.

To summarize, the perception in most AACC is that the decentralization of the last 30 years has improved everyone's position but, at the same time, it is believed that the most developed territories have achieved better and more complete social protection systems for their populations. Therefore, it is felt that the 'original' or pre-existing inequalities in the State of Autonomies have increased. The truth is that, despite these perceptions, and as we have seen in this chapter, the existing data confirm that the basic core of rights and benefits is essentially shared by the whole country, and that the existing differences do not decisively affect this common base.

On the other hand, the data we have been able to collect (Gallego and Subirats 2010), which coincide with the outcomes of other studies conducted from different perspectives (Rodríguez Pose and Gill 2004; De la Fuente 2008; Goerlich and Villar 2009), suggest that the gaps between the AACC that existed in

---

the periphery generally oppose such 'closure', while the main state-wide political parties – centre-right PP and socialist PSOE – promote it.

1979 in such areas as disposable income, education levels and access to basic services have shown a notable tendency to decrease over the last 30 years, even though the differences in productive capacities between the more and the less developed regions have tended to increase. The political decentralization of Spain has favoured greater equality among Spaniards, or at least has not reduced it.[8] It would be interesting to examine in more depth the deviation between perceptions on the one hand and existing indicators and data on the other, to find out the extent to which the perception of inequality is derived from the lack of transparency in the tradition of bilateral agreements, is rather the result of as yet unresolved issues between AACC, or simply reflects confusion between equality and uniformity.

Conclusions

The analysis we have presented here asks whether decentralization has led to territorial differences in relation to the welfare policies deployed by the AACC in Spain. We have focused on education and health policies, as they are not just still central areas of welfare, but are also those that bear the greatest budgetary weight in these territorial regional governments. For both policies, we have analysed the main differences that have been detected in what we have defined as their symbolic, substantive and operative dimensions.

In relation to the symbolic dimension, according to what can be gleaned from the evolution of legislation, there is a remarkably high degree of homogeneity when it comes to a declaration of the governing principles and recognition of rights by both the central state and regional governments. In this sense, processes of both diffusion and convergence can be inferred (by following the time scales involved in the adoption of the regulations) in the cognitive frameworks that form the foundations of public interventions in each area. Sometimes the itineraries of diffusion circulate among the AACC and from them towards higher government bodies, sometimes from central government or even from international bodies towards sub-state governments.

In similar fashion, clear homogeneity is identified in a substantive core of the extent and intensity of public coverage for a range of services in the cases of education and health. Hence, the diversity of substantive options (what needs and demands are to be covered) appears only in relation to services complementing the nucleus defined by central government legislation as being common to the

---

8   In this sense, the recent study by the researchers at the Consejo Superior de Investigaciones Científicas (CSIC) concludes that, if in 1975 the regional distribution of income presented a major divide between the richest regions (then the Basque Country, Madrid, Navarre and Catalonia) and the less rich ones (then Extremadura, Galicia, Andalusia and Castile-La Mancha), at present (2005 data) the AACC at each extreme are still the same, but the distance between them has been very significantly reduced (De la Fuente 2008: 689).

whole state (a range of basic services). The extent to which this diversity should be interpreted as inequality or rather as an indicator of the capacity for response and for prioritizing the distinct needs or demands in each territory is a matter of ongoing debate that is subject to future modulations or intensifications.

Along the same lines, the operative dimension of the policies analysed shows divergences when we observe the persistence of structures of provision of inherited services that were initially different in each territory. But we also observe a tendency to expand and consolidate methods for indirect provision of services, with the private and non-profit making sectors playing an increasing role in all of the AACC.

Undoubtedly, indicators such as the evolution in expenditure per capita dedicated to a particular policy area and the relative weight of this effort in the budget of each regional government tell us a lot about the degree of that government's commitment to certain services and problems. This clearly includes political decisions to define and/or prioritize more or fewer areas of intervention within their competences. Even so, certain factors distort this reasoning and limit the interpretation of these conclusions, such as, for example, the finance system of autonomous regions and the resources per capita that each of them finally commands in its budget. In Spain, the redistributive effort has led not only to a high degree of convergence in terms of the availability of public resources to the AACC, but also often to the radical alteration of the original positions that they held in terms of their contribution to the state's overall budget. Moreover, the special finance systems in the Basque Country and Navarre may inspire, for example, these AACC to systematically dedicate more resources per capita to the services analysed and, in passing, also contribute to their populations' perception that the level of benefits and the quality of those services are much better than those of the other AACC. It is also significant that the autonomous regions, even when evaluating these aspects in the other regions, consider their own systems to be superior.

In short, 30 years on from the establishment of the State of the Autonomies, the general picture painted here suggests that there is a remarkable shared core of principles, values, benefits and services, and a periphery in which the differences between regions in certain benefits and the existence (or absence) of certain services is more manifest. The deployment of these options is occurring against a background in which we observe the persistence of territorial differences in relation to certain characteristics of the population, such as structure by age groups and the degree of urbanization, or even the intensification of differences in relation to new phenomena such as immigration and new social habits that might involve new social risks. However, a tendency has been observed towards convergence with respect to economic development in some cases, and with respect to the availability and dedication of public resources per capita to welfare policies in others, although there is no positive correlation between the two.

The general data suggest that the gaps in terms of welfare have narrowed, but at the same time the general publics in the respective regions still consider that differences existed before the creation of the AACC and that these differences are still present. We therefore have here the classic case of evidence suggesting one thing but perceptions suggesting quite another. This all implies that we should continue to discuss convergence and divergence in the decentralized construction of welfare policies in Spain. We understand that, for the moment, the value of equality has not been altered by the capacity to serve the value of diversity, both of which values are present in the constitutional foundations of the democratic state of Spain. It remains to be seen whether the convergence process in the basic aspects of the policies analysed, and even the coming together of benefits that appear to be the most diverse today, stems from dynamics of emulation and learning between AACC or from the logic of hierarchical decision-making in the central state.

References

Banting, K.G. 2006. Social Citizenship and Federalism: Is a Federal Welfare State a Contradiction in Terms?, in *Territory, Democracy and Justice. Regionalism and Federalism in Western Democracies*, edited by S. Greer. New York: Palgrave Macmillan, 44–66.

Börzel, S. 2002. *States and Regions in the European Union*. Cambridge: Cambridge University Press.

Bosch, N. and Duran, J.M. (eds) 2005. *La Financiación de las Comunidades Autónomas: políticas tributarias y solidaridad interterritorial*. Barcelona: Universitat de Barcelona.

Castells, A. and Bosch, N. (eds) 1999. *Desequilibrios Territoriales en España y Europa*. Barcelona: Ariel.

De la Fuente, A. 2008. Dinámica regional de la renta y la población, in *España Siglo XXI. La Economía*, edited by J. Velarde Fuertes and J.M. Serrano Sanz. Madrid: Biblioteca Nueva, Fundación Sistema, 679–719.

Gallego, R., Gomà, R. and Subirats, J. (eds) 2003. *Estado de Bienestar y Comunidades Autónomas*. Madrid: Tecnos-UPF.

Gallego, R., Gomà, R. and Subirats, J. 2005. Spain, from State Welfare to Regional Welfare?, in *The Territorial Politics of Welfare*, edited by N. McEwen and L. Moreno. London: Routledge, 103–26.

Gallego, R. and Subirats, J. 2010. *Descentralització i desigualtat en l'estat de benestar: Evolució sòcio-estructural, percepcions i polítiques autonòmiques*. Barcelona: Institut d'Estudis Autonòmics.

Goerlich, F.J. and Villar, A. 2009. *Desigualdad y Bienestar en España y sus Comunidades Autónomas (1973–2003). Revista de Economía Aplicada*, 17(50), 119–52.

Grau, M. 2000. Spain: Incomplete Federalism, in *Federalism and Political Performance*, edited by U. Wachendorfer-Schmidt. London: Routledge/ECPR, 58–78.

Grau, M. 2010. The Spanish Lower Chamber of Parliament: An Intergovernmental Arena? The Representation and Integration of Territorial Interests within the Congreso de los Diputados, in *Legislatures in Federal Systems and Multi-level Governance*, edited by R. Hrbek. Baden-Baden: Nomos, 11–33.

Marshall, T.H. [1950] 1992. Citizenship and Social Class, in *Citizenship and Social Class*, edited by T.H. Marshall and T. Bottomore. London: Pluto Press, 1–85.

Navarro, V. and Freixanet, M. 2007. Observatori Social d'Espanya. *Informe 2007. Atenció sanitaria.* [Online] Available at: http://seggroupspublic/documents/binario/51940.pdf [Accessed: 20 October 2010].

OECD (Organisation for Economic Co-operation and Development) 2007. *PISA 2006: Science Competencies for Tomorrow's World. Vol. 1: Analysis.* Paris: OECD.

Rodriguez Pose, A. and Gill, N. 2004. Is there a Global Link between Regional Disparities and Devolution? *Environment and Planning*, 36(12), 2097–117.

Subirats, J. and Gallego, R. 2002. *Veinte años de autonomías en España: Leyes, políticas públicas, instituciones y opinión pública.* Madrid: Centro de Investigaciones Sociológicas.

Vilalta, M. 2007. Los problemas actuales de la financiación autonómica, in *Nueva Financiación autonómica*, edited by S. Lago. Madrid: Instituto de Estudios Fiscales, 11–40.

Watts, R. 1999. *Comparing Federal Systems.* Kingston, ON: Institute of Intergovernmental Relations.

Chapter 7
Assessing the Welfare Mix: Public and Private in the Realm of Social Welfare

Teresa Montagut

Introduction

The European social model has been affected by changes brought about by neoliberal globalization and by social and demographic transformations. The non-profit and for-profit private sector's role in the management of services and programmes has expanded, which in turn has reduced the proportion of the services provided directly by general government. To understanding this private-sector expansion, we must examine factors within societies, such as changes in their structures, and external pressures caused by the definitive globalization of the economy.

Although the direct state provision of social programmes was a key characteristic of the European model of social protection, at no time has there been just one dimension of social welfare. Instead, as Johnson (1987) concluded, we should talk of a 'welfare mix' as welfare provision has been channelled through four sectors, in varying proportions in different countries: the state, the market, the informal sector and the voluntary sector. In recent years the size of the role played by each of these sectors has changed. In addition, an organized voluntary sector has emerged and become a new social actor that can influence public policies. Although comparable changes have taken place in all countries, they have occurred differently depending on each country's specific characteristics and its adherence, as an 'ideal type', to a certain model of society, welfare regime or group of similar countries (for example, Titmuss 1968; Esping-Andersen 1990; Trigilia 2002; Seeleib-Kaiser 2008). Therefore, despite the unifying trends, the interrelation between a country's specific social and productive structure, its shared beliefs and norms, and its history not only have an effect on its current structures but also guide the framing of its public policies. Spain, which like other southern European countries has a family-based welfare regime, appears to have weak state structures in comparison with the role that the family plays in protecting its members, particularly in the area of social welfare. Nevertheless, social protection policies are also being redesigned, and programmes that are directly provided by general government are declining (Guillén and Petmesidou 2008).

Social protection is based on the health, education, pension and social services systems. Each one of these pillars has undergone changes, depending largely on two variables: how developed it is as a social protection system (that is, whether it is a consolidated system or one that is still being structured) and the authority that governs it (that is, whether it is a national system for the whole of Spain or the responsibility of the autonomous regional governments created to decentralize political affairs). Changes in the health, education and pension systems are closely correlated with the state's financial difficulties. The search for efficiency and a reduction in budget pressure are the main reasons for the appearance of the quasi-markets and the decentralization of management.

The social service system has specific characteristics.[1] Today, civil society's involvement in the management of its services through numerous non-profit organizations is bringing about a new situation. The consolidation of social service policies in Spain has been possible since the recovery of democracy and particularly in the last 15 years of the twentieth century. This chapter is focused on the public and private realm that is now consolidating a new system of social services in Spain. It analyses the rapid changes in Spanish social service policies. The next section addresses the various phases that political activities have passed through in just a few years – not in the sense of government, but in broader terms of action in the public arena. First, we examine the role of the laws and policies of general government. Second, we look at the role of civil society and its recent organization as a political actor. Finally, we turn to the influence that Europe has exerted since Spain became a Member State of the European Union. The following section gives a general overview of the current public and private realms in social service policies. A summary is provided by way of conclusion in the final section, which enables us to begin to see and understand some of the problems that have arisen as this new situation has emerged.

From the Design to the Redesign of Social Service Policies

Spanish social service policies have been structured since the Constitution of 1978. Prior to this date and during the Franco dictatorship, there were no social services, in a strict sense. Social involvement was basically channelled in three ways. First, the treatment of 'social maladjustment' was an objective of public policies aimed at containing and controlling the 'deviant behaviour' of certain young, socially marginalized people. The paradigmatic case was that of the large-scale institutions for the custody of minors. The work of these reformatories was

---

1   The social service system in Spain is understood as the set of both social care services and social assistance (economic transfers for the most needy).

closer to repression than re-education. The second form of assistance or care was provided in the broad field of disabilities. Because of a lack of government resources, mutual aid organizations played a very important role in this area, and particularly associations of parents of children affected by disorders or disabilities. In fact, this field was the first to be addressed by civil society, and was the first resource or commitment of a private, secular nature. Finally, a third way of meeting social needs during the dictatorship involved the care provided mainly by the Catholic Church through the Caritas organization for groups or individuals who were poor or vulnerable. This institution played a considerable role in the last years of the Franco regime, as it fostered a design of social services that went beyond mere charity. Although this social protection was not then considered a response to social rights, it did represent an important step as it involved the design of a set of services whose professional providers, and particularly the social workers, proposed a form of community activity that could mobilize the resources of the groups themselves or the affected regions.

The recovery of democracy in Spain made it possible to channel the concerns of many citizens, claiming an active political role. General government could assume an active role in caring for the most disadvantaged members of society and make a commitment to redistributing resources. The democratic state was considered to be responsible for meeting social needs. Hence, social services needed to be public, which meant – at that time – that they should be provided by the various state administrations. The idea of the state meeting all public needs was considered a victory, a step towards democratic modernity. It was a democratic achievement since, under the supposition that democracy creates social rights, the state had to provide social services on behalf of society. To varying degrees and intensities, other European states passed through the same stage soon after the Second World War. However, in Spain it occurred at the beginning of the 1980s. This was a time of economic crisis that coincided with the modernization of Spain's political institutions and the productive structure itself. In short, social services were designed at a time of economic crisis in which there was a sharp increase in the social needs to be met, basically for two reasons: the loss of employment and job instability caused by the economic situation; and the 'visibility' of many shortages which had previously been ignored, controlled or left to the family to deal with.

This period, in which 'public' was almost synonymous with 'governmental', progressively changed, and led, first, to civil society gradually taking responsibility for the management of public services – 'public' in the sense that is a sphere that belongs to everyone – and second, to the very recent entry of the market into this area of social protection, as in other European countries. Perhaps what is different about Spain is that the changes have occurred in a very short period, as the country has passed through the three phases in less than 25 years. In the first stage, it was considered that only the state should offer social protection services. Then non-profit organizations began to manage services, with a high level of public funding and, in many cases, state supervision. Finally, in recent years some commercial companies have begun to provide social services.

Social services can be defined as the set of services provided to the community to prevent or eliminate the causes of marginalization. Because of the decentralization of political power, social services are not regulated by the central state. Article 148 of the Constitution allocates to autonomous regional governments exclusive powers over 'social services' (*asistencia social*). However, some articles[2] of the Constitution establish a series of state obligations for services that, if required, should subsequently be introduced with specific laws. Thus, social services are differentiated from other services linked to 'social security', which are contribution-based and are therefore the same throughout Spain and come under the central state's authority. In addition, as Spain signed the European Union's Social Charter in 1980, it made a commitment to establish a social service system. During the 1980s, almost all of the regional governments passed their Social Services Acts and designed a series of political measures and services to meet the social needs of their respective populations.

At the beginning, from the time of the first municipal elections in 1979, the town councils or local governments were the bodies that began to plan social service programmes. Subsequently, these programmes became part of the political structure of the regional governments as they were constituted and their laws implemented. Each region drafted and approved its own Social Services Act. This led to variations in the designs of the specific policies and the conditions of access to resources, depending on each geographic region, its inertia, strengths and weaknesses.

The services were practically created from scratch and were therefore designed from the perspective of government responsibility. Each regional government planned its programmes on the basis of its material and professional resources alone (except in sectors in which civil society had already been active, for example in the case of mutual aid organizations for specific disabilities, or Caritas and other religious organizations that continued to provide care for the most destitute). The regional governments' budgetary effort in this area over ten years was huge. As shown in Table 7.1, spending increased from 2.1 billion pesetas in 1981 (just over 12 million euros) to almost 231 billion in 1990 (almost 1.4 billion euros). In other words, the amount allocated to social welfare increased over one hundredfold in just 10 years. As mentioned above, this occurred at a time of considerable economic and ideological turmoil.

Spain's incorporation into the European Union in 1986 meant that the country was influenced by mature democracies whose social protection systems had already been consolidated for many years. Together, these democracies gradually devised new ways to transform and adapt their policies in the new era of post-Fordism, in which the definitive globalization of the economy complicated the role of states as redistributors of resources within their borders (and the pressure of the neoliberal trend influencing the functions that the state should perform).

---

2   Specifically, Articles 25, 39, 40, 41, 48, 49 and 59.

Table 7.1   **Total regional governments spending on social services, 1981–90, in percentages**

Groups	1981	1985	1990
Elderly	48.86	16.50	17.61
Care for disabled people	35.18	9.96	19.16
Protection of minors	8.92	11.33	14.77
Young people	0	4.15	5.04
Advancement of women	0	0.80	1.87
Other groups	6.12	3.24	8.66
General social welfare spending	0	53.99	31.90
Fight against poverty	0	0	0.97
Total (*)	2,106,000,000	59,604,574,215	230,960,326,199

Note:(*) Pesetas.
Source: Barea (1997).

The current welfare mix in social services is basically the result of three main factors: political will and action to boost the development of non-profit organizations and to promote voluntary work; people's new interests and their involvement in voluntary work and membership of the European Union, which also had a considerable influence. We now analyse these three factors in turn.

Political Action: Policies and Laws

A review of public policies shows that some of the Spanish laws and regulations passed in recent years, which today constitute the legal framework for social services, have played a considerable role in promoting and assisting the development of non-profit organizations and, to a lesser extent, the participation of commercial companies in the management and provision of services. Next, we will analyse the policies that have had the greatest direct or indirect impact on the current welfare mix of social services.

The Allocation of 0.52 per cent of Personal Income Tax   The 'allocation of 0.52 per cent of personal income tax' is an annual notice of funding availability that is linked to the population's income. The policy was established in 1988, when the socialist government of that time created the Ministry of Social Affairs. The establishment of this ministry by the state government may seem a little contradictory, as the Spanish Constitution does not confer upon the central state direct responsibilities for this area. However, the reason for forming the ministry could lie in precisely this regional distribution of powers. The Spanish government's desire to recover some of its responsibilities in this area is understandable, as it needed to address the potential risk of differences in the social rights of people in the various regions. In addition, the Constitution prescribes that the state should 'guarantee the principle of solidarity and equality so that all Spaniards have the same rights and obligations in any part of the state territory'[3] (Articles 138 and 139).

One of the most notable consequences of forming the Ministry of Social Affairs was the promotion of social participation. This was a proposed objective and it was related to one of the two new policies that emerged at state level after the creation of the ministry: that of allocating 0.52 per cent of personal income tax (IRPF) to social welfare programmes.[4] This policy is regulated by a Decree issued in 1988, with two subsequent modifications. It represented an opportunity to boost the role of private entities in the management of various social services programmes. To a large extent, it contributed to the considerable development of the voluntary sector and of non-profit organizations in the 1990s, which was explicitly stated as one of the new ministry's objectives.[5]

The 1998 General State Budget (PGE) Law for 1988 established that a fixed percentage of income tax collection would be allocated to religious interests (funding for the Catholic Church) or to other social interests, depending on the option selected by each taxpayer. This law stipulated that when citizens filed their taxes they could decide whether they wanted to donate 0.5239 per cent of their tax to one of the two options. If no option was selected, the government would by default allocate the percentage to non-profit entities. The Ministry of Social Affairs (or the Directorate-General for Social Affairs after the ministry was disbanded) was responsible for distributing to the entities 80 per cent of the total received. The remaining 20 per cent was allocated to development cooperation projects by the Spanish Agency for International Cooperation (AECI), which came under the Ministry of Foreign Affairs.

Since its establishment, the programme has undergone some changes. Since 2000, taxpayers have been able to opt to contribute to one of the two options or to both options at the same time. In the latter case, 0.52 per cent is assigned to each option. In addition, the allocation of funds on behalf of those who do not select an option has changed. In this case, the amount is no longer awarded to non-profit organizations but instead forms part of the PGEs.

---

3   Translation for the author from original.

4   The second policy was the 'Concerted plan for the development of the basic provision of social services', which, among other measures, aims to establish a municipal network of social services that are the same for all Spaniards and involve the various regional governments.

5   The document *La política del Ministerio de Asuntos Sociales* (The policy of the Ministry of Social Affairs), published in 1990, contains a notable proposal to present a Bill of Foundations and Associations to 'channel human and financial resources in a charitable way to improve the quality of life of citizens in general and of the most disadvantaged sectors, in particular'. In addition, it mentions 'the desire to work on a regulation with the greatest possible scope to regulate the voluntary sector and thus promote its presence in social services programs and assistance' (Ministerio de Asuntos Sociales 1990: 5).

Table 7.2 **Options selected by taxpayers (per cent) on income tax returns, 1995–2004**

Financial year	Catholic Church	Other social interests	Both options	Not allocated
1995	36.6	21.1	—	42.3
1996	33.4	18.0	—	48.6
1997	37.0	25.6	—	37.5
1998	36.6	29.2	—	34.1
1999	29.4	29.6	10.3	30.7
2000	27.5	30.0	11.7	30.9
2001	22.0	31.6	11.3	35.1
2002	22.5	32.6	11.9	33.0
2003	21.9	32.4	11.6	34.2
2004	22.1	33.5	11.5	32.9

Source: Ministry of Employment and Social Affairs (2008).

These changes have been influenced by pressure from the Catholic Church, which has been assigned less by taxpayers every year. With this modification, the government has also guaranteed a minimum amount and fixed a maximum. The minimum currently stands at 123.6 million euros and the maximum at 132.2 million euros. If taxpayers' contributions do not reach the minimum quantity, the state provides the difference. In contrast, if more than the maximum is contributed, the surplus is allocated to the PGE.

Another change has been an increase in the proportion that is allocated individually. Since 2009, the amount that each citizen assigns to one or both options has stood at 0.7 per cent instead of 0.52 per cent. This change is the result of an agreement between the entities and the government, as well as the addition of environmental protection as an activity of social interest (so some of the funds will be managed by the Ministry of the Environment).

Table 7.2 shows how Spaniards' tax allocation choices have changed over time. Over 10 years the percentage of taxpayers who opted to allocate funds to the Catholic Church fell continuously, while the percentage selecting non-governmental organizations (NGOs) rose. Since its introduction, the possibility of donating to both the Church and NGOs has mainly been selected by those who previously donated to the Catholic Church. In addition, although the proportion is decreasing, a third of the population still does not use this direct source of funding social care. It is difficult to assess whether this is out of personal choice or due to a lack of awareness of the facility.

Hence, we can see this law's contribution to, and impact on, promoting both the voluntary sector and social work by civil society organizations. However, yet another factor has had a considerable influence on the role of non-profit organizations. One of the requirements of the 1988 Decree is that 'programs that receive funding must be executed in various autonomous regions. When they are implemented in just one region, the subsidy can be obtained only if the programme is declared of general interest by the regional government of the area in which the activity is carried out'.[6] Hence, the Decree has fostered coordination between organizations at state level for two reasons: to attract subsidies and to have a presence and strength as a sector. The Spanish NGO Platform of Social Action is now a collective actor that represents entities in the third sector.

The Law for the Promotion of Personal Autonomy and the Care of Dependent Persons approved in December 2006   The General State Budget Law led to the consolidation of the role of the third sector. (We define the 'third sector' as the set of civil society entities or organizations that provide not-for-profit public services and are linked to varying degrees with voluntary work.) The law discussed below has also fostered, although perhaps indirectly, the entry of private companies into the management of social care services. This law brings about significant changes in social protection and in private participation in public social services. It is a universal law promoted by the Spanish government for all Spaniards. It is the first law that defines the meeting of personal needs as a universal right for the entire population, regardless of income, and it aims to eliminate the stigma that has been attached to users of social protection programmes in the past. The law aims to lay the foundations for the construction of this *fourth pillar* of the Spanish welfare system. The law recognizes a new right of citizens: the right to be cared for when personal autonomy has been violated. Although this is a central state law, the decentralization of power means that its implementation requires the collaboration and participation of all levels of government – central, regional and local.

Although this law at the time of writing is still in a development phase – the text itself states that it will not be fully implemented until 2015 – its universality is leading to the creation of new services, in terms of both institutions and home care professionals.

New Regional Social Service Acts   Finally, the new regional social services Acts that have gradually been legislated have had a further major influence on the consolidation and strengthening of the public–private welfare mix. Since the first social services regulations were approved, most of the regional governments have progressively changed and modified their Acts, in accordance with the process of democratic consolidation and social transformation. The most recent changes involve a considerable modification that strengthens the private sector's role in the provision of social welfare. As an example, we will discuss the 2007

---

6   As stated in the 2009 notice of funding availability on the Ministry of Health and Social Policy's website: http://www.msps.es/politicaSocial/ongVoluntariado/subvenciones/IRPF/home.htm.

Catalan Social Services Act, which was drawn up with the collaboration of experts from organizations and the academic world. Article 14 of this Act defines the public system of social services as being 'made up of the set of resources, services, activities, programmes, projects and facilities for the social care of the population that are run by the Catalan regional government, local entities and other administrations, as well as those provided by social or private entities and approved by the government'. Article 68 of the Act explicitly recognizes that individuals and private legal entities (subject to prior authorization) have the right to set up social service centres and establishments and to manage their programmes and services.

Spanish Civil Society

Spanish civil society, like civil society in other countries in southern Europe, was characterized in the past by its lack of organization and, perhaps, by its belated awakening. Nevertheless, there are notable differences between countries, which also have a historical aspect. After the regime of General Franco ended in 1975, modern democracy was built through institutional agreements between the parties in the absence of other political actors. In other words, it was created by means of a top-down approach. As this approach focused on the way that the parties – which had just become legal again – could participate, other channels of citizen participation were not incorporated to a sufficient degree (see Subirats 1999 for more detail). Modern Spain was constructed without reducing the gap between political and civil society. (However, the fragility of civil society parallels the weakness of the public institutions.) In the past, levels of group identification in Spain were very low. This factor still appears in highly varied assessments: the Spanish fear everything to do with the state and simultaneously expect everything from it; there is 'a strange dependence on the state, accompanied by a deeply rooted mistrust of everything public' (see Subirats 1999 for more detail). It could be said, in general terms, that the public arena has been more closely linked to the 'political' sphere than to a space for collective responsibility. Civil society has not had a strong and organized presence, which could explain the delay in establishing a network of associations that work for the common good.

Despite this traditional and historical lack of collective responsibility, in recent years considerable changes have taken place. Regional ways of organizing civil society have become more similar, and an area of public responsibility has gradually been consolidated by the entities involved in the management of social welfare services that involve voluntary work. The increasing expansion of voluntary organizations has also been influenced by the prestige or social recognition given, in recent years, to the solidarity with which they are associated. This process has taken place not only in Spain (see Kendall 2009). In fact, Spain has moved in the same direction as other European countries. However, a different structure has been created, in accordance with the parameters of the country's social structure and the values and beliefs that its community shares. In

Spain, the development of civil society is clearly fostered by general government. As a result, it is interesting to describe its process of consolidation. The term 'civil society' covers a wide field that includes a set of entities and structures that make up an institutional network (schools, churches, newspapers, companies and voluntary associations). In other words, it encompasses the relationships between citizens who are not part of the sphere of government. However, in this section we address the composition of the *social third sector*, which is linked to the problems of welfare states and is fostered in some way by EU institutions.

The process of Spanish modernization has been spectacular since the recovery of democracy in 1977. This can be seen in Spain's consolidation of democracy, its welfare policies, its inclusion in EU bodies and its changes in customs and social institutions, among other factors. In just a few years, Spain has passed through the same stages as other European countries, but the changes have occurred extremely rapidly. This is particularly true of the social services system, in which modifications have been introduced even though the system is still not fully developed. It could be said that the system has been reformed before it has been consolidated. The third sector's role in welfare provision has gradually developed as policies have been implemented. The new 'public–private' arena has been made possible by the public policies analysed above and by the 'awakening' of Spanish civil society, and all of this in very few years. The number of NGOs grew most rapidly from 1978 to the mid-1990s. However, these associations established a client-based relationship with general government. Over half of the organizations included in the survey of voluntary organizations in Spain (*Plataforma Promoción Voluntariado* 1997) were formed after 1986, and only 16 per cent were established before 1975. In recent years they have begun to play a very active role, particularly since the creation of the Platform of Social Action NGOs. Today, this Platform represents the wide-ranging sector and constitutes a network made up of 25 federations and state networks that bring together thousands of local or regional entities[7] and, together with other international alliances, form part of the European Social Platform.

European Convergence

The entry of Spain into the European Union coincided with a period in which the coordination between the various countries became stronger. During this time, the Member States' political institutions and the measures that they implement developed according to the general political and economic environment and situation, as a result of their participation and involvement in Europe. This influence of the European Union on Member States has come to be called the process of *Europeanization.* Various studies have shown how each state's political institutions evolve as a result of its position within the context of EU policies (Cowles, Caporaso and Risse 2001; Knill 2001; Featherstone and Radaelli 2003).

---

7   http://www.plataformaongs.org/.

References to the third sector, and the EU's influence on the function that it is developing, are fairly recent (Kendall and Anheier 1999; Kendall 2009). The role that the non-profit sector could play in the creation of a new Europe is discussed in the Fontaine Report,[8] which was published in 1986 and explicitly states: 'Europe needs inspiration to take a further step towards its destiny as a Community. Non-profit making associations are an opportunity to be taken in this respect. Inertia must be overcome and this opportunity must be boldly seized' (quoted in Kendall and Anheier 1999: 283). In the 1990s various initiatives were devised that were implemented in different countries; for example, DG XXIII established the social economy unit; regulations were drawn up and approved for a European Statute of Association; the Maastricht Treaty (Appendix 23) discussed the promotion of cooperation between the European Community and the voluntary associations and foundations for social welfare, as a result of which DG V promoted dialogue in the Social Policy Forum; DG XXIII and DG V jointly presented a communication for promoting the role of voluntary organizations and foundations in Europe and their already active role of participating in the distribution of structural funds.[9]

In short, despite each country's specific characteristics, 'European convergence' has promoted paths that can be shared and routes that can be followed by all Member States. One good example of this that is related to the third sector in the current decade is the National Action Plans (NAPs), particularly the one on social inclusion. These measures have helped Spain to reinforce the ways in which it had already begun to function. The NAP for Social Inclusion, which was introduced during the Lisbon EC meeting in March 2000,[10] has perhaps played the most important role. In this NAP, the fight against social exclusion is highlighted as one of the steps required for the cohesion of European states. Four basic objectives are set out: to facilitate participation in employment and access to resources; to prevent the risk of exclusion; to assist the most vulnerable population; and to mobilize all relevant actors who are involved in social inclusion programmes.[11] The NAP for Social Inclusion has strengthened the role of the third sector in various ways. For example, the sector was given a leading role in the design and assessment of the NAP itself. In addition, the mobilization of non-profit entities is facilitated, which has led to the strengthening, or in some cases the creation, of networks of actors within the sector.

---

8   The report was written by Mrs N. Fontaine who served as the rapporteur of the European Parliament's Committee of Legal Affairs and Citizens' Rights.

9   See, for example Commission of the European Communities (1997).

10   European Council (2000).

11   For an analysis of this policy, see Bradsen, T. et al. (2009).

The Public and Private Structure of Social Services at the Beginning of the Twenty-first Century: An Overview

The consolidation of the Spanish system of social care in the first decade of the twenty-first century occurred at the same time as the private, non-profit sector started to manage services, and more recently, as commercial companies also entered the arena. Hence, the public–private mix was formed. As discussed above, Spanish civil society had a weak structure in the past and its emergence and organization in non-profit entities is relatively recent. A sharp increase in the number of non-profit organizations occurred at the end of the 1980s and the beginnings of the 1990s, and their development has been fostered by the public sector. Such organizations depend to a great extent on public funding, at national, regional and local levels. In some cases it could be said that the third sector is more of an extension of the public services on which it is dependent than a sufficiently independent sector. However, the Spanish third sector is not homogeneous. Because of the decentralization of power, it is closely linked to the strength of civil society in each geographic area. Certain Spanish regions have historically been more involved in associations than others, which has led to more structured development of non-profit social services organizations today.

There is still a lack of agreement on how to define the organizations that make up the Spanish third sector. There are various reasons for this difficulty in coming up with an exact number. One factor is that the registration processes of voluntary organizations are highly diverse. There are various legal forms of entities, the main ones being associations, foundations and cooperatives. Each of these legal forms has its own specific register. In addition, registers are decentralized and do not indicate the activity that the registered entities carry out. Consequently, the most recent studies do not analyse the same universe and so have disparate results – from 10,000 to 253,000 entities (see Montagut 2009). Nevertheless, some of the regional governments have more recent data, which are perhaps closer to the reality. Specifically, the Observatory of the Third Sector[12] in Catalonia and the Observatory of the Third Sector of Bizkaia[13] in the Basque Country are two non-profit organizations that, among other objectives, aim to gain through their databases an approximate overview of the structures of non-profit organizations in their respective regions. Thus, we know that there are now 7,000 entities in Catalonia and around 5,000 in the Basque Country. On the basis of these data, the number of entities in Spain is probably higher than that stated in the aforementioned studies.

Despite this difficulty in gathering information on the number of non-profit entities involved in social services, we have accurate data on one specific, important sector: organizations that have received subsidies through the programme to allocate 0.52 per cent of income tax. The information on these organizations is

---

12   http://www.tercersector.net/php/index.php.

13   http://www.3sbizkaia.org/.

comprehensive and the most recent data are on the 2007 programme. They are found in the unpublished *Encuesta a las entidades sociales convocatoria 2007*, which was undertaken by the Centro de Estudios Económicos Tomillo for the Ministry of Employment and Social Affairs. The survey sample corresponds to 80 per cent of the entities that received subsidies in the 2007 programme. Below is an analysis of the main characteristics of these institutions, drawn from the latest available data. This provides a general idea of their importance, in economic and social terms.

As can be seen in Figure 7.1, almost half of the entities are associations (46.2 per cent) which, when added to the federations (19 per cent) and confederations (4.8 per cent), make up 70 per cent of the total number of entities. Foundations represent 26.4 per cent of the total and, in a lower proportion, 2.9 per cent of the entities are religious. The remaining 0.7 per cent include singular entities as specific as the Spanish Red Cross or Caritas.

The 2007 programme of allocating 0.52 per cent of income tax to third sector entities produced a total of 101,974,859 euros for distribution. The way that this amount was distributed reflects the convergence between government priorities in areas of specific social needs and the services provided by organizations to meet these needs. No group was the focus of a high proportion of the subsidized programmes. Instead, the subsidies were spread across different groups, and the numbers of programmes for each one group ranged from a maximum of 15 per cent of the total to a minimum of 4 per cent. As shown in the following figure, over 10 per cent of the total number of subsidized programmes were for the following groups: childhood and family (14.9 per cent), young people (12.2 per cent), and promotion of voluntary work (12 per cent).

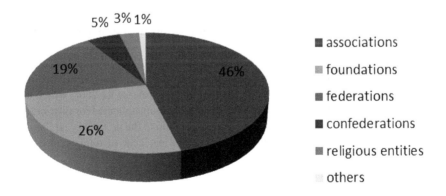

Figure 7.1   Legal forms and percentage shares of third sector entities in the 0.52 per cent programme, 2007

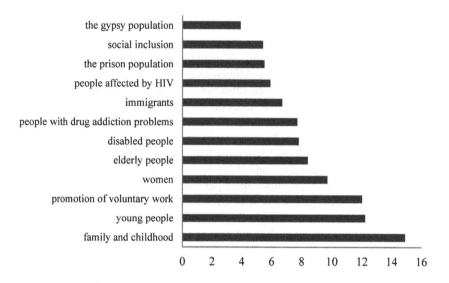

Figure 7.2   Percentages of the total of subsidized programmes by group, 2007

These groups were followed by women (9.7 per cent), elderly people (8.4 per cent), disabled people (7.8 per cent), people with drug addiction problems (7.7 per cent), immigrants (6.7 per cent), people affected by HIV (5.9 per cent), the prison population (5.5 per cent), social inclusion programmes (5.4 per cent) and the gypsy population (3.9 per cent). The number of programmes subsidized is not related to the amount of money received. For example, most programmes that were subsidized were for family, childhood and young people. However, the greatest amount of money was allocated to elderly people. This group received 23.5 per cent of the total subsidy (almost 24 millon euros). Over the years, we can see that this group has been awarded the highest proportion of funds in all of the notices of funding availability.

The most recent data, which correspond to the distributions of subsidies in 2008 and 2009, can be found in the press releases for these two years that are posted on the Ministry of Health and Social Policy website. The press release for 2008, which was posted on 23 December 2009,[14] states that the total amount collected for distribution was 190,782,795 euros. This was 56 million more than in the previous year, largely because of the increase from 0.52 per cent to 0.7 per cent of total income tax.

---

14   http://www.msps.es/gabinetePrensa/notaPrensa/desarrolloNotaPrensa.jsp?id=1708.

Table 7.3 Percentages of the total subsidy that groups have received in each notice of funding availability, 1996–2007

Groups	1996	1998	2000	2004	2007
Elderly people	24.0	20.7	20.5	22.8	23.5
Disabled people	17.0	16.4	15.9	17.2	14.3
Family and childhood	9.0	11.3	10.8	10.6	12.0
Young people	9.0	8.3	8.5	8.1	8.2
Women	9.0	9.9	8.8	8.4	8.5
Refugees and immigrants	8.0	8.7	8.6	9.6	9.8
Drug addicts	6.0	6.4	6.7	5.0	5.0
Promotion of voluntary work	4.0	4.4	4.8	4.0	4.2
Social inclusion programmes	4.0	4.0	4.2	5.7	5.8
Gypsy population	4.0	3.3	3.4	*	2.8
People affected by HIV	3.0	3.0	3.0	*	2.9
Prison population	3.0	3.1	3.0	*	3.0
Emergency fund	1.0	0.0	1.9	0.0	0.0

Note: *No figures are available, but the percentage is less than 3 per cent of the total.

Source: Ministry of Employment and Social Affairs (2008).

The ministry's three main priorities were: entities that carry out programmes for people in situations of poverty and exclusion; entities that work for personal autonomy and combat situations of dependency; and the promotion of voluntary work. Over 1,800 programmes were implemented by 378 entities, of which 1,013 were subsidized. The Spanish Red Cross and Caritas are the two largest voluntary organizations. The Spanish Red Cross received over 33 million euros (for 47 programmes) and Caritas received almost 19 million euros (for 38 programmes).

The notice of funding availability for 2009 was published in a press release on 14 June 2010.[15] The Ministry stated that the amount allocated to NGO programmes had increased to over 205 million euros, 7.69 per cent more than in the previous year. The amounts were distributed in a pattern similar to that of the previous year, although with substantial gains to elderly people (29.14 per cent of the total) and to programmes for people with disabilities (23.48 per cent); and 10.76 per cent was allocated to family and childhood programmes.

The programme for allocating subsidies from income tax is probably the NGOs' main source of funding. However, NGOs also receive public subsidies through other channels. Each local government and each regional government has arrangements with the entities that work in its respective area. In addition, as mentioned previously, the implementation of the Law for the Promotion of Personal Autonomy is an extremely important channel at the local level. It could be said that the private, non-profit sector in Spain is 'protected' by general government in

15   http://www.msps.es/gabinetePrensa/notaPrensa/desarrolloNotaPrensa.jsp?id=1827.

two ways: the government has fostered its creation; and it is financially dependent on different areas of government.

As a result of the pressure of economic and political forces in recent years, such as globalization and the neoliberal trend, the public sector has gradually introduced market values and methods in its policies, in order to increase its efficiency in times of difficulties. In the social care sector, this has led to the involvement of the private commercial sector in outsourced services. Some non-profit organizations have taken on commercial forms that enable them to ensure their continued existence. This process is now called 'marketization'. In addition, for-profit companies have entered the sector, some of which previously worked in the field of general services. Such companies expanded their area of activity to the social services when they saw the opportunity to win a government contract. As market companies have only recently entered the social services field, there is little data on this topic. No studies show their specific weight in the field or assess their potential future development. However, we know that in the main cities public tenders have involved considerable amounts of money in order to outsource the management of the services that must be provided by way of implementing the Law for the Promotion of Personal Autonomy. In Madrid and Barcelona (the two largest Spanish cities) the management of 'home care' services by the non-profit or commercial private sector in 2009 cost a total of 180 million euros. Some of the tenders were won by commercial service companies, and some by the financially strongest third sector entities. As the amounts of money involved are considerable, the government requires bidders to demonstrate sufficient financial solvency. It could be said that these services have enabled commercial companies to seize a business opportunity. Prior to this law, commercial and social initiatives displayed a certain degree of specialization. Commercial companies were reasonably focused on services for which there was a solid demand, such as residential homes for the elderly; in contrast, third sector entities were centred on other services whose supply did not have to be financially profitable.

Conclusion

In short, and to conclude, it could be said that in just a few years Spain has gone through the same stages of social services provision as other European countries, but the changes have occurred extremely quickly. Like other transformations in Spanish social structures that have led to modernization, and as shown above, Spanish social services have moved through four stages in very little time. In 30 years, a situation in which no system of protection existed in the field of social services has been transformed by the development of a network of government-run services and centres, by the entry into the market of non-profit entities and, finally, by the entry of commercial companies into the provision of social services.

Spain differs in this area in that social service policies had to meet new social needs even though the social protection system was still not fully developed.

The structure of the protection system today is similar to that in other European countries, although it is perhaps still not mature. A mixed system of service provision has been consolidated in which the main supplier is the central state, but other providers include non-profit organizations and, in some cases, private companies. Another notable aspect is the multi-level coordination of social services. The map of social services presents a highly fragmented picture. The powers of the governments of the autonomous regions should be coordinated with the Law for the Promotion of Personal Autonomy at state level and with the powers that the Local Government Law invests in the city councils of the large cities, as well as with some comprehensive, interdepartmental programmes.

We already have good information on the extent of the social third sector's role in programmes to meet social needs. However, at the time of writing this article, and due to the recent emergence of the phenomenon, no studies existed on the effects that the entry of commercial companies into social services management may have on collective responsibility. Likewise, little information exists on the dimensions of the role that families play as a buffer to cushion many young peoples' insufficient resources and the lack of services for the elderly. Studies are required to estimate the proportion of total service provision that is provided by families, and the needs that would not be met in the population if the informal sector – basically, families – did not carry out this important function.

In this new situation, no consensus has yet emerged on whether the private provision of public services will diminish the responsibilities that the state has assumed over time in relation to the redistribution of resources. The redesign of social care policies involves a readjustment of public responsibilities. The central state should take on another kind of responsibility – one that involves coordinating the welfare mix and controlling and evaluating programmes and services. In short, the central state should be the ultimate guarantor of social rights. Therefore, it should establish new functions that make up a new framework of collaboration, together with the new responsibilities in the public sphere assumed by civil society. Perhaps the *third sector* is closest to this new commitment; at least, this new responsibility appears to be ubiquitous in its discourse. The question is whether the commercial sector can take on this responsibility. How will it serve profit and society at the same time? At the moment this seems to be a rather difficult task, but not impossible. Corporate social responsibility, which is becoming more common in companies, could be a good framework for demonstrating that, without losing sight of profit, services can be offered for the 'common good'.

References

Brandsen, T., Pavolini, E., Ranci, C., Sittermann, B. and Zimmer, A. 2009. National Action Plans on Social Inclusion: An Opportunity for the Third Sector?, in *The Handbook on Third Sector Policy in Europe*, edited by J. Kendall. Cheltenham: Edward Elgar, 253–75.

Commission of the European Communities. 1997. *Promoting the Role of Voluntary Organisations and Foundations in Europe*. Luxembourg: Office of Official Publications of the European Commission.

Constitution of Spain of 1978. [Online] Available at: http://es.wikisource.org/wiki/Constituci%C3%B3n_espa%C3%B1ola_de_1978 [Accessed: 10 October 2010].

Cowles, M.G., Caporaso, J. and Risse, T. 2001. *Transforming Europe: Europeanization and Domestic Change*. New York: Cornell University Press.

Esping-Andersen, G. 1990. *The Three Worlds of Welfare Capitalism*. Cambridge: Policy Press.

European Council. 2000. *Lisbon. Presidency Conclusions*. [Online] Available at: http://europal.europa.eu/summits/lis1_en.htm [Accessed: 14 July 2010].

Featherstone, K. and Radaelli, C. (eds) 2003. *The Politics of Europeanization*. Oxford: Oxford University Press.

Guillén, A.M. and Petmesidou, M. 2008. The Public–Private Mix in Southern Europe: What Changed in the Last Decade?, in *Transformations of the Welfare States*, edited by M. Seeleib-Kaiser. Basingstoke: Palgrave, 56–78.

Johnson, N. 1987. *The Welfare State in Transition: The Theory and Practice of Welfare Pluralism*. Brighton: Wheatsheaf Books.

Kendall, J. (ed.) 2009. *Handbook on Third Sector Policy in Europe*. Cheltenham: Edward Elgar.

Kendall, J. and Anheier, H. 1999. The Third Sector and the European Union Policy Process: An Initial Evaluation. *Journal of European Public Policy*, 6(2), 283–307.

Knill, C. 2001. *The Europeanisation of National Administrations: Patterns of Institutional Change and Persistence*. Cambridge: Cambridge University Press.

Ministry of Employment and Social Affairs (*Ministerio de Trabajo y Asuntos Sociales*) 2008. *¿Quién es quién? Convocatoria 2007*. Madrid: Ministerio of Employment and Social Affairs.

Ministry of Health and Social Policy (*Ministerio de Sanidad y Política Social*). [Online] Available at: http://www.msps.es/politicaSocial/ongVoluntariado/subvenciones/IRPF/home.htm [Accessed: 18 April 2010].

Ministry of Social Affairs (*Ministerio de Asuntos Sociales*). 1990. *La Política del Ministerio de Asuntos Sociales*. Madrid. Ministerio de Asuntos Sociales.

Montagut, T. 2009. The Third Sector and the Policy Process in Spain: The Emergence of a New Policy Player, in *Handbook on Third Sector Policy in Europe*, edited by J. Kendall. Cheltenham: Edward Elgar, 119–39.

Observatorio del Tercer Sector. [Online] Available at: http://www.tercersector.net/php/index.php [Accessed: 10 November 2010].

Observatorio del Tercer Sector de Bizcaia. [Online] Available at: http://www.3sbizkaia.org [Accessed: 10 November 2010].

Plataforma de ONG de Acción Social. [Online] Available at: http://www.plataformaongs.org/ [Accessed: 10 November 2010].

Plataforma Promoción del Voluntariado. 1997. *Las organizaciones de voluntariado en España*. Madrid.

Seeleib-Kaiser, M. (ed.) 2008. *Transformations of the Welfare States*. Basingstoke: Palgrave.

Subirats, J. (ed.). 1999. *¿Existe sociedad civil en España?* Madrid: Estudios de la Fundación Encuentro.

Titmuss, R. 1968. *Social Policy: An Introduction*. London: Allen & Unwin.

Trigilia, C. 2002. *Economic Sociology: State, Market and Society in Modern Capitalism*. Oxford: Blackwell.

Chapter 8

Are Spaniards Different?
European Convergence and
Regional Divergence in the Evaluation of the
Welfare State

Inés Calzada and Eloísa del Pino

Introduction

There are reasons to believe that Spaniards' attitudes towards the Spanish welfare state have converged with those of other Europeans in recent years. As explained in earlier chapters of the book, the Spanish welfare state was developed belatedly. However, very significant advances have occurred with social policies since the return of democracy. Furthermore, the Spanish welfare state is now facing the same challenges as are the welfare states elsewhere in Europe (Starke 2008; Palier and Martin 2008; Seeleib-Kaiser, van Dyk and Roggenkamp 2008): an aging population, growing doubts about the future viability of public old-age pensions systems, Europeanization and the arrival of a significant number of new citizens from developing countries who become new beneficiaries of social services and benefits.

Spaniards, like other European citizens, view this situation with some concern, and the new challenges may affect attitudes to the welfare state across all countries (Goul Andersen 1999; Van Oorschot 2006; Guillén 2007). Hence, the common risks and problems that beset welfare policies may have made Spaniards quite similar to other Europeans in their opinions of the welfare state.

However, other features of the Spanish welfare state suggest that some issues peculiar to Spain may still exist. Some experts argue, for example, that the Spanish welfare state has failed to catch up with others in their European environment (Navarro 2003, 2007; Rodríguez Cabrero 2004). Indeed, its belated and incomplete development, along with other specificities in welfare provision, such as the important role played by the family, especially by women, have led some to classify the Spanish welfare state as a distinct, 'Mediterranean' type of welfare regime (Moreno 2000), distinct from Esping-Andersen's (1990) three types. Moreover, although the pressures on the Spanish welfare state are similar to those experienced by other welfare states, in Spain they appear to be more intense than in other countries. For example, Spain has already one of the most aged populations in the world; and although the share of immigrants in the total population is similar to those in neighbouring countries, their arrival has occurred in a shorter period of time.

In addition to the convergence of the Spanish welfare state with its European counterparts, researchers have recently started to study the internal divergences in welfare provision that are appearing within the country. Since the 1990s the development of the Spanish welfare state has remained strongly conditioned by the process of devolution. The central government continues to maintain primary responsibility for old-age pensions and other social security programmes. However, at least since 2002, the 17 Autonomous Communities (AACC from now on) have exercised primary responsibility for health, education and social services. As a result, several tiers of government must now interact with each other in complex ways. Sub-national governments implement dissimilar policies in the welfare programmes they control. Spain is now witnessing the emergence of regional variations in levels of welfare expenditure, eligibility criteria and the extent to which private providers are contracted to deliver publicly funded services. Not surprisingly, various recent studies have found disparities in the educational and health outcomes in the AACC (CES 2000; OECD 2007), which has intensified public debate among social policy experts on the potential emergence of inequalities across citizens and regions.

The study of citizens' attitudes towards social policies becomes especially important in a context of multi-level government. On the one hand, in a multi-level system citizen satisfaction with the functioning of welfare policies may differ in each of the levels of government. On the other hand, citizens' attitudes and preferences can help us to forecast developments of welfare programmes in the near future in every AACC. Finally, it is important to know the extent to which citizens are aware of the level of government that must be electorally rewarded or punished for good or bad policy performance.

This chapter presents an overview of Spanish attitudes to the Spanish welfare state. In doing so, it aims to answer certain questions closely related to the debates on public welfare outlined above. Are Spaniards different from other European citizens in their welfare preferences? Is the underdevelopment of the Spanish welfare state reflected in lower levels of popular support for welfare programmes than those found in countries with older and larger welfare states? How do Spaniards face the challenges to their welfare programmes? Are they more prone to support retrenchment than other European citizens? After the intensive process of decentralization experienced in Spain, can attitudinal divergences be found within the country's different regions?

As data sources, we use the two most important comparative surveys available on welfare issues, *The Role of Government IV* (ISSP 2006) and the fourth round of the *European Social Survey* (ESS 2008), as well as several national surveys carried out by the Spanish Sociological Research Centre (CIS) over the years. *The Role of Government* is a comparative and longitudinal survey that focuses on welfare attitudes. It was conducted by the International Social Survey Programme (ISSP) in 1980, 1985, 1996 and 2006. We use primarily the last round of the survey. The *European Social Survey* is also comparative and longitudinal (2002, 2004, 2006 and 2008), and although not devoted to welfare state, in its fourth round (2008) it included a module on welfare attitudes. The *Centro de Investigaciones Sociológicas* (CIS) is an independent entity assigned to the Ministry of the Presidency with the purpose of studying Spanish society, mainly through opinion polls. All CIS surveys mentioned in this chapter involve in-person household interviews of at least 2,500 (designed sample) randomly selected adult residents in Spain, with a margin of sampling error of plus or minus 2 per cent at a confidence level of 95 per cent.

To supplement the quantitative information provided by surveys and to achieve a more profound understanding of Spaniards' discourses on welfare, we also use data from eight focus groups carried out in July 2006 by a team from the Spanish National Research Council (CSIC), within a research project funded by the Spanish National Research Plan: 'Welfare State Reforms: Stakeholders and Citizen Support' (REBAAC). The aim of this project was to provide evidence with which to assess the degree of societal consent and dissent for welfare reforms. It focused on the public perception of new challenges and problems arising from external factors (Europeanization, globalization and internationalization of the economy) and internal factors (changes in value systems, demographic transitions, new roles for women, transformations of the labour market or integration of immigrants). These focus group meetings were held in Madrid and covered the left–right ideological spectrum and people of different social classes, ages and genders; unemployed people, wage earners and professionals; and, finally, payers and receivers of welfare services and benefits.

Spanish Attitudes to the Welfare State in the European Context

Compared with most of its European counterparts, the Spanish welfare state may appear embryonic and underdeveloped (Navarro 2002). However, when we change our focus from the substantive reality of welfare programmes to the ideas, attitudes and expectations Spaniards have regarding the welfare state, neither of these terms applies. Several data indicate that a large majority of Spaniards have a clear view of what type of welfare model they prefer, what the problems of the existing public programmes are and how they should be solved by the government. For instance, most survey questions on welfare topics have a very low level of 'No answer' and 'Don't know' responses; temporal comparisons find a substantial stability in aggregate attitudes across time, and individual discourses on welfare appear quite consistent. All these findings indicate that the Spanish welfare state is one of the more important political issues to Spaniards and that their ideas are worth studying and listening to.

But although it is common to speak about 'attitudes to the welfare state', various scholars have shown that people do not have one single opinion on this topic but rather distinct opinions concerning different dimensions of welfare policies (Roller 1995; Sihvo and Uusitalo 1995). In a recent study, Van Oorschot and Meuleman (2009) identified six 'dimensions' of attitudes to the welfare state: (*a*) guiding principles of the welfare state, (*b*) scope of government's responsibilities in welfare, (*c*) level of expenditure, (*d*) underuse and overuse of services and benefits, (*e*) outcomes of social provision and (*f*) unintended consequences.

We follow this 'dimensional' scheme in elaborating a brief overview of Spanish attitudes to the welfare state and comparing Spain with a set of seven other European countries (France, Germany, Norway, Portugal, Switzerland, Sweden and the UK). The sample of countries was selected to include geographical and cultural variation across western Europe, as well as different traditions in the organization of welfare institutions. Although it is not the aim of the chapter, the data presented can be read from a 'welfare regime' perspective. We have representatives of Esping-Andersen's (1990) three welfare regimes and also of a fourth 'Mediterranean regime' (Ferrera 1996; Moreno 2000): Norway and Sweden (social democratic), France and Germany (conservative), the UK and Switzerland (liberal, though the position of Switzerland is somewhat ambiguous; see Arts and Gelissen 2002), and Spain and Portugal (Mediterranean).

Attitudes to the Guiding Principles and Scope of the Welfare State

A welfare state can be designed to pursue a range of goals. In its more developed version it should guarantee a decent standard of living for all citizens 'from cradle to grave' and decrease social inequality, hence constituting a central institution of society. In its minimalist form, it is a marginal mechanism to take care temporarily of those who fail to provide for themselves through the normal channel, namely, the market. If we understand these ideal types as the two poles of a continuum, Spaniards' desires fall clearly closer to the former.

To a question presenting three prototypical forms of the welfare state, 74 per cent of Spaniards answered that 'The government should be responsible for the welfare of all citizens' (universal welfare state), 15 per cent answered that 'The government should be responsible only for the welfare of underprivileged citizens' (targeted welfare state), and just 7 per cent chose the option 'The citizens must be responsible for their own welfare' (minimal welfare state) (CIS 2008).

Given their preference for a universal welfare state, it is no surprise that Spaniards stand out among Europeans in supporting far-reaching state intervention that includes coverage of universal risks (health care, old-age pensions), labour market risks (unemployment) and help in combining work and family life (childcare, paid leave to care for sick family members). Table 8.1 suggests that Spain is among the most 'welfarist' of the eight countries included, especially in respondents' support for state intervention in the labour market. This finding refutes the idea that the relative underdevelopment of the Spanish welfare state would be reflected in lower levels of popular support for it.

Table 8.1 Preferred goals of the welfare state, eight European countries (2008)

Country	Jobs for everyone	Health care	Std. living for old	Std. living unemployed	Childcare services	Paid leave from work	Mean of six aspects
Norway	6.03	8.96	8.66	7.34	7.97	8.19	7.86
Sweden	6.04	8.66	8.48	7.39	7.92	7.90	7.73
Germany	6.26	8.40	7.60	6.46	8.02	7.37	7.35
France	5.86	8.02	7.94	6.12	7.14	7.17	7.04
Spain	7.66	8.96	8.83	7.73	8.30	8.20	8.28
Portugal	7.29	8.77	8.88	7.33	8.25	8.17	8.12
United Kingdom	5.94	8.74	8.53	6.00	6.93	7.16	7.22
Switzerland	4.84	7.66	7.23	6.28	6.47	6.11	6.43
Average	6.32	8.54	8.28	6.82	7.66	7.55	7.53

Notes: Questions posed: Should it or should it not be the responsibility of government to: Ensure adequate health care for the sick?; Ensure a reasonable standard of living for the old?; Ensure a reasonable standard of living for the unemployed?; Ensure sufficient childcare services?; Provide paid leave to people who have to care for sick family members?

0 = not government responsibility at all; 10 = entirely government responsibility.

Source: ESS (2008).

It may be of interest to mention that Spaniards' preference for a government burdened with numerous responsibilities has frequently been interpreted as a residue of the 40 years of Francoist dictatorship (1939–75), a period that was characterized, among other things, by significant state intervention in the economy, but not in welfare. The explanation may sound plausible but it turns out to be incorrect. If the Spanish preference for a universal welfare state were grounded in the experience of dictatorship, we should find that older people favour a big welfare state more than younger cohorts. This is not the case. In fact, younger cohorts are slightly more supportive of state intervention in welfare than older ones, indicating also that welfare-state legitimacy is not endangered by generational change (Arriba, Calzada and del Pino 2006).

In Spain, citizens believe that their young welfares state should be further developed. Although recent Spanish governments have made significant effort to increase social resources, social expenditure as percentage of GDP is still four points below the EU-15 average. The same is true of tax, which is lower than that in most European countries (OECD 2009). As shown in the following quotation from a focus group, citizens are capable of recognizing the differences between the Spanish welfare state and other welfare states around Europe in respect of generosity and taxes:

W: Well, I wish that the government would do its best for a welfare state to exist.

M: It would be wonderful ... but in only four countries has it worked, in Northern Europe ...

M: Here, In Spain there has never been a welfare state. The welfare state is only from Sweden ...

W: [The Nordic countries] They pay a lot of taxes ...

M: France and the United Kingdom enjoy more social services ...

M: [In Spain, social services] are directed primarily on women, in particular women. I mean, because the authorities are unable to reach certain sectors of society and then automatically it is women who are responsible for caring for the elderly, childcare, caring, right? And that should be covered by the government.

Outcomes, Expenditure and Finance

Table 8.2 reveals that Spaniards are satisfied with the performance of their national health service, which is popularly perceived as the most important policy sector. On a scale from 0 to 10, where 0 means that the state of health services is *extremely bad* and 10 means it is *extremely good*, the average evaluation of Spaniards falls slightly more than 6. Satisfaction with public health care is therefore similar to what we find in Sweden, Norway, France or the UK. The state of education and the standard of living of pensioners are evaluated worse, with means around 5, which could be interpreted as a 'pass',[1] and are not far from the averages of France, Sweden or the UK. On the standard of living of unemployed people, the welfare state receives a 4, a clear 'fail', shared with Germany and, again, with France. It is only in their evaluation of the provision of childcare services that Spain is outstandingly dissatisfied among European countries, together with Portugal, the only country in Table 8.2 where citizens evaluate the outcomes of all welfare programmes quite negatively (with scores between 3 and 4).

The main conclusion that can be drawn from Table 8.2 is that Spaniards are not particularly different from other Europeans in their evaluation of welfare programmes. They rate health care and the standard of living of pensioners slightly above the average, and the provision of child-care services and the level of living of unemployed slightly below it. It is interesting that these results coexist with a perceived increase in the demands for high-quality public services. A CIS survey from 2009 (n° 2.809) shows that 60 per cent of Spaniards deem that Spanish citizens are more demanding with respect to social services than in 1999. Asked if they were personally demanding when dealing with public services and benefits, 53 per cent considered themselves as 'quite' or 'very' demanding, 38 per cent answered that they were 'a little' demanding, and only 6 per cent perceived themselves to be 'not at all' demanding.

The fairly positive evaluations of health care, education and the standard of living of the elderly do not imply that Spaniards have no criticisms of their welfare programmes. In 2008 the percentage of citizens who said that welfare programmes were performing 'quite' or 'very' inefficiently was 39 per cent for health service primary care, 42 per cent for health service hospital care, 42 per cent for education, 34 per cent for the 'management of old-age pensions' and 37 per cent for the 'management of unemployment benefits' (CIS 2008).

Interestingly, although some politicians assume that citizens' criticisms to the welfare state reveal their desire to privatize the management of the programmes, in fact this is not the case: a large majority of Spaniards want the programmes to continue to be publicly funded and publicly provided. In 2008 a survey by the Spanish Sociological Research Centre presented citizens with three different ways of organizing welfare programmes: (*a*) public funding and public provision; (*b*) public funding but private provision; and (*c*) private funding and private provision (privatization). Of the respondents, 87 per cent and 86 per cent preferred public funding and public provision for education and health care respectively. In pensions 68 per cent opted for 'a model like the present one, where pensions are public and funded through contributions', and 25 per cent preferred 'a model like the present one but where workers are allowed to devote part of their social contributions into a private pension plan'. Only 2 per cent were in favour of privatization (CIS 2008).

---

1   In Spain it is very common in evaluations to use a scale of 0–10, where 5 is a 'pass'. This is the case, for example, in all stages of the education system.

Table 8.2   Citizen evaluation of welfare services in eight European countries (2008)

Country	State of education	State of health services	Standard of living of pensioners	Standard of living of unemployed	Childcare services
Norway	6.32	6.01	5.80	4.97	6.12
Sweden	5.69	6.05	4.70	4.18	6.40
Germany	4.42	4.65	5.59	3.75	4.41
France	4.98	6.00	4.35	3.77	4.87
Portugal	3.98	4.32	2.67	3.01	3.92
Spain	5.24	6.07	4.93	3.70	4.19
Switzerland	6.54	6.94	6.21	4.86	4.49
United Kingdom	5.70	5.95	4.29	4.63	4.42
Average	5.25	5.67	4.76	4.03	4.76

Note: Question: What do you think overall about …? the state of education nowadays; the state of health services nowadays; the standard of living of pensioners; the standard of living of unemployed?; the provision of affordable childcare service for working parents. 0 = extremely bad; 10 = extremely good.
Source: ESS (2008).

Data show that citizens attribute some of the programmes' inefficiencies to inadequate funding by government. There is a strong statistical association between perceiving a welfare programme as inefficient and considering it underfunded; but there is no statistically significant association between perceiving a programme to be inefficient and wanting to turn its management over to private hands (Calzada and Del Pino 2008).

For many Spaniards, the inefficiency of welfare programmes could to a certain extent be solved with more money, something that might partially explain the majority demand for an increase in the budget devoted to the welfare state. Almost 90 per cent of citizens want the government to spend 'more' or 'much more' in health care, education and old-age pensions; 59 per cent also want more money devoted to unemployment benefits.

Although the figures in Table 8.3 seem to mirror and be grounded in the comparatively moderate levels of social spending in Spain, the Spanish people are not alone in asking for more in this direction. Table 8.4 includes the percentage of citizens who wants the government to spend 'more' or 'much more' in four core welfare programmes. Even though the table includes some of the most liberal welfare states (the US and Australia), we can see how a desire for more social expenditure is shared by many Western countries.

**Table 8.3   Spaniards' preferences for government spending on some
welfare programmes (2006)**

	Health care	Education	Unemployment benefits	Old-age pensions
Spend much more	34	33	12	28
Spend more	53	54	47	55
Spend the same as now	12	12	33	16
Spend less	1	1	6	1
Spend much less	0	0	1	0
Total	100	100	100	100

Note: Question: Listed below are various areas of government spending. Please show
whether you would like to see more or less government spending in each area. Remember
that if you say 'much more' it might require a tax increase to pay for it.
Source: ISSP (2006).

It may be worth mentioning that respondents who want to see less money put
into health care amount to less than 10 per cent in the 11 countries listed, and
those who want less spending on education or old-age pensions amount to less
than 8 per cent (ISSP, 2006). Only on unemployment benefits do we find, in some
countries, sizeable groups of citizens that would support a decrease in public
expenditure (close to 40 per cent in France, the United Kingdom and Australia).

**Table 8.4   Percentage of the respondents in 11 western countries favouring
'more' or 'much more' government spending on some welfare
programmes (2006)**

2006	AUS	CDN	FRA	GER	IRE	NOR	SPA	SWE	SWI	UK	US
Health care	90	77	60	66	93	86	87	80	48	82	80
Education	80	66	59	82	88	62	87	53	70	73	83
Old-age pensions	54	53	46	52	90	59	83	61	55	74	64
Unemp. benefits	12	26	14	33	54	19	59	25	29	16	37

Notes: AUS: Australia; CDN: Canada; FRA: France; GER: Germany; NOR: Norway; SPA:
Spain; SWE: Sweden; SWI: Switzerland; UK: United Kingdom; US: United States of
America. Question: *Listed below are various areas of Government spending. Please show
whether you would like to see more or less government spending in each area. Remember
that if you say 'much more' it might require a tax increase to pay for it.*
Source: ISSP (2006).

Spaniards are not alone in wanting a better funded welfare state; but if such preferences are to be put into practice someone has to pay the bill. As in several other countries, Spanish citizens are not keen on tax increases, but that does not mean that they suffer from any kind of 'tax aversion'. In 1993, 1994 and 1995 around 73 per cent of interviewees disagreed with the sentence 'It would be better to pay less in taxes and reduce a little the quantity or quality of public services' (Calzada and Del Pino 2008, based on CIS data). In 2005 the question was asked again, slightly reworded to offer two response options, but with similar results. That year 69 per cent of Spaniards believed that 'It is better to spend more in social services and benefits even if that means paying more in taxes', and only 31 per cent thought that 'It is better to pay less taxes even if that means spending less on social services and benefits'. These data suggest a historical acceptance of the drawbacks of extending the welfare state, but the survey (CIS 2009) shows that the economic crisis has had a heavy impact on Spaniards attitudes towards the level of taxation. In 2009 only 44 per cent preferred to increase taxes to improve public services rather than to reduce taxes and spend less on public services. Previous studies on the impact of economic crises on welfare attitudes have shown that, although a crisis depresses support for welfare expenditure, once it is over attitudes return to their normal pattern (Forma 1999). Time will tell whether this is the case also in Spain, or whether we are witnessing the initial moments of a trend change regarding attitudes to the trade-off between taxes and services. In any case, focus groups allow us to better understand the reasoning of citizens in relation to tax. The following quotations from focus groups show that people believe it is possible to improve public services by upgrading its management and without raising taxes:

> First Woman: Well, people are very afraid of tax increases. I am certainly not concerned about it. If I see, I mean, if I see results ... Of course, I don't mind paying more taxes if I know that some day those taxes will be useful for paying to this young lady a maternity leave or a benefit when she needs it.

> Second Woman: If that takes you to a better quality of life.

> First Woman: Every time someone says they will lower taxes, I get the creeps, because I start thinking they [National Health System] will not have the money to cure me in case I get some disease.

> Man: The fact is that the welfare state is paid for with taxes. People will have to be clear about that.

> Second Woman: Yes, but also with a proper management.

> Man: Yes, with the two things. I mean ...

Second Woman: We think that if there is a more efficient management that would allow for better service for significantly less money.

As for the way taxes are raised, Spain is one of the European countries with strong popular support for progressive taxation. In 2008, 57 per cent of respondents considered that 'higher earners should pay a higher share of their earning in taxes', versus 38 per cent thinking that 'higher and lower earners should pay the same percentage of their earnings in taxes' (ESS 2008).

Fraud and the Costs and Benefits of Social Provision

Social provision can have costs and benefits for a society. Benefits seem to outweigh costs in the eyes of Spaniards. While a majority agree on the benefits, those who believe it has economic or moral costs are always less than 50 per cent (see Table 8.5). To start with the positive aspects, 53 per cent consider that the welfare state 'prevents widespread poverty', 56 per cent consider that it 'leads to a more equal society' and 58 per cent agree with the sentence: 'social services and benefits make it easier to combine work and family life'.

The negative effects could be of an economic or moral nature. Spaniards seem more concerned about the economic costs than the moral costs. Of all respondents, 46 per cent think that social benefits and services 'cost businesses too much in taxes'; 40 per cent believe that they 'place too great a strain on the economy' and 'make people lazy'. In comparison, the percentages who feel that social provision negatively affects the extension of mutual help are low (between 33 per cent and 20 per cent). Finally, we should note that 67 per cent of Spaniards deem that 'social benefits and services encourage people from other countries to come and live here'. The interpretation of this effect can be positive or negative depending on the individual's position in the labour market (employer, employee or unemployed), and possibly also on her or his degree of tolerance for other cultures. In the present context of economic crisis and high unemployment, the arrival of new immigrant workers is possibly not seen in a good light by those who are already in the country.

Compared with those from other countries, the Spanish data are not eye-catching. Concerns about the negative effects of the welfare state on the economy are more extensive than in the Nordic countries but less extensive than in France and the UK. As for the moral effects, respondents in Spain and Sweden are the least concerned that social benefits and services might make people less willing to care for each other. But if Spain does not stand out for its concern about the cost of welfare, neither is it among those countries most convinced of its virtues. Those who believe that welfare programmes 'prevent widespread poverty' amount to a weaker majority (53 per cent) than those in the Nordic and Continental countries (around 65 per cent). This popular appraisal actually may reflect the inability of the Spanish welfare state to bring poverty levels close to European standard.

Table 8.5   Perceived social costs and benefits of the welfare state in six European countries (2008)

Social benefits and services ...	Percentage of respondents agreeing with the statements in					
	Germany	*Spain*	*France*	*UK*	*Norway*	*Sweden*
Economic costs						
Place too great strain on economy	38	40	53	52	25	26
Cost businesses too much in taxes/charges	44	46	59	51	34	36
Encourage people from other countries to come live here	82	67	71	76	71	57
Make people lazy	39	40	48	66	43	37
Moral costs						
Make people less willing care for one another	41	33	50	49	39	26
Make people less willing look after themselves/ family	33	20	55	50	22	24
Social benefits						
Prevent widespread poverty	66	53	67	57	65	67
Lead to a more equal society	42	56	59	42	67	64
Make it easier to combine work and family	58	58	65	58	71	74

Note: Question: Please tell me to what extent you agree or disagree that social benefits and services in (country) ...
Source: ESS [2008].

The final aspect of attitudes to the welfare state we examine has to do with beliefs about the overuse and underuse of public services and benefits. In the eyes of Spaniards, both problems affect welfare programmes. To start with beliefs about underuse, 64 of respondents believe that many poor people receive less benefit than they are legally entitled to, and a large majority (72 per cent) believe that there are insufficient benefits in Spain to help those in real need. Once again, people complain of the insufficient development of the welfare state, whose coverage, this time related to certain groups, is inadequate.

Table 8.6   Perceived underuse and overuse of social services and benefits in six European Countries (2008)

	Percentage of respondents agreeing or strongly agreeing with the statements in					
	Germany	*Spain*	*France*	*UK*	*Norway*	*Sweden*
Most unemployed people do not really try to find a job.	35	30	43	46	19	16
Many with very low incomes get less benefit than they are legally entitled to.	48	64	50	52	24	23
Many manage to obtain benefits/ services they are not entitled to.	67	70	64	78	48	51
Benefits in this country are insufficient to help people in real need.	52	72	59	57	51	33
Employees often pretend they are sick to stay at home.	23	48	32	66	32	21

Note: Question: Please say how much you agree or disagree with each of the following statements about people in [country].
Source: ESS (2008).

> W: I think we are talking about welfare crisis when, actually, there is a great number of groups in Spain that are still deprived of welfare, because there are no appropriate services.

Similar percentages believe that the Spanish welfare state suffers from overuse or 'free riding'. 70 per cent of interviewees believe that 'many manage to obtain benefits or services they are not entitled to'. We do not have information on what specific social programmes are perceived as being more prone to generate 'free-rider' problems but, interestingly, it is not abuse of unemployment benefits that causes the most concern: Table 8.6 shows that only 30 per cent of Spaniards consider that 'most unemployed people do not really try to find a job', the lowest percentage in the six countries surveyed. The ceaseless references in the economic debate to the 'lazy unemployed' and to the negative effect of subsidizing those looking for work foreshadowed a worse popular image of unemployed people.

Up until now we have studied Spaniards' attitudes to different aspects of the welfare state from a comparative perspective. Although the data may be open to different interpretations, it seems clear that Spain does not differ markedly from other European countries in this respect. Within this context of similar attitudinal patterns, Spaniards stand out in their support for a big welfare state and in their desire for an increase in the funds devoted to this institution. This could reflect the fact that, although the Spanish welfare state has similar principles and organizational rules to other European welfare states, it is still lagging behind in terms of funding.

The Territorial Organization of Welfare Provision

As mentioned in the introduction, the development of the Spanish welfare state has been conditioned by the process of devolution. As a result of this process, several tiers of government must now interact with each other in complex ways to deliver welfare services. Indeed, the 17 AACC currently have the main responsibility for providing citizens with health, education and social services, and regional' governments have started to implement dissimilar policies in these areas.

In this context, the degree of citizens satisfaction with decentralized public services can be a subjective indicator of regional performance and, eventually, of (in)equality across regions. Table 8.7 shows important differences between the regions in the evaluation of welfare programmes. In the case of health care, Asturias is the community in which citizens are the most satisfied. People from Asturias are 20 points above the average Spanish level of satisfaction, and 36 points above the level in the Canary Islands, whose citizens are the least satisfied with their public health care. As for public education, 80 per cent of the citizens in Asturias feel very or quite satisfied, compared with only 44 per cent of the people in Madrid, the community with the most negative evaluation of this policy. People in Navarre ranked social services more positively, especially in comparison with the inhabitants of Murcia, Madrid and Valencia.

Finally, a recent analysis comparing citizens satisfaction with decentralized policies (public health and education) to the satisfaction with centralized policies (public pensions), showed that indeed there are differences across AACC. These differences are bigger in those policies where the jurisdiction belongs to the AACC. Although reduced, these differences persist in all policies even when controlling for the effects of individual variables and some socio-economic environmental characteristics. It is therefore likely that part of the satisfaction is due to the effects of different management models in education and health conducted by the regions (Diaz-Pulido, Del Pino and Palop 2010).

Citizens' preferences for one model of service management over another (for example, private versus public) can, in the long term, be partly determined by their perceptions of the present performance of the services.

Table 8.7 Percentage of citizens who are 'very satisfied' and 'quite satisfied' with welfare services, by Autonomous Communities in Spain (2009)

Autonomous Community	Public health	Public education	Social services
Asturias	83	80	62
Basque Country	78	72	52
Navarre	77	72	72
The Balearics	69	59	59
Aragon	68	66	62
Castile and León	64	57	55
Castile la Mancha	64	60	65
Spain	*60*	*57*	*53*
Cantabria	60	59	56
C. Valencian	60	58	49
Rioja	60	76	66
Catalonia	59	51	50
Andalusia	59	56	57
Galicia	57	60	50
Madrid	56	44	49
Murcia	52	62	47
Extremadura	50	61	54
Canary Islands	36	50	49

Note: Question: Regardless of whether you have used them or not, are you very, quite, not very or not at all satisfied with how these public services work: Public Health, Public Education, Social Services?

Source: Prepared by authors using CIS and AEVAL (2009).

Table 8.7 indicates that dissatisfaction with public services is extensive in some AACC; and, although Spaniards are not particularly inclined to transfer the management of public welfare programmes to the private sector, this attitude could change if inefficiency persists. Some theoretical models suggest that protracted perceived inefficiency might change citizens' preferences (Lyons, Lowery and DeHoog 1992). In other words, citizens' patience is limited.

In fact, in 2009 regional differences began to appear in citizens' preferences concerning model of provision. For example, over 70 per cent of the inhabitants of Asturias would use public health care if they could choose between public and private provision. However, only 39 per cent of the Canary Islands population would choose the public option.

Table 8.8   Opinions (%) about the level of government that is and should be responsible for the management of various welfare programmes (2008)

	European Union ...		Central government		Autonomous Regions		Local government	
	... is the main responsible	... should be responsible	... is the main responsible	... should be responsible	... is the main responsible	... should be responsible	... is the main responsible	... should be responsible
Health	2	4	37	56	59	37	1	2
Pensions	1	3	79	66	19	29	1	2
Education	3	4	43	57	52	37	3	2
Social services	1	3	37	45	45	38	16	14
Disability benefits and services	1	3	44	48	40	35	14	14
Housing	1	3	47	49	42	36	10	12

Note: Question: Which of the following institutions do you think is mainly responsible for the management of: health care, old-age pensions; education; social services, care for dependent; housing. Question: Which one do you think it should be responsible for the management of these programmes?

Source: Prepared by authors from CIS (2008).

Similarly with education: while almost 70 per cent of citizens in Asturias would choose a public school for their children, only 55 per cent of Madrid's inhabitants would do the same.

Clarifying which level of government is responsible for each welfare programme is of utmost importance if we expect citizens to reward or punish policy performance in this area. As can be observed in Table 8.8, in 2008 a majority of citizens knew that health care and education were the responsibilities of the AACC, while responsibility for pensions for the elderly still lay with the central government. As one can gather from the following exchange between three citizens, in general, they evaluate these areas positively but they are afraid of an increase in the differences among the autonomous communities.

Man: I believe that the gover ... all levels of government can be blamed, all of them: the city council, the community government and the central government. In the case of Madrid, the community government is solely guilty, because it is the one that has the responsibility for these policies ...

First Woman: ... the central government gives money to each region. Then each region runs it as it wants ... and the differences in health care are immense. Why? Mrs. Esperanza Aguirre [the President Madrid's regional government] receives money for health, then the lady with the money does what she wants.

Second Woman: Regarding the old people's homes ... In Madrid there are 25,000 elderly ... they are waiting to have a place in an old people's home, and when they obtain it they are already dead ... what happens is it depends on the Autonomous Community of Madrid. The government should make a law in which all AACC are included ...

In Spain, popular attitudes to the territorial organization of the welfare state are ambivalent. On the one hand, citizens support the development of the regions and they are generally satisfied with the one they belong to. On the other hand, there is some concern about the territorial inequality that can be generated by the devolution of welfare policies. It is perhaps for this reason that most of the population would prefer health-care, education and pensions be managed by the central government, leaving sub-national bodies in charge of social policies that affect fewer people and cost less money, such as social services, disability benefits and social housing. Of course, neither welfare programmes nor welfare attitudes are identical across the AACC. In 2005, for example, 61 per cent of those living in the Basque Country and 56 per cent of those living in Catalonia preferred health care to be run by the community government, but only 41 per cent of Andalusians shares this preference. The same divergence of preference applies to education and old-age pensions for the elderly, but for the latter programme fewer than 50 per cent of citizens in the Basque Country and Catalonia would hand the responsibility over to their community governments (Arriba, Calzada and del Pino 2006). Focus groups show that these results can be explained by the fact that, in some AACC, citizens have to reconcile their concerns about departures from equality in welfare state provision with their support for a territorial model of government better adapted to their regional identities.

A Look into the Future

After reviewing the possible convergence of Spaniards' attitudes towards the welfare state with of those of other European populations, and assessing the divergences among Spanish regions, it is appropriate to conclude with a look into the future or, at least, at what Spaniards forecast for their welfare programmes. Recent changes in European societies have fuelled public debates on the sustainability of the welfare state and, additionally, have provoked a certain scepticism about the durability of popular support for a social model that some economists believe is doomed to fail. Economic prognoses abound, as usual contradicting one another. Less frequently are ordinary citizens' ideas about the future of the welfare state taken into account. In 2008, a CIS survey invited interviewees to make predictions on the situation of various welfare programmes in 10 years' time, and gave them a choice among three options: improvement, maintenance and deterioration. From their answers to this question, we know that Spaniards are generally optimistic regarding the future of their welfare state. A majority believe that governments will offer services or benefits of equal or superior quality to that which prevails today. This is true for all the programmes on which a forecast was invited – health care, elderly care, unemployment protection, education and old-age pensions – although for this last area the percentage of pessimists is slightly higher than for the rest. One third of Spaniards believe that public old-age pensions will deteriorate in 10 years' time but, even if this is a substantial percentage, when compared with corresponding results in other countries it reveals that the Spanish are strikingly optimistic about the future of public pensions and health care (ESS 2008).

Rather than the welfare state as a whole, it is precisely with regard to public retirement pensions that citizens perceive a serious risk to sustainability. There is no agreement, though, on the cause of the problem. Some people believe public pensions will suffer a serious crisis because of population ageing. Others assume that this 'crisis' is mostly a tall tale fabricated to serve the interests of the private insurance sector. In any case, focus groups show disquiet about this issue. People are not sure whether we will be able to afford public pensions in the future, or whether the amount will be lower than it is today:

M: The Social Security is paying the current pensions with social contributions. It is very dangerous, above all, if we bear in mind the ageing of the population.

W: I listen to highly trained people from the university ... saying no, you don't have to be afraid ... Pensions are guaranteed with the economic growth we have ... What happens is that maybe somebody can take advantage of the opportunity ... you manipulate the situation a little bit ... Because if you manipulate and say danger, danger, danger ...

M: You say 'I am going to the private system'.

M: ... social retrenchment.

Several solutions are being discussed in the political and academic arenas to deal with the 'financial crisis' of the public pension systems. In 2008 a CIS survey invited respondents to evaluate six of them. Three of the options received majority support: promotion of women's integration in the labour market, legalization of jobs for migrant workers so that they can pay contributions and taxes, and increasing the birth rate. More than two-thirds of citizens considered at least one of these policies as 'positive' or 'very positive'. The other three measures presented as possible ways to help the pension system were strongly rejected: increased social security contributions, extension of the minimum period of contributions needed to receive a pension, and an increase in the retirement age (the last of these was the central proposal of a new plan launched by the Spanish government at the time of this writing). They were rejected probably because they implied cuts in welfare rights or tougher eligibility requirements. As in 2005, in 2008 the first of these restrictive options was evaluated as 'negative' or 'very negative' by more than 50 per cent of the population, and around 70 per cent also opposed the other two. Apparently, in the eyes of the citizens the future of our public pensions system now rests on the shoulders of women and immigrants.

Finally, immigration is one of the issues that more frequently emerges in focus groups on welfare state' future. Citizens have ambivalent feelings. On the one hand, it is believed that immigrants contribute to the sustainability of the social protection system. On the other hand, they are seen as big consumers of public resources (scholarships, benefits, etc.) and, for some groups, as competitors in the race for a scarce commodity like jobs. In 2008, for example, more than 50 per cent of the Spanish population felt that immigrants were receiving 'quite a lot' or 'a lot' of public help, what makes them the only population group considered to be well protected by the State. These results are in line with other studies in showing that nationality is a clear divide in citizens' perceptions about who deserves, or not, public help (van Oorschot 2006).

Conclusions

This chapter has tried to present an overview of Spanish attitudes towards the welfare state. The main question that it addresses is whether the attitudes of Spaniards are similar to those of citizens of other European welfare states subject to equal challenges or, conversely, whether they are different because of the peculiarities of the Spanish model. We compared attitudes towards the welfare state in Spain with those in a set of European countries selected to include institutional, geographical and cultural variation across western Europe. For data sources we used the two most important comparative surveys on welfare issues, *The Role of Government* (ISSP 2006) and the 2008 round of the *European Social Survey*. Moreover, we utilized several Spanish national surveys and focus groups.

Spain is among the countries where more extensive support for state intervention in welfare areas can be found, and citizens seem to believe that the welfare state has a certain leeway to increase the quality of some of its public services and the amount of its public expenditure (although a desire for more expenditure in health care, education and pensions for the elderly is common to Western countries). On the whole, Spaniards' evaluation of the performance of welfare services is similar to the average of the eight countries studied, and quite close to those of French, Germans or Swedish citizens However, the standard of living of unemployed people and the provision of childcare services are evaluated more negatively than in other countries. Indeed, unemployment protection and childcare are two traditional deficiencies in the Spanish welfare. Spanish opinion polls show that high unemployment is most frequently perceived by citizens as the country's most pressing problem. Although Spain was the first country of the EU-27 to create employment since the turn of the millennium, it never reduced its unemployment rate below the 8.3 per cent it achieved in 2007 (the average in EU-27 was 7.1 per cent and in EU-15 7 per cent). Likewise, the insufficient public spending on childcare policies, one of the lowest levels among OECD members, is a traditional complaint in a country that has one of the lowest rates of fertility among Western countries.

Spaniards believe that, with the exception of immigrants, numerous social groups are still poorly protected by the government. Fewer Spaniards than citizens in Nordic and Continental countries believe that welfare programmes 'prevent widespread poverty'. A large majority think that many poor people get fewer benefits than they are legally entitled to and that there are insufficient benefits to help those in real need.

Spain does not present extensive alarm about the alleged negative consequences of the welfare state. There is some concern about its negative effect on the economy, although less so than in France and the UK. As for the future of their welfare programmes, Spaniards are generally optimistic. Nevertheless, there exists a certain pessimism concerning public pensions. Moreover, this pessimism will perhaps increase following the Spanish government's proposal in autumn 2010 for retrenching pensions, based on assumptions about the future effects of population ageing on the system.

As we have seen, some divergences and convergences exist between Spanish citizens' attitudes towards their welfare regime and those in other, more consolidated welfare states throughout Europe. The divergences seem to be related to the incomplete development of the Spanish welfare state, where citizens are perhaps more demanding, especially with regard to certain policy sectors. The convergences in attitudes are a result of the common challenges and pressures that Western welfare regimes are experiencing.

Despite all this, when we break down Spaniards' attitudes according to the AACC where they live, we find some divergences within the country. For years, the primary responsibility for implementing some of the main welfare policies has belonged to the regional governments. Sometimes they have implemented different policies. As a result, there are important differences among the AACC in citizens' evaluation of public services. While in some AACC citizens are mainly satisfied with public welfare services, in others they are preponderantly dissatisfied. Based on some theoretical models and recent data from the communities, we believe the traditional Spanish preferences for a public model could change in the regions where citizens' perception of inefficiency is prolonged. Perhaps in future years we will find differences in attitudes corresponding to the diverse welfare regimes among the 17 AACC.

References

Arriba, A., Calzada, I. and del Pino, E. 2006. *Las Actitudes de los Españoles hacia el Estado de Bienestar, 1985–2005. Opiniones y Actitudes*. Madrid: Centro de Investigaciones Sociológicas.

Arts, W.A. and Gelissen, J.P.T.M. 2002. Three Worlds of Welfare Capitalism or More? A State-of-the-art Report. *Journal of European Social Policy*, 12(2), 137–58.

Calzada, I. and Del Pino, E. 2008. Perceived Efficacy and Citizens' Attitudes toward Welfare State Reform. *International Review of Administrative Sciences*, 74(4), 555–74.

CES (Consejo Económico y Social de España) 2000. *Unidad de Mercado y Cohesión Social, Informe 3/2000*. Madrid: CES.

CIS (Centro de Investigaciones Sociológicas) 2002. *Instituciones y Autonomías II*, Estudio n. 2544. [Online] Available at: http://www.cis.es/cis/opencms/-Archivos/Marginales/2440_2459/2455/e245500.html [Accessed: 1 February 2010].

CIS 2005a. *Barómetro de febrero*. Estudio n. 2.594. [Online] Available at: http://www.cis.es/cis/opencm/ES/1_encuestas/estudios/ver.jsp?estudio=4536 [Accessed: 1 February 2010].

CIS 2005b. *Barómetro Autonómico*. Estudio n. 2.610. [Online] Available at: http://www.cis.es/cis/opencm/ES/1_encuestas/estudios/ver.jsp?estudio=5338&cuestionario=5651&muestra=9964 [Accessed: 1 February 2010].

CIS 2008. *Actitudes hacia el Estado de Bienestar*. Estudios n. 2.765. [Online] Available at: http://www.cis.es/cis/opencm/ES/1_encuestas/estudios/ver.jsp?estudio=8860 [Accessed: 1 February 2010].

CIS 2009. *Opinión Pública y Política Fiscal*. Estudio n. 2.809. [Online] Available at: http://www.cis.es/cis/opencms/-Archivos/Marginales/2800_2819/2809/es2809.pdf [Accessed: 1 February 2010].

CIS and Agencia de Evaluación de Políticas y Calidad de los Servicios (AEVAL). 2009. Calidad de los Servicios Públicos IV. Estudio n. 2.813.

Diaz-Pulido, J.M., Del Pino, E. and Palop, P. 2010. *Los Determinantes de las Actitudes Ciudadanas hacia las Políticas de Bienestar en las Comunidades Autónomas*. II Congreso Anual de la Red Española de Política Social. Crisis Económica y Políticas Sociales, October, Madrid.

Esping-Andersen, G. 1990. *Three Worlds of Welfare Capitalism*. Cambridge: Polity Press.

ESS (*European Social Survey*). 2008. [Online] Available at: http://ess.nsd.uib.no/ [Accessed: 17 January 2010].

Ferrera, M. 1996. The 'Southern Model' of Welfare in Social Europe. *Journal of European Social Policy*, 6(1), 17–37.

Forma, P. 1999. *Interests, Institutions and the Welfare State: Studies on Public Opinion Towards the Welfare State*. STAKES (National Research and Development Centre for Welfare and Health) Research Report 102. Turku: University of Turku.

Goul Andersen, J. 1999. Changing Labour Markets, New Social Divisions and Welfare States Support, in *The End of the Welfare State? Responses State Retrenchment*, edited by S. Svallfors and P. Taylor-Gooby. London: Routledge, 12–33.

Guillén, A.M. 2007. Spain: Starting from Periphery, Becoming Centre, in *The Europeanization of Social Protection*, edited by J. Kvist and J. Saari. Bristol: Policy Press, 117–36.

ISSP (International Social Survey Programme) 2006. *The Role of Government*. [Online] Available at: http://www.issp.org [Accessed: 17 January 2010].

Lyons, W.E., Lowery, D. and DeHoog, R. 1992. *The Politics of Dissatisfaction: Citizens, Services and Urban Institutions*. New York: M.E. Sharpe, Inc.

Moreno, L. 2000. The Spanish Development of Southern European Welfare, in *Survival of the European Welfare State*, edited by S. Kuhnle. Londres: Routledge, 146–65.

Navarro, V. 2002. *Bienestar Insuficiente, Democracia Incompleta*. Barcelona: Anagrama.

Navarro, V. (ed.) 2003. *El Estado del Bienestar en España*. Madrid: Tecnos/UPF.

Navarro, V. 2007. *Observatorio Social de España*. [Online] Available at: http://www.observatoriosocial.org/ [Accessed: 1 November 2010].

OECD 2007. *Programme for International Student Assessment (PISA) 2006 Science Competencies for Tomorrow's World.* [Online] Available at: http://www.oecd.org [Accessed: 21 November 2009].

OECD 2009. *Taxing Wages 2007/2008* (2008 Edition). París: OECD.

Palier, B. and Martin, C. 2008. *Reforming the Bismarckian Welfare System.* Oxford: Blackwell.

Rodriguez Cabrero, G. 2004. *El Estado del Bienestar en España: debates, desarrollo y retos.* Madrid: Fundamentos.

Roller, E. 1995. The Welfare State: The Equality Dimension, in *The Scope of Government*, edited by O. Borre and E. Scarbrough. New York/Oxford: Oxford University Press, 169–97.

Seeleib-Kaiser, M., van Dyk, S. and Roggenkamp, M. 2008. *Party Politics and Social Welfare: Comparing Christian and Social Democracy in Austria, Germany and Netherlands.* Cheltenham: Edward Elgar.

Sihvo, T. and Uusitalo, H. 1995. Attitudes Towards the Welfare State have Several Dimensions. *Scandinavian Journal of Social Welfare*, 4, 215–23.

Starke, P. 2008. *Radical Welfare State Retrenchment.* New York: Palgrave.

Van Oorschot, W. 2006. Making the Difference in Social Europe: Deservingness Perceptions among Citizens of European Welfare States. *Journal of European Social Policy*, 16(1), 23–42.

Van Oorschot, W. and Meuleman, B. 2009. *Welfarism and the Multidimensionality of Welfare State Legitimacy. Evidence from The Netherlands 2006 based on Confirmatory Factor Analyses.* Paper presented at the ESPANET Conference, Urbino, 18 September.

PART III
Key Challenges to the Spanish Welfare State

Part-time Employment in Spain: A Victim of the 'Temporality Culture' and a Lagging Implementation

Zyab Ibáñez

Introduction

Since 1990, Spanish employment figures have shown a clear trend towards narrowing the gap with European averages.[1] However, by 2010, together with the cyclical return of unemployment to around 20 per cent, as in the mid-1980s and mid-1990s, two other exceptions to convergence with Europe remain, and these two, unlike unemployment, have changed little in good times or bad: first, the very high percentages of fixed-term contracts, which seems stuck at a third of total employment, more than double the EU average; and second, the slight development of part-time employment (PT). In 2008 PT in Spain amounted to 12 per cent of total employment as opposed to 21 per cent for the EU-15.

It will be argued in the following section that these two distinctive traits in the Spanish labour market – high levels of short-term contracts and low levels of PT – are closely related. The extension of temporary contracts as the main form of flexibility, together with other forms of precarious employment, has excluded the consolidation of flexible but secure employment alternatives such as stable PT contracts.

The next section claims that access to PT is institutionally constrained. An inconsistent regulatory trajectory coupled with serious implementation deficits at the collective bargaining level has played a crucial part in hindering access to good PT jobs, either through transitions from full-time (FT) to PT or as initial contracts. This is even more striking in the public sector, where the government's and the trade unions' expressed concern with the promotion of normalized PT could have materialized in greater incentives to make PT an available and attractive option. Nevertheless, individual measures and legislative initiatives in labour law and

---

1   The employment rate grew from 49 per cent in 1992 to 64.3 per cent in 2008, mainly because of a spectacular increase in female employment, from around 30 per cent of women in 1994 to more than 50 per cent at present, and 65.9 per cent for those aged 25–54 years (EC 2009).

social policy to promote work–life balance and access to PT as an early retirement arrangement may mark the start of a different approach.

The succeeding section explores how these (to some extent unintended) realities have constrained the agendas of the main actors on these issues, while an emergent awareness of the interactions among different policies could lead to more strategic developments.

The deepening links between welfare and labour market policies in the pursuit of the aims of modern welfare states is widely recognized. This chapter intends to enhance the understanding of such a relationship by focusing on two areas where PT plays a key role: work-life balance (WLB) and activation policies. A central dilemma of Spanish employment and welfare policies is how to substitute a combination of flexibility and security for the prevailing mixture of rigidity and vulnerability; the development of PT that is voluntary, stable and enjoys pro rata conditions will be a key step towards resolving it. This is all the more so given that PT is the most common form of working-time flexibility across Europe and stable pro rata PT is increasingly demanded not just by working mothers but also by other groups of employees in 'transitional' biographical periods, whether between education and employment, between different jobs, or between employment and retirement.[2]

Factors behind Low Levels of Spanish Part-time Employment

As in other southern European countries, social, cultural and political backgrounds affect the lack of a tradition of formal PT in Spain. PT may have long been present in the Spanish informal economy, but it has always been marginal in the formal economy. As relatively recently as 1980, the Spanish Workers Statute restricted access to a PT contract to very limited groups of the working population, namely, the unemployed and people aged under 25. Only in 1984, with the first statutory reform of PT, was the option of PT opened up to the entire working population. This almost complete lack of PT until the mid-1980s certainly affects the recent evolution of PT and how the different institutions have adapted to it.

The explanation of the restrictions on PT in Spain in the early 1980s is surely related to the mix of factors behind the very recent entry of Spanish women into the labour market, but it may also be related to the pre-welfare state 'Durkheimian' view that the same FT job from early youth to old age for each (male) individual was a key ingredient of social order. This view prevailed across Europe, and it also found indirect support in the interest of trade unions in a standardized (though rigidly hierarchical) labour force to support the growing welfare state. In Spain, the idea of a single FT job from adolescence to old age as a core element of social

---

2   For details of research design and methodology see Ibañez (2007, 2011a). The research for this chapter is based on a total of 20 in-depth interviews of experts and representatives of social partners, documents and secondary data. See Appendix 1.

order was certainly reinforced by the industrial relations system that prevailed in the pre-democratic era before 1975. These cultural and historical factors are very difficult to operationalize but they cannot be ignored, especially when most of the Spanish working population in the 1980s, in the 1990s and in present times began shaping their attitudes towards labour market participation in that historical context.

Industrial Relations and the Welfare System

From a wider institutional perspective, Spain is not among the countries where various regulatory contexts have favoured PT. Starting with industrial relations, Crouch (1993) describes the Spanish system as one of pluralistic bargaining or contestation, where organized labour has little power and low levels of organizational articulation on the one hand, but a high level of social recognition and great mobilizing capacity on the other. This situation has not helped to sustain a consensual approach to contentious issues such as working-time flexibility. In addition, the segmentation of the labour market, especially strong since 1990 (see Chapter 5), has further weakened collective bargaining, at the same time as bargaining at the company and individual levels is displacing wider spheres of agreement (Miguéléz and Rebollo 1999). As regards the mode of regulating working time, Anxo and O'Reilly (2002) include Spain among the 'statist' regimes characterized by the major role played by the state as regulatory agent and by low levels of PT.

In relation to the welfare state, the income maintenance model, whereby most social benefits are linked to the recipients' employment record, has, at least until recently, discriminated against part-timers. Furthermore, the model has also contributed to keeping levels of youth participation in the labour market low, as Spanish families have traditionally supported long periods of dependence for children in the family home, with a contradictory combination of generational solidarity within the household and generational segmentation in the labour market, where seniority plays a central role and where the strong protection of insiders has particularly discriminated against young people (Cebrián et al. 2000).

This wider institutional and socio-economic context certainly shapes the working-time options for Spanish employees. However, recently growing female and youth labour market participation in a context of high employment growth (which has taken place at the same time as fertility rates have plunged below the replacement rate, as in most other European countries) might have been a favourable scenario for the development of PT, as happened in the Netherlands or the UK in the late 1970s and early 1980s (Ibáñez 2011b).

In Spain a 'childcare provision' argument may have also forecast significant growth of PT as female employment rates started to increase, given some important similarities to the British and Dutch systems in terms of welfare provision: for example, a traditional male breadwinner system combined with insufficient levels of childcare and short spells of maternity leave (León 2007). However, low levels of Spanish PT, as in other southern and Continental European countries, may cast doubt on the generalizability of childcare provision in explaining levels of PT (Ibáñez 2011a).

Before Spanish PT could have developed, flexibility had already taken the form of temporary contracts. Given that experts and principal actors assume that the extension of temporary contracts is the main obstacle to PT growth, I will comment on this issue before discussing other matters.

Labour Market Dualization and Segmentation

The general divide between permanent and temporary contracts may be a major reason behind the low levels of Spanish PT, as the use of fixed-term contracts is so extensive that it leaves little room for other forms of flexibility (CES 1996, 2005; Cebrián et al. 2000, 2003; Blanco et al. 2001; Senise 2001; Martín and Zarapuz 2002; Valdés dal-Ré 2004; MTAS 2005).

The high degree of flexibility allowed by temporary FT contracts has favoured organizations that have adapted to this modality of flexibility to the detriment of the possibilities that stable PT may offer. At the same time, trade unions, given the unexpected massive use of temporary contracts, have become highly resistant to any new forms of flexibility. These processes seem very difficult to reverse despite recent efforts to promote stable PT, and the permanent recommendation made by the European Employment Strategy, in its yearly assessments of the Spanish situation, to substitute this heavy use of fixed-term contracts for more stable PT.

On the labour demand side, the personal and social services sectors, together with intensive agricultural and building sectors that have the largest potential for job creation, include activities where high flexibility is needed in the form of fixed-term, PT or other working patterns. In Spain, these sectors, especially for low-skill occupations, have traditionally obtained flexibility either through the informal economy, with its related weaknesses, or through low-quality temporary contracts.

It is remarkable that, even though various governments have made regulatory efforts to promote stable PT (see below), in the public sector temporary contracts are more numerous and faster-growing than PT. In fact, the extension of public-sector employment in social and personal services, which are considered to be among the main sources of future employment, has involved a large percentage of temporality, especially at the local level.

Together with the division between permanent and temporary employees, there is evidence that other dimensions of segmentation in the Spanish labour market also hinder PT growth, such as the differences between private-sector and public-sector employees, the expansion of precarious forms of employment among young people, and the growing evidence of unpaid overtime for certain groups of employees.

The differences between the public and the private sectors have been a traditional factor of inequality in the Spanish labour market (Recio 1999), in terms of significant income differences per hour worked, different occupational structures, and different working time arrangements (the actual average working week for private-sector FT employees is more than 40 hours, whereas for public-sector employees it is fewer than 35 hours).

As for the vulnerability experienced by young people, their over-representation in the group of temporary employees is further compounded by the problems they face in the transition from education to employment. This involves in many cases long periods in diverse forms of 'training contracts' (*contratos de formación* for those with high-school qualifications; *contratos en prácticas* for university graduates; and non-formal grants, *becas no-convenidas*, for university graduates) that are increasingly used to fill regular job vacancies (OECD 2007). These training contracts have notably worse conditions than average temporary contracts, often becoming employment traps rather than stepping stones to stable jobs. These 'training' arrangements were initially introduced to facilitate first entrance into the labour market for groups of young workers (aged 16–30) with varying qualifications. However, they were soon extended to a much larger group of employees than they were originally conceived for, across a variety of sectors – including public administrations – and for lengthening durations. Since 1990, it has not been uncommon to encounter people with successive 'training' contracts. These arrangements have been increasingly seen as a form of 'cheap labour'. Although in theory they provide training jobs, most do not involve detailed training paths that lead to specific jobs. In practice, many '*becarios*' perform tasks that are equivalent to those performed by employees on standard contracts, but with much lower salaries and without most entitlements to social protection. A Work Council trade unionist, referring to the *becarios* problem, put it this way:

> They are paid around 300 euros per month; they don't really learn much and many of them have high-responsibility tasks, equivalent to a permanent employee. However, once the 'training period' finishes they cannot continue, very few of them are rehired …[3]

By 2004, the Spanish Ministry of Education reported that there were around one and a half million of these trainees (a rough estimate given that no clear statistics are available).[4] Most of them received a gross annual income of less than 6,000 euros, which is less than 40 per cent of the Spanish average gross income. Thus, it may not be a great exaggeration to claim, as some trade unionists do, that more than one million young people are working FT with a PT income. This is further aggravated by the heavy weight that 'seniority' has in determining final

---

3   Transcription from RNE 1, 'El ombligo de la luna' 17-02-05.

4   *El País*, 03-10-04.

employment conditions, which prejudices new entrants into the labour market and employment transitions, as women and young people often are.[5]

A further factor that obstructs the use of integrated forms of PT is the extensive use of unpaid overtime. The regulations limit overtime to a maximum of 80 hours per year, but qualitative studies suggest a growth in the number of employees who work much longer hours than either permitted by regulation or agreed, including a significant increase in unpaid overtime, while employees may be losing control over working time in collective bargaining (Miguélez et al. 1996; Prieto et al. 1996). According to the 2005 CIS Barometer,[6] 22 per cent of employees work unpaid overtime. A leading Spanish politician, Ramón Jauregui, involved in working time policies at various levels since the early 1990s, wrote:

> We find people working easily 10 to 12 hours per day in thousands of Spanish firms, banks and small businesses and nobody thinks about claiming income for those extra hours.[7]

At the same time, the extension of a culture of 'presenteeism' among career jobs in the private sector is particularly damaging the career opportunities for women, who, because of family responsibilities, find it more difficult to work long hours.

So far, the groups of Spanish employees that could have benefited more from working-time 'flexicurity' have been those most affected by precariousness: women reconciling work and family life, young people in the transition from education to work, workers close to retirement age and workers with retraining needs. These segmentation processes facilitate the extension of various forms of precarious FT contracts where there are no clear links between performance, rewards and time units; this creates an unfavourable context for PT, as good PT needs precisely transparency in the wage-effort bargain. The erosion of benchmark notions of FT employment contracts makes it more difficult to guarantee the corresponding conditions for part-timers.

A wide consensus therefore exists among the main Spanish labour market actors, though at a very general level, that there is a pressing need to combine flexibility and security. As said before, the central dilemma of Spanish employment policies could be expressed as how to substitute a combination of flexibility and security for the mixture of rigidity and vulnerability now in place, and which three major labour reforms (in 1984, 1994, and 2002) have been unable to resolve.

---

5   In the case of Spain, when referring to segmentation between a core group of FT, permanent and qualified adult and young workers unemployment and precariousness, Cebrián et al. (2003: 231) pointed out: 'this is a system where seniority pays and it is through seniority that most social rights are acquired'.

6   May 2005/n° 2607, Centro de Investigaciones Sociológicas (CIS) is the main government research centre for sociological surveys.

7   *El País*, 27-05-05.

In fact, it would be misleading to consider Spanish labour-market regulation and policies as either rigid or flexible. At present it actually combines very rigid and very flexible elements, as often happens in dualized contexts. The Spanish labour market combines, on the one hand, some of the highest severance costs for permanent employees with, on the other hand, spectacular levels of temporary contracts. The same happens in relation to working-time regulation, where big gaps in the development of procedures for PT access coexists with a very high degree of flexibility for annualized computing of working time and its irregular distribution over the year. The evolution of PT regulation and policies over recent decades is an illustrative example of these contradictions.

Regulatory and Policy Changes Affecting Part-time Employment

The formulation of strategies that made it possible to increase flexibility has been on the agenda of Spanish labour market reform since 1984 (see Table 9.1). However, faced with high levels of unemployment, Spanish employment policies in the 1980s and '90s mainly focused on a single element of flexibility: fixed-term contracts. This marked the beginning of a strong growth in the use of temporary contracts by employers, who eventually adapted to a 'temporality culture' (*cultura de la temporalidad*) and were reluctant to explore other forms of flexibility, especially stable PT (Rhodes 1997; Toharia et al. 1998; MTAS 2005).

The 1994 reform aimed to extend employers' use of PT as another strategy to increase employment. This led to authors like Ruivo, González and Varejao (1998: 206) and Prieto and Ramos (1999: 472) to expect, in a context of deregulation and de-standardization, significant increases in PT levels, however 'precarious'. However, this did not happen. PT remained at a very low level, and the trade-off between the quantity and the quality of PT remained a real policy dilemma.

The Agreement on Stable Part-time Employment Promotion (*Acuerdo para la promoción del empleo estable a tiempo parcial*), signed in 1998 by the centre-right government and the main trade unions, signified an important change of direction. The origin, method and content of this agreement were significantly influenced by the European Council Directive 97/81/EC of 15 December 1997, implementing the European Framework Agreement on PT employment between the European social partners (Rodríguez-Piñero 1998). Spanish trade unions, which were more sceptical about PT than their European counterparts mainly because of the experience of the massive recent growth in temporary contracts, signed this agreement and assumed that PT in Spain would grow to European levels in the immediate future (UGT 1998).

Table 9.1   Main policy developments in Spain concerning part-time employment contracts

1984 Law 32/1984   First statutory reform of PT. Abolished restrictions on eligibility, liberalization of fixed-term contracts.
1993 Royal Decree-Law 18/1993   Greater flexibility for PT. Increase security of fixed-term contracts. Introduction of temporary agencies.
1994 Law 11/1994   Increased deregulation and flexibility in employment. Incentives for employers to use PT, by changing PT definition and the measurement of working-time distribution.
1997 Royal Decree-Law 8/1997, Law 63/97   Aimed at decreasing levels of temporality and greater stability in employment.
1998 Royal Decree-Law 15/1998   Promotion of stable and voluntary PT by recognizing the principle of proportionality. Transposition of the social contract signed between the government and the main trade-unions – though against employers' opposition; and incorporation into national law of EU Directive 97/81/EC on PT work.
1999 Law 39/1999   Promoted reconciliation of family and working lives of employees. Various modifications were introduced in Article 37.5 of the Workers' Statute to give parents of children under the age of six the entitlement to reduce from one-third to a half their working hours within a FT employment contract. This Article 37.5, seems to have had a bigger impact on the evolution of PT than the successive changes to Article 12, which is concerned with PT.*
2001 Royal Decree-Law 5/2001, Law 12/2001   It changed substantial elements of the 1998 reform to make PT more flexible, in line with employers' demands, but against the opposition of trade-unions.
Royal Decree Law 16/2001 on PT retirement   Agreed by the government, one of the main trade unions (CC.OO), and the employer's organization (CEOE). Has given a very beneficial access to PT for workers over 60.

Note: *Both articles leave open the possibility of introducing new alternatives and details in collective agreements or in employer–employee contracts.
Source: Own elaboration from Cebrián et al. (2003); Valdés dal-Ré (2004); MTAS (2005).

This 1998 Spanish reform of PT shared the flexicurity objectives of the European Employment Strategy, introducing some key innovations. It changed the definition of PT again, restoring a time limit for PT contracts (no more than 77 per cent of the FT working day); it required employment contracts detail precisely and in advance the monthly, weekly and daily distribution of working time, so that PT contracts would not become 'on-call' jobs; it stressed the principle of 'voluntariness' in access to PT, and in the mobility from FT to PT and vice versa; and it laid down the principle of proportionality with full-timers in the treatment of part-timers in any of the key employment conditions.

However, Spanish employers strongly opposed the 1998 reform and did not sign the agreement, claiming that it involved unnecessary rigidities and administrative hurdles that were present neither in the European Directive 97/81 on PT nor in the International Labour Organisation (ILO) Convention on PT work. Employers opposed elements such as a narrow definition of a PT contract or the complicated procedures to arrange schedules, which could make the use of PT unattractive at the organizational level, especially for small and medium-sized firms (CEOE 1998a, 1998b).

The employers' opposition to the 1998 reform of PT, and the reality of stagnating low PT levels, induced the centre-right government to look for a new reform that would again modify substantially the regulation of PT. This fact undermined the final impact of the agreement on the evolution of PT (Pérez Infante 2000). As noted above, PT figures have remained more or less the same since 1995, at around 10 per cent of employment (recent levels of 12 per cent are due to methodological changes since the 2005 survey), though there has been some substitution of permanent PT for temporary PT. The 2001 reform (laws 5/01 and 12/01) was an attempt to accommodate some of the employers' demands by introducing greater flexibility in the conditions of PT contracts. It abolished the limit of 77 per cent of the normal FT contract, avoiding any clear boundary between FT and PT; it significantly softened the requirements to specify the distribution of working hours in monthly, weekly and daily patterns; and it changed the treatment of the extra hours worked by part-timers. This time, trade unions strongly opposed the reform, and advised their members to use collective bargaining to try to restrain the new flexibility by including more specific procedures on working-time schedules in collective agreements, and supporting the creation of permanent PT (CCOO 2001b; UGT 2001a, 2001b).

Furthermore, despite the 1998 reform to strengthen collective and individual bargaining against a tradition of state 'regulationism', this new space for collective bargaining did not materialize in actual rules and arrangements to develop PT contracts. Very few agreements deal with PT, and very little, if any, progress has been made on the detailed procedures to guide the use of PT contracts (González del Rey 1998: 337, quoted in Valdés dal-Ré 2004: 248). This absence is of special relevance given that issues as important for the promotion of PT as the implementation of the requirements and procedures for voluntary transfer from FT to PT and vice versa are supposed to be developed in collective bargaining and collective agreements.

As for the regulation of transitions from FT to PT and vice versa, present and past regulations have focused on protecting the voluntary character of the transition from employer pressures to transfer FT employees into PT. However, in relation to the procedures FT employees interested in a PT position should follow, the national regulation considers only the employer's obligation to inform them of PT vacancies available, and it leaves the drafting of more detailed procedures to collective agreements.[8] Interviewees (IS1, IS5, IS9, IS16) believe that because of the scarcity of PT vacancies and the little weight given to employees preferences,

---

8   Art. 12, section (e) of the Workers' Statute (Ley del Estatuto de los Trabajadores, Law 63/1997 and Law 12/2001) (*Texto refundido de la ley del estatuto de los trabajadores, texto actualizado a 15 de Julio de 2002, de www.ugt.es. Extractos del artículo 12. Contrato a tiempo parcial y contrato de relevo (redactado según ley 63/1997 y ley 12/2001)*).

these transitions from FT to PT have received little attention so far in collective agreements in sectors and firms, resulting in a very low presence of actual FT–PT transitions. In addition, section (g) of art. 12 of the Workers' Statute explicitly assumes that PT is mainly an option aimed at employees who need to reconcile family responsibilities with paid employment or who are combining work with training and education, instead of opening this arrangement to a wider range of interests and circumstances (as has happened in the Dutch case and is being discussed in the UK and Germany).

By 2004, though clauses in collective agreements referring to PT contracts were growing rapidly, they were present in fewer than 10 per cent of collective agreements, at either sector or firm level (CES 2004: 359), and most of them merely alluded to the PT replacement contracts for employees aged above 60 as a form of job-share. This situation led to Valdés dal-Ré (2004: 233) to evaluate the various Spanish policies on PT during the former decades in the following terms:

> In addition to a lack of firm and consistent policy approaches, the statutory regulation of PT work has been characterised even more, at least until relatively recently, by a manifest lack of correspondence between the rhetorically professed objectives being pursued and the techniques used to put them into practice.

In a similar direction, the report published by the Ministry of Labour and Social Affairs in 2005 (MTAS 2005) argued that the rapid succession of contradictory and short-sighted PT reforms, often accompanied by opposition from one of the main social partners, had not helped PT. In fact, according to the report, PT contracts were the form of contract that had experienced the greatest number of hasty and ad hoc reforms in the previous ten years, to the extent that at some point they were taken by the main actors as transitory changes that would not last long (MTAS 2005: 67, 202). Certain elements, like for example the number of hours required to define a contract as PT, have changed with each reform. This report also linked the low levels of PT to the extension of the 'temporality culture', and predicted that PT and temporary contracts would in future form a system of 'connected chambers', in which an increase in stable PT would be accompanied by an equivalent fall in temporality.

The regulatory reforms that have so far had a clearer impact in the growth of PT are the 1999 law on reconciling work and family life and the 2001 law on PT retirement,[9] both of which provide specific entitlements to apply for reduced working hours. As a result of the law 39/1999 on reconciling work and family life,[10] various modifications were introduced in article 37.5 of the Workers' Statute

---

9   These changes in entitlements to PT particularly affect specific groups of employees. Mothers of small children (aged under six) and workers aged 60 or more seem to be behind a significant growth of PT in the period 2003–2005.

10   Law 39/1999 'to promote reconciliation of family and working lives of employees', BOE n. 6 of November 1999.

to give parents of children under the age of six the entitlement to reduce their working hours within an FT job from one third to a half of average FT hours (Guillén et al. 2009).[11] Article 37.5 seems to have had a bigger impact on the evolution of PT than the previously mentioned article 12, which was specifically concerned with PT.[12] In 2007 the Law on Equality between men and women further enhanced access to reduced working hours, though again, as with previous PT reforms, consensus was not achieved. The main employers' organization opposed this reform, advising its members to limit the impact of this law as much as possible in collective bargaining (CEOE 2006).

As for PT retirement, Royal Decree Law 16/2001 on PT retirement – agreed by the government, one of the main trade unions (CCOO), and the employer's organization CEOE – has given a very beneficial access to PT for workers aged over 60. These older workers can receive a salary proportional to the hours they work, which they can reduce to just 15 per cent of average FT hours, while beginning to receive a proportion of their pension equivalent to the hours reduced. The full pension is given once they reach the retirement age of 65. This generous system had been so successful, well beyond initial expectations, that subsequent reforms in 2007 and 2008 have tried to restrict this option. However, despite the possible imbalances in this mechanism, its success, in terms of applicants, shows that many employees older, and perhaps younger, than 60 would consider seizing an opportunity to work PT, depending on the conditions of the trade-offs involved.

Since the entitlements introduced by these specific reforms on work-family reconciliation and on early PT retirement helped to increase those particular forms of PT in the following years, this would back the argument that the very low levels of PT in both public and private sectors before these reforms are closely related to constrained access to PT and are not just a result of employees' lack of interest in PT.

The general balance, however, points to a lack of success of the consecutive reforms of PT regulation during recent decades, which is matched by an equivalent failure of the various reforms during that same period to limit the use of temporary contracts. In both lines of regulation (PT and temporary contracts), subsequent Conservative (PP) and Socialist governments (PSOE) have tried different formulas that were on some occasions closer to the trade unions' perspective and on other occasions closer to the employers' perspective. The different governments used legislation by decree on the majority of occasions, as attempts to frame a consensus for reform often failed.

This sequence of failed attempts to promote stable PT in Spain supports the idea that the underlying problems of promoting PT are part of a wider regulatory context, characterized by the difficulties Spanish employment policies and reforms have faced since around 1990 in forging better balances between flexibility and

---

11   It also entitles those in care of dependent relatives.

12   Both articles leave open the possibility of introducing new options and details in collective agreements or in employer–employee contracts.

security. This lack of success is recognized by the main political parties, successive governments and the social partners; though, as one might expect, they differ in their detailed diagnosis and reform strategies.

Views and Perspectives of Social Actors on PT

The initial steps towards flexibility took place in the mid-1980s in a context of spectacularly high unemployment (close to 20 per cent of the labour force, with youth unemployment well above 30 per cent), which put job creation at the top of the agenda of labour market actors. However, and in contrast to other European countries, neither working-time flexibility nor collective working-time reductions were considered plausible strategies to promote employment, though these issues sporadically appeared in general debates.

PT started to be seen in Spain as a convenient instrument for labour market flexibilization only after the early 1990s (Cebrián et al. 2003: 212). By that time, the levels of temporary contracts were already very high. The arguments regarding PT put forward by the main actors and most experts mainly referred then, as they do now, to PT as a convenient employment creation tool (Cebrián et al. 2003; CES 2004; MTAS 2005), and very rarely as promoting quality of life or diverse lifestyle options. This helps to explain the lack of emphasis on the constraints on access to PT. Exceptions to this somewhat narrow-minded approach are the previously mentioned new reforms on reconciling work and family life and those on early PT retirement. However, even if the main element of these reforms is easier access to reduced working hours, the topic is often considered as a completely different area from PT, and, in fact, the issues are dealt with in different sections of the regulation. As a trade unionist said:

> One thing is to have a FT contract with 50% of the working hours, and a completely different thing is to have a PT contract. (IS5)

This kind of statement shows a concern with the different nature of the contracts regardless of the number of working hours, and reflects a dual labour market context. Similar working-time arrangements are considered intrinsically different depending on the type of contract, and are dealt with in different sections of the regulation, relating to separate policy agendas. These two facts have not favoured a coordinated perspective that includes all the interactions and complementarities affecting PT.

Scepticism towards individualized working-time flexibility was common among other European trade unions; but whereas in other countries these views have evolved towards more supportive attitudes to stable PT, Spanish trade unionists still resist any form of flexibility. This precariousness has made trade unions subordinate PT claims to the main priority of tackling temporality. As a trade unionist argues:

> We [CCOO education representative] think it is interesting to explore new ways of access to voluntary part-time, though we are not working with any specific proposals or measures ... our main concern now is how to tackle the problem of temporality, which has grown beyond all expectations. (IS8)

For employers, on the other hand, PT contracts designed by the regulations up to 2001 did not provide the flexibility they had expected. They felt the contracts contained certain rigidities and regulatory specificities that made them difficult to apply, mainly in relation to how the different hours were distributed and scheduled and to the possibility of increasing the actual number of hours to meet organizational needs. In addition, when reforms that introduce important changes are considered, for example the recent regulations on work-life balance, employers are reluctant to accept general national regulations. As one CEOE representative put it:

> Progress on work–family balance cannot be dealt with in a general manner, given the peculiarities of each sector. These [changes] should be introduced within the framework of collective agreements. The interests of firms and their competitiveness should also be protected.[13]

Nevertheless, as said before, regulation on working-time flexibility at the collective agreements level has not yet developed in Spain sufficiently to provide clear frameworks of action.

Trade unions and employees have meanwhile been sceptical about the actual guarantees offered by PT contracts to employees in terms of income, access to social security and control over actual working-time arrangements. Trade unions have stressed in every bargaining process the links between the evolution of PT and the evolution of temporality, and have problems in considering any increase of PT separately from the issue of temporality. According to them, the first victim of a flexibility based solely on precarious temporality is the lack of space for any form of stable PT. A UGT representative argued:

> A (fixed-term contract) worker is more likely to do two things to avoid losing the job: to perform tasks that do not correspond to her or his category and to work longer hours, that is, extra unpaid hours.[14]

In a similar vein, a CCOO trade unionist said:

> To enhance the voluntary character of PT, we would need to promote it as a permanent contract but also guarantee equal treatment in terms of remuneration and social rights.[15]

---

13   *El País*, 19-12-05.
14   Carlos Martín, CC.OO. *El País*, 21-12-03.
15   Antonio Ferrer, UGT, *El País*, 21-12-03.

Since the end of the 1990s the need to promote stable PT has become a common topic among the main political parties, social partners and principal experts. This goal appeared in the national employment plans of various governments, in the main reports of the Socio-Economic Council (*Consejo Económico y Social*, CES),[16] social partners' documents and experts' recommendations (MTAS 2005). All the relevant actors interviewed also shared the general objective of substituting higher percentages of stable PT for the high levels of temporality. However, most interviewees could not detail specific proposals in relation to any factor concerning PT. A good example of this is the statement by the trade unionist quoted above. At the same time, the promotion of PT has never been a top priority among the main actors. The potential for regulatory measures to affect any further growth of PT is also related to issues of socioeconomic structure, like the future evolution of public and private care services (CES 2005).

Interviewees often referred to the need for a 'cultural change' a 'change of mentality', suggesting that it is not going to be a short-term predictable change, and stated that, after the various reforms during the previous decade, there seemed to be little scope for further regulatory intervention. A Spanish expert on human resources management concluded that to promote PT in firms:

> we would have to change the whole cultural reasoning of the employers, who have difficulties in understanding that many of the jobs could actually fit within this form of employment contract. They think that a PT worker is someone not fully committed to the firm or organization, which is absolutely false.[17]

According to an employers' representative who was interviewed (IS9), most employers' resistance to stable PT and their preference for fixed-term contracts has to do with 'lack of habit' and lack of familiarity with PT more than with a rational decision. This factor might also explain why the use of fixed-term PT is not so extensive either, and it seems related to the Spanish employers' perception of part-timers as less involved than those on fixed-term contracts (as suggested by recent research: Blanco et al. 2001; Senise 2001). Several documented international examples point in the opposite direction.

In Spain there are also examples of firms where employers and employees have agreed access to different working-time arrangements and this has had positive effects; but they are still exceptional.[18] Yet even if the entitlement to reconcile

---

16   The main Spanish advisory board for social dialogue on labour market issues among social partners.

17   Sandalio Gomez, Professor of Industrial Relations at IESE, University of Navarra, *El País*, 21-12-03.

18   Roberto Armanado, human resources director of a company which has recently introduced the possibility of a 25-hour working week, stated 'it pays off in many ways ... their work has been optimized and this has resulted in indices of productivity similar to a full day ... the economic loss in Gres de Valls (a competitive tile firm) is minimal, because

work and family life is gaining ground, many employees are afraid of using it. At the end of 2005, a consultant on family-friendly working time arrangements stated that:

> ... Firms should change their culture and workers should dare to ask for the work-life balance measures which are contemplated by the law. There are a few of these but people do not use them (because) they're afraid of the consequences.[19]

Modifying entrenched prejudices against PT among the main actors may prove a more difficult step than implementing specific reforms. The scepticism of many trade unionists about the possibilities of PT is often expressed in the following terms:

> We [CCOO] have had huge internal disputes to understand whether we had to support PT or not, because PT work is not the ideal job where I choose to work four hours when I want to, and every day I work those same four hours. PT is not this, a PT worker in this country is the woman who works over the counter at El Campo [superstore], who works one week in the mornings and the following one in the afternoons. In Spain, PT work is the most precarious thing that exists and therefore, within the trade union we've had very strong disputes to decide what was the position of the organization in relation to PT. (IS10)

> (...) PT work has been at the same 8 per cent for more than ten years, despite the fact that in those ten years we've made five reforms of PT time regulation. Employers in those sectors with stable and well-paid employment do not even think about PT as a form of organizing working time, and in those sectors where PT is taken into consideration people do not want to work PT. That is, those who want to work PT, their employer doesn't want it and those (workers) who do work PT would rather be working FT. Employers' and employees' interests are never in agreement when it comes to part-time. (IS5)

> ... we think that this is something ..., we are not hugely enthusiastic about but that it has to be done. (IS6)

Spanish employers and trade unions were latecomers in familiarizing themselves with working-time flexibility issues; and whereas employers seem to have adapted to a single form of flexibility, namely the extensive use of temporary contracts, as an option to avoid paying the costs of firing permanent employees, trade unions have interpreted the high levels of fixed-term contracts as a warning against other forms of flexibility.

---

if workers earn 900 euros in a full day, with the reduced one they are paid about 780' (*El País*, 21-12-03).

19   *El País*, 19-12-05.

Conclusions

Whereas annual working hours have been reduced significantly in Spain since the beginning of the twentieth century, from around 2,500 hours in 1931 to fewer than 1,800 hours by 2009, the eight-hour working day has functioned as the main normative reference since at least when it was first imposed by regulation in 1919.[20] This certainly seems a difficult reference to challenge. Likewise, although the maximum annual working time (including overtime) fell from 2,552 hours in 1931 to 1,926 hours in 1983, the average working week for the core group of male full-timers has remained almost stable since 1977, with a slight reduction in the average number of working hours per week, from 44.6 in 1977 to 43 in 2002.[21] In addition, collective working-time reductions since the 1980s have not been as important in Spain as in most other European countries, which makes Spain the EU country with the third-longest working hours, after Portugal and Greece, even though in quality-of-life surveys a significant proportion of employees express their interest in more free time (CIS 2005).

Spanish labour market regulatory decisions since the 1990s have tilted the balance towards a single form of flexibility: high levels of temporary contracts. This did not help to make PT attractive to the trade unions and many employees. Employers' extensive use of fixed-term contracts and their resistance to PT is an important factor explaining a low level of PT in the private sector, as interviewees from political parties, government and trade unions attest.

However, it does not explain the even lower levels of stable PT in the public sector (6.8 per cent, compared with 15.8 per cent in the private sector; see Table 9.2), where government and trade unions have a huge say. Institutional constraints have to be taken into account in explaining why in a country like The Netherlands public sector PT is 44 per cent (Ibáñez 2011b), whereas in Spain PT in the public sector is at a much lower level than in the private sector.

The Spanish public sector could have pioneered the promotion of PT, as other European countries have, by creating initial PT job offers and by offering wider working-time options to its employees. So far, however, very few initial PT jobs have been offered in the Spanish public sector, and the opportunities to reduce working hours have been deliberately restricted by making the loss of real income bigger than the proportion of hours reduced, by restricting the organizational availability of reduced-hours positions, and by limiting the concession of reduced hours to considerations of family responsibilities alone.

Various governments, as public-sector employers, have pioneered important advances in the organization of working time for their FT employees, such as a more flexible distribution of working time or the promotion of the 35-hour week. However, they have not taken equivalent key steps in promoting PT, even though

---

20   Real Decreto de 3 de Abril de 1919, in Alonso Olea, 1960, t. II: 456; quoted in Prieto and Ramos 1999: 468.

21   These figures are taken from Cebrián et al. 2003: 211.

the growth of stable PT may have been a more desirable form of flexibility than the growth in the number of temporary contracts that has actually taken place in the public sector.

A more difficult step is to identify the political and institutional causes behind the reality of these regulations and their implementation. Possibilities include path dependency or institutional inertia; the conflicting interests of trade unions, government, and political parties; the different social background of these actors, with an over-representation of core employees at the expense of those more interested in PT; and different negotiating and learning capacities. These are certainly key issues for further research.

To conclude the chapter, the future evolution of Spanish PT is surely linked to such factors as the growth of the personal and social-services sectors or the increasing labour-market participation of women and young people. Nonetheless, there is still significant room for improvement at the regulatory level, for example in terms of developing the details and procedures around the opportunities to change from FT to PT, and extending this entitlement to all employees.

Table 9.2   Percentages of part-time employment in the private and the public sectors

	1996	**2005**	**2010**
Private sector			
Total	9.4	14.2	15.8
Female	25.8	29.6	28.5
Public sector			
Total	4.8	7.3	6.8
Female	7.3	10.7	10.0

Note: In 2005, methodological changes increased PT figures.
Source: INE, Encuesta Población Activa (2010).

References

Anxo, D. and O'Reilly, J. 2002. Working-time Transitions and Transitional Labour Markets, in *The Dynamics of Full Employment: Social Integration Through Transitional Labour Markets*, edited by G. Schmid and B. Gazier. Cheltenham, UK and Northampton, US: Edward Elgar, 339–65.

Blanco, J., Caprile, M., Elvira, C. and Moreno, D. 2001. *Balance Histórico de da Contratación d Tiempo Parcial en España*. Madrid: Ministerio de Trabajo y Asuntos Sociales.

CCOO 2001. *Informe y Recomendaciones sobre las Modificaciones Introducidas por el Real Decreto-ley 5/2001*. Madrid: CCOO.

Cebrian, I., Davia, M.A., Herranz, V. and Moreno, G. 2003. Flexibility in the Spanish Labour Market: Working Time and Temporary Employment, in *Regulating Working-time Transitions in Europe*, edited by J. O'Reilly. Cheltenham: Edward Elgar, 201–39.

Cebrian, I., Gash, V., Moreno, G., O'Connell, P.J. and Toharia, L. 2000. Peripheral Labour in Peripheral Markets? Mobility and Working Time within Transitional Labour Markets among Women in Ireland and Spain, in *Working-time Changes: Social Integration Through Transitional Labour Markets*, edited by J. O'Reilly, I. Cebrián and M. Lallement. Cheltenham: Edward Elgar, 205–50.

Confederación Española de Organizaciones Empresariales (CEOE) 1998a. *Consideraciones Empresariales sobre la Nueva Regulación del Contrato de Trabajo a Tiempo Parcial*. Madrid: Documento CEOE.

CEOE 1998b. *El Trabajo a Tiempo Parcial en la Unión Europea e en España. Algunas Consideraciones*. Documento CEOE.

CEOE 2006. *Criterios para la Negociación Colectiva*. Madrid: CEOE.

CES 2004. *La Temporalidad en el Empleo en el Sector Público*. Informe 3/2004 Madrid: CES.

CES 2005. *Memoria Socioeconómica y Laboral de España 2004*. Madrid: CES.

Centro de Investigaciones Sociológicas (CIS) 2005. *CIS Barometer of May*, No. 2607. Madrid: CIS.

Consejo Económico y Social (CES) 1996. *El trabajo a Tiempo Parcial*. Informe 4/96. Madrid: CES.

Crouch, C. 1993. *Industrial Relations and the European State Traditions*. Oxford: Clarendon Press.

Encuesta de Población Activa (EPA) 2010. [Online] Available at http://www.ine.es Madrid: Instituto Nacional de Estadística (INE) [Accessed: 12 November 2010].

El País, 3 October 2004. [Online] Available at: http://www.elpais.com/ [Accessed: 12 November 2010].

El País, 27 May 2005. [Online] Available at: http://www.elpais.com/ [Accessed: 12 November 2010].

El País, 19 December 2005. [Online] Available at: http://www.elpais.com/ [Accessed: 12 November 2010].

El País, 21 December 2003. [Online] Available at: http://www.elpais.com/ [Accessed: 12 November 2010].

European Commission (EC) 2009. *Employment in Europe 2009*. Directorate-General for Employment, Industrial Relations and Social affairs. [Online] Available at: http://europa.eu.int/comm/dg05/empl&esf [Accessed: 12 November 2010].

González del Rey, I. 1998. Ordenación del tiempo de trabajo: trabajo a tiempo parcial, in *Condiciones de empleo y de trabajo en la negociación colectiva*, edited by J.G. Murcia. Madrid: Consejo Económico y Social.

Guillén, A.M., Moreno-Manzanaro, N. and González, S. 2009. Conciliación de la vida laboral y familiar en España. El impacto de las políticas de la Unión Europea. *Documentación Social*, 154, 119–38.

Ibáñez, Z. 2007. *Access to Non-vulnerable PT Employment in the Netherlands, Spain and the UK, with Special Reference to the School and Local Government Sectors*. Published thesis. Florence: European University Institute.

Ibáñez, Z. 2011a. Part-time in Skilled Jobs: The Case of Teachers in the U.K., Spain and The Netherlands, in *Work–Life Balance in Europe. The Role of Job Quality*, edited by S. Drobnic and A.M. Guillén. Hampshire: Palgrave, 149–73.

Ibáñez, Z. 2011b. Part-time: Beyond Second Best? *Time and Society*, 20(2), 171–96.

León, M. 2007. Speeding or Holding Back?: Institutional Factors in the Development of Childcare Provision in Spain. *European Societies*, 9(3), 315–39.

Martín, C. and Zarapuz, L. 2002. *Los Retos del Empleo y el Paro en España tras la Cumbre de Barcelona*. Madrid: CCOO.

Miguélez, F., Prieto, C. and Castaño, C. (1996) *Recursos humanos y relaciones laborales en el sector bancario español*. Universidad Autónoma de Barcelona y Universidad Complutense de Madrid, mimeo.

Miguélez, F. and Rebollo, O. 1999. Negociación colectiva en los noventa, in *Las Relaciones de Empleo en España*, edited by F. Migueléz and C. Prieto. Madrid: Siglo XXI, 325–46.

MTAS 2005. *Más y Mejor Empleo en en Nuevo Escenario Socioeconómico. Por una Flexibilidad y Seguridad Laborales Efectivas. Informe de la Comisión de Expertos para el Diálogo Social*. (Authors: J. Cruz, F. Duran, J. Jimeno, M. Olalla, S. Ruesga, C. Sáez, L. Toharia and F. Valdés dal-Ré). Madrid: MTAS.

OECD 2007. *Jobs for Youth. Spain*. Paris: OECD.

Pérez Infante, J. 2000. La duración de la jornada de trabajo. Situación y evolución reciente. *Revista del Ministerio de Trabajo y Asuntos Sociales*, 16, 13–54.

Prieto, C. (dir.) (1996) *Trabajo e identidad social femenina*. Madrid: Escuela de Relaciones Laborales/Dirección General de la Mujer (Comunidad Autónoma de Madrid), mímeo.

Prieto, C. and Ramos, R. 1999. El tiempo de trabajo: entre la competitividad y los tiempos sociales, in *Las Relaciones de Empleo en España*, edited by F. Miguelez and C. Prieto. Madrid: Siglo XXI, 463–87.

Recio, A. 1999. La segmentación del mercado laboral en España, in *Las Relaciones de Empleo en España*, edited by F. Miguélez and C. Prieto. Madrid: Siglo XXI, 125–50.

Rhodes, M. 1997. *Southern European Welfare States: Between Crisis and Reform*. London: Frank Cass.

Rodríguez-Piñero, M. 1998. El trabajo a tiempo parcial, entre normalización e incentivación. *Relaciones Laborales*, 15/16, 1–9.

Ruivo, M., González, M.P. and Varejao, J.M. 1998. Why is Part-time Work so Low in Portugal and Spain?, in *Part-time Prospects. An International Comparison of Part-time Work in Europe, North America and the Pacific Rim*, edited by J. O'Reilly and C. Fagan London: Routledge, 199–213.

Senise Barrio, M.J. 2001. *El trabajo a Tiempo Parcial como Instrumento de Creación de Empleo*. Madrid: Tecnos.

Toharia, L., Albert, C., Cebrián, I., García Serrano, C., García Mainar, I., Malo, M.A., Moreno, G. and Villagómez, E. 1998. *El Mercado de Trabajo en España*. Madrid: McGraw Hill.

UGT 2001a. *Valoración de UGT al Real Decreto-Ley 5/2001 de Medidas Urgentes de Reforma del Mercado de Trabajo*. Madrid: UGT.

UGT 2001b. *La Nueva Reforma Laboral: incidencia en la negociación colectiva y criterios de actuación*. Madrid: UGT.

Unión General de Trabajadores (UGT) 1998. *Informe sobre el Acuerdo de 1998 para la Promoción del Trabajo a Tiempo Parcial*. Madrid: UGT.

Valdés dal-Ré, F. 2004. Spain: The Difficulty of Marrying Flexibility with Security, in *Employment Policy and the Regulation of Part-time Work in the European Union: A Comparative Analysis*, edited by S. Sciarra, P. Davies and M. Freedland. Cambridge: Cambridge University Press, 224–57.

Appendix 1: Interviewees

IS1: National employment authority representative.
IS2: PSOE representative.
IS3: PP representative.
IS4: National education authority representative.
IS5: CCOO representative.
IS6: UGT representative.
IS7: National education authority representative.
IS8: CCOO teachers' representative.
IS9: CEOE representative.
IS10: CCOO representative.
IS11: Secondary school teacher.
IS12: Secondary school teacher.
IS13: Local government employee.
IS14: Personnel/HR manager local government.
IS15: Catholic education employers' representative.
IS16: Education employers' representative.
IS17: Secondary school teacher.
IS18: Secondary school teacher.
IS19: Human resources manager.
IS20: Local government human resources manager.

Chapter 10

Female Employment and Policies for Balancing Work and Family Life in Spain

Olga Salido

Introduction

Recent socio-demographic changes, like the increase in life expectancy and the decline of fertility rates, represent a deep challenge to the traditional balance of European welfare states, threatening the sustainability of their pensions systems in the mid-term and requiring a radical reorganization of the prevailing welfare mix. These pressures are especially strong in a country like Spain, which has experienced an extraordinarily deep and rapid process of economic, social and cultural change over recent decades. Spanish women are playing a leading role in this process of change, especially through a strong and permanent commitment to the labour market, together with radical changes in reproductive and marriage behaviour.

The activation of female employment appears to be a way to tackle the most pessimistic scenarios in this respect. The Lisbon Agenda (2000), and its update by Agenda 2020, made female employment a touchstone for economic growth and the sustainability of European welfare states, moving it to the top of the political agenda. However, the express goal of the European Employment Strategy to achieve a female employment rate of 60 per cent by 2010 seems still distant to many country members[1]. Moreover, female employment lags well behind male levels. In fact, wide differences between female and male employment levels are still the rule across the European Union: female rates of economic activity are lower than men's in every country, with an average gap of 14 points (European Commission 2009a). The picture worsens dramatically when we consider married women and mothers. Women with small children suffer from an average employment penalty of around 12 points with respect to childless women, a gap that persists in spite of the significant increase in their employment rates in recent years.

---

1   Agenda 2020 has recently raised this threshold to 75 per cent, a goal which obviously lies even more distant for many countries, especially southern European countries. In spite of a rapid process of change since 2000, Spain is still far from the stated threshold for 2010, with a female employment rate of 54.9 per cent compared with 59.1 per cent for EU-27 in 2008 (European Commission 2009a: 19, Table 4).

The spreading awareness that the goal of female economic activation cannot be accomplished without a radical reorganization of family life – together with the formal goal of advancing gender equal opportunity – has made of the reconciliation of work and family life a crucial step towards removing any disincentive to female labour force participation, turning it into one of the main topics of the European social agenda. Moreover, the reconciliation of work and family life has become a burgeoning policy area at the national level as well as the EU level. The country-specific answers given to the new challenges depend on a complex set of variables, ranging from market structure and the gender relations system to family policies and institutional inertias, which conform with the national welfare architecture (OECD 2004; Moreno Mínguez 2008; Salido and Moreno 2009). As part of the Mediterranean welfare regime, Spain perfectly exemplifies the 'familialistic paradox': a weak policy system to support the family in a country where the family has traditionally been assumed to play a central role in welfare provision (Esping-Andersen 1999). Given that Spain has one of lowest fertility rates in the world and is still lagging in female employment in Europe, it seems clear that the traditional role played by the family in the Spanish welfare state is in crisis (Bernardi 2005; Baizán 2007). Numerous legislative initiatives and regulations at both central and regional levels have been implemented since 2000 in order to address this situation. Nevertheless, they seem still insufficient to meet the new needs of working mothers and children (León 2005), as the demographic imbalance and the still low levels of female labour force participation indicate.

The absence of an institutional vocation to assume caring tasks as a public responsibility leads to major imbalances in women's lives, making women find individual solutions to the challenge of combining work and family responsibilities. In spite of deep social changes in Spanish society over recent decades, reconciliation strategies rely on the help of relatives or use the informal commercialization of caring tasks by migrant women (Flaquer and Escobedo 2008). Although both childcare and old-age care services have recently grown sharply, parental networks – formed mainly by grandmothers – are still the main way in which working mothers reconcile the needs of family and work. A recent study shows that still 30 per cent of working mothers would not be able to work and another 30 per cent would work only with great difficulty if their relatives did not care for their children during working hours. Even if we consider such care as a form of altruistic solidarity between generations in a time of rapid social change, it is clearly an unsustainable strategy in the mid- to long term (Fernández and Tobío 2005: 32).

As numerous studies have shown, female employment is highly sensitive to the implementation of labour market and family policies, which favour different arrangements to deal with the dilemma (Boje and Leira 2000; Gornick 2000; OECD 2004; European Commission 2009b). In this sense, part-time work is the key to explaining the especially high labour force participation rates of females in some countries, such as the Netherlands or Sweden (European Commission 2009a) (see Chapter 9). This is not the case in Spain, where, in spite of the increasing importance of part-time employment over recent years, most women who work do so on a full-time basis.[2] Besides, as well as a measure that helps reconcile work and family life, part-time work, with its usually lower benefits and coverage than regular full-time employment, has in Spain been part of a general strategy to fight the high rates of unemployment that have characterized the Spanish labour market. This too is common to southern European countries, and goes hand with hand with low rates of female participation and a strong gender division of roles.

This lack of flexible work arrangements oriented to female employment and of family-friendly policies has for decades pushed married women to make a stark choice between work and family, preventing them from being adequately incorporated into the workforce (European Commission 2005; Moreno Mínguez 2008). The steep fall in fertility rates since the 1980s is with no doubt a reflection of this unresolved dilemma. As part of a general tendency towards low levels of fertility in advanced societies, the change has been especially intense in Spain and other southern European countries, suggesting the existence of structural constraints. The abrupt decline of fertility rates over recent decades might be at least partly explained by these labour constraints on women with dependent children at home.[3] It is mainly explained by a delay in the first maternity age for women, which has jumped from an average of 25.3 in the mid-1970s to 29.3 in the early 2000. Although this postponement can be considered as part of a general demographic tendency common to all advanced societies, in Spain it has a peculiar and dramatic character. The crucial difference is that this 'delay' means a real 'loss' of reproductive chances due to a significant reduction in second and third children among Spanish women (Esping-Andersen 2004; Delgado et al. 2009). Spanish women nevertheless show the same desire to have children as women in other European countries, although the gap between the desired and actual number of children they have is greatest amongst them (European Commission 2006).

This chapter addresses the main developments in work-family balance policies in Spain over recent decades, trying to highlight their flaws and pointing to possible ways for future improvement. The chapter is organized as follows. First, it outlines recent trends and particularities of female employment. Second, it reviews the main policy measures adopted in work-family balance policies in Spain since the 1980s. Finally, the effectiveness of the work-family policies implemented is critically assessed, with suggestions of possible future improvement.

---

2   By 1998, the Spanish rate of female part-time employment was 17 per cent, almost half the EU-15 average of 32.7 per cent. Partly because of methodological changes, the Spanish rate had increased to 22.9 per cent by 2009, still far behind the European average (36.5 per cent) (Eurostat database, online).

3   In 1975, Spain had one of the highest fertility rates among European countries, with a value of 2.780, but it had fallen to 1.637 by the mid-1980s. Just one decade later, Spain had joined the 'club' of the lowest-fertility countries, with a rate of 1.187, far below the replacement rate of 2.1 (Delgado et al. 2009).

Spanish Women on the Move: Female Labour Force Participation Trends in Recent Decades

As part of a general process of social and cultural change, women have increasingly entered the labour force in most advanced societies over recent decades. In Spain, partly because of a delayed process of modernization and access to democratic rule, women have joined this general tendency late but with extraordinary intensity. As we can observe in Figure 10.1, from the mid-1970s until the late 2000s, the share of women who were active rose from one third to one half.[4] Moreover, the sharp increase in female activity rate and the moderate decline in the male rate helped to reduce the gender activity gap to one third during that period. Even during periods of recession in the Spanish economy (that is, 1976–85, 1993–5 and, more recently, since 2008), women's demand for employment has continued to increase, resulting in strikingly high rates of female unemployment (Figure 10.1). Moreover, unemployment rates are significantly higher among women than among men, indicating a significant gender imbalance in the Spanish labour market. Only since 2000 has the female rate of unemployment reverted to the previous tendency, successively declining from 30.4 per cent in 1995 to 19.8 per cent in 2000, and again to 11.6 per cent in 2005, narrowing the gender gap from 12 to 5 percentage points.[5]

In fact, the unprecedented growth of employment that the Spanish economy experienced from the mid-1990s until the crisis that erupted in 2008 was largely driven by the surge of female employment. Half of the eight million net new jobs created over the period of expansion (1995–2007) were taken up by women,[6] increasing their employment rate by 15 points in the short span of just a decade (from 26.3 per cent to 41.5 per cent). Moreover, female employment seems to be weathering the recent crisis much more successfully than male employment.[7]

These trends in women's activity can be largely explained by the dramatic increase in women's educational level over recent decades. In 1987, only 6 per cent of women aged 16 and older had tertiary education, while 8 per cent were illiterate, and another 16 per cent had an incomplete primary education.

---

4   Over the period, female activity rates rose from 28.5 per cent to 51.7 per cent, while male rates experienced a moderate decline: from 77.6 per cent to 68.1 per cent (Labour Force Survey, 1976–2009, fourth quarter).

5   The greater impact of the recent employment crisis in Spain (partly induced by the bursting of the housing bubble) on traditionally male-dominated sectors, like construction, have had the effect of *artificially* closing the unemployment gender gap (rates for 2009, fourth quarter: 19.1 per cent for women and 18.6 per cent for men).

6   During this period, the Spanish employed population grew from 12,626,000 to 20,510,000, the fastest growth in the EU (www.ine.es).

7   Concretely, 1,755,000 of the total of 2,033,000 jobs lost since 2008 were occupied by men.

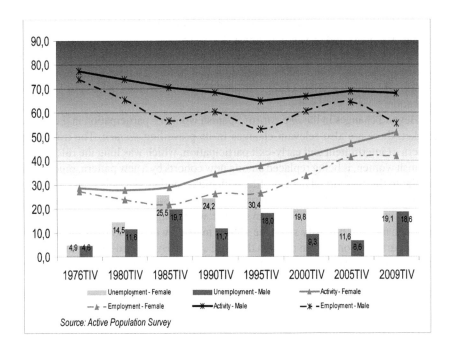

Figure 10.1 Activity, employment, and unemployment rates by sex (1976–2009)

By 2007 these figures had changed radically: the proportion of women who were illiterate and had received incomplete compulsory education had been reduced to 3 per cent (mainly concentrated among the oldest age cohorts), while 16 per cent had received tertiary education (INE database, www.ine.es). Moreover, these trends have an important generational component, enhancing the employment chances of women under 50 years old.[8]

According to economic theory, highly educated women are bound to have a higher economic return for their work, a factor that will likely alter the frame for human capital investment and labour force participation choices, inducing changes in women's preferences for employment and maternity. This would be especially true for southern Mediterranean countries, where policies supporting families and children are clearly underdeveloped, making educational level the

---

8   The impact of change is even stronger on the younger cohorts. To compare 30-year-old women in different time spots, the percentage of women educated at tertiary level rapidly rose from 3 per cent in 1965 to 12.6 per cent in 1985, and then to 22.7 per cent in 1995 and 31 per cent in 2005. Conversely, the proportion of 30-year-old women without elementary education fell abruptly from 31.3 per cent in 1965 to 3.9 per cent in 1985, and then, to 1.6 per cent in 1995 and 0.6 per cent in 2005 (Delgado et al. 2009: 94).

most salient explanatory variable for female participation in the labour market (De Henau, Meulders and O´Dorchai 2006). As we can see in Figure 10.2, the highest increase in activity rates occurred among those educated to secondary level (24.8 percentage points), followed by those educated to tertiary level (12.2 percentage points). However, smaller changes occurred among women with low levels of education.

Beyond changes in the *intensity* of Spanish women's participation in the labour market, there are also relevant changes in its prevailing *pattern*. The traditional pattern of intermittent and early-exit participation, which was long the rule among Spanish women, is being replaced among new cohorts by a new pattern, much more similar to the age-curved male profile, with higher and more stable rates of activity in the central ages. Furthermore, married women are leading the change. Comparing panels A and B of Figure 10.3, we can see that, while single women experienced only minor changes in intensity since the 1990s, married women radically altered their labour participation pattern through their life cycles. By the mid-1980s, the activity rate for married women peaked at the age range of 25–29 years, falling sharply for the next age group onwards, with a decline of 20 points for women only ten years older (aged 35–39). By 1990, only three years later, the activity gap between these two age groups had been reduced to less than ten points, which would point to a new pattern among middle-age women of longer spells in the labour market.

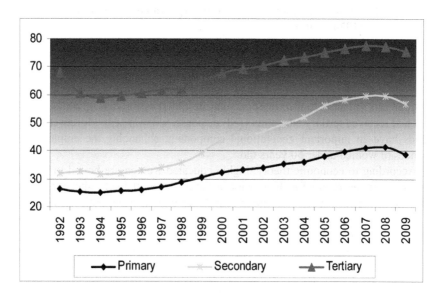

Figure 10.2   Female activity rates by educational level:
women aged 15–64, 1992–2009

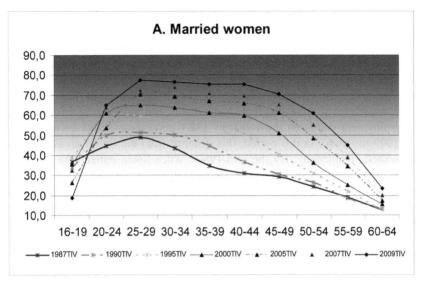

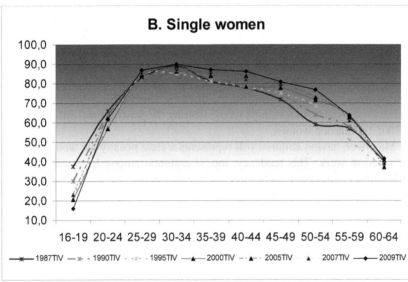

Figure 10.3 **Female activity rates by marital status and age cohort (1987–2009)**

This change is especially relevant given that the 25–49 age range coincides with a moment in the life cycle in which maternity is bound to happen. Moreover, the change seems to have consolidated over the following years, reaching an almost constant and high activity rate (of around 75 per cent) in the central ages (married women aged between 20 and 44) at the following moments in time considered (1995, 2000, 2005 and 2009).

Nevertheless, despite the changes described, Spain still lags behind the European average. Table 10.1 shows employment rates of women aged 25–49, the ages when work and family responsibilities are most likely to conflict, and therefore when the effects of changes in female behaviour are more relevant. Spain, together with Ireland and the Netherlands, is a country where female rates of employment increased most sharply (32.1 percentage points between 1987 and 2009 in Spain). In this period, this distance from the European average has diminished significantly. By the mid-1980s, when Spain entered the European Union (then called the Economic Community), the Spanish rate of female employment was 33.3 per cent, the lowest in the European context, and 21 points below the European Union average. This gap remained stable until 1995 (42 per cent for Spain against 62.3 per cent for the EU), falling afterwards quickly to five points by 2007 (and back to seven points by 2009 as a result of the recent employment crisis).

But in spite of the stated general advances, being married still significantly reduces women's chances of labour force participation. Although a gap between the employment rates of single women and married women is common to all European countries, it is very wide in Spain (if not the widest). As is graphically summarized in Figure 10.4, Spanish married women (aged 25–49) on average suffered from an almost constant penalty of 19 points vis-à-vis single women throughout the recent expansive period of employment (1995–2005),[9] approximately double the European average. Moreover, while the distance between Spain and the European Union almost vanished for single women during the period, it was still remarkable in 2005 for married women.

Moreover, having children still represents a clear penalty for women who are dedicated to work. This tendency, too, is common among European countries, with almost no exceptions. The largest difference is associated with the third child, without a clearly distinguishable pattern by country. On average, the employment rate for one-child women in Europe (again, aged 25–49) is 6.6 percentage points lower than that of childless women, for women with two children it is 9.5 points lower, and for those with three or more children it is 24.1 points lower (Table 10.2). For Spain, the equivalent differences are wider: 9, 13 and 24.3 points, respectively. Having a third child is critical to participation across countries, but it is in the simple fact of maternity that southern European women in general, and Spanish women in particular, make a difference. The persistence of a traditional pattern of the gender division of roles among the older cohorts of Spanish women would help to explain this fact.

---

9   The selected 1995–2005 period taken for this comparison responds both to data comparability restrictions, and to the intention to control the disturbing effects of growing unemployment from 2007 onwards.

Table 10.1   Female employment rate (25–49 years) by number and age of children in the EU (1987–2009)

	1987	1990	1995	2000	2005	2007	2009	1987–1995	1995–2005	2005–2007	2007–2009	1987–2009
European Union(a)	54.3	58.7	62.3	67.1	70.3	72.4	72.4	8.0	8.0	2.1	0.0	18.1
Belgium	53.7	58.8	63.9	71.8	73.0	74.8	75.8	10.2	9.1	1.8	1.0	22.1
Denmark	81.8	81.4	77.4	80.9	80.7	82.8	83.0	-4.4	3.3	2.1	0.2	1.2
Germany	56.5	63.1	67.4	72.2	73.0	75.7	77.3	10.9	5.6	2.7	1.6	20.8
Ireland	35.5	40.5	51.4	65.2	68.8	70.5	67.6	15.9	17.4	1.7	-2.9	32.1
Greece	46.1	49.3	51.1	55.1	60.7	63.0	64.3	5.0	9.6	2.3	1.3	18.2
Spain	33.3	38.9	42.0	53.4	63.6(b)	67.6	65.4	8.7	21.6	4.0	-2.2	32.1
France	63.9	66.0	68.5	70.3	74.5	76.4	76.9	4.6	6.0	1.9	0.5	13.0
Italy	46.6	49.0	49.0	53.0	59.4	60.6	59.9	2.4	10.4	1.2	-0.7	13.3
Luxembourg	49.3	51.3	53.6	65.6	70.6	74.0	73.2	4.3	17.0	3.4	-0.8	23.9
Netherlands	48.7	53.8	62.8	73.7	77.0	80.1	82.0	14.1	14.2	3.1	1.9	33.3
Austria	–	–	72.3	75.5	77.4	78.1	80.6	–	5.1	0.7	2.5	8.3
Portugal	61.3	66.5	71.0	76.4	76.3	76.5	76.6	9.7	5.3	0.2	0.1	15.3
Finland	–	–	71.1	77.1	78.6	80.0	79.7	–	7.5	1.4	-0.3	8.6
Sweden	–	–	81.6	80.3	80.8(b)	83.0	81.7	–	-0.8	2.2	-1.3	0.1
United Kingdom	63.1	69.1	69.9	73.6	74.9	74.5	74.5	6.8	5.0	-0.4	0.0	11.4

Notes:
(a) EC6–1972, EC9–1980, EC10–1985, EC12–1994, EU15–2004, EU25–2006, EU27–2007.
(b) Break in series due to methodological changes in the definition of unemployment.

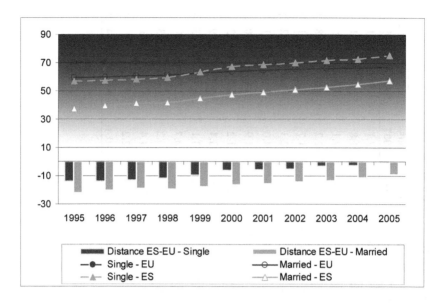

**Figure 10.4   Female employment rates by civil status:
women aged 25–49 years, 1995–2005**

Work–Family Balance Policies on the Political Agenda

Spain is one of the European countries where public spending on family benefits is relatively low, at 1.1 per cent of GDP against a European average of 2.1 per cent. As for in-kind support, there is a shortage of caring services, especially for those aged 0–2 years (European Commission 2008). Furthermore, family transfers are usually targeted in response to need, and designed to protect exclusively low-income households and families with disabled children. However, the rate of children at risk of poverty (24 per cent) is among the highest in Europe (European Commission 2009b). On the other hand, low cash benefits and an inadequately developed system of childcare services are among the main features of the Spanish welfare regime.

The low percentage of GDP dedicated to family policies in Spain is only a minor feature of a situation characterized by the lack of a fully developed institutional framework for family protection, with inadequate levels of maturity and effectiveness (Flaquer 2000: 14), which can be taken as part of the aftermath of the ultra-conservative Francoist regime (Valiente 1995, 2005). Indeed, scarcity of resources and fragmentation were the most salient traits of the family policy system at the end the dictatorship.

Table 10.2 Female employment and maternity in the European Union* by the number of children aged under 12 (2008): women aged 25–49

	Female rate 2008	Zero children	One child	Two children	Three + children	Dif. Zero– One	Dif. Zero– Two	Dif. Zero– Three+
European Union	73.1	78.6	72.0	69.1	54.5	-6.6	-9.5	-24.1
Germany	76.4	83.7	77.2	72.4	53.0	-6.5	-11.3	-30.7
Ireland	78.4	81.5	68.2	61.5	49.1	-13.3	-20.0	-32.4
Greece	76.8	70.0	62.5	59.7	54.4	-7.5	-10.3	-15.6
Spain	70.1	73.2	64.2	60.2	48.9	-9.0	-13.0	-24.3
France	64.0	80.4	78.6	77.8	59.0	-1.8	-2.6	-21.4
Italy	67.8	67.3	59.5	53.4	40.3	-7.8	-13.9	-27.0
Luxembourg	77.6	83.7	74.4	70.8	52.6	-9.3	-12.9	-31.1
Netherlands	61.1	86.6	79.8	81.4	71.3	-6.8	-5.2	-15.3
Austria	71.4	85.2	82.1	77.3	60.0	-3.1	-7.9	-25.2
Portugal	81.8	78.2	77.5	75.5	66.6	-0.7	-2.7	-11.6
Finland	79.5	84.0	77.0	83.0	67.4	-7.0	-1.0	-16.6
United Kingdom	77.5	84.0	75.1	71.8	48.6	-8.9	-12.2	-35.4

Note: * No data available for Sweden and Denmark.

Source: Eurostat Statistics Database, on line: http://epp.eurostat.ec.europa.eu.

When democracy was restored by mid-1970s, one of the main issues on the political agenda was the achievement of formal equality between the sexes, a topic largely neglected by a complex system of rules and practices that had virtually turned women into second-class citizens (see Chapter 4). In this context, family issues were left behind, treated as part of a conservative agenda. Also, the critical character of other economic and social issues (such as the economic crisis, territorial integration and the political stability of the new democratic regime) worked against any priority being accorded to family issues. Consequently, women, not families, were the political focus of social policy during the period. In this context, the Plans for Equal Opportunities between Women and Men, and later, the Action for Employment Plans, both drawn up in the image of their European counterparts, were the most salient instruments driving the development of policies concerning gender and women issues, with just a limited recognition of the need for an adequate balance between work and family life (Instituto de la Mujer 1997: 41).

In one of the crudest scenarios of low fertility and population ageing among EU Member States, and in an open public debate on the sustainability of the pensions system, the problem of reconciling work and family life finally moved belatedly to the forefront of public concern in the late 1990s. In 1997 the first parliamentary debate on family issues since the beginning of the democratic period took place, which resulted in an explicit mandate to the government to elaborate a comprehensive family policy plan in order to cope with family issues from a global perspective. This initiative materialized four years later in the National Plan for Family Support (*Plan Integral de Apoyo a la Familia*), which covered a wide variety of policies, ranging from taxation to social security and child benefits. Furthermore, the accession to government of the conservative Popular Party (PP) in 1996 helped family issues to find a significant place on the political agenda. However, the first piece of legislation explicitly to address the work–family balance, the Act to Promote the Reconciliation of Work and Family Life of Employed Persons (Act 39/1999), lacked the expected strength, being a mere transposition of two European Union Directives[10] designed to enhance parental leave and maternal protection at work as a way to reconcile professional and personal life and promote gender equality. The Act recognized the need to develop new measures to accommodate social changes resulting from increasing female participation in the labour force.

Among other measures, the 1999 Act reinforced the protection of expectant and breastfeeding mothers at work, establishing new paid leave entitlements in the event of health risk and declaring 'null and void' dismissals related to parental leaves and leaves by pregnant women and new mothers.[11] Maternity leave regulations remained unchanged in 1999, with the entitlement of 16 weeks of

---

10   Namely, the European Council (EC) Directive 92/85/CEE on maternity protection and the EC Directive 96/34/EC on parental leave.

11   In addition, the Act extended all the existing entitlements to adoptive and foster parents, thereby granting them the same leave rights as biological parents.

leave paid at 100 per cent of previous earnings. Although there were no changes in the existing two-day remunerated paternity leave, fathers could now take up to ten weeks of the mother's leave, provided there was no risk to her health. Nonetheless, the new father's right is detrimental to the mother's right, leaving intact the assumption that childcare is mainly a maternal responsibility (Bustelo and Lombardo 2007). Also, new 'family care' leave schemes were introduced, allowing existing flexible-time and parental-leave schemes to be extended to take care of a relative in the event of severe illness, accident or old age. Both family and parental leaves were recognized for the first time as individual rights instead of family rights, allowing both mothers and fathers to take them simultaneously.

One of the distinctive traits of the southern European welfare regimes is the fiscal character of their family policies (Flaquer 2000). In Spain, fiscal deductions for home acquisition have traditionally played a major role, operating in fact as a deferred mechanism of social protection and a substitute for the precarious public coverage of social risks that families can face. PP governments implemented two fiscal reforms that consolidated most of the pro-home ownership measures, namely, tax breaks for home purchase and for renovation. The reforms were declared to have the explicit purpose of making the Spanish tax system more family friendly. The introduction of the concept of a 'vital minimum' can be considered a novelty in this sense, leaving untaxed the minimum income threshold needed to meet families' basic needs. This way, personal and family circumstances were taken into account in order to assess taxpayers' real disposable incomes. Also, child benefits were considered non-labour-related income and so were exempted from income tax. In addition to the standard personal and family fiscal deductions, new special tax breaks were introduced for sole parents. Finally, the same income tax rate was to be applied to individual and family annual income returns, a reform which allowed married couples to combine in one family statement all the tax breaks that the husband and the wife were entitled to. At the end of its period in office in 2004, the PP introduced some additional fiscal reforms, increasing the existing family benefits, which had been frozen since 1991, by 35 per cent. Besides, it introduced a new means-tested benefit for third and further children as well as for multiple births, although the amount remained still quite low. Nevertheless, these fiscal measures do not benefit families with one income-tax payer or where husband and wife earn very different salaries (Instituto de Política Familiar 2004). Moreover, this kind of policy is criticized for its negative effect in terms vertical social equity, since it usually favours taxpayers in the medium and upper income deciles.

The policy that had by far the greatest public impact was a new subsidy for working mothers, known as the '100 Euros cheque'.[12] The policy was aimed at

---

12   Monthly payments of €100 were made available to working mothers who are gainfully employed full time, employed part-time for at least 50 per cent of full-time working hours, or self-employed with social contributions paid for a minimum of 15 days per month. The benefit is payable to working mothers with children up to three years of age, and it can be received either monthly in cash or as a deduction from annual income tax.

providing working mothers with cash support, and it was the first measure introduced explicitly to 'stimulate the incorporation of women into the labour market' and 'compensate for the social and labour costs associated with maternity'.[13] However, it has been subject to several criticisms. First, as it excludes women working part-time, in the informal economy or not in the labour market, it would introduce a class selection bias, discriminating against the most vulnerable groups of working mothers. Second, the low level of benefit is not likely to compensate fully for the expenses associated with maternity, and, with labour market conditions unchanged, it is doubtful whether it will have a significant impact on women's decisions on whether to participate in the labour market. Finally, the measure has been criticized for reinforcing a traditional model of domestic responsibilities (Bertelsmann Stiftung 2004: 51–2).

The legislative impulse of the Popular Party, though necessary and long due, left unattended most of the demands of policy actors. The most conservative sectors, led by the Catholic Church, were unsatisfied with the steps towards the individualization of rights on parental leave, and demanded policies that were more explicitly designed to sustain fertility rates. Additionally, the employer's organization, the Spanish Confederation of Entrepreneurship Organizations (*Confederación Española de Organizaciones Empresariales*, CEOE), expressed its concern about the negative effect of the measures that were supposed to reconcile work and family life. These measures were deemed to limit employers' freedom, introducing constraints on productivity, with an eventually perverse effect on women's employment. For their part, feminist and labour organizations criticized the government's lack of sensibility to the goal of gender equality with respect to reconciling work and family life.

In spite of these criticisms, one of the clearest merits of the PP policy initiatives is that they made family issues a matter of public concern. By the time of the 2004 general election, parties across the political spectrum had incorporated family issues in their political programmes. The PP announced that the family would become the key axis of its political activity for the next mandate if it was re-elected. The Socialist Party (PSOE), meanwhile, criticized the PP policy measures because of their lack of economic funding, which left the legal framework in limbo. In general, left-wing parties demanded a more generous family policy designed to create a safety net of social services and to increase the low level of expenditure on social and family issues, and criticized the steps taken towards privatization of rights and reinforcement of the conventional model of the family during the PP's term of office.

The political programme of the new PSOE government that came to office in 2004 also included family issues as a specific policy focus, considering them for the first time as a touchstone for welfare policies. The improvement of families' welfare, as well as that of each of their individual members, became the main

---

13   Royal Decree 27/2003, which elaborates the partial reform of the Income Tax (*Impuesto sobre la Renta de Personas Físicas* – IRPF) established by Law 46/2002.

goal of these policies. For this purpose, the concept of family is redefined so as to include households other than the conventional heterosexual family based on marriage, such as *de facto* marital unions as well as homosexual unions, and all are guaranteed equal rights. The legislative initiative to give homosexual couples the right to marry encountered strong resistance from the most conservative groups, led by the Catholic Church. This lively debate provided evidence of both the relevance of the family institution in Spanish society and the divergence of points of view on its significance and functionality.

Even though family issues were retained as a priority on the new policy agenda, they were subject to a profound reorientation, which made gender equality its touchstone. Policies reconciling work and family life become for the first time associated with the policies promoting equality, instead of being considered a substitute for them (Salido and Moreno 2009: 292). In this way, policies reconciling work and family are considered to go beyond 'women's issues', making them a crucial question for the welfare equilibrium of a society. On the other hand, such policies are also increasingly linked to the European goal of full employment, which means that they will be significantly modified towards activation.

The Act for Effective Equality Between Women and Men (*Ley Orgánica 3/2007, para la Igualdad Efectiva entre Mujeres y Hombres*) introduced important measures to reconcile work and family life explicitly designed to alter the conventional decision framework in this area and to remove the obstacles to achieving effective equality between men and women. Among these measures is the relaxation of the previous requirement to make Social Security contributions to maternity leave schemes, with the introduction of non-contributory maternity leave for women with no labour experience.[14] Furthermore, in order to facilitate access to maternity benefit of young female employees, age was introduced as a criterion to determine eligibility for maternity benefit.[15] The duration of family leave and parental leave was extended, but they remained unpaid. It has been demonstrated that unpaid leaves have an undesirable effect on women's employment, reinforcing the traditional division of tasks between the sexes, with women assuming the main responsibility for caring for children as well as for sick or elderly relatives

---

14   This non-contributory maternity benefit is equivalent to 100 per cent of the official annual reference income (*Indicador Público de Rentas de Efectos Múltiples*, IPREM), which in 2010 amounts to €7,455.14.

15   Before 2007, to qualify for maternity leave benefit a mother needed to be employed immediately before the leave and to have contributed to Social Security for 180 days during the previous five years. Under the new regulations, mothers aged under 21 years do not need to show previous employment to qualify for the maternity benefit, while mothers aged between 21 and 26 need to have only 90 days' contributions to Social Security in the seven years prior to the date of birth, adoption or fostering, or 180 days during their entire working life. Mothers aged over 26 years need previous contributions of 180 days in the seven years prior to the date of birth, adoption or fostering, or 360 days during their entire working life.

(Jaumotte 2004; European Commission 2009b). The most innovative measure in this area was the introduction of paid paternity leave of 15 days for fathers on a 'take it or leave it' basis. In spite of its novelty, it nevertheless left unattended the old claim for longer paternity leave made by feminist and labour organizations.

Another priority of the new policy map was to give a response to the increasing demand for public caring services. Trying to cope with the problems associated with a growing elderly population, the PSOE government drafted an Act to Promote Personal Autonomy and Attention to Dependent People (Act 39/2006, *Ley para Promover la Autonomía Personal*), which was intended to create a national long-term care system to cover the caring needs of the growing elderly and dependent population. It can be considered as one of the most innovative initiatives on the policy agenda, as it provides care services independently of the health, gender or age status of the dependent population, and irrespective of people's labour status or work trajectories. However, the articulation of the care system still makes women the keystone of the caring tasks,[16] reinforcing the role of women as carers in the family, and leaving untouched the traditional sexual division of work (Kriz and Salido 2008). Also, remedying the endemic shortage of childcare for children under three years of age was taken as another priority for the new design of policies reconciling work and family life. However, the stated goal of providing 300,000 additional publicly subsidized childcare places for children aged up to three years by 2010 has not been achieved, and is one of the weakest points in policies reconciling work and family life developed during recent years (INECSE 2009; European Commission 2008). Nevertheless, the coverage goals of 90 per cent of children aged between three years and the mandatory school age, and 33 per cent for children under three years of age by 2010, announced by the Barcelona Summit of the European Council (2002), were fulfilled in Spain (although with some regional disparities; see Chapter 6), reaching 91 per cent and 39 per cent, respectively, by 2006 (European Commission 2008: 4). However, these figures hide the fact that more than 50 per cent of the care service for under-threes is provided for less than 30 hours a week, which does not necessarily enable parents to work full time. Furthermore, around 33 per cent of the services are provided on a private funding basis, which increases their cost and makes them unaffordable by most parents (González 2004).

Finally, the Socialist government in 2007 introduced a new child policy measure, consisting of a one-off cash benefit of €2,500 for the birth or adoption of a child (Act 35/2007).[17] In spite of the substantial increase in the budget, the policy drew severe criticism from parties across the ideological spectrum as well as from social partners (CES 2007: 5; EIRO 2007). Thus, while the conservative PP

---

16   The help is provided in two ways: either as day-care services and residential homes or as economic compensation to the main care provider in the household. See Chapter 12 for an extensive discussion of the dependence system.

17   The measure was cancelled in May 2010 as one of the 'anti-crisis' measures, with effect from January 2011.

argued that the 'baby cheque' – as it is popularly known – should be increased up to €3,000, and criticized the opportunistic character of a measure that was so remote from the left's traditional policies, the left-wing parties – Izquierda Unida (IU) and Esquerra Republicana de Catalunya (ERC) – detected with scepticism its direct pro-natalist character, and demanded a progressive tapering of the benefit depending on the household income level, as well as a radical reorientation of family policy towards the provision of social services for dependants. Moreover, the real goals of the measure are unclear: it could be 'compensation to families for the expenses associated with the birth of a new child', as the law states, or a milestone on the road to guaranteeing a universal right of citizenship to all newborns, as the government itself states, or a pure pro-natalist measure, as some its critics maintain. Several studies have shown that fertility rates are impervious to measures of this nature, especially if other circumstances remain unchanged (Jaumotte 2004; Bernardi 2005). Still, even if the benefit manages to raise the fertility rate, by being made available to mothers only it is by no means certain to help promote gender equality in earning and caring, and guaranteeing a universal right.

Challenging the Spanish Welfare State

The fall in fertility rates and the ageing of population, together with changes in the patterns of family organization and women's orientation to employment, have generated new needs for public services, as well as a general concern with reconciling work and family life, making reconciliation policies one of the most dynamic areas of social policy in Spain. Accordingly, family policies have undergone significant changes in Spain in recent years.

Nevertheless, Spain can still be largely characterized as an 'outstanding' example of the Mediterranean welfare regime. With a clearly underdeveloped public system of social services, especially for children under the age of three, low cash benefits, and long and unpaid parental leaves, individual informal arrangements are the most common strategy to reconcile work and family life. In this context, the opportunity cost of having children is still excessively high for working women. Conversely, working on a regular basis is too costly for women with a family orientation. As a result, Spain has in a relatively short period of time become the leader among low-fertility countries, while female rates of activity and employment, despite having dramatically increased in recent times, are still among the lowest in Europe.

Furthermore, the increase in female employment can be considered one of the most radical changes in Spanish society since the mid-1980s. It is important to note that the increasing incorporation of Spanish women into the labour force is part of a continuous tendency of change in women's role in society that has been manifested even more strongly in recent times. The trade-off between family and work seems to be increasingly resolved in favour of the latter, evidence of a process of profound reorientation in women's values and behaviour. As we have seen, the generalized increase in female educational levels and the consequent increase in the rewards to female salaried work are undoubtedly among the most salient variables to be taken into account. Also, more egalitarian attitudes towards family roles seem to be taking root among the Spanish population. The dual-earner family, in which both men and women work equally outside the home, appears increasingly as the preferred model (64 per cent), while the traditional family based on the husband's work covers a reduced proportion (13.9 per cent) (CIS 2006). However, only 44 per cent of households are actually organized on a two-earner basis, still fewer than the EU average, while another 43 per cent remain with the traditional male breadwinner model (Eurostat 2005: 5).

Even though the movement of women into paid employment can potentially open the door to women's economic independence, the structures of inequality both inside the household and in the labour market can remain unaltered (León 2002; Bustelo and Lombardo 2007). Moreover, some policies designed to help women both perform caring tasks and undertake paid employment, such as parental leave and other flexible working schemes, may preserve the traditional division of labour by sex, reinforcing the role of women as carers. The real impact of policies reconciling work and family life on gender equality will depend primarily on the predominant conception of women's role in society and in public policies (Lewis 1997). Where the predominant stereotype of women makes them responsible for family care, policies reconciling work and family life mainly promote flexible work arrangements, leaving the solution to the work–family dilemma as a private matter, and indirectly reinforcing the traditional sexual division of labour.

In this sense, Spain still appears as one of the countries with a more unequal gender welfare regime (Cousins 2005). One can say that while revolutionary changes are taking place in women's working behaviour, correlative changes in the gender division of labour have yet to begin. Several recent studies on the use of time by men and women show clearly that as a rule of thumb the bulk of the domestic work is done by women, pushing them into much long working days than men's, and with high levels of stress. This strategy is especially 'popular' among Spanish women, with one of the longest working days in the European Union. Spain is also one of the countries with the greatest distance between men and women in terms of caring for children (European Commission 2009c). When reconciling work and family life is approached in individual terms, as a problem affecting mainly women or, to put it boldly, as a 'women's problem', overwork appears the most frequent resort of women to manage work and family tasks (Fernández and Tobío 2005; Saraceno 2000). As we have seen in this chapter, Spain is a good example of the 'overburden model' of female employment and fertility.

Gender equality has not been given priority in the measures reconciling work and family life developed in recent years in Spain. Most of recent developments in policies promoting work-family life balance have been associated with exogenous forces, chiefly the European drive towards employability and activation, leaving the goal of gender equality in second place and lacking the effectiveness needed to adequately facilitate women's entrance into the labour market. Policy changes introduced by the conservative PP government help *de facto* to reinforce the traditional male earner-female carer division of roles by gender, re-privatizing caring tasks within the family through the extension of parental leave and the introduction of a monthly cash benefit for working mothers. And although the Socialist government made significant inroads into gender equality by implementing the Equality Act, some critical issues remain unresolved. The adequate articulation of the new national dependency system, which ultimately leaves caring responsibilities as a women's issue, giving priority to concerns about fertility and an ageing population, is one of the most controversial issues.

Moreover, the increased commitment of women to paid work means that caring needs will also increase in future decades. This will generate a stronger demand for social provision which, if not met, will result in an unsustainable situation from the point of view of personal and collective well-being. Women's employment is bound to be considered a key element for both economic growth and competiveness, but also for social cohesion. As a recent study by the European Commission on the cost of raising children has pointed out, the modernization of policies to adequately support families is crucial not only to allowing Europeans to have the number of children they want, but also to achieving the goal of equality of opportunities between women and men and to reducing child poverty (European Commission 2009b: 7). Also, the success of the Lisbon Employment Strategy is highly dependant on the successful incorporation of women into the labour market, which will not be possible unless the existing imbalances in attempts to reconcile work and family life are removed. As we have seen, in the case of Spain these imbalances are manifested in the crudest possible way, placing on women's shoulders the main burden of reconciling work and family life, and giving rise to individual strategies that prove to be inefficient from both personal and collective points of view. This is, with no doubt, one of the main challenges that the Spanish welfare state faces in the mid-term.

References

Baizán, P. 2007. The Impact of Labour Market Status on Second and Higher Order Births: A Comparative Analysis based on the European Community Household Panel, in *Family Formation and Family Dilemmas in Contemporary Europe*, edited by G. Esping-Andersen. Madrid: Fundación BBVA, 93–127.

Bernardi, F. 2005. Public Policies and Low Fertility: Rationales for Public Intervention and a Diagnosis for the Spanish Case. *Journal of European Social Policy*, 15(2), 27–42.

Bertelsmann Stiftung (ed.) 2004. *International Reform Monitor. Social Policy, Labor Market Policy, Industrial Relations*, Issue 9. [Online] Available at: http://www.bertelsmann-stiftung.de/cps/rde/xbcr/SID-0A000F14-90D82142/bst_engl/refmon_9e.pdf [Accessed: 26 November 2010].

Boje, Th.P. and Leira, A. (eds) 2000. Citizenship, Family Policy and Women's Patterns of Employment, in *Gender, Welfare State and the Market: Towards a New Division of Labour*, edited by T.P. Boje and A. Leira. Florence, KY: Routledge, 41–69.

Bustelo, M. and Lombardo, E. (eds) 2007. *Políticas de Igualdad en España y en Europa: Afinando la Mirada*, Madrid: Cátedra.

CES (*Consejo Económico y Social*) 2007. Dictamen sobre el proyecto de ley por el que se establece la deducción por nacimiento o adopción en el impuesto sobre la renta de las personas físicas y la prestación económica de pago único por nacimiento o adopción de la Seguridad Social. Madrid: CES. [Online] Available at: http://www.ces.es [Accessed: 26 November 2010].

CIS (*Centro de Investigaciones Sociológicas*) 2006. *Encuesta de Fecundidad y Familia 2006*, Estudio n° 2639. Madrid: CIS.

Cousins, C. 2005. The Development of a Gendered Social Policy Regime, in *Gendering Spanish Democracy*, edited by M. Threlfall, C. Cousins and C. Valiente. New York: Routledge, 55–77.

De Henau, J., Meulders, D. and O'Dorchai, S. 2006. The Childcare Triad? Indicators Assessing Three Fields of Child Policies towards Working Mothers in the EU-15. *Journal of Comparative Policy Analysis*, 8(2, Special Issue), 129–48.

Delgado, M. et al. 2009. *Fecundidad y Trayectoria Laboral de las Mujeres en España*. Madrid: Instituto de la Mujer, Ministerio de Igualdad.

EIRO 2007. *Spain: Social Partners Critical of New Family Support Allowance*. [Online] Available at: http://www.eurofound.europa.eu/eiro/2007/10/articles/es0710019i.htm [Accessed: 26 November 2010].

Esping-Andersen, G. 1999. *Social Foundations of Post-industrial Economies*. Oxford: Oxford University Press.

Esping-Andersen, G. 2004. Política familiar y la nueva demografía, *Información Comercial Española, Consecuencias de la evolución demográfica en la economía*, 815, 45–60.

European Commission 2005. *Reconciliation of Work and Private Life: A Comparative Review of Thirty European Countries*. Luxembourg: Office for Official Publications of the European Communities. [Online] Available at: ec.europa.eu/social/Blobservlet?docId=2488&langId=en [Accessed: 17 August 2011].

European Commission 2006. *Childbearing Preferences and Family Issues on Europe, Special Eurobarometer 253 / Wave 65.1 – TNS Opinion & Social*. Luxembourg: Office for Official Publications of the European Communities. [Online] Available at: http://ec.europa.eu/public_opinion/archives/ebs/ebs_253_en.pdf [Accessed: 17 August 2011].

European Commission 2008. *Implementation of the Barcelona Objectives Concerning Childcare Facilities for Pre-school-age Children* {COM(2008) 598}.

European Commission 2009a. *Employment in Europe 2009*. Luxembourg: Office for Official Publications of the European Communities.

European Commission 2009b. *The Costs of Raising Children and the Effectiveness of Policies to Support Parenthood in European Countries: A Literature Review*. Luxembourg: Office for Official Publications of the European Communities.

European Commission 2009c. *Report on Equality between Women and Men*. Luxembourg: Office for Official Publications of the European Communities.

Eurostat 2005. Gender Gaps in the Reconciliation between Work and Family Life, in *Statistics in Focus. Theme: Population and Social Conditions*, 4/2005. Luxembourg: Office of Official Publications of the EU. [Online] Available at: http://epp.eurostat.ec.europa.eu/cache/ITY_OFFPUB/KS-NK-05-004-EN. PDF [Accessed: 17 August 2011].

Fernández, J.A. and Tobío, C. 2005. *Conciliar las Responsabilidades Familiares y Laborales: Políticas y Prácticas Sociales*, Documento de Trabajo 79/2005. Madrid: Fundación Alternativas.

Flaquer, L. 2000. *Las Políticas Familiares en una Perspectiva Comparada*. Barcelona: Fundación 'la Caixa' (Colección Estudios Sociales, 3).

Flaquer, L. and Escobedo, A. 2008. The Metamorphosis of Informal Work in Spain: Family Solidarity, Female Immigration and Development of Social Rights, in *Formal and Informal Work: The Hidden Work Regime in Europe*, edited by B. Pfau-Effinger, L. Flaquer and P. Jensen. London: Routledge.

González, M.J. 2004. La escolarización de la primera infancia en España: desequilibrios territoriales y socioeconómicos en el acceso a los servicios, in *El Estado del Bienestar en España*, edited by V. Navarro. Barcelona: Editorial Tecnos, 291–312.

Gornick, J. 2000. Family Policy and Mothers' Employment: Cross-national Variations, in *Gender, State and the Market: Towards a New Division of Labour*, edited by T.P. Boje and A. Leira. Florence, KY: Routledge, 111–32.

INECSE (Instituto Nacional de Evaluación y Calidad del Sistema Educativo) 2009. *Sistema Estatal de Indicadores de la Educación*. Madrid: Ministerio de Educación. [Online] Available at: http://www.educacion.gob.es/ dctm/ievaluacion/indicadores-educativos/seie-2010-completo-imprenta. pdf?documentId=0901e72b8062e4f6 [Accessed: 17 August 2011].

Instituto de la Mujer 1997. *III Plan para la Igualdad de Oportunidades entre Mujeres y Hombres*. Madrid: Ministerio de Trabajo y Asuntos Sociales, Instituto de la Mujer.

Instituto de Política Familiar 2004. *Evolución de la Familia en España*. Madrid: Instituto de Política Familiar. [Online] Available at: http://www.ipfe.org/ informe_evolucion_familia_esp_2003_1.pdf [Accessed: 26 November 2010].

Jaumotte, F. 2004. *Female Labour Force Participation: Past Trends and Main Determinants in OECD Countries*. Paris: Economics Department, OECD.

Kriz, K. and Salido, O. 2008. *Family Policy Changes in Germany and Spain (1997–2007): Uneven Developments towards Gender Reconstruction*, paper presented at the Meeting of the American Sociological Association. Boston, 3 August.

León, M. 2002. The Individualisation of Social Rights: Hidden Familialistic Practices in Spanish Social Policy. *South European Society & Politics*, 7(3), 53–79.

León, M. 2005. Welfare State Regimes and the Social Organisation of Labour: Childcare Arrangements and the Work/Family Balance Dilemma. *The Sociological Review*, 53(2), 204–18.

Lewis, J. 1997. Gender and Welfare Regimes: Further Thoughts. *Social Politics*, 4(2), 160–77.

Moreno Mínguez, A. 2008. El reducido empleo femenino en los Estados del Bienestar del sur de Europa, *Revista Internacional de Sociología*, 65(50), 129–62.

OECD 2004. *Labour Force Participation of Women: Empirical Evidence on the Role of Policy and Other Determinants in OECD Countries*, OECD Economic Studies No. 37. Paris: OECD.

Salido, O. and Moreno, L. 2009. Familia y género, in *Reformas de las Políticas del Bienestar en España*, edited by L. Moreno. Madrid: Siglo XXI, 281–308.

Saraceno, Ch. 2000. Gendered Policies: Family Obligations and Social Policies in Europe, in *Gender, Welfare State and the Market*, edited by T.P. Boje and A. Leira. London: Routledge, 135–56.

Valiente, C. 1995. Rejecting the Past: Central Government and Family Policy in post-Authoritarian Spain (1975–94), in *The Family in Social Policy and Family Policy*, edited by L. Hantrais and M.T. Letablier. Cross-National Research Papers, 4(3). Loughborough: European Research Centre, Loughborough University of Technology, 80–96.

Valiente, C. 2005. The Changing Roles of Men in Family in Spain, in *Gendering Spanish Democracy*, edited by M. Threlfall, C. Cousins and C. Valiente. New York: Routledge, 187–203.

Chapter 11

Immigration and Social Policy in Spain: A New Model of Migration in Europe

Miguel Laparra

Introduction

Spanish society has made a commitment of extraordinary dimensions with regard to immigration, the implications of which can be seen in practically all spheres of social life. To a large extent, many of the social features and tendencies of the Spanish social policy that will have to be outlined in the future will depend on how this commitment unfolds.

Social policies have not been excluded from this influence. Rather the opposite: recent transformations of the Spanish welfare state are difficult to explain without the immigration factor. On the one hand, the general increase in wealth, especially in social security contributions, has made possible a great expansion of certain social services and pensions. On the other hand, immigration has brought a marked growth in the demand for several services and required them to adapt to the new needs and the peculiarities of the recently settled population. Moreover, the Spanish welfare state, with all its limitations in comparison with the countries of north and central Europe, has become a fundamental component of this new migratory model in the south of Europe.

In this chapter our aim is, first, to show the emergence of Spain in the international migratory system as one of the primary global destinations. We then examine how migratory policies have evolved. Policies of integration have quickly acquired special prominence. These are economic and social rather than cultural policies, firmly based on labour market integration, although they also give access to different systems of social protection, so extending social rights to the immigrant population overall. Finally we look at the (provisional) results of this migratory model, its main limitations and the most important challenges that confront it in the future.

The Emergence of Spain as a Destination in the International Migration System

As the first decade of the twenty-first century closes, Spain has come to the end of a long period of immigration, which started in the mid-1990s.[1] It covered a period of sustained, and at times spectacularly high, economic growth, which led very directly to an increase in employment, especially in unskilled work, within a pattern of growth which is now pejoratively referred to as *del ladrillo* (based on bricks). A significant feature of this model was the intensity of the flow of immigrants into Spain. The rate of net migration for much of the decade was between one and two immigrants per hundred inhabitants, a spectacular level which made Spain one of the principal destinations for migrants in Europe and, in relative terms, in the OECD countries as well. Within the European Union, since 2000 immigration to Spain has been exceeded only by immigration to Germany, and in relative terms it is only just below immigration to some small countries. Spain stands out even in comparison with countries traditionally described as having 'populating' immigration patterns (Australia, Canada and New Zealand), with an inflow four times greater than that into the United States (see Figure 11.1).

Currently immigration is not significantly affecting half the countries in Europe, in particular the eastern European states, which in some cases have experienced negative net migration. But other countries in the centre and north of Europe with a stronger tradition of immigration and with high levels of wealth and generous welfare systems have also remained below the European average in this respect, at 3.8 per cent for the period 2001–2005 (the United Kingdom, France and Germany having an annual average of between 2 per cent and 3 per cent) according to Eurostat[2] (Laparra 2008b).

At the end of the decade, Spain, together with Ireland, had the largest foreign-born populations of the EU-15 countries (Luxembourg, with 42.3 per cent foreign-born residents, is undoubtedly a special case, because of its unique characteristics). But this is less significant than the speed with which this transformation has occurred. In 1998 Spain, together with Finland (1.6 per cent), was the country with the lowest proportion of immigrants within the EU-15. Ten years later it was the third-highest (after Luxembourg and Ireland). During this period, and especially in the years immediately before the economic crisis, Spain undoubtedly experienced the greatest increase in foreign-born population (see Figure 11.2).

---

1   The phenomenon had already been noticed (Izquierdo Escribano 1996).

2   The figures provided by the OECD show significant differences in some cases and consequently it is not easy to make a precise comparison of these countries. But in the case of immigration into Spain, the difference is clear.

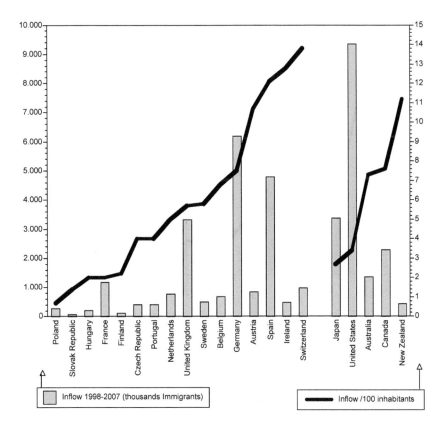

**Figure 11.1   Total inflow (thousands of immigrants) and inflow per
100 inhabitants in several EU and other OECD countries
(1998–2007)**

What we wish to highlight here, however, is the extent of immigration in southern Europe: six out of every 10 immigrants who come to Europe each year entered Spain, Italy, Portugal, Greece, Cyprus or Malta. With the exception of Greece, immigration for all these countries is above the European average and in some cases the rate is four times higher than the average.

With these absolute and relative figures and the data on immigration flow and the stock of foreign-born population taken into account, Spain is undoubtedly a remarkable case in the international context, as it has undergone one of the most intense immigration processes of the industrialised countries.

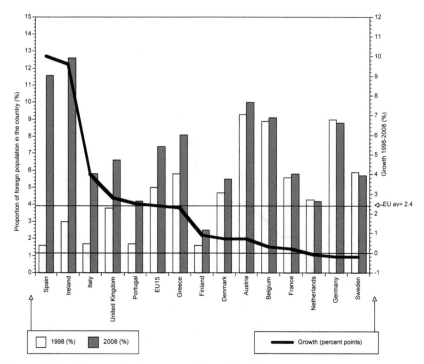

Figure 11.2   Changes in the proportion of foreign-born population in various European countries, 1998–2008

This extraordinary process, from the demographic point of view alone,[3] has had a very marked impact on Spanish society as a whole, its institutions and social policies (labour market, taxation, social security contributions, and so on). Within one decade immigration into Spain has been the equivalent of receiving the whole population of Denmark (almost five million). This has affected, for better or worse, all aspects of employment, housing, education and health care, as well as other infrastructural needs that may be considered less relevant to this chapter, such as water supply and electricity, public transport and telecommunications.

We are witnessing, therefore, *a new model of migration in southern Europe* which was already noticed some time ago (Baldwin-Edwards 1998). This is the result of a combination of factors, principally the geographical position of southern European countries as either bordering or near to immigrants' countries of origin; their affinity with Latin America (a greater influence in the case of Spain), the economic dynamism that creates a need for unskilled labour, and the existence of a large irregular economy.

---

3   For a detailed analysis of the demographic impact of immigration, see (Izquierdo et al. 2006).

If we look back at the classic approach (Ravenstein 1885), southern European countries should play the role of the southern gateway to Europe and countries of passage to the north, where there are better salaries and more highly developed welfare states. However, nowadays the countries of southern Europe have become the preferred destination for many migrants, not only from Africa or Latin America but also from Eastern Europe.

Even if we are not describing a new model of migration, the stage at which southern European countries currently find themselves as compared with countries in the centre and north of Europe involves certain significant characteristics. This is what Dassetto conceptualized as the 'migratory cycle' (Bastenier and Dassetto 1990; Cachón 2009). In Spain, for example, the immigrants have arrived so recently that most of the population of immigrant origins has not yet acquired Spanish nationality. Consequently, the difference between the proportion of people born abroad and those who have foreign nationality is still small. Most immigrants in traditional destination countries have been naturalized, though more in some countries than in others (see Figure 11.3).

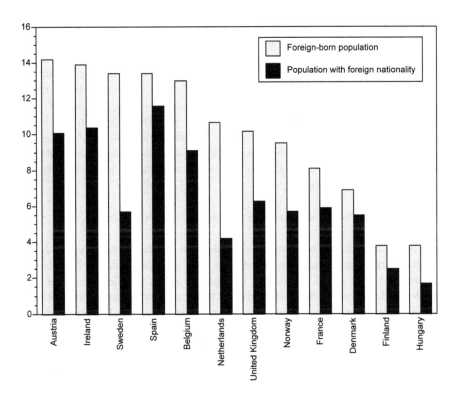

Figure 11.3 Percentage of population with foreign nationality and of foreign-born population, in some EU countries, 2007

These differences in the tempi of immigration processes also means notable differences in the social policy contexts. This is evident, first, in the limitations to political participation by immigrants (note the differences between Sweden and the Netherlands) and therefore in the way in which questions about immigration or the management of cultural diversity are framed. It also affects, second, to the restrictions on recognising certain social rights of the non-national population.

Along with access to nationality, certain other changes that normally arise from immigration are still almost imperceptible in Spain. The speed, intensity and recent nature of this process of immigration has meant that some of the dynamics associated with immigration, such as the institutionalization of immigration policies or the increasing social integration of immigrants, are not sufficiently valued in Spain, as can be seen in the following sections.

The Institutionalization of Immigration Policy in Spain and its Consequences for Social Policy

From 2000 onwards the question of immigration was 'institutionalized' in Spain (Cachón 2002). Immigration has become consolidated 'as a political question, perhaps one of the key political questions' (de Lucas et al. 2002). It is worth highlighting the most noticeable aspects of this process of institutionalization that resulted from the change of government in 2004. These were: (*a*) the construction of a model for gradually bringing immigration flows under control by reducing the number of illegal immigrants (as a result of the new immigration law of 2004 and the 'regularization' of 2005); (*b*) the stimulus given to integration policies as a result of the Strategic Plan for Citizenship and Integration 2007–10,[4] and (*c*) the implementation in 2005 of the Fund for Receiving and Integrating Immigrants and for Educational Support, which financed specific activities by town councils and Autonomous Communities.

Regularization and the Maturing of the Immigration Process: 2004–2008

The Spanish model of immigration since the first 90s has been firmly based on irregular immigration and consequently the flow of immigrants has been barely controlled by the public authorities. But the key is not the illegal entrants who evade border controls; these still amount to a minority of immigrants. Rather it is the existence of an irregular employment market, which has provided real opportunities for employment without the necessary work permits. In the long term, it would continue to be difficult to control immigration flows if a large black economy and irregular employment sector continued to exist.

---

4   The plan was approved by the government in February 2007 but the preparatory work began in December 2004 (MTAS 2007).

The rate of irregular immigration in Spain has been amongst the highest in the European Union, and is therefore a significant characteristic of the country's immigration pattern. The difference between the number of current residence permits and the number of foreigners registered as resident with their local councils has been used as an approximation that enables us to identify at least the trend in irregular immigration in Spain. However, it is extremely difficult to calculate the number of irregular immigrants.[5]

With these caveats, we analysed the difference between the Register of Inhabitants and the register of residence permits for non-EU citizens only, who are in a more vulnerable position legally.

The Figure 11.4 shows how in recent years irregular situations have been reduced significantly, although there could still be a significant number (albeit a minority) of non-EU citizens without residence permits.

In recent years this pattern of intense and irregular immigration (both dominant features of immigration in southern Europe, especially Spain) seems to have been changing (Laparra 2008b). First, the increase in formal employment from the mid-1990s was significant, and this trend could have led to a reduction in irregular employment, at least in relative terms. Second, the introduction and implementation of new instruments for regulating the flow of immigrants was steering most of them through regular channels.

---

5 Registration with the local council ('*padrón*') is compulsory even for irregular immigrants, almost all of whom are actually registered since the door to certain social rights is thereby opened. The estimate, based on a comparison between the local Register of Inhabitants and residence permits, does not take into account applications for residence that are in progress. The population of citizens of EU countries also tends to be incompletely registered, although this may not be significant for the social integration of immigrants. It is necessary to be aware of the distortion in the register, whereby some residents in Spain are not registered and some people who appear on the register are no longer in the country. Within these limitations it is necessary to recognize that the municipal register of inhabitants is a high-quality source of data for estimating the number of immigrants that are actually living in the country, including those whose presence is irregular. It is a characteristic which is absent from censuses and registers in other European countries do not have and which can on occasions make comparison difficult.

The updating of the register improved as the result of a regulation from 2005 that requires people from outside the European Union to renew their entries in the register every two years. As for residents from other European Union countries, updating the register improved as the result of the passing of Royal Decree 240/2007, which requires all people from other EU countries who reside in Spain and do not have a residence card to request entry in the Central Register of Foreigners.

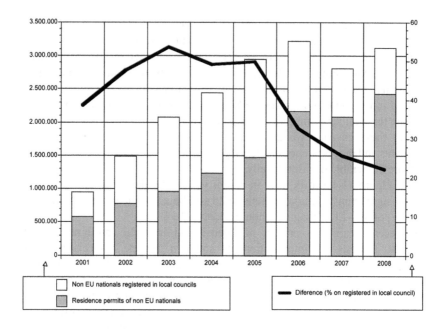

Figure 11.4   Changes in the number of non-EU citizens in Spain entered in the register of inhabitants and those who have a residence permit, 2000–2008

A number of factors seemed to be especially significant here: access to work and residence permits by means of contracting in the country of origin, organized by the employing companies themselves (between 2006 and 2007 this involved 440,000 people); widening the range of activities open to work-permit claims; access by immigrants without papers to the right of residence through established roots in the community or in employment, and through family reunification.

From 2004 onwards, a new political discourse about immigration emerged in the central government that was to be embodied in the Strategic Plan for Citizenship and Integration (PECI).[6] This represented a break from the earlier 'Programa Greco' (Global Programme of Regulation and Coordination of Immigration in Spain) approved by the Popular Party in 2001–2004, which was strongly focused on establishing security and control measures but lacked a strategy for integrating the immigrant population. In parallel with this a Support Fund for the Reception and Social Integration of Immigrants (Fondo de Apoyo a la Acogida e Integración Social de Inmigrantes) was established. The fund began to be distributed to the

---

6   The PECI was finally approved by the Council of Ministers in 2007, but its lines of action and political orientation had an impact from the preparatory phases in 2005.

Autonomous Communities and to town and city councils from 2005 onwards, and grew to a total of 200 million euros.

But the most important change during this period was that immigration into Spain ceased to be predominantly irregular. Between 2004 and 2008 the pattern gradually shifted from irregular immigration (which eventually involved almost half the non-EU immigrants) to regular immigration. Most of the existing population of immigrants without papers became regularized, and forms of regular immigration were developed at the same time, thereby increasing the government's ability to control the flow of immigrants into the country.

The 2005 'normalization' process led to almost 600,000 immigrants accessing residence and work permits. This was possibly the largest regularization process to occur in Europe in a long time. The bulk of irregular immigration that had been accumulating since the previous regularization in 2000–2001 was thus regularized.[7] In addition, the enlargement of the European Union meant the implicit regularization of more than half a million immigrants from Eastern Europe from 2007 onwards. In the long term, however, if the trend is not reversed,[8] the regularization of the flow of immigrants through three very different mechanisms may be of greater significance. These mechanisms are: contracting in the country of origin, which has increased very significantly in recent years; family reunification, which channels a progressively larger proportion of the flow of immigrants, and the progressive regularization of residents through the right to residence as a result of having established roots in the community or in the labour market (*arraigo social y laboral*).

As a result of all this, the number of immigrants without permits, which was estimated to involve half the non-EU immigrants in 2003, was reduced to an almost residual level of around 10–15 per cent, in a period when the foreign population in Spain had doubled. In contrast to a situation in which there was a substantial number of *margizens* at the start of this period, there has been a very substantial increase in *denizens* (1.1 million immigrants with permanent residence permits) and even *quasi-citizens* (1.9 million citizens from the European Union) (Hammar 1990; Martinello 1994; Castles y Davidson 2000). That is, 53 per cent of foreign residents in Spain now have a permanent right to remain, and a large proportion of these have the right to vote in local and European elections.

Thus, the main obstacle to promoting integration (it is practically impossible to develop processes of social integration in irregular situations) was gradually overcome during this period. It would be regrettable if the social goal of integration were lost as a result of the reforms proposed by the Law on the Rights and Freedoms of Foreigners and the management of immigration flows. Quite

---

7   This is the direct consequence of the passing of Immigration Law 2394/2004.

8   This is the change that might be indicated in the statement from the Ministry of Employment at the beginning of the 2008 legislature. The minister focused on the reduction in family reunification and contracting in country of origin, the principal mechanisms that have made it possible to increase the number of regular immigrants in recent years.

the reverse: it would be better to consider how to fully resolve the situation of irregular non-EU immigrants who are still in Spain.[9]

As a consequence of all these changes, together with the extremely rapid process of social change that Spain has undergone since the 1960s, the Spanish immigration system has also developed very rapidly and is already showing definite signs of maturity despite its very recent appearance on the international scene. This is reflected in the migration routes, which do not lead to Spain by chance as a place of passage or as a temporary alternative destination. It is also reflected in the composition of the flow, which is increasingly complex and more selective, and progressively involves family reunification; and it can be seen in a large number of plans for the future of the population already established in the country.

An Immigration Policy Structured on Two Levels

In Spain the control of immigration is in the hands of the central state but, nevertheless, most of the responsibilities that affect integration belong to the Autonomous Communities (a similar division of responsibilities can be found in some other countries). The central state is responsible for issuing and reviewing of work and residence permits, family reunification, recognizing refugee status, controlling the frontiers, establishing quotas of legal entries, as well as initiating deportation procedures and repatriations. Meanwhile the Autonomous Communities manage current policies on employment, housing, health, education and social services.

This model for implementing immigration policy has been shown to be ineffective in dealing with the diversity of situations in each Autonomous Communities (see Table 11.1) and is seen to involve very significant contradictions.

In reality, the Autonomous Communities have not completed the construction of a clearly defined integration model adapted to their needs; and the central state has not been capable of introducing entirely efficient mechanisms for controlling the immigration flow and the legal presence of immigrants in the country.

Perhaps in response to these limitations, in recent years both levels of administration (i.e. the central state and the Autonomous Communities) have sought to extend their influence over issues that initially were not their responsibility. The central state is trying to exert more influence on social policies and to participate in the construction of a model (or several models) for social integration, while Autonomous Communities aspire to increase their decision-making capacity over policies for controlling the inflow of immigrants.

---

9   It is not easy to estimate the number of these irregular situations, but the difference between the numbers in the Register of Inhabitants and the number of residence permits suggests a figure of less than half a million.

Table 11.1   **Foreign population in Spain per 100 inhabitants, according to nationality (grouped into large region of origins)**

	Foreign population	Total EU-15	Total EU-12	Total EU-27	Magreb	Rest of Africa	Latin America	Total non-EU nationals
Murcia	16.31	2.51	1.68	4.18	4.61	0.53	5.98	12.13
Catalonia	15.91	2.33	1.78	4.11	3.19	0.89	5.37	11.80
Madrid	16.66	1.41	4.12	5.53	1.35	0.59	7.53	11.13
The Balearic Islands	21.69	8.67	2.47	11.15	2.27	0.86	6.08	10.54
Melilla	10.34	1.43	0.06	1.49	8.38	0.01	0.18	8.85
La Rioja	14.59	1.84	3.96	5.80	2.85	0.49	3.71	8.78
Valencia	17.46	5.58	3.92	9.50	1.80	0.46	3.98	7.96
Navarre	11.20	1.46	2.15	3.61	1.86	0.53	4.48	7.59
All Spain	12.08	2.51	2.36	4.86	1.68	0.47	3.88	7.22
The Canaries	14.32	6.86	0.77	7.63	1.04	0.42	4.07	6.68
Aragon	12.79	0.87	5.54	6.41	1.74	0.96	2.93	6.38
Castilla-La Mancha	10.85	0.45	5.11	5.56	1.69	0.23	2.82	5.29
The Basque country	6.12	0.84	0.78	1.62	0.80	0.37	2.80	4.50
Cantabria	6.47	0.82	1.24	2.06	0.33	0.21	2.97	4.41
Ceuta	4.51	0.37	0.04	0.41	3.79	0.01	0.14	4.11
Andalusia	8.13	2.65	1.41	4.05	1.34	0.32	1.73	4.08
Castilla and Leon	6.54	0.90	2.37	3.27	0.82	0.13	1.98	3.27
Asturias	4.34	0.68	0.90	1.58	0.25	0.19	1.98	2.76
Galicia	3.81	1.08	0.31	1.40	0.23	0.14	1.80	2.42
Extremadura	3.38	0.67	0.91	1.58	0.80	0.05	0.76	1.80

Note: EU-15: Austria, Belgium, Denmark, Finland, France, Germany, Greece, Ireland, Italy, Luxembourg, Netherlands, Portugal, Spain, Sweden, United Kingdom.

EU-12: Bulgaria, Cyprus, Czech Republic, Estonia, Hungary, Latvia, Lithuania, Malta, Poland, Romania, Slovak Republic, Slovenia.

Source: Calculations by the author based on the Register of Inhabitants as of 1 January 2009 (National Institute of Statistics, INE).

The state monopoly on the management and control of immigration and conditions for residence, which left the Autonomous Communities with a much reduced ability to influence decisions regarding the level of immigration, seems to be a source of contradiction that the Autonomous Communities at times feel to be an unjustified imposition by the central authorities.

The 'Programa Greco' 2001–2004 did not meet the needs of the local and regional administrations in this respect, largely because its philosophy was one of control and not integration. The change of government in 2004 initiated a change in the level of intervention by the central state, whereby it influenced the social policies of the Autonomous Communities and fostered the social integration of immigrants with standard criteria throughout the country. The principal instrument used was the Strategic Plan for Citizenship and Integration 2007–10 (PECI), approved by the government in February 2007 with a budget of 2,005 million euros for the whole period.

After the approval of a new Immigration Law in December 2004 and the consequent 'regularization' of the position of immigrants in 2005, the Support Fund for the Reception and Social Integration of Immigrants and Educational Support was the first step in a move to link the central state with the integration policies of the Autonomous Communities. This fund for specific actions was distributed to the regions on the basis of a variety of parameters related to the impact of immigration. The aim is to provide specific funding to the Autonomous Communities and municipalities for actions that lead to increased integration.

This fund for specific actions (a small part of the total budget for the PECI, the Strategic Plan) increased to 200 million euros in 2007 and 2008, although afterwards it was reduced because of national budgetary restrictions. This fund was used for specific actions with the immigrant population; the general cost of the services used by the immigrants (education, health care, and so on), was financed from the ordinary sections of the Budget. This amount, although reduced, has had a significant impact in relation to the specific measures that were developed, and for this reason it is an important instrument in the hands of the central state for influencing regional and local policies.

At the same time, the Autonomous Communities approved various plans for the integration of the immigrant population which, directly or indirectly, sought to influence the ways in which immigration is controlled (Martínez de Lizarrondo 2006). As one more step in this process, responsibility for the management of work permits has been added to the new Statutes of Autonomy in an attempt to adapt immigration policy to the reality of each regional labour market. This is the case in Catalonia and Andalusia.

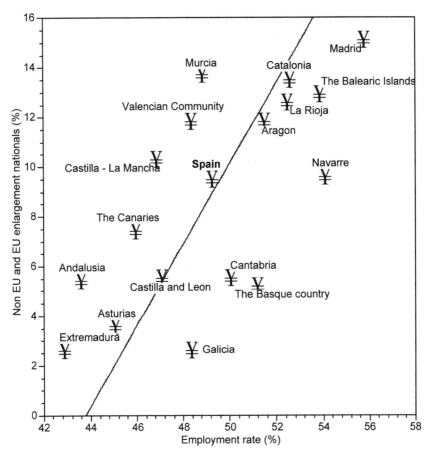

Figure 11.5   Immigration and employment in the Autonomous Communities in 2009

An Integration Model Based on (Precarious) Employment

The contribution to the Spanish labour market made by foreigners has been clear to see. The positive development of the economy until 2008 cannot be understood without reference to their contribution. Figure 11.5 demonstrates the significant correlation between immigration and employment. Immigrants have mainly chosen to settle in the Autonomous Communities with the most employment, although this relationship does not fit perfectly. Some regions, such as Andalusia, the Canary Islands and Extremadura, are experiencing pressure on the labour market as a result of the flow of immigrants, while others (the Basque Country, Cantabria, and Navarre among others) seem to have a greater capacity to absorb the new workers (although they have also experienced a loss of employment during the economic crisis that began in 2008). In general, in the regions with the greatest economic dynamism the business world has generally adopted a more open policy towards legal immigration.

Another issue is the type of jobs that the immigrant population performs. Immigration has normally been associated with extremely precarious employment; and the media are full of news about high levels of exploitation and the quasi-slavery of certain workers.[10] There has come to be talk of 'invisible workers', characterized by their very precarious employment and poverty, a model that was to lead to El Ejido,[11] a municipality in Andalusia, being described as 'an authentic icon of the basic trends in Spanish capitalism' (Martínez Veiga 2001, 2004).

However, it is necessary to recognize that labour mobility has been intense and that many immigrant workers, after relinquishing the hardest and least protected employment, have managed to gain access to more regulated employment with better working conditions, although their presence in the most skilled positions is still very limited.

In an immigration process as intense as that experienced by Spain, the overwhelming majority of immigrants have been in the country for only a short time. Their labour market situation, therefore, could not be expected to be very favourable, and this fact has to be taken into account. A more dynamic perspective that enables us to see trends in the employment of foreign workers over time and, therefore, the employment trends for those who have been settled for some time gives us a rather different impression (Laparra 2008a; García de Eulate 2009).

The Figure 11.6 shows the labour transitions of the immigrant population, both between different sectors and between different qualification levels, over the two inter-survey periods in Navarre: 2000–2003 and 2003–2008.[12] This diachronic perspective, based on retrospective information in each of the surveys carried out, provides us with a snapshot of the dynamics of immigration in the labour market and, in doing so, enables us to anticipate a future in which immigrants do not have always to be automatically condemned to situations of precarious employment and over-exploitation.

---

10   An analysis of immigration surveys in Navarra reveals an association between illegal immigration and precarious conditions of employment, associated with abusive strategies on the part of employers.

11   A reference to the immigrant population of south-east Spain that works in intensive agriculture in greenhouses.

12   This Autonomous Comunity in northern Spain serves as a reference, with the presence of an immigrant population that is similar to that of Spain as a whole, although with a more dynamic labour market and a significantly higher income level.

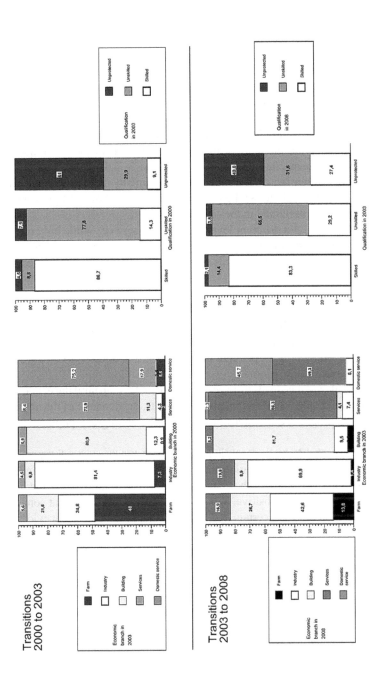

Figure 11.6 Labour market transitions of the immigrant population in Navarre, 2000–2008

To make a comparison between the two periods, it is necessary to note their different durations (three years and five years). This is a limitation that is difficult to circumvent with the information available, but it does not invalidate the conclusions reached. We must also stress that the meaning we give to the notion of 'qualification' is extremely broad here; we are referring to any employment level higher than that of labourer, in agriculture, industry and construction, and its equivalent in the service sector. It refers to highly qualified employment in only a very few cases.

The figure shows how mobility from the most precarious labour market sectors, such as agriculture, is substantial in the first period (with 52 per cent of immigrants changing sector between 2000 and 2003), while nearly half of all immigrants remained trapped in their sector of origin, which is normally more precarious. But in the second period (2003–2008) the process intensifies and only 14 per cent of workers in agriculture remained in the same sector.

The same happens, at a different level, in domestic service. While only one in five domestic workers managed to find other (normally better) employment in the first period, 54.4 per cent managed this potentially positive move in the second period.

Once employment at a higher qualification level is achieved, it is relatively difficult to regress to a lower level (eight out of 10 maintain the higher level). The differences between the two periods may arise from their different lengths. However, progress to a higher qualification level from unqualified work (labourer or similar) achieved by only 14 per cent in the first period, doubled to 29 per cent in the second period.

This empirical evidence leads us to conclude that, at least up until the economic crisis, and despite strong social and institutional limits, the dynamic of the upward labour mobility progressively intensified among the immigrant population in employment.

Despite many problems that continue to exist in the process of the social integration of the immigrant population, many positive elements can be highlighted in the period immediately before the economic crisis. The trend over the medium to long term was especially positive. What is especially worrying is that some of these trends have become less certain and, although there is no consistent evidence of effective regression, we cannot ignore this possibility.

However, we must not adopt the simplistic belief that *all social problems are a consequence of this economic crisis*. On the contrary, it is the crisis which in many cases is magnifying some of the structural problems that Spain has not adequately addressed and which is making them more visible. One such problem is unemployment among the immigrant population. It is true that the economic crisis has particularly affected immigrants and that foreigners make up a large part of the newly unemployed. However, unemployment amongst immigrants was already a problem before the crisis and was largely explained (and continues to be explained) as the obverse of the flexibility and mobility which immigrants contribute to the labour market.[13] Both during and before the crisis, the foreign active population has functioned as a shock absorber in the labour market, incurring the costs of flexibility in the form of precarious employment and periodic unemployment. What the crisis does is to put this shock absorber fully into effect and to impose a large part of the market pressure on the foreign labour force.

Nevertheless, it is essential to recognize that the economic recession is having a substantial impact on the labour market and especially, as discussed above, on the immigrant population, which in many cases is seeing the hard-won achievements of previous years disappearing and its standards of living deteriorating. In mid-2009 the number of unemployed immigrants was 2.7 times greater than the number in 2007, exceeding one million. According to the Labour Force Survey (EPA), one in every four unemployed people was a foreigner in mid-2009.

The Integrating Potential of Universalism in a Limited Welfare State

Beyond the labour market (in any case on the basis of our model of integration), improvements in the social situation of the immigrant population have been extended to other areas. In general the Spanish welfare state, despite its inadequacies, has shown itself to have a great potential for the social reception and integration of the immigrant population. This has been possible, among other things, because public opinion is more disposed to accept the incorporation of foreigners into social programmes (Mau and Burkhardt 2009), an aspect of a comparatively positive attitude towards immigration.[14]

Education was provided quickly and within the mainstream school structure, despite the growing number of foreign minors and the diversity of their origins. In compulsory education, practically all of the foreign population was incorporated without any problems worthy of particular mention. For example, families with minors expressed a high level of satisfaction with the process of integrating their sons or daughters in the educational process.[15] However the positive aspects described here must not be allowed to conceal serious problems of overload in the system, the excessive concentration of immigrant children in some schools, and an insufficient response to the emerging diversity of social and academic backgrounds (Anaut 2009; Pérez and Rahona 2009).

Universal health care was also extended to the immigrant population. Only a small minority[16] – in general a small group of recent arrivals who are free from

---

13   Real unemployment among the immigrant population was 25 per cent in Navarre in the first half of 2008, before the effects of the economic crisis were felt (Laparra, Martínez de Lizarrondo and García 2009).

14   Spain was in seventh position out of 23 European Union countries (Masso 2009).

15   A satisfaction rate of 90 per cent was expressed by the immigrant population in Navarre (Survey III 2008. Immigration in Navarre).

16   In Navarre, 6.5 per cent (Survey III 2008. Immigration in Navarre).

health problems – does not have a health card. It is notable that when they settle down they will be incorporated into the system without major problems. It is possible to say that the process of extending and universalizing the right to public health care, which began in 2002, has been successfully extended to people of all nationalities, sexes and ages. However, problems of overload in certain more sensitive services and a lack of adaptation to immigrants' needs (Jimeno and Moreno 2007; Lasheras 2009) have also emerged.

The living conditions of immigrants have improved over this period, for example in enhanced access to housing, in the reduction of house sharing, in the type of tenancy and in the ownership of general domestic equipment. Nevertheless, the current economic crisis has to be taken into account, as it may have the effect of decelerating or reversing these positive trends. Taking Navarre as a reference, sub-letting in 2008 had decreased in frequency (15.5 per cent) compared with data collected for 2003 (31 per cent). In addition, the proportion living in overcrowded conditions decreased (2000: 47.5 per cent, 2008: 28.9 per cent). Even so, these problems continue to be significant. Fewer than 0.5 per cent of homes lacked the most basic facilities (hot water or bathroom). Homes lacking heating fell to 13 per cent (less than half the figure for five years earlier) and almost one in every two immigrant households had its own vehicle (double the figure from the previous survey in 2003). Beyond these most basic indicators, however, the immigrant population has a long way to go before it reaches a situation of equality with the Spanish population (Iturbide and García 2009).

It never ceases to be surprising that in just one decade some five million people arrived in Spain and have been housed and that, despite the absence of policies implementing measures appropriate for such large numbers of people, this has not noticeably increased the problem of slums or sub-standard housing. To a large extent the immigrants have occupied a major part of the empty housing that existed at the beginning of the process and housing that has become available as a result of property development during the property bubble, with the native Spanish population accessing better-quality housing. The market has been the principal way for immigrants to access housing; public policies have had little impact.

In accordance with the political and administrative framework,[17] and also with the improvements in living and working conditions, social relations between the host population and the immigrant population have been progressively less characterized by ethnic discrimination. The share of immigrants claiming to have suffered from discrimination fell by more than 22 per cent from 2000, to 45.6 per cent of the immigrant population surveyed in 2008. The number of complaints received by social bodies such as SOS Racismo has also fallen. Almost half the people surveyed in Navarre in 2008 considered that discrimination had decreased

---

17   On other occasions we have stressed the socially constructed character of racist attitudes. Now, by contrast, it must be understood that there is a relationship between a more positive political context for the immigrant population and a more receptive attitude by the local population towards the presence of immigrants.

since 2003, compared with only 7 per cent who thought that discrimination had increased since 2003 (Andueza 2009). This reduction in discrimination could be seen in practically all areas. In some areas such as employment or housing, it can be explained by the rationality of financial relationships. This rationality has developed with the acceptance of the presence of immigrants both in the labour market and in the housing market when the immigrants demonstrate they are useful, satisfy specific needs, or provide supplementary income. Curiously, it is in public premises where a reduction in discrimination is least reported, and it is in the streets that the perception of discrimination reaches one of its highest levels (affecting one in four immigrants). By contrast, when real socializing occurs and immigrants become better known, such as through being neighbours, discrimination is noticeably reduced, to only 13.5 per cent.[18] The presence of immigrants becoming accepted as normal, and immigrants and locals getting to know one another and interacting, therefore seem to be the key factors in strengthening equality of treatment in all areas. This process of normalization and the immigrant population's own perception of decreased discrimination have without a doubt been influenced by the experience of equal treatment in the main systems of social protection, namely, the health and education systems. In both, the perception of discriminatory treatment is minimal amongst the foreign-born population.

In short, one might think that the more clearly universal welfare areas in Spain (the educational and health systems) have played an important role in the social integration model for the new immigrant population, with other social programmes playing a lesser role. These systems have accompanied a process based more on economic rationality, befitting the labour market as well as the housing or consumer markets. Altogether this has prompted important feedback for a reasonably positive reception by the Spanish population as a whole.

An Undefined Cultural Integration Model: Between Interculturality and Civic Integration

In recent times some European countries such as Germany, the Netherlands, Sweden and France have introduced, with a wide degree of variation, changes in their immigration policies with the objective of achieving what has come to be referred to as 'civic integration'. This is established through a series of repressive policies towards immigrants (Joppke 2006), which consist of the introduction of certain obligatory activities and commitments aimed at guaranteeing an adequate understanding of the language, customs, laws and basic institutions of

---

18   It has even been suggested that attitudes towards foreigners do not depend so much on whether immigrants are present in greater or smaller numbers, or even on how much the host population knows about immigration, but instead reflect ideological factors and beliefs (Aierdi and Bilbao 2009).

the host country. They also aim at ensuring the incorporation of the immigrant population into the democratic values of tolerance and respect for individual freedoms and human rights. These measures are usually justified as providing immigrants with the real possibility of integrating socially and improving their employment levels. These policies, however, which emphasize the most cultural aspects of integration, gradually come to be understood in an authoritarian way, and are then converted into devices for controlling the flow of immigration and for selecting immigrants. The issue of civic integration raises at least three issues: (*a*) the paradox that certain countries, such as the Netherlands and France, with relatively low levels of immigration (although with substantial established ethnic minorities) are those that most insist on directing these policies, theoretically, at recently arrived immigrants; (*b*) pragmatic doubt about the efficiency of these policies in achieving their professed objectives and in improving the levels of social integration of the immigrant population; and (*c*) a methodological (and ethical) contradiction between the liberal objectives of these policies and the authoritarian methods that they use.

Curiously, despite a supposed Europeanization of policies aimed at integrating immigrant populations (Rosenow 2009), the debate about civic integration has not been seriously taken up in Spain. It has only occasionally appeared in the public debate, based on some proposals from the parliamentary opposition, and has only occasionally resulted in specific measures or the design of programmes or protocols for action.[19] Neither learning the Spanish language nor knowledge of Spanish society on the part of the immigrant population has been considered an objective for which significant resources would have to be provided.

In Spain, the substantial amount of immigration from Latin America is an element that leads to the question of integration being posed differently. In a way, the option of strengthening Latin American immigration first and European immigration second (de facto selectivity, never made explicit in the design of immigration policies) was the principal instrument used as a (preventive) policy for cultural integration and against the African 'threat' (see Figure 11.7).

As a consequence of this selectivity in immigration flows, the issue of civic or cultural integration arose as a serious political and civic concern only in relation to the immigrant population from the Maghreb. Curiously, however, no cultural integration policy is specifically proposed for this group.

The political discourse that has been constructed in the European Union on the cultural dimension of integration (i.e. civic integration) introduces a legitimate debate which seems necessary from various points of view. In Spain it could have a positive influence leading to actions aimed at facilitating knowledge of the language and institutions of the destination society. However, there is always a significant risk of reinforcing repressive elements that introduce new symbolic barriers to social integration.

---

19   Only the question of the veil features frequently in public debate, as the result of some conflict that has occurred, generally in a quite decontextualized way.

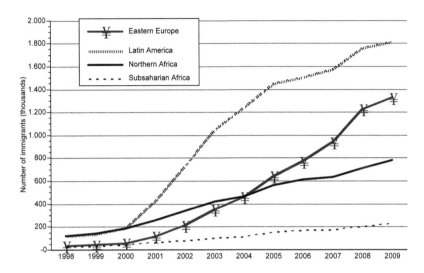

Figure 11.7 **Principal origins of the foreign population settled in Spain, 1998–2009**

Conclusion: The Results of a Precarious Integration Model Applied to Immigration

The migratory flow experienced in Spain since mid-1990s has had profound economic implications which, in the context of an economic crisis, seem to have been forgotten. Economic growth and the increase in tax revenue and social security contributions, which accompanied immigration, represent a significant support (at least provisionally) for the sustainability of the welfare state in Spain. For example, the regularization in 2005 alone brought into the open 565,000 irregular workers, and their corresponding social security contributions increased revenues by €1,500m for 2006. Calculations made by the Economic Office of the President (OEP 2006) estimate that 50 per cent of the increase in GDP could be explained by immigration in Spain during the five years prior to the economic crisis that began in 2008. Immigration would have caused an increase in the rate of activity, especially for women (one-third of the 12 percentage points increase) and a two percentage point reduction in the rate of unemployment. As a result, in 2005 immigration would have generated a surplus of €5,000m in the Central Government budget (0.5 per cent of GDP).

Other regional estimations had previously come to similar conclusions. In Navarre, for example, the increase in aggregate demand and the subsequent commercial expansion was quantified as a fiscal surplus of €15m in 2003, including social security contributions (Rodríguez Cabrero 2005).

Table 11.2   Percentage of households affected by exclusion processes in different areas in Spain, 2007

	Spanish and EU-15 nationals	Non-EU and EU-12 enlargement nationals
Exclusion from employment	12.5	27.2
Exclusion from consumption	8.0	17.6
Political exclusion	4.3	89.1
Exclusion from education	6.0	3.5
Exclusion from housing	17.8	37.0
Exclusion from health	10.8	16.6
Social conflict	12.3	16.4
Social isolation	7.5	9.2

Source: FOESSA Survey (2008) (Laparra and Pérez Eransus 2009).

The investment of between €180m and €250m in the purchase of housing in the period 1998–2003, aside from the immigrants' strategic contribution to the active population in quantitative terms and in flexibility have also been underlined (Laparra 2005). Even during the crisis, in spite of the increase in unemployment rates already mentioned, the employed foreign-born population remained quite stable: an average of 2.63 million in 2009, compared with 2.78 million in 2007.[20]

It should be stressed that, in spite of the relative general success in the immigrants' incorporation into the labour market in Spain, the process of social integration of immigrants in Spain is far from consolidated, as can be seen from the list of 35 exclusion indicators, divided into eight large dimensions defined in the FOESSA Report 2008 (see Table 11.2). In nearly all the dimensions, the households in which there is a non-EU foreigner or a foreigner from the enlarged EU-12, the distance from the local population (EU-15 included) is very considerable. If we leave aside the exclusion of political rights (a priori for foreigners) in other aspects of social and economic rights, the impact of social exclusion is double that on the host population.

Of the households of non-EU immigrants or from the enlarged EU-12, 28 per cent would be below the relative poverty threshold, compared with 18 per cent of the native-born population; and 43 per cent had several problems of exclusion, compared with 14 per cent for Spanish or EU-15 households. The most severe social exclusion, which would only affect 3.5 per cent of Spanish, reaches 14.2 per cent of non-EU nationals or people from the enlarged EU (see Figure 11.8). These are the failed migration projects, which reveals the limits of the model of the social integration of immigrants in Spain. This is the genuinely unresolved issue of immigration policy.

---

20   INE: EPA, yearly average.

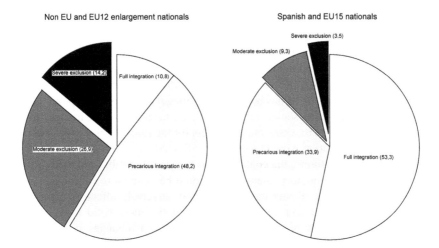

Figure 11.8 **Social integration of non-EU immigrants (and immigrants from countries in the recently enlarged EU-12) with the population of Spanish nationality (and with the EU-15)**

Perhaps the crisis that began in 2008 further highlights the extent of these limits to Spain's social integration model. The way it is tackled will very significantly mark Spanish society in the future. The property and financial crisis has decisively affected the evolution of these trends. It has had a very rapid effect in destroying employment, especially in sectors such as construction, which has a considerable number of foreign workers. This could be reducing the attraction which the expansion of the labour market had experienced since mid-1990s (if networks transmitting information about the new context work) but it could also represent a risk of repeating past strategies of adaptation to bad times, so 'submerging' the economic activity of companies and expanding irregular contracting (of Spanish and, possibly to a greater extent, of foreign workers). As a first consequence, a hardening of the political debate on immigration could be questioning some of the ways in which irregularity has been reduced in recent years (such as contracting in country of origin, or family reunification). It remains to be seen how these migratory flows evolve and what routes, regular or irregular, they mainly use.

As a consequence of the increase in unemployment, the economic situation of immigrants has rapidly worsened. In the first quarter of 2009 the proportion of 'households without an income' among the immigrant population[21] was 2.7

---

21 Households whose main breadwinner is a foreigner and in which there is no employment, pension, unemployment allowance or benefit. Data from the EPA, Spanish Labour Force Survey (2009 1st quarter).

times that of Spanish households, the equivalent of more than one in 10 immigrant homes in an extremely complicated social situation.

More delicate may be the effect which the reduction in employment, more specifically regular employment, might have on the process of renewing residence permits. If this process of *irregularization befalling the unemployed immigrant population*, or, as has been said, of 'illegalization of unemployment'[22] intensifies, a significant social achievement, painstakingly constructed since 2005, would have gone to waste, and prospects for the future social integration of the immigrant population would be seriously affected.

In the immediate future, the context could be less favourable and, with it, the management of the migratory phenomenon could become more conflictual. It is not only the economic climate that has changed, adversely affecting especially immigrant employment and undermining one of the most solid bases of the model of integration that has been collectively built. The changes announced in migratory policies could destroy the progress made both in the regularization of the migratory flow (contracting in country of origin, family reunification) and in the regularization of the stock of irregular immigration (extraordinary regularizations, case by case reguralization because of labour or social, rooted, settlement). If there are fewer employment opportunities, it would seem reasonable to try to reduce the flow of new immigrants and to facilitate a process of voluntary return as far as possible. Beyond this interim adjustment to the crisis, it is necessary to give thought to a long-term migratory strategy: after the crisis, immigration will continue to be necessary in Spain (and migratory pressure will continue in many countries of origin).

One of the questions for the long term is precisely what role immigration and migratory policy should have in a new, post-crisis model of growth, based more than the previous model on knowledge, investment and productivity. The migratory system in this possible new model would need to be more selective (in quantity and quality), attracting a more qualified population and encouraging training processes for resident immigrants. It is not clear, however, that a structural transformation of Spanish economy and society will unavoidably come about after the crisis. We do not know whether it is viable or whether an attempt to implement it would be successful, much less in what time frame. What does seem reasonable to assume is that important sectors of the economy, such as agro-food, tourism and social care, will continue to demand a considerable volume of labour which the resident population may be unable to supply, even if unemployment rates increase (Oliver 2006; Jimeno and Moreno 2007). It seems reasonable, therefore, to believe that Spain will participate in the *dual tendency* (qualified and unskilled immigrants) that has been proposed for the migratory-labour system in Europe (Favell 2008).

The demographic imbalances in the Spanish population, furthermore, will continue to need a migratory flow to make a contribution to ensuring the

---

22   Antonio Izquierdo, *Público* Newspaper.

sustainability of the system (Jimeno and Moreno 2007). This prospect of the transformation (but also of the maintenance) of some of the structural characteristics of the society must be considered very seriously when decisions are made on matters of migratory policy, in an attempt to respond not only to the economic and political imperatives of the present situation, but also to future structural needs.

The crisis, in the short and long terms, raises a whole series of misgivings that we cannot resolve here. In any case, an alternative prospect free of immigration could possibly be worse for all. It would have to be recognized that the settled immigrant population already forms part of Spanish society and is destined to be fully integrated in it. For this reason, it remains a priority to continue promoting social rights (and also political rights), equality of opportunities (removing the barriers that block social mobility) and equality of treatment (avoiding ethnic discrimination). Whether we like it or not, immigrants and host population alike have to live through the crisis together; and the resulting model of society depends, among other things, on an awareness of what this implies. It would seem reasonable, in this sense, to continue to build migratory policy while giving thought not only to present economic circumstances but also to long-term economic and social trends.

References

Aierdi, X. and Bilbao, S. 2009. La opinión de la sociedad de acogida sobre las políticas sociales dirigidas a los inmigrantes, in *Inmigración y Políticas Sociales*, edited by L. Cachón y M. Laparra. Barcelona: Bellaterra, 105–48.

Anaut, S. 2009. Educación, in *Encuesta 2008 Inmigración en Navarra*, edited by M. Laparra, A. Martínez de Lizarrondo and J.R. García de Eulate. Pamplona: Cátedra UNESCO de Ciudadanía, Convivencia y Pluralismo (Universidad Pública de Navarra) y Oficina de Atención a la Inmigración (Gobierno de Navarra), 235–68.

Andueza, I. 2009. Discriminación, in *Encuesta 2008 Inmigración en Navarra*, edited by M. Laparra, A. Martínez de Lizarrondo and J.R. García de Eulate. Pamplona: Cátedra UNESCO de Ciudadanía, Convivencia y Pluralismo (Universidad Pública de Navarra) y Oficina de Atención a la Inmigración (Gobierno de Navarra), 323–50.

Baldwin-Edwards, M. 1998. Where Free Markets Reign: Aliens in the Twilight Zone. Special Issue on Inmigrants and the Informal Economy in Southern Europe, *South European Society and Politics*, 3(3), 1–15.

Bastenier, A. and Dassetto, F. 1990. *Inmigrations et Nouveau Pluralismes. Une confrontation de societes*. Bruselas: De Boeck-Wesmael.

Cachón, L. 2002. La formación de la 'España inmigrante': mercado y ciudadanía. *Revista Española de Investigaciones Sociológicas*, 97, 95–126.

Cachón, L. 2009. *La 'España Inmigrante': Marco Discriminatorio, Mercado de Trabajo y Políticas de Integración*. Barcelona: Anthropos.

Castles, S. and Davidson, A. 2000. *Citizenship and Migration. Globalization and the Politics of Belonging*. New York: Palgrave.

de Lucas, J., Mestre, R. and Solanes, A. 2002. *Inmigrantes: una Aproximación Jurídica a sus Derechos*. Valencia: Germania.

Favell, A. 2008. The New Face of East–West Migration in Europe. *Journal of Ethnic and Migration Studies*, 34(5), 701–16.

García de Eulate, J.R. 2009. Empleo y Formación, in *Encuesta 2008 Inmigración en Navarra*, edited by M. Laparra, A. Martínez de Lizarrondo y J.R. García de Eulate. Pamplona: Cátedra UNESCO de Ciudadanía, Convivencia y Pluralismo (Universidad Pública de Navarra) y Oficina de Atención a la Inmigración (Gobierno de Navarra), 121–208.

Hammar, T. 1990. *Democracy and the Nation-state: Aliens, Denizens and Citizens in a World of International Migration*. Aldershot: Avebury.

Iturbide, R. and García, Á. 2009. Vivienda, in *Encuesta 2008 Inmigración en Navarra*, edited by M. Laparra, A. Martínez de Lizarrondo y J.R. García de Eulate. Pamplona: Cátedra UNESCO de Ciudadanía, Convivencia y Pluralismo (Universidad Pública de Navarra) y Oficina de Atención a la Inmigración (Gobierno de Navarra), 209–34.

Izquierdo Escribano, A. 1996. *La Inmigración Inesperada: la Población Extranjera en España (1991–1995)*. Madrid: Trotta.

Izquierdo, A. et al. 2006. *Demografía de los Extranjeros. Incidencia en el Crecimiento de la Población*. Bilbao: Fundación BBVA.

Jimeno, J.F. and Moreno, F.J. 2007. *La Sostenibilidad Económica y Social del Modelo Migratorio Español*. Madrid: Centro de Estudios Políticos y Constitucionales.

Joppke, C. 2006. Beyond National Models: Civic Integration Policies for Immigrants in Wertern Europe. *West European Politics*, 30(1), 1–22.

Laparra, M. (coord.) 2005. *El Impacto de la Inmigración en una Sociedad que se Transforma*. Pamplona: Gobierno de Navarra. Dirección General de Bienestar Social.

Laparra, M. 2008a. La dinámica de la integración social de los inmigrantes y su impacto en la sociedad de acogida. La perspectiva desde Navarra. *Política y Sociedad*, 45(1), 167–86.

Laparra, M. 2008b. Southern Europe in the Mirror of European Traditional Immigration Countries. *Italian Journal of Social Policy*, 1/2008, 207–32.

Laparra, M., Martínez de Lizarrondo, A. and García de Eulate, J.R. (eds) 2009. *Encuesta 2008 Inmigración en Navarra*. Pamplona: Cátedra UNESCO de Ciudadanía, Convivencia y Pluralismo (Universidad Pública de Navarra) y Oficina de Atención a la Inmigración (Gobierno de Navarra).

Laparra, M. and Pérez Eransus, B. (eds) 2009. *La Exclusión Social en España: Un Espacio Diverso y Disperso en Intensa Transformación*. Madrid: Fundación Foessa.

Lasheras, R. 2009. Salud, in *Encuesta 2008 Inmigración en Navarra*, edited by M. Laparra, A. Martínez de Lizarrondo and J.R. García de Eulate. Pamplona: Cátedra UNESCO de Ciudadanía, Convivencia y Pluralismo (Universidad Pública de Navarra) y Oficina de Atención a la Inmigración (Gobierno de Navarra), 269–88.

Martinello, M. 1994. Citizenship of the European Union: A Critical View, in *From Aliens to Citizens*, edited by R. Bauböck. Aldershot: Avebury, 29–48.

Martínez de Lizarrondo, A. 2006. ¿Un modelo español de integración de inmigrantes?: una mirada a los planes de las Comunidades autónomas, in *Migrations and Social Policies in Europe*. Pamplona: Departamento de Trabajo Social. Universidad Pública de Navarra. [Online] Available at: http://www.unavarra.es/migraciones/ [Accessed: 10 November 2010].

Martínez Veiga, U. 2001. *El Ejido: Discriminación, Exclusión Social y Racismo*. Madrid: La Catarata.

Martínez Veiga, U. 2004. *Trabajadores Invisibles*. Madrid: La Catarata.

Masso, A. 2009. A Readiness to Accept Immigrants in Europe? Individual and Country-level Characteristics. *Journal of Ethnic and Migration Studies*, 35(2), 251–70.

Mau, S. and Burkhardt, C. 2009. Migration and Welfare State Solidarity in Western Europe. *Journal of European Social Policy*, 19(3), 213–29.

MTAS 2007. *Plan Estratégico de Ciudadanía e Integración (2007–2010)*. Madrid: Ministerio de Trabajo y Asuntos Sociales. [Online] Available at: http://www.mtas.es/migraciones/Integracion/PlanEstrategico/Docs/PECIDEF180407.pdf [Accessed: 29 August 2011].

OEP (Oficina Económica del Presidente) 2006. *Inmigración y Economía Española: 1996–2006*. Madrid: Oficina Económica del Presidente. 15 de noviembre de 2006.

Oliver, J. 2006. *España 2020: un Mestizaje ineludible*. Barcelona, Institut d'Estudis Autonòmics.

Pérez, C. and Rahona, M. 2009. La inmigración en el sistema educativo español y sus implicaciones en la política educativa, in *Inmigración y Políticas Sociales*, edited by L. Cachón y M. Laparra. Barcelona: Bellaterra, 149–80.

Ravenstein, E.G. 1885. The Laws of Migration. *Journal of the Royal Statistical Society*, 48, 167–227.

Rodríguez Cabrero, G. 2005. El impacto económico. Norma de consumo y acceso a los sistemas de bienestar, in *El impacto de la inmigración en una sociedad que se transforma*, edited by M. Laparra. Pamplona: Gobierno de Navarra: 77–136.

Rosenow, K. 2009. The Europeanisation of Integration Policies. *International Migration*, 47(1), 133–59.

Chapter 12

Long-term Care:
The Persistence of Familialism

Sebastián Sarasa

Introduction: Is Spanish Long-term Care Undergoing a
Process of European Convergence?

The Spanish transition to a post-industrial society has developed following a low-fertility equilibrium model, like many other conservative welfare regimes (Esping-Andersen 1999). From 1981 onwards, the fertility rate remained below 2.1 births per woman, reaching its lowest point of 1.2 in 2000; and demographic ageing is rapid. EUROSTAT projections in 2008 estimated that a 6.4 per cent of the population will be aged 80 years and older in 2030, making Spain the fourth most aged country in the European Union (Giannakouris 2008). Simultaneously, female participation in the labour market, though still below the EU average, is steadily increasing, rising from 25 per cent at the beginning of the 1980s to almost 52 per cent in 2009.[1] Therefore, the rising ratio of older people to women aged 45 to 69 (the bulk of carers) and the greater partipation of women in paid work makes the familialist model of long-term care unsustainable in the near future. Familialism is a pattern of welfare organization in which the family provides more social care than the two other providers, namely, the state and the market. It is characterized by high ratios of intergenerational co-residence, low rates of female integration in the labour market and, paradoxically, low public expenditure on family policies, the bulk of them based on means testing and also on cash transfers and tax deductions rather than on services provision. As a result, social inequalities are important, specially those linked to gender roles. High degrees of familialism are common among nations governed by conservative welfare regimes, especially Mediterranean nations (Esping-Andersen 1999).

Population ageing involves a greater demand for care services, and more paid jobs, but also unhappy predictions about the financial sustainability of public health services and retirement pensions. The steady increase in the ratio of the retired population to the active population suggests that the funding of health and long-term care services, as well as retirement pensions, will be increasingly difficult, unless the quantity and the quality of the employed population dramatically increases (Esping-Andersen and Sarasa 2002). Before demographic

---

1   Own estimates from Labour Force Survey.

ageing became so evident, most welfare states had based the care of the frail elderly on expensive institutional services such as hospitals, nursing homes and residences. Since the 1970s in the Scandinavian nations, and the 1980s in other developed countries, the core of long-term care has been shifting towards communitarian services that are cheaper and that delay the entry of the old into institutions. The prioritization of communitarian care, however, involves a trade-off related to the role of women. Demographic ageing raises the question of the capacity of middle-aged women to remain employed if they have to retain their traditional role as carers; hence, reducing the cost of institutional services may have little, if any, effect on the public deficit because, if women withdraw from the labour market, tax revenue and Social Security contributions fall. Such a strategy may be more efficient if a large network of community care services is developed with state subsidies increasing women's opportunities to obtain permanent paid employment. Hence, action to deal with the future fiscal deficit implies increasing social expenditure today.

In December 2006 the Spanish Parliament passed a long-term care law that put an end to a long-standing tradition of means-tested social services inasmuch as it establishes universal eligibility criteria for those in need of long-term care. The law as published in the *Boletin Oficial del Estado* (BOE-A-2006-21990) includes an introduction explaining why it is needed; it cites demographic ageing, the expansion of paid employment for women, and the consequent reduction in the capacity of informal care networks to cope with the needs of the frail elderly. It also stresses the need to expand social services and it recalls the constitutional mandate to do so. Therefore, the new law states that one of its main goals is to set up regions with enough resources to provide a system of universal social services, of which the universal coverage of dependent people is the first step. As was said, what is commonly known as the 'Dependency Law' purported to construct the 'fourth pillar' of the Spanish welfare state to complement the three existing pillars of universal coverage, that is, of health, education and retirement pensions.

From the perspective of welfare regimes theory, such a legislative innovation raises an interesting question. How may familialistic welfare regimes evolve when the state's unwillingness to support the family as a source of welfare becomes so out of date and inefficient as to force it to intervene? Defamilialization is urged in Spain[2] but so it is also in many other nations whose welfare regimes limit the state to a subsidiary function. The social costs of familialism, in terms of low fertility and loss to the labour force, may be very acute in the Spanish case, as well as in all of southern Europe, but they arise also with different intensities in most of Continental Europe (Esping-Andersen 1999). Therefore, one may wonder whether

---

2   'Defamilialization' refers to policies that reduce the dependency of individuals on their families, giving them access to economic resources independently of family reciprocity (Esping-Andersen 1999).

European nations will experience a process of convergence, at least in the field of family policies.

Convergence of welfare regimes is supposed to be forced by structural constraints, mainly economic and demographic ones that leave little room for path dependency, political ideologies, power resources and cultural values. Economic constraints, however, are cited in arguments both against and in favour of social spending on family policies. The *race-to-the-bottom* thesis predicts a convergence to residual welfare states, given the pressure of international trade and financial markets (Rodrik 1997; Gilbert 2002); capital mobility would erode national sovereignty, constraining the ability of national governments to maintain ratios of social spending higher than those mantained by globally hegemonic countries as the United States (Ohmae 1995; Standing 1999). However, the empirical evidence in favour of the race-to-the-bottom thesis has been problematic; conversely, what has been shown is that the response of some small European nations to demographic ageing and economic globalization has been quite successful, as economic productivity and demographic fertility have been enhanced trough public spending on family services and job-training programmes (Esping-Andersen 1999; Hall and Soskice 2001).

A specific variant of this debate has been applied to family policies and, more specifically, to long-term care. At least in Europe, the development of family policies has been a firm pattern of social policy at the end of the twentieth century, in spite of warnings of a welfare state crisis (Gornick and Meyers 2001). European Union directives have recommended activating people for employment, especially women, and reconciling work and family life. In recent years the EU Member States have tried to contain the growth of health and pensions spending but, at the same time, they have increased public expenditure on social care. The reforms implemented in social care policies concerning eligibility criteria, and the nature of both the benefits and the providers of services, have made some sociologists envisage the obsolescence of classical welfare regimes in the foreseeable future (Daly and Lewis 2000). The convergence of care regimes would be characterized by the equalizing of nations' social expenditure (Daatland 2009), the decentralization of policies and a greater presence of home-based care allowances, which would lead to an increase in informal and semi-formal caring as well as quasi-markets in the provision of care services (Ungerson 1997; Behning 2005; Geissler and Pfau-Effinger 2005). Furthermore, the institutional changes in care arrangements do not clearly follow the typology of welfare regimes (Geissler 2005: 311–13). In fact, one of the most salient events since 1990 has been that provision for older people, as well as provision for children, is no longer to be understood as a natural part of the family's life style in conservative and liberal welfare regimes, in which the state does not need to intervene. Whatever the welfare regime, care today would be conceived as work and employment (Geissler 2005: 309).

However, there are doubts that such a convergence is happening in long-term care (Burau, Theobald and Blank 2007). Kröger, Anttonen and Sipilä (2003) argue that, in spite of the trends in Scandinavian countries since the 1990s onwards in favour of marketization, targeting and home-care allowances, it would be an exaggeration to maintain that any convergence of care regimes has occurred. The OECD (2005: 80) concludes that, while policymakers in all countries are concerned about how to sustain their systems of long-term care, their strategies have been so different as to widen differences between OECD countries in their provision of long-term care within their social protection systems.

This chapter explores the steps taken by the Spanish welfare regime towards defamilialization in the field of long-term care, and contrasts these reforms with those elsewhere in the European Union. It concludes that the implementation of the new law is constrained by the persistence of familialism, and that this outcome is shared by other conservative welfare regimes. The chapter first shows that care needs, family burdens and formal resources were unequally distributed among gender and social strata before the law was passed. Second, it considers the alternative policies that the Spanish welfare state could have adopted to overcome the negative effects of ageing. Such alternatives are selected from nations representing different welfare regimes in Europe; and our data show that a typology of welfare regimes is still useful for understanding how labour market, family, gender and state are related in long-term care. Third, the chapter analyses some of the major problems in the implementation of this new Spanish legislation, and shows how familialism persists through the provision of cash transfers in spite of the law's intended objective of defamilializing long-term care by the expansion of social services. Finally, it concludes with some remarks summarizing the main contributions of the chapter.

Spanish Long-term Care before the Dependency Law was Passed

Before the Dependency Law was passed in 2006, long-term care needs were covered by a mixture of contributory Social Security benefits and means-tested benefits provided by the autonomous regions. At the end of twentieth century the coverage was clearly inadequate, and families were overwhelmed with caring duties. Such a situation has had damaging effects on women's health status and life opportunities, especially those who do not belong to the upper social strata.

Needs and Resources in International Perspective

The ageing process of the Spanish population is increasing the need for long-term care. A third of elderly persons have some form of disability, and of these half have severe difficulties in performing activities of daily living (IMSERSO 2008). However, the need for long-term care is not circumscribed by age; 40 per cent of Spaniards with some form of disability are younger than 65 years, and one-third of people requiring more than 30 hours per week of personal care are also younger than 65 (Sarasa 2003). Hence, any view of social care for dependent people must include not only the elderly, but also younger people suffering from limitations in daily activities.

The Spanish welfare state dealt with those needs before the twenty-first century as other familistic welfare regimes did. Like most social services in Spain, long-term care is provided by a mixture of public, private non-profit and private for-profit sources, the last supplying the bulk of the services. Data from 1999 obtained from the Disabilities, Impairments and Health State Survey (EDDES) collected by the National Statistics Institute (INE 1999) shows that among people in need 7.5 per cent receive services provided by the market, 4.9 per cent services from the public sector, and 2.6 per cent services from volunteers. Before the new law was passed in 2006, the public provision of long-term care had been means-tested and insufficiently funded; consequently, since the provision of public services was targeted to poorer families, the market had become the main provider, but accessible only to the well-off. Table 12.1 shows the relative probabilities of receiving help from different providers, depending on the disposable income of the household where the dependent person resides. Buying services in the market is strongly conditioned by income, as expected, and public services are focused on the poor, while volunteering does not show any significant trend. As a result, families in the middle range of the income distribution are the most burdened, since they are relatively excluded both from the market and from the public services.

Hence, the meagre supply of long-term care services, most of them provided by the market, has been mainly concentrated on the richest strata of Spanish society. This pattern of long-term care service consumption is shared by other *familistic* welfare regimes, where dependent people have a lower probability of receiving services other than those provided by relatives and friends. Considering Italy, Greece and Spain altogether, Sarasa and Billingsley (2008) estimate that people older than 50 years with bad health or having difficulties with activities of daily living have less than half the probability of corresponding Danes and Swedes of receiving external support, and 23 per cent less probability than Germans and Austrians. Furthermore, while in those nations access to long-term care services is not significantly conditioned by disposable income, in southern Europe dependent people in the richest quintile of the income distribution are four times more likely to access services than dependent people in the lowest quintile (Sarasa and Billingsley 2008).

Table 12.1   Odds ratios from logistic regressions on using different providers of care depending on disposable income

	Market	Public services	NGOs	Family
First quartile	Category of reference			
Second quartile	1.12	1.04	0.85	1.13**
Third quartile	1.57***	0.88	0.96	1.19**
Fourth quartile	2.57***	0.73*	0.75	1.09

Note: ***Significant at 99 per cent. **Significant at 95 per cent. *Significant at 90 per cent. Estimates controlled for by dependence severity, age, sex, household size, region and size of town, marital status and educational credentials.
Source: INE (1999).

Unequal Distribution of Burdens between Gender and Social Strata

The weakness of service provision forces Spanish families, as in other southern European welfare regimes, to provide physical care instead of focusing their efforts on housekeeping and dealing with the authorities, as happens in northern Europe (Brandt, Haberkern and Szydlik 2009). As a result, of people looking after dependent relatives, the share of those who care more than 20 hours per week rises to 72 per cent in Spain, a figure dramatically distant from the 20 per cent of Danish carers, and distant enough from Germany and Austria (40 per cent) and the UK (48 per cent).[3] IMSERSO (2005) estimates that many informal carers of the elderly are their spouses (17 per cent), but most of them (57 per cent) are their children, many of them constituting a 'sandwich generation' that has to care for their parents and for their own children too (36 per cent of them care for the elderly as well nurturing their own children). Such a double role of carers is growing along with changes in the Spanish family; the dramatic reduction of extended families that occurred in the second-half of the twentieth century (Del Campo and Rodriguez-Brioso 2002) is still going on, as the IMSERSO (2005) data show us, and the share of informal carers other than children and spouses who are related to the elderly (grandchildren, brothers, nephews and so on) declined from 28 per cent to 14 per cent between 1994 and 2004. Conversely, the share of children has grown by 10 per cent in the same period. One of the main factors affecting the involvement of children in caring for their parents is extended intergenerational co-residence. The share of young people in Spain co-residing with parents older than 50 is among the greatest of Europe, and such co-residence is greater among the lower strata (Kohli and Albertini 2008), who are least able to afford formal services from the market.

The burdens of social care are not evenly distributed among gender and social strata. Spain shows one of the highest levels of gender inequality in the

---

3   Own estimatess from European Household Panel (1994–2001).

distribution of caring among children with care-dependent parents (Keck 2008). The bulk of social care is provided by middle-aged women, especially by those with less education and less disposable income, who are compelled to remain outside the labour market. Sarasa (2009) estimates the probability in several European nations of employed middle-aged women abandoning the labour market when they assume adult care responsibilities. He concludes that women try to reconcile the two demands, but, since adult care takes more than 14 hours per week and lasts longer than some months, many women cannot cope with both and decide to work part-time or to abandon the labour market. Women with low education credentials are at a high risk of unemployment, suffer from bad health or who care for children are the most likely to quit the labour market. It is easy to infer that Spanish carers are very likely to pay such a penalty inasmuch as most of them allocate more than 20 hours per week to caring for their parents; hence, 42 per cent of women looking after their parents assert that their caring activity has damaged their employment careers and 30 per cent assert that it prevents them from undertaking paid work (IMSERSO 2005).

Health deterioration is another reward many carers receive in exchange for their altruism. One third of carers say that their health status has worsened since they began their caring activity. Demoralization affects them as well; even though most carers feel their activity is a moral duty they have to perform, 47 per cent consider they cannot afford private caring services, and 22 per cent feel themselves trapped into carrying a very heavy burden (IMSERSO 2005).

Therefore, neither means-tested programmes of social care implemented by the different regional governments nor Social Security benefits were the optimal way of reducing the risk of exclusion suffered by such households where one member was severely dependent. Social care, as institutionalized before the new law was passed in 2006, had a very limited capacity for generating employment and for reconciling informal care with paid employment among women with little education. Now the question is: has the new legislation meant a significant step forward? But before analysing this issue, let's look at which alternatives could be chosen.

Institutional Alternatives

Long-term care is a difficult field of comparative research since most of the subject matter transcends the distinction between formal services and informal relationships, especially since care can be delivered by trained professionals, untrained paid helpers, relatives or friends (Burau, Theobald and Blank 2007: 172). Furthermore, the lack of uniformity in the way long-term care is measured makes international comparison a risky task (Comas-Herrera et al. 2006). Nevertheless, reviewing national studies and quantitative reports from different international institutions gives one a rough overview of the main institutional options in long-term care available in the European Union. Most comprehensive reviews of long-term care have arisen from both the Esping-Andersen's work on welfare regimes, and from the social care perspective (Daly and Lewis 2000) focusing on how childcare and long-term care are arranged in different nations.

The collection edited by Pfau-Effinger and Geissler (2005) shows how care arrangements differ among countries depending on how much care has been formalized as paid work or as semi-formal care, or even on how much care is provided by precarious forms of undeclared work. Bettio and Plantenga (2004) compare social care arrangements among the European nations, introducing two more indicators of the degree of formalization of services provided to children and the elderly, namely, the time allowed off work to informal carers and public spending on cash transfers to the beneficiaries (including pensions in the case of the elderly). Their analyses identify five clusters or care regimes, more or less equivalents to those identified previously by Anttonen and Sipilä (1996) and Gauthier (1996). The Scandinavian nations, including Finland, rely on formal services; their retirement pensions are not very high, but enough to keep poverty rates relatively low among elderly people, and other cash transfers to dependent people are rare. At the opposite extreme, southern European nations rely mostly on informal care provided by relatives, and retirement pensions are low (except in Italy, where they are among the highest in Europe).

Between the north and the south, three clusters of states appear: one, whose best representatives are Germany and Austria, has recently implemented universal coverage of long-term care, but relies mostly on cash transfers to the disabled without controlling their final destination (Wiener 2007). Such a provision may be understood as compensation for the additional exigencies suffered by the disabled and their relatives because of their impairment,[4] but also as an incentive for women to stay at home, out of the labour market. German beneficiaries may choose between in-kind services and cash allowances; most beneficiaries choose cash benefits, but such a choice reflects preferences that are more structurally constrained than culturally determined, since cash beneficiaries are over-represented among working-class households and beneficiaries opting for home-based care services are more frequent among the upper social strata (Theobald 2004).

Another cluster of states, represented by France and Belgium, has moved towards a greater formalization of services by delivering universal cash allowances or vouchers, that is, cash transfers to disabled people that are not designed to protect them from the additional exigencies of their impairment or to ameliorate the particular likelihood of poverty linked to disability, but intended to fund the

---

4   Some analysts defend a flat payment for care because it compensates for carers' lost earnings and promotes informal care, at the same time discouraging expensive formal care in nursing homes (Johnson and Lo Saso 2000). That option would be preferred to subsidizing formal care because the latter 'will distort relative prices and lead to under use of informal care' (Ettner 1996) and will have substantial effects on intergenerational living and care arrangement decisions (Pezzin and Steinberg 1999).

purchase of services, especially personal care services (Ungerson 1997). In France, for example, the *allocation personnalisée à l'autonomie* implemented in 2002 is paid to finance a specific care package, determined by a team of professionals according to their diagnosis of the needs of the recipient. The use of the benefit is therefore controlled; it can be used only to finance services identified as necessary by the professionals. This is based on a universal principle whereby the recipient contributes to the care package according to his or her level of income; below a fixed income threshold, recipients do not contribute at all to the funding of their care packages (Da Roit, Le Bihan and Österle 2007).

Finally, in the UK Attendance Allowances for people older than 65 and Disability Living Allowances for the younger disabled are provided universally, in cash, with no control on their final destination. These benefits seem to be akin to those provided in Austria or Germany; however, their value is lower than those offered in conservative welfare regimes.[5] Furthermore means-tested home help and residential care are provided by local governments, except in Scotland.

As a result of those different care arrangements, long-term care in some nations is biased towards formal services and in others towards informal care. The latter concentrate long-term care expenditure on cash transfers. Table 12.2 shows the structure of long-term care expenditure, and distinguishes those countries where such expenditure is biased towards in-kind home services from those where it is biased towards cash allowances. Scandinavian nations invest most of their high expenditure on long-term care in in-kind benefits, rendering cash allowances to a marginal option. Conversely, Austria, Germany and England belong to the cluster of nations that spend more on cash allowances transferred to disabled people. However, France and Belgium promote the development of formal in-kind services and have become separated from the other conservative welfare regimes. Therefore long-term care developed during the 1990s following the same patterns of childcare programmes institutionalized in previous decades; and in the process long-term care reforms have reinforced and not diluted the social-care regime typology constructed by Anttonen and Sipilä (1996) and Gauthier (1996). Gauthier identifies four childcare regimes: the French pro-family/pronatalist, the German pro-traditional, the Swedish pro-egalitarian and, finally, the pro-family non-interventionist (UK, USA). State-organized childcare is common in Scandinavian nations, but also in France and Belgium, while is hardly available at all in the other nations (Knijn and Kremer 1997). All in all, the EU Member States still can be clustered following the classical typology of welfare regimes, but it should be recognized that family policies among conservative regimes vary in their degree of familialism, which is highest among southern European countries and lowest in France and Belgium.

---

5   The Attendance Allowance in the UK ranges in 2010 from a minimum of 237 euros to a màximum of 350 euros per month (www.direct.gov.uk). Such benefits were worth on average 419 euros in Austria in 2008, and from 216 to almost 700 euros in Germany (Heinike and Thomsen 2010).

Table 12.2   Percentage of GDP expended on long-term care

	Total	Institutions	Community in-kind care	Cash allowances
Denmark	2.7	0.73	1.98	—
Sweden	3.9	2.28	1.49	0.13
Norway	2.3	1.15	0.97	0.18
Finland	1.0	0.48	0.45	0.07
Belgium	1.5	1.08	0.42	—
France	0.9	0.52	0.38	—
England	1.2	0.57	0.29	0.34
Germany	0.9	0.52	0.16	0.22
Austria	1.3	0.56	—	0.74
Spain	0.3	0.18	0.08	0.04

Source: Own elaboration from Huber et al. (2009: 99) Table 7.1.

Spanish policymakers, who had already opted for universal coverage, could choose among three institutional arrangements, given that English long-term care is means-tested. Each of them has different effects on the status of long-term care jobs, women's employment opportunities and household caring burdens. The intensity of informal care provided by relatives differs among nations, depending on how long-term care has been arranged. The elasticity of the women's time allocated to informal care is more sensitive to social expenditure on formal services than to expenditure on cash transfers (Sarasa 2008), making the provision of services more efficient than cash transfers in reducing women's probability of allocating many hours to adult care. Hence, the intensity of informal care provided by women is the less when the supply of formal services is greater, so much so that the average number of hours of care provided weekly by middle-aged women is 11.6 in Denmark, 14.5 in France, 21.8 in Austria and 31.8 in Spain.[6]

Furthermore, opting for in-kind benefits has better consequences for the status of caring jobs, so improving the working conditions and career opportunities of employed women; and that status declines as the activity shifts from care formally provided by organizations to care formally contracted by beneficiaries and hence to informality. As Simonazzi (2009) describes, Scandinavian nations offer an important supply of formal services provided by relatively skilled and well-paid workers. France has opted to develop a formal but dual labour market: on the one hand trained and skilled workers are employed by organizations where they find career opportunities; on the other hand unskilled and low-paid workers are contracted directly by the recipients of benefits. In Germany and Austria the formal sector is less developed, but it is also divided between qualified and unqualified workers; moreover, the increasing numbers of informal providers,

---

6   Author's own estimates from ECHP (2000).

mainly immigrants, are adding a complex labour segmentation. Finally, Italy and Spain have also experienced a dramatic increase in irregular immigration that has fuelled informal elderly care services (Bettio et al. 2006).

The Spanish Option

The law aproved by the Spanish Parliament guarantees universal coverage to nationals older than six years.[7] It recognizes three degrees of dependency – moderate, severe and great – each divided into two levels of severity. The applicant is assessed as moderately dependent when he or she needs assistance with basic activities of daily life (BADL) at least once a day, or needs intermitent support for personal autonomy. When assistance with BADL is needed two or three times a day and the applicant does not want a permanent carer, then he or she qualifies as severely dependent. Finally, great dependency is reserved for people who need permanent support from a carer. The law implements seven categories of benefit to cover these needs: four in-kind benefits and three cash benefits. In-kind benefits include (*a*) institutional care, (*b*) day and night centres, (*c*) alarm-call service and (*d*) home-help services, the last including personal and household help. Cash benefits include (*e*) vouchers for services contracted in the market when public services are in short supply, (*f*) allowances for hiring personal assistants, especially for greatly dependent disabled young and adults in need of help to be autonomous and to attend education courses or a workplace, and, finally, (*g*) allowances paid to relatives or non-professional carers who may contribute to Social Security.[8] Services are not freely provided since the users have to pay a part of the cost depending on their personal income. This involves a move towards defamilialization inasmuch as services provided before the new law required co-payments assessed in the light of household income rather than personal income.

The law explicitly asserts the priority of in-kind care over any other benefit. Depending on the needs and preferences of beneficiaries, formal services directly supplied by the public sector or by subcontracted private organizations (profit and non-profit) must be provided first, and allowances paid to relatives and other informal workers are limited to exceptional cases. Under exceptional circumstances – such as a supposed initial and transitory period until a network of in-kind care providers can be consolidated – the beneficiary may receive a cash allowance to finance a specific formal care package previously agreed to and controlled by local authorities. Cash allowances not linked to formal carers are paid only in very exceptional situations. Formally, the new Spanish long-term care arrangement looks more similar to the French equivalent than to the German or the Austrian, since in-kind care is planned to be the preferred benefit, allowing a significant reduction in households' burdens and a growth in social services jobs,

---

7   In practice, however, the bulk of beneficiaries are elderly people.
8   A more detailed description of this law can be found in León (2009).

both for the benefit of women with little education. At the same time, it should improve the labour status of many carers, most of them immigrants, engaged by families in the grey market, and it should increase tax and Social Security revenues. However, the implementation of the law has been difficult, and the expansion of cash transfers has undermined the development of social services.

As Table 12.3 shows, 50 per cent of benefits are paid allowances and almost 18 per cent are payments to subsidize institutional help. Only 33 per cent of beneficiaries are receiving services (like home help, vouchers, personal assistants and day/night centres) that help them to remain in their communities without overloading their relatives. That is not the scenario one might have imagined when the law was first passed. Paid allowances were defined as an *exceptional* benefit to be provided only under special conditions, but quite the reverse has been the case. Certainly, three years after the law was passed insufficient services providers are available, and some observers are wondering what is in store for long-term care services. If nothing changes dramatically in the near future, the so-called fourth pillar of the Spanish welfare state will be no more than a rhetorical formula used in a transitory period in the history of Spain's social services. Of course, as of 2010 the law is still not completely implemented since the legislator has provided for a period of eight years until coverage is completed, ending in 2014. However, given that the law is being implemented in phases, focusing benefits on the most dependent during the first years and the less dependent in the last years, what recent data are showing is how benefits have been delivered to most dependent applicants who, by definition, are most in need of services. Hence, one can expect an even greater proportion of cash transfers in the medium term. Furthermore, the background of economic crisis, with its pressure to control the public deficit, does not seem to favour services provision, though it is not clear whether the development of formal long-term care services would be a better or a worse option than cash allowances in times of crisis. Cash allowances generate public expenditure with low tax revenues, while long-term care services generate employment, benefiting households with little education where unemployment has grown more dramatically, and increase tax revenues.

Why has this distortion of goals happened? There are several possible explanations, some of them foreseen by the authors of the White Paper that inspired the law (León 2009). They include the effects of partisan competition in a quasi-federal state, the weakness of the social services infrastructure together with the inadequacy of the bureaucracy, and, last but not least, the persistence of a strong familialistic culture among citizens. We examine these explanations, but it should be understood that no empirical research has been undertaken to test them.

Table 12.3   Benefits provided as at 1 February 2010

Benefit	Number of cases	% of cases
Institutional care	102,208	17.5
Day/night centres	29,816	5.1
Paid allowances	291,664	50.0
Alarm call services	53,437	9.2
Vouchers	39,819	6.8
Home help	62,788	10.8
Personal assistance	693	0.1
Others	3,045	0.5
Total	444,476	100.0

Source: IMSERSO (2009). Available at: http://www.imserso.es/dependencia_01/documentacion/
estadisticas/datos_estadisticos_saad/index.htm.

Partisan and Territorial Competition

Though the previous Conservative government of the Popular Party – PP – had already inquired into the reform of long-term care, the new law was a compromise that the Socialist PSOE had adopted in the electoral campaign of 2004 when it promised to establish a National System of Care for Dependent People that would achieve universal coverage within two parliaments. This proposal was in tune with Spanish public opinion, which overwhelmingly preferred ageing at home rather than in residences, and preferred the state rather than private entities to ensure that option (Walker 1999).

The law won the support of the trade unions and most political parties, except the Catalan and Basque nationalist parties, CiU, PNV and EA, which were against what they judged to be an intrusion of central government power into the regions' responsibilities. The law gives the central government the power to organize long-term care, but this is a disputed issue because health and social services are responsibilities of the autonomous regions, and Social Security benefits are the responsibility of central government. Inasfar as the new long-term care services were defined as Social Security benefits, the responsibility for the programme lay with central government, though the Catalan nationalist party, CiU, has challenged this in the Constitutional Court. Nevertheless, the role of the autonomous regions in developing the law is crucial since they are in charge of implementing it as well as partially funding it. Each beneficiary has a minimum level of need that is covered by central government funding, but the intensity of the benefit is supplemented by the autonomous regions. The regions are in charge of evaluating applicants' degree of dependency and deciding which kind of benefit should be provided to them. Furthermore, how far in-kind care is extended depends on the regional governments' commitment to implementing formal services.

This role for the Autonomous Communities – AACC – has become one of the main obstacles to offering homogeneous benefits throughout the national territory. Each region has its own system of health and social services, with different degrees of development and of coordination; furthermore, some regions are governed by the Popular Party, which in the national Parliament is in strong opposition to the Socialist government; hence, those autonomous regions where the new law has been least developed, such as Madrid, Murcia, Valencia and the Canaries, are all governed by the Popular Party. The number of applications managed in those four autonomous regions range from 1 per cent to 1.7 per cent of the total population, below the national average of 2.5 per cent[9] and far below the number in the most active regions, such as Andalusia (4.11 per cent) or the Basque Country (3.6 per cent).[10]

An Underdeveloped and Rigid System of Social Services

Another serious difficulty in the implementation of the law has been the poor development of social services in Spain. Securing universal coverage of long-term services demands a much higher level of organizational resources and supply of human capital than had been developed in the Autonomous Communities. Such a deficit was probably the cause of the initial chaos, when the assessment and admission of applications lasted a year or more, a problem widely publicized by the media that has contributed to exacerbating public dissatisfaction with the law. Although the Act came into force in January 2007, it was not until May 2007 that citizens could initiate the processes. Certainly, the number of applications has exceeded the provisions of the White Paper, on which the central government based its forecasts, but social services organization has been lacking, too; many regions have not yet received clear protocols on how to handle the demands, the distribution of responsibilities and the coordination of the services. As a result, citizens have made numerous complaints about the lack of information, the slow resolution of cases and the inadequate amount of cash benefits dispensed.

Other difficulties have arisen related to the adaptation of benefits to beneficiaries' needs. Generally speaking, two ways of evaluating needs may be identified among the current programmes of long-term care in several countries. One is led by case managers who maintain continuous contact with dependent persons and adapt resources and services to the evolution of needs, which is hardly predictable among frail elderly people. This way of identifying and following dependent persons' needs is currently followed in the Nordic countries and the UK; it allows services to be adapted to the changing situations of beneficiaries and

---

9   Data obtained from IMSERSO http://www.imserso.es/Presentacion/groups/imserso/documents/binario/solcasaad.pdf.

10   Such an association between the Popular Party and the performance of the new law is not to be understood as a strict political strategy shared by all the regional governments dominated by the party. La Rioja, which is also governed by the PP, is an autonomus regions that is more involved in the performance of the law.

their families. The other way, more rigid and bureaucratic in my view, involves teams of professionals who, after checking applicants' limitations, try to rank them against a closed list of dependency standards as previously defined by the authorities; each rank equates to a number of hours of care or to another measure of need translatable into units of cost. Such a procedure has been implemented in Spain, following examples from other Conservative welfare regimes.

In the Spanish case, once the applicant has been evaluated and accepted, a personal care programme is drawn up in consultation with the beneficiary. However, this procedure gives rise to inconveniencies, as has been made clear by the Committee of Experts which was set up by the government and which the Spanish Parliament asked to assess problems in the implementation of the law (Comité de Expertos 2009). The first inconvenience is the rigidity and the delays in any process to adapt services to changing needs. Each time his or her needs change, the beneficiary must apply for a new evaluation by the Committee of Experts, a procedure that may take months. Second, the way standards have been defined makes it difficult to accept basic and instrumental limitations on daily living arising from mental disability, insanity, and organic illnesses generating episodes of severe loss of autonomy. In addition, the vague definition of available services makes it difficult for the professionals to arrange the optimal combination of them; some Autonomous Communities explicitly refuse such combinations, such as where a person needs some hours of home help in combination with attendance at a day centre. The Committee of Experts also calls attention to the lack of coordination between health and social services.

The historically poor development of social services at the community level, specifically those related to long-term care, in addition to the aforementioned difficulties in assigning specific services, explain why the bulk of benefits take the form of cash transfers to beneficiaries; professionals facing difficulties in assigning services may find easier to pay cash allowances. Moreover, as the services require co-payments from the beneficiaries, some beneficiaries prefer to accept money rather than pay for the service. Last but not least, paid allowances cost local and regional governments less than services.

Traditional Gender Values Rooted in Families

However difficult it may be to assess the effect of cultural values on social behaviour, there is some evidence in favour of the cultural theory of welfare regimes. The same cluster of countries we have identified in relation to childcare and long-term care is identified by Kohli and Albertini (2008) in relation to parental support strategies for adult children's projects, thus supporting the thesis that different values govern intergenerational relationships inside families (Kalmijn and Saraceno 2008).

Some professionals and experts argue that the familialistic culture, still so deeply rooted in Spanish families, explains the long-term care users' preference for cash transfers. The idea is consistent with the still low ratios of middle-aged women active in the labour market, and assumes that such inactive women, because they have been socialized in more traditional gender roles, are likely to look after their parents and parents-in-law.

However, these explanations have weaknesses. The partisan and territorial hypothesis explains well the unequal territorial development of the law, but not why cash transfers are so large. Even autonomous regions governed by centre-left coalitions have been reluctant to provide services instead of cash transfers. The inadequacy of inherited social services and the persistence of familialistic ideology among middle-aged citizens are perhaps the best hypotheses, but they are not free of problems in terms of counterfactuals. Table 12.4 shows some indicators related to long-term care coverage among people older than 64 years and to women active in the labour market for two autonomous regions that share centre-left coalition governments but with different degrees of modernization. Catalonia, richer than Andalusia, began modernizing a long time before Andalusia, and developed a network of social services that is a little larger than Andalusia's. As well, women are more integrated in the formal labour market in Catalonia, which means that the Catalan family is supposed to be less traditional and women less likely to accept the gender division of roles. However, the ratios of long-term care coverage before and after the implementation of the law show that home help has expanded more in Andalusia and cash transfers have increased more in Catalonia. These two cases may be outliers, exceptions of the rule, but they are a signal of warning against a common hypothesis that no one has tested with empirical data.

Path dependency, though strong, is not a deterministic factor preventing the choice of any option other than the inherited one (Crouch and Farrell 2004). Experience in the Netherlands during the 1990s is the best example of how welfare regimes may experience dramatic institutional change (Visser and Hemerijk 1997). But this does not seem to be the case at present with the reform of long-term care in Spain.[11] Nevertheless, why long-term care in Spain has been bound to path dependency is still unknown. Future research is necessary in order to identify how constituencies and expectations created under the familialistic regime are undermining the reform.

Even though long-term care services have not developed as the law intended, some advances in inequality reduction are happening, of course. We do not have yet reliable estimates on the newly generated employment and changes in the distribution of benefits by social strata, but the experience of Germany and Austria may be indicative of the changes taking place. In those countries where the state has been financing semi-formal family-based care work, this kind of work is not replacing formal employment but rather informal family-based care work (Geissler 2005: 312).

---

11   If the trend evident during this first stage does not change, the Spanish long-term care arrangement will be at most similar to the German one. In that case one could say that the care arrangements of different welfare regimes had converged, but there are doubts as to whether conservative and familialistic regimes are really different (Esping-Andersen 1999).

Table 12.4   Long-term care development and gender roles in Andalusia and Catalonia, 2004–2010

	Andalusia		Catalonia	
	2004	*2010*	*2004*	*2010*
Coverage ratios				
Home help	3.5	17.4	3.9	11.8
Cash transfers	na	45.6	na	57.1
Day centres	0.2	na	0.4	na
Institutional care	1.1	na	1.8	na
Women's labour activity ratios by age				
Women 25–54	–	0.7	–	0.8
Women older than 54	–	0.1	–	0.2

Sources: Coverage ratios in 2004: Utrilla de la Hoz (2007). Women's labour activity: INE (2009). Coverage ratios in 2010: own estimation from IMSERSO (2010) and INE (2010).

In Germany, employment in social long-term care services has really grown after the legislative reform in the 1990s. In home-based care services the number of jobs increased by almost three times between 1996 and 2001, and in residential services they more than doubled (Theobald 2004). Furthermore, despite the social class bias of benefit choices, with lower strata choosing cash allowances and upper strata choosing in-kind benefits, Germany and Austria do not suffer such huge inequalities in accessing professional care as southern European countries do (Sarasa and Billingsley 2008).

Conclusion

Long-term care in Spain has been provided mainly by the family, with the state providing a meagre supply of means-tested services and the market covering the needs of the richest families. As a result, an unequal distribution of burdens among social classes and genders has limited women's opportunities in the labour market. Demographic ageing is making clear the limits of such a care regime, and the Spanish state has launched a major reform that could be read as a big step towards defamilialization. However, having been implemented, the reform is showing itself to be more familialistic than the government anticipated. The Spanish case illustrates how difficult it is to escape from path dependency.

The Dependency Law, as it was designed, seemed to represent progress in so far as formal services were planned to lighten women's care burdens and to increase the amount and quality of paid jobs in long-term care. However, the result of its first three years since implementation is disappointing. Several explanations of this failure have been proposed, but none has yet been empirically tested. The way path dependency has exerted its influence in Spanish long-term care is an open field of research.

At the same time, in comparing the Spanish reform with others recently implemented in the European Union, one can conclude that, so far from converging, different care arrangements linked to different welfare regimes are still clearly distinguishable. Certainly, all welfare regimes are accepting a greater involvement of the state in family affairs; all are also introducing programmes dealing with semi-formal care and quasi-markets. But they are still a long way from any convergence, and the trends observed do not alter the structure of family policies that characterized welfare regimes in the second half of the twentieth century.

References

Anttonen, A. and Sipilä, J. 1996. European Social Care Services: Is it Possible to Identify Models? *Journal of European Social Policy*, 6(2), 87–100.

Behning, U. 2005. Changing Long-term Care Regimes: A Six Country Comparison of Directions and Effects, in *Care and Social Integration in European Societies*, edited by B. Pfau-Effinger and B. Geissler. Bristol: Policy Press, 73–91.

Bettio, F. and Plantenga, J. 2004. Comparing Care Regimes in Europe. *Feminist Economics*, 10(1), 85–113.

Bettio, F., Simonazzi, A. and Villa, P. (2006). Change in Care Regimes and Female Migration: The 'Care Drain' in the Mediterranean. *Journal of European Social Policy*, 16(3), 271–85.

Brandt, M., Haberkern, K. and Szydlik, M. 2009. Intergenerational Help and Care in Europe. *European Sociological Review*, 25(5), 585–601.

Burau, V., Theobald, H. and Blank, R.H. 2007. *Governing Home Care: A Cross National Comparison*. Cheltenham: Edward Elgar.

Comas-Herrera, A., Wittenberg, R., Costa-Font, J., Gori, C., Di Maio, A., Patxot, C., Pickard, L., Pozzi, A. and Rothgang, H. 2006. Future Long-term Care Expenditure in Germany, Spain, Italy and the United Kingdom. *Ageing and Society*, 26, 285–302.

Comité de Expertos 2009. *Informe final del grupo de expertos para la evaluación del desarrollo y efectiva aplicación de la Ley 39/2006 14 de diciembre de promoción de la autonomía personal y atención a las personas en situación de dependencia*. Madrid: IMSERSO. [Online] Available at: http://www. imsersomayores.csic.es/documentacion/biblioteca/registro.htm?id=53313 [Accessed: 20 November 2010].

Crouch, C. and Farrell, H. 2004. Breaking the Path of Institutional Development? Alternatives to the New Determinism. *Rationality and Society*, 16(1), 5–43.

Da Roit, B., Le Bihan, B. and Österle, A. 2007. Long-term Care Policies in Italy, Austria and France: Variations in Cash-for-Care Schemes. *Social Policy and Administration*, 41(6), 653–71.

Daatland, S.O. 2009. Taylor, Target, Tinker, Tune. Estrategias recientes en la protección de la dependencia en la vejez bajo el modelo escandinavo del Estado de Bienestar, in *El Tratamiento de la Dependencia en los Regímenes de Bienestar Europeos*, edited by A. Arriba and F.J. Moreno. Madrid: IMSERSO, 145–64.

Daly, M. and Lewis, J. 2000. The Concept of Social Care and the Analysis of Contemporary Welfare States. *British Journal of Sociology*, 51(2), 281–98.

Del Campo, S. and Rodriguez-Brioso, M.M. 2002. La gran transformación de la familia española durante a segunda mitad del siglo XX. *Revista Española de Investigaciones Sociológicas*, 100(2), 103–65.

ECHP. 2000. *European Community Household Panel*. Brussels: Eurostat. [Online] Available at: http://epp.eurostat.ec.europa.eu/portal/page/portal/microdata/ echp [Accessed: 20 November 2010].

Esping-Andersen, G. 1999. *Social Foundations of Post-industrial Economies*. Oxford: Oxford University Press.

Esping-Andersen, G. and Sarasa, S. 2002. The Generational Conflict Reconsidered. *Journal of European Social Policy*, 12(1), 5–21.

Ettner, S.L. 1996. The Opportunity Costs of Elder Care. *Journal of Human Resources*, 31, 189–205.

Giannakouris, K. 2008. Ageing Characterises the Demographic Perspectives of the European Societies, in *EUROSTAT Statistics in Focus. Population and Social Conditions*, 72/2008. Luxembourg: Statistical Office of the European Communities (Eurostat).

Gauthier, A.M. 1996. *The State and the Family. A Comparative Analysis of Family Policies in Industrialized Countries*. Oxford: Oxford University Press.

Geissler, B. 2005. Welfare State and the Family in the Field of Social Care, in *Care and Social Integration in European Societies*, edited by B. Pfau-Effinger and B. Geissler. Bristol: Policy Press, 307–16.

Geissler, B. and Pfau-Effinger, B. 2005. Change in European Care Arrangements, in *Care and Social Integration in European Societies*, edited by B. Pfau-Effinger and B. Geissler. Bristol: Policy Press, 3–20.

Gilbert, N. 2002. *Transformation of the Welfare State*. New York: Oxford University Press.

Gornick, J.C. and Meyers, M.K. 2001. Lesson-drawing in Family Policy: Media Reports and Empirical Evidence about European Developments. *Journal of Comparative Policy Analysis: Research and Practice*, 3, 31–57.

Hall, P. and Soskice, D. 2001. *Varieties of Capitalism: The Institutional Foundations of Comparative Advantatge*. Oxford: Oxford University Press.

Heinicke, K. and Thomsen, S.L. 2010. *The Social Long-term Care Insurance in Germany: Origin, Situation, Threats, and Perspectives*. Mannheim: Centre for European Economic Research Discussion Paper 10–12.

Huber, M., Rodrigues, R., Hoffman, F., Gasior, K. and Marin, B. 2009. *Facts and Figures on Long-term Care. Europe and North America.* Vienna: European Centre for Social Welfare Policy and Research.

IMSERSO (Instituto de Mayores y Servicios Sociales) 2005. *Cuidados a las Personas Mayores en los Hogares Españoles. El entorno familiar.* Madrid: IMSERSO.

IMSERSO 2008. *Las Personas Mayores en España. Informe 2008.* Madrid: IMSERSO.

IMSERSO 2009. *Información estadística del sistema para la autonomía y atención a la dependencia.* Paper presented at the International Expert Meeting on Monitoring Long-term Care for the Elderly. Jerusalem, 7–9 September.

IMSERSO 2010. *Datos estadísticos del sistema para la autonomía y atención a la dependencia.* Madrid: IMSERSO. [Online] Available at: http://www. imserso.es/InterPresent1/groups/imserso/documents/binario/prestarecsaad.pdf [Accessed: 20 November 2010].

INE (Instituto Nacional de Estadística) 1999. *Encuesta sobre Discapacidades, Deficiencias y Estado de Salud. Avance de Resultados.* Madrid: INE.

INE 2009. *Spanish Labour Force Survey.* Madrid: INE.

INE 2010. *Series de Población desde 1996. Cifras Oficiales de la Revisión Anual del Padrón Municipal a 1 de enero de cada año.* Madrid: INE.

Johnson, R.W. and Lo Saso, A.T. 2000. *The Trade-off between Hours of Paid Employment and Time Assistance to Elderly Parents at Midlife.* The Retirement Project. Urban Institute. [Online] Avalaible at: http://www.urban. org [Accessed: 1 November 2010].

Kalmijn, M. and Saraceno, C. 2008. A Comparative Perspective on Intergenerational Support: Responsiveness to Parental Needs in Individualistic and Familialistic Countries. *European Societies*, 10(3), 479–508.

Keck, W. 2008. The Relationship between Children and their Frail Elderly Parents in Different Care Regimes, in *Families, Ageing and Social Policy: Intergenerational Solidarity in European Welfare States*, edited by C. Saraceno. Cheltenham: Edward Elgar.

Knijn, T. and Kremer, M. 1997. Gender and the Caring Dimension of Welfare States: Toward Inclusive Citizenship. *Social Politics. International Studies in Gender, State and Society*, 4(3, Special Issue), 328–61.

Kohli, M. and Albertini, M. 2008. The Family as a Source of Support for Adult Children's Own Family Projects: European Varieties, in *Families, Ageing and Social Policy. Intergenerational Solidarity in European Welfare States*, edited by C. Saraceno. Cheltenham: Edward Elgar, 38–58.

Kröger, T., Anttonen, A. and Sipilä, J. 2003. Social Care in Finland: Stronger and Weaker Forms of Universalism, in *The Young the Old and the State: Social Care Systems in Five Industrial Nations*, edited by. J. Anttonen, J. Baldock and J. Sipilä. Cheltenham: Edward Elgar, 25–54.

León, M. 2009. Recent Developments in Long-term Care in the Spanish Welfare State: Restructuring 'Familistic' Practices. *VII Annual ESPAnet Conference: The Future of the Welfare State.* Urbino, Italy, 17–19 September.

OECD 2005. *Long-term Care for Older People.* Paris: OECD.

Ohmae, K. 1995. *The End of the Nation State: The Rise of Regional Economics.* London: HarperCollins.

Pezzin, L.E. and Steinberg, B. 1999. Intergenerational Household Formation, Female Labour Supply and Informal Caregiving: A Bargaining Approach. *Journal of Human Resources*, 34, 475–503.

Pfau-Effinger, B. and Geissler, B. (eds) 2005. *Care and Social Integration in European Societies.* Bristol: Policy Press.

Rodrik, D. 1997. *Has Globalization Gone Too Far?* Washington, DC: Peterson Institute for International Economics. [Online] Available at: http://bookstore.piie.com/book-store/57.html [Accessed: 20 November 2010].

Sarasa, S. 2003. *Una Propuesta de Servicios Comunitarios de Atención a Personas Mayores.* Madrid: Fundación Alternativas, Documentos de Trabajo 15/2003.

Sarasa, S. 2008. Do Welfare Benefits Affect Women's Choices of Adult Care Giving? *European Sociological Review*, 24(1), 37–51.

Sarasa, S. 2009. Labour Supply and Adult Care-giving. Paper presented at the EQUALSOC/FAMNET Workshop, Berlin, 11–12 May.

Sarasa, S. and Billingsley, S. 2008. Personal and Household Caregiving from Adult Children to Parents and Social Stratification, in *Families, Ageing and Social Policy: Intergenerational Solidarity in European Welfare States*, edited by C. Saraceno. Cheltenham: Edward Elgar.

Simonazzi, A.M. 2009. Care Regimes and National Employment Models. *Cambridge Journal of Economics*, 2, 211–32.

Standing, G. 1999. *Global Labour Flexibility: Seeking Distributive Justice.* Basingstoke: Macmillan.

Theobald, H. 2004. *Care Services for the Elderly in Germany Infrastructure, Access and Utilisation from the Perspective of Different User Groups.* Discussion Paper. Public Health Research Unit. Berlin: Social Science Research Center.

Ungerson, C. 1997. Social Politics and the Commodification of Care. *Social Politics*, 4(3), 362–81.

Utrilla de la Hoz, A. 2007. La financiación de los servicios sociales en las Comunidades Autónomas. *Revista de Estudios Regionales*, 78, 135–60.

Visser, J. and Hemerijck, A. 1997. *A Dutch 'Miracle'.* Amsterdam: Amsterdam University Press.

Walker, A. 1999. *Actitudes hacia el envejecimiento de la población en Europa.* Madrid: IMSERSO.

Wiener, J. 2007. Commentary: Cash and Counselling in an International Context. *Health Services Research*, (42)1, 567–76.

Chapter 13

Tackling Poverty

Luis Ayala

Introduction

There is more poverty in Spain than in most European countries. Despite the huge development of the main redistributive policies of the Welfare State, Spain's income poverty levels and inequality indices stand out among EU Member States. Relative poverty tended to decrease in Spain throughout the period 1973–90; but the initial levels were so high that the proportion of households below the poverty threshold was still greater than in other Western countries. Poverty rates remained practically unchanged when the Spanish economy experienced a strong and rapid economic expansion in the following decades.

There are many reasons why poverty is still widespread in Spain. On the one hand, unemployment is much higher in Spain than in Western Europe. Although there is no evidence of statistical association between higher unemployment rates and higher poverty rates – because of unemployment benefits and the singular intra-household distribution of unemployment – surveys show especially high levels of poverty in those households with more unemployed individuals. On the other hand, there are remarkable singularities of social protection in Spain regarding both the general levels of social expenditure and the institutional design of policies that specifically target low-income households. The system of anti-poverty policies is more fragmented, and the scope of most actions aimed at combating social exclusion is more limited than their equivalents in other European countries. These features are at the heart of both the visible barriers to claimants becoming self-sufficient and the persistent inequalities among recipients.

These difficulties do not, however, mean that the anti-poverty system has not undergone substantial reforms. As compared with the schemes in force at the beginning of the 1980s there is no doubt that the system has expanded substantially in terms of both recipients and expenditure, and has become more complex. Both outcomes are intrinsically tied to a long-standing strategy of enlarging social protection by gradually enforcing selectivity in benefits. As a result, there is a wide range of benefits, with different population groups receiving unequal levels of coverage. As well, rather large territorial inequalities are embedded in the current system. Since their beginning, regional initiatives have been handicapped by serious problems of coordination and financing. This shortcoming, over and above the natural regional differences, has produced a mosaic of highly varied schemes, with a striking disparity of regulations and results.

These general characteristics of the long-term development of the Spanish anti-poverty system raise numerous interesting questions. Has the safety net grown enough to substantially reduce inequality and poverty? Which population groups receive higher coverage? Are there sizeable territorial inequalities in benefits? Which are the main challenges the system faces in an era of economic downturn? These and other questions make it necessary to review different issues related to the programmes' characteristics – including expenditure trends, adequacy or future challenges – as well as the changes in poverty in the Spanish society.

This chapter analyses the main characteristics and results of this model of guaranteeing sufficient resources to low-income households. First, we review the long-term changes in poverty levels and patterns, using available micro-data. Second, we review the most relevant shifts in the design of welfare policies in Spain. We focus narrowly on the results of the system in terms of poverty reduction. We then evaluate the main challenges faced by welfare policies in Spain. The chapter ends with a brief list of conclusions.

Long-term Changes in Poverty

Poverty Trends

A global analysis of the effects of social policies on poverty requires first a comprehensive picture of long-term changes in social needs and economic insecurity. Over recent years, the development of survey and administrative data in many countries has contributed to a better understanding of the changes in poverty and their underlying causes. In Spain, the scarcity of consistent data has constituted a major constraint on the study of poverty, severely limiting the range of possible answers to basic questions about changes in poverty.

Empirical work prior to the development of the European Community Household Panel (ECHP) and the Living Conditions Survey (ECV) mainly relied on the Family Budget Surveys (EPFs). These surveys – conducted in 1973/4, 1980/81 and 1990/91 – are the only sources offering comparable data on income poverty for the 1970s and 1980s. There is substantial agreement about changes in poverty in these decades. Many studies using the EPFs have confirmed two characteristic patterns of change from the early 1970s to the 1990s.[1] First, relative poverty tended to decrease in Spain throughout the period 1973–80. Poverty changes, however, were not constant over these two decades because

---

1   See for instance Ruiz-Castillo (1987); Bosch, Escribano and Sánchez (1989); Ayala, Martínez and Ruiz-Huerta (1993); García Lizana and Martín Reyes (1994); Ruiz-Huerta and Martínez (1994); Martín-Guzmán (1996); and Cantó (1997). These studies generally define the poverty line as half the equivalent average income.

of simultaneous countervailing forces. During the 1970s the unemployment rate grew steadily after a period of near-full employment. However, a consistent growth in earnings and the late development of certain basic welfare state services led to a slight reduction of poverty. Second, poverty fell sharply during the 1980s. Changes were not uniform throughout the whole period, with the sign and magnitude of the reduction varying significantly between the two halves of the decade. Job destruction caused poverty indicators to remain high in the early 1980s. The second half of the decade was characterized by the opposite trend, with a very marked decrease in the unemployment rate and an increase in social spending. Poverty tended to fall significantly, at a considerably higher rate than that experienced in other European countries in the same period.

The analysis of long-term changes in poverty after 1990 is not an easy task. There are no homogeneous Datasets to identify possible changes. For many years no new Family Budget Surveys were conducted, and the new Datasets that were compiled some years later do not cover the complete period and were developed with different methodologies. It is possible, however, to put together the different pieces of information in order to collect and interpret the changes in poverty from 1990 up to 2010. A Continuous Family Budget Survey (ECPF) covered the period between the mid-1980s and the mid-1990s. This survey was replaced by a new one covering the next 10 years. As in other European countries, the European Community Household Panel (ECHP) was conducted in Spain from 1993 to 2000. This survey was replaced by the new Living Conditions Survey (ECV); and recently an annual Family Budget Survey with a similar sample to those of the basic EPFs has been also developed.

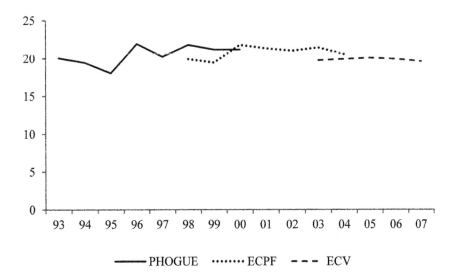

Figure 13.1   Poverty rates in Spain, 1993–2007

The joint analysis of these data sets shows a certain shift in the long-term trends of poverty in Spain (Figure 13.1). The set of poverty measures estimated show a rather stable trend from the mid-1990s. Cantó, Del Río and Gradín (2003) found a moderate reversal of poverty trends in 1985–95 using the ECPF. Between 1985 and 1992 a substantial increase in earnings and employment resulted in declining poverty rates. A sluggish economy in 1993–4 gave rise to an upsurge of poverty. Martínez, Ruiz-Huerta and Ayala (1998) reached a similar conclusion for 1990–95 using the same data set. Oliver, Ramos and Raymond (2001) also found negative growth rates of income among the lowest deciles in the first half of the 1990s using the ECPF. Available evidence, therefore, shows a halt in the historical trend of poverty reduction in the first half of the 1990s. Although it cannot be said that there was a notable increase of poverty during this period, there was a break in the downward trend. Neither the vulnerability generated by extremely high unemployment rates – close to 25 per cent – nor the stringent reforms of unemployment benefits could be offset by the gradual introduction of new means-tested benefits.

There is no strong consensus about the changes in later years. The mild recession of 1992–4 was followed by strong aggregate growth from 1995 to 2007. A natural hypothesis should be that poverty fell. A stylized fact of income distribution processes in Spain had so far been the lessening of inequality and poverty in periods of economic growth. GDP growth rates were increasing from 1995 to 2007, and dramatic employment growth could be expected to pull thousands of households out of poverty. However, the available data from ECHP and ECV show that poverty rates were rather stable from the mid-1990s to 2007, just when economic expansion came to a halt.

The observed stability in poverty rates raises questions about some of the traditional assumptions in analyses of long-term poverty in Spain. First, although there were no marked changes in poverty during 2000–2007, there was a break in the trend towards lower poverty rates during 1973–93. Second, for the first time poverty did not fall in a period of economic growth. It must be stressed that the strong employment growth that took place in this period was not translated into falls in poverty and inequality. A substantial part of the growth was based on low-wage jobs and fixed-term contracts. Third, in contrast to the trend towards social convergence in the 1980s, when most European countries registered higher inequality and poverty rates, the gap between Spanish poverty rates and the EU average widened. Figure 13.2 gives general support to the notion that the level of poverty in Spain remains among the highest in EU countries. Spain has a 33 per cent higher risk of income poverty than the EU-25. The gap has remained stable in recent years, and only four countries among the 27 Member Estates have a higher incidence of poverty.

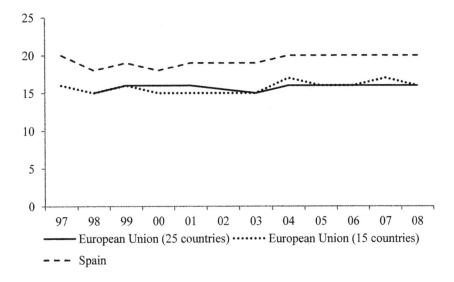

Figure 13.2 Poverty rates in the European Union, 1997–2008

A final issue is a somewhat permanent characteristic of poverty: there is still a segment of severe poverty (households whose income is below 30 per cent of the median income) in the Spanish social structure. Our own estimates with the new Family Budget Survey are of an incidence of this risk of poverty in the range of 2.5–3.0 per cent (Table 13.1). This poverty risk has fallen at a faster rate than the one resulting from the standard thresholds. However, more than one million people in Spain are still facing severe difficulties in meeting basic needs. A similar percentage – around 3 per cent – is also found by different studies analysing chronicity in Spanish poverty (Cantó, Gradín and del Río 2009).

Table 13.1   Poverty rates in Spain, 1980–2008

	60% median income	30% median income
1980	19.0	3.5
1990	16.9	2.7
2008	17.9	2.3

Source: Family Budget Survey.

In sum, Spain still has one of the highest levels of poverty among EU countries. Poverty did not fall in the extended period of economic growth; and there also is a nucleus of severe poverty that the spread of income support policies seems not to have substantially alleviated. All these traits could have been exacerbated by the economic downturn that started in 2007. Although there is no updated information on poverty indicators showing the effects of the current economic crisis, it is possible to infer from indirect measures a worsening of poverty rates. In recession periods, the change in the number of unemployed heads of households or of jobless households has been a good predictor of poverty in Spain (Ayala and Palacio 2000). Updated information on these variables allows us to foresee an upsurge in the incidence of poverty.

Changes in Poverty Patterns

A key question in the analysis of possible interactions between poverty and social policy in Spain is whether changes in poverty patterns have increased the potential demand for social benefits. The aforementioned sources, administrative records and research studies agree in describing a set of common features in poverty patterns in Spain over time. The most relevant is a change in some of the basic features of the structure of poverty in the last decades. In terms of demographics, the main changes have been a double reversal of poverty profiles by age group, the consolidation of a high risk of poverty in households headed by women, the difficulties of families of extreme sizes and the drastic increase in poverty among single-parent households.

On the first issue, one outstanding feature of the changing poverty profiles in Spain has been the particular evolution of the poverty risk of the elderly. At the beginning of the 1990s, information available from EPF-90 and ECHP-93 showed for the first time a reversal of the traditional picture of higher poverty rates among the elderly. Substantial improvements in the coverage of transfers for people aged over 65 had turned around the position of this group, reducing its poverty rate systematically well below the average. Twenty years later, however, the positions had been inverted again (see Table 13.2). The growth of social benefits was noticeably lower than the improvement in median income.

On the other side of the population pyramid, child poverty has also become well established in the Spanish social structure. Since 1990, Spain has one of the highest child poverty rates in the European Union. Family benefits that are very low by European standards and a growing dependency of families with children on labour outcomes are at the heart of this vulnerability. Youth poverty is another of the disadvantageous social processes that have become well-established in recent decades. Spiraling housing prices, employment instability and high unemployment rates have led to a glut of youths stuck at home.

Table 13.2 Changes in poverty patterns, 1980–2008

	EPF 80–81	**EPF 90–91**	**EPF 2008**
Gender			
Male	18.95	16.86	17.48
Female	19.11	16.93	18.41
Age			
< 18	21.65	21.60	23.13
18–65	16.74	15.00	15.28
> 65	22.02	14.51	23.42
Gender and age			
< 18, male	21.37	22.11	22.77
< 18, female	21.94	21.05	23.50
18–65, male	16.66	14.45	14.77
18–65, female	16.83	15.54	15.80
> 65, male	23.45	15.38	23.54
> 65, female	20.95	13.83	23.32
Household size			
1	27.33	20.52	18.61
2	20.91	19.83	17.82
3	12.47	10.18	10.84
4	11.63	10.28	16.39
5	15.87	16.66	23.81
6	20.08	20.52	31.34
7	30.72	32.04	45.43
Household composition			
Single person, > 65	30.17	19.06	26.94
Single person, < 65	23.06	23.11	9.44
Individual or couple, > 65, no children	31.86	25.00	30.61
Individual or couple, < 65, no children	14.30	14.23	7.23
Single parent	24.79	44.70	38.94

Table 13.2   Continued

	EPF 80–81	EPF 90–91	EPF 2008
Educational level of household head			
Illiterate	48.37	43.34	57.67
Without formal education	32.68	26.65	30.89
Primary education	6.66	12.59	19.70
Secondary education	2.18	7.85	11.39
Technical secondary	2.80	6.98	10.20
Pre-university level	2.23	2.13	5.72
University education	0.52	3.27	2.61
Labour force status of household head			
Employed	14.48	9.10	13.45
Unemployed	46.09	47.65	55.55
Retired	32.50	14.94	19.67
Total	**19.03**	**16.89**	**17.94**

Source: Family Budget Survey.

The increase in rates among single-parent households is also a noticeable trait of the new pattern of poverty in Spain. Unlike the situation at the beginning of the 1990s, when this group was marginal among household structures, its number has increased, although it is lower than in other European countries, as is its poverty, which has registered the greatest rate of growth among the demographic categories.

As for education and labour, the main changes have been a marked process of differentiation in the labour market, caused by the high proportion of fixed-term contracts, the increase in low-wage jobs and the changes in the risk of poverty of people with university-level qualifications. It cannot be said, however, that earnings differences have widened since 1990. The increase in educational attainment compensated for differences in income among groups with different levels of education. Another important change is the incidence of poverty among households with employed heads. In the 1980s, the rise in youth unemployment was not translated into drastic increases in income inequality or poverty, because most of these situations were mitigated through the intra-household distribution of unemployment. From the early 1990s, however, the specific poverty rates for households with unemployed heads have reached their highest levels ever.

A last relevant dimension in the analysis of changes in poverty in Spain is their territorial distribution. The changes have been less visible in this respect, although poverty has become more concentrated in certain areas of the country. The results for rural areas and large urban areas differ markedly.

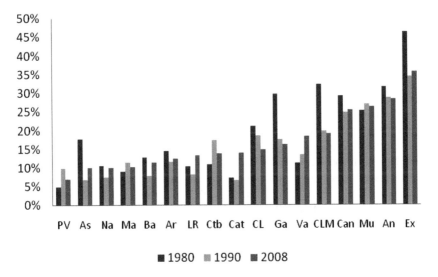

Figure 13.3 Regional poverty rates, 1980–2008

In rural areas, the exodus of the young has led to the gradual aging of the population, which is relatively well-covered economically by the social protection system, although with severe limits to substantially reduce the extension of relative income poverty. In large urban areas, some new forms of poverty have been observed, such as the aforementioned increase in single-parent families, and wage earners with incomes below the poverty threshold. The main characteristic, however, is the persistence of a very well-defined map of poverty. Although poverty has become less concentrated than in the 1980s, there is still a substantial regional dispersion of rates (Figure 13.3). Furthermore, the available evidence shows a clear linear relationship with the regional mean level of income for the different poverty measures, with the richest regions having substantially lower indicators.

Means-tested Benefits and Poverty

The Mosaic of Welfare Benefits in Spain

The Spanish system of social protection has drastically changed over recent decades, and a variety of forces have shaped government policy. It is usually argued that changes in unemployment determine the ratio of welfare benefits claimants to the total population. Both the number of social assistance claimants and the number of unemployment grew during the 1980s. Whereas there was certain asymmetrical behaviour between unemployment rates and the relative volume of assistance-type benefits, these indicators evolved similarly during the 1990s. After the mid-1990s, the relative importance of assistance benefits fell, although more moderately than unemployment. The economic crisis of the last few years, however, has placed the system under unprecedented stress.

Economic conditions are not the only reason for changes in the number and types of welfare benefits in Spain.[2] A characteristic trait of the system of means-tested benefits has been the gradual coverage of different demographic groups by means of specific welfare subsystems. From the mid-1980s, there has been an attempt to resolve the apparent contradiction between two objectives that seem hard to reconcile, namely, the desire to make the various welfare benefits universal and the need to contain the increase in public spending. The solution was to increase the coverage of social needs with those benefits that led to the lowest possible public expenditure (Rodríguez Cabrero 2004). This strategy has also been reinforced by strong ideological pressure to make welfare spending more selective.

The expansion of the system has not been sufficient, however, to guarantee a safety net offering universal coverage. The Spanish case is a good example of the difficulty of institutionally ensuring the universal right to a minimum income. Despite the reduction in poverty in recent decades described above, a significant number of Spanish households still suffer from economic insecurity. This reality raises doubts about the current organization of social protection and requires possible alternatives to be proposed. Two questions arise regarding the possible shaping of policy. The first relates to the current structure of non-contributory income-maintenance programmes and their evolution in recent years. The second has to do with the redistributive effect of the system and the impact of means-tested benefits on poverty.

On the first issue, the majority of studies on the development of the welfare state in Spain have concluded that the political transition provided a definitive stimulus to the consolidation of the public provision of welfare. While some basic guarantees and social rights already existed in the 1960s, increasing demands for their universalization in the framework of political change and, above all, social consensus linked to the restoration of democracy accelerated the consolidation of some of the fundamental institutions of a modern welfare state. Initially, contributory benefits were considerably widened, both in terms of levels and the number of beneficiaries. Since the mid-1980s, however, means-tested cash benefits have become increasingly relevant. Means-tested benefits have been set at a much lower level than contributory benefits for reasons of efficiency and economic viability, thereby containing public expenditure.

---

2   Focusing only on minimum income benefits, Ayala and Pérez (2005) found that both unemployment and institutional variables were strong and significant factors explaining caseloads.

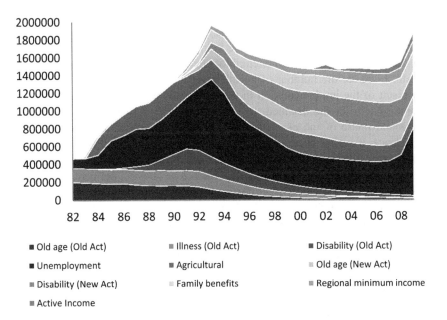

Figure 13.4 Number of means-tested benefits

Changes in the labour market were especially important in driving the growth of means-tested benefits. The problems of job creation stimulated the establishment of alternative mechanisms to guarantee incomes; non-contributory protection for the unemployed increased notably, while the increase in temporary work and the extension of the informal economy added new pressures. The result was an increase in the number of means-tested benefits. This led to a certain softening of social conflict, but created additional social segmentation by adding differences in the types of income guarantee to existing differences in earnings and income mobility. Furthermore, the creation of new benefits was insufficiently coordinated, producing a highly complex non-contributory system in which different benefits aimed at the same groups still coexist. These are, in general, highly selective benefits, whose principal criteria of eligibility are age, illness and economic activity.

The figures clearly demonstrate the aforementioned complexity of non-contributory protection and its sharp growth,[3] its total quantity having multiplied almost fourfold since the mid-1980s (Figure 13.4). It is possible to demarcate

---

3   Although not included in Figure 13.4, retirement pensions include a very high proportion of supplements that are non-contributory.

distinct stages in the expansion of non-contributory benefit programmes.[4] The first half of the 1980s may be considered as an initial period of expansion, with the number of benefits doubling. In the following five years, the reduction in the rate of unemployment and tighter eligibility requirements caused a more moderate growth. Even so, the number of beneficiaries increased by over half a million, as a result of the implementation in the mid-1980s of the guaranteed minimum income system for the disabled. It was to be in the first half of the 1990s that the second phase of the expansion of non-contributory benefits occurred. The coexistence of earlier benefits with the new Non-contributory Pensions Act and the new regional minimum income schemes was the primary cause of the dramatic increase in the number of beneficiaries, which rose above 5 per cent of the total population. Another factor was the decline in economic activity and in the capacity to create jobs, to which must be added various cost-cutting measures affecting the contributory protection scheme's coverage of the unemployed, which transferred an increasing number of beneficiaries to the non-contributory system. The economic recovery that followed gave rise to a long period of relative stability. From 2008, however, the economic crisis pushed the figures upward again.

The final result of this expansion is a close-woven network of welfare benefits. Despite attempts at rationalization, a complex mixture of overlapping benefits survives, and significant gaps in the system's overall coverage persist. The most important of the latter is probably the lack of a general minimum income mechanism, a shortcoming that deprives specific groups – a significant number of temporary workers, the unemployed who have exhausted their unemployment benefit entitlements or have not fulfilled the minimum requirements for eligibility, elderly people aged under 65 with no means of their own, some disabled individuals and young people unable to enter the labour market – of any form of minimum income guarantee, depending on where they live.

Poverty Alleviation

One of the questions arising from the complexity of the current structure of social transfers in Spain is whether the development of benefits has been efficient in reducing the risk of poverty. Although the inequality and poverty effects of public expenditure are now examined relatively infrequently in Spain, the available evidence shows contemporary results that are similar to those found in previous decades. Many studies undertaken some years ago showed that social expenditure had redistributive effects and that non-contributory benefits in particular were remarkable progressive, and, moreover, increasingly so in the 1980s. Most of the empirical work focused on the 1980s and confirmed this redistributive effect and its broadening over that decade (Gimeno 1993, Bandrés 1993). The growth of the relative share of social transfers in households' income gave rise

---

4	A detailed review of the institutional process can be found in Arriba and Guinea (2009).

to an unprecedented redistributive effect, affecting not only generations but also individuals and regions. The analysis of purely means-tested benefits made clear their progressivity (Pazos and Salas 1996; Martín-Guzmán, Bellido and Jano 1995).

Existing studies from the 1990s also showed an improvement in beneficiaries' purchasing power resulting from means-tested benefits, which, however, did not produce significant decreases in inequality (Ayala and Martínez 2005). In fact, although the small sums alleviated severe poverty, they were insufficient to reduce moderate poverty, as the income of the poor was increasingly falling below that of the rest of the population.

Do these singularities still hold in the current setting? Table 13.3 presents estimates of poverty rates before (no attention is paid to possible modifications in individual behaviour which would be implied by such a radical change) and after social transfers. The results mirrors those traditionally obtained from other sources. Poverty rates 'after' transfers fall to a half of those simulated with pre-transfer income. There are, however, large age differences in the poverty-reducing effects of benefits. While children register reductions in the range of 20–25 per cent, poverty falls to one third of the initial value among people aged over 65. The reduction in poverty is smaller than that observed in previous periods; our own estimates with the ECHP reveal that in the mid-1990s the effect was close to 60 per cent. These differences are smaller when stricter poverty thresholds are used. This last result confirms the reality of the problem that social benefits do less to sustain the growth rate of average incomes than to alleviate the crudest situations of economic insecurity.

A key issue is that each of the benefits has a different impact on poverty reduction. The complex net of benefits may cause fragmentation in terms of adequacy and effectiveness. As stressed by Laparra (2009), guaranteed minimum income schemes have been created at very different moments of time and backed by different types of political and ideological justification. On the one hand, individuals who are absent from the labour market – the disabled and the elderly people – are clearly differentiated from those who are potentially active.

Table 13.3   Risk of poverty 'before' and 'after' transfers, 2004–2008

	2004		2008	
	Before transfers	*After transfers*	*Before transfers*	*After transfers*
Total	41.3	19.9	38.3	19.6
Children	32.2	24.3	29.8	24.0
Elderly	84.9	29.6	83.1	27.6

Source: Living Conditions Survey.

On the other hand, there have been different routes to access to the available benefits as some programmes have been defined as natural extensions of contributory protection while other systems have been designed with no regard whatsoever to Social Security benefits. As a result, the current net of subsystems yields substantial differences in both the concepts of social need that justified the benefit and the economic protection received by each household.

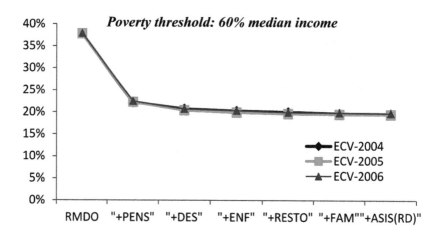

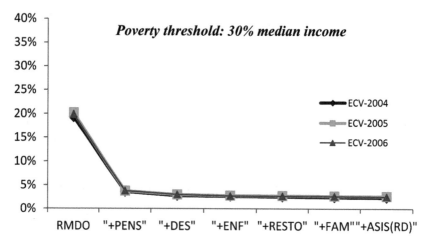

Figure 13.5   Cumulative impact of social benefits on poverty, 2004–2006

Figure 13.5 differentiates the effects of each social benefit on poverty reduction. First, the results confirm the aforementioned claim that the system drastically reduces severe poverty, even though a non-negligible proportion of households below the threshold (3 per cent) persists. Second, social transfers also contribute to reducing more moderate forms of poverty, but the effects are rather smaller than in the case of severe poverty. Third, pensions still are the main mechanism for reducing poverty in Spain. This result also holds in other countries and can be considered a stylized fact of social protection. The poverty incidence of other benefits is clearly lower, with welfare benefits having very limited effects.

A final question is the prospects for the continuity of the current effects of the system. A key issue for achieving higher levels of success in fighting poverty is how to close the gap between social benefits and average incomes. In fact, the usual way to test the impact of social transfers – including means-tested benefits – on poverty is to estimate the gap between average amounts of benefits and the mean or median income. Figure 13.6 plots the ratio of monthly benefits as a proportion of per capita GDP. The result somewhat contradicts the assumption of a continuous improvement of benefits over time – an outcome that holds in the case when benefits are compared to inflation or changes in the minimum wage. Social benefits have not only not followed the path of average incomes but the gap has widened since the mid-1990s. Only in very recent years has the gap shrunk, because of higher minimum pensions, the economic crisis and the sluggish growth in per capita income.

Three Dilemmas of Anti-poverty Policies in Spain

Despite the remarkable growth of means-tested benefits in Spain, the system is still characterized by comparatively low adequacy, its potential impact on poverty is diminished by the heterogeneity and fragmentation of sub-programmes, and the expansion did not keep up to pace with the country's economic growth. Inequality embedded in regional minimum income programmes also acts as a limit to poverty reduction. This set of difficulties necessarily restricts the possibilities of the system and introduces the need for reform.

While it is important to emphasize that changes are necessary from adequacy and equity perspectives, the need for reform goes far deeper. The Spanish welfare state faces challenges that are similar to those in most Western countries, where, among the different lines of reform, welfare programmes have been modified in the light of core beliefs about work and personal responsibility (Blank and Haskins 2001). The major economic rationale for welfare reform in many countries has revolved around encouraging labour-market participation and transitions from welfare to work. The work incentives of welfare programmes have been a subject of increasing concern to voters and policymakers, and in most countries increasingly stringent requirements to participate in welfare-to-work programmes have been imposed.

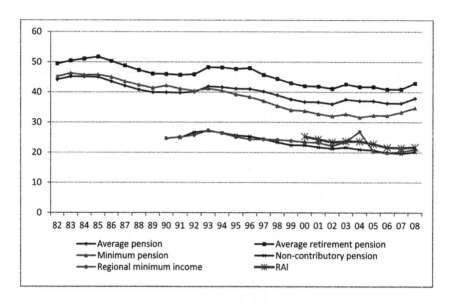

Figure 13.6   Average benefits as a proportion of per capita GDP

There is no doubt that the dynamics of participation is a major public concern, and Spain is no exception in the European and international contexts. Existing findings for current programmes, however, are subject to a great deal of uncertainty. There is therefore a need for reform that addresses the necessity of reducing the current fragmentation of the system, the problem of territorial inequality, and the need to improve the economic situation and labour opportunities of low-income families.

Towards a Unified Safety Net?

One of the most striking paradoxes in the development of means-tested benefits in Spain is the lack of a last-resort safety net for households or individuals who have exhausted their entitlement to other economics resources. The Spanish safety net has been developed on a fragmented and cumulative basis; but the existence of a varied set of specific non-contributory minima has not helped to define an ultimate net of economic security with similar objectives and a similar outreach to those of other countries in the European Union (Moreno 2007). Progressive development of the regional minimum-income systems has hardly made up for this deficiency. As a result, the coverage of certain households – especially those of the long-term unemployed – largely depends on the differing extent of regional minimum-income schemes. A first issue in the reform of welfare programmes in

Spain is therefore how to ensure a guaranteed income for any individual at risk of poverty.

There is also a growing, if somewhat less heated, debate about the equity problems that may be caused by the current level of fragmentation. The observed differences in the poverty incidence of each benefit are strongly linked to the different level of economic security provided in each case. It seems necessary to reform the system in order to define more homogeneous criteria that avoid current inequalities. Existing differences give rise to different rights among low-income households, causing severe horizontal equity problems.

Therefore, a global reform of the system seems reasonable, addressing the double necessity of guaranteeing a minimum level of resources and harmonizing the different amounts embedded in the current variety of means-tested programmes. This reform should also include tackle other causes of the observed fragmentation. Access criteria, protection levels, and even equivalence scales should be made more uniform. A more integrated system is needed that takes into account both contributory and non-contributory benefits in order to make the system more coherent.

These reforms, however, while contributing to a reduction of internal inequalities, are not enough to substantially improve the adequacy of the system. As mentioned, the economic protection provided by most benefits falls far short of the level required to substantially reduce poverty. Further steps should be taken towards higher levels of benefits, most of which clearly below European standards. Especially striking are the general minimum-income programmes, whose levels are much lower in Spain than in other EU countries (Figure 13.7).

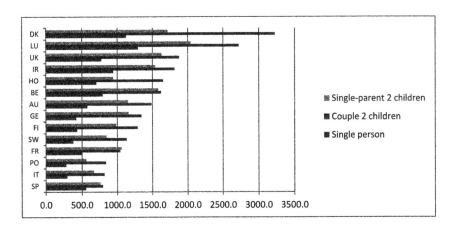

**Figure 13.7   General minimum income benefits in
purchasing power parity, 2009**

Source: MISSOC.

These disparities go beyond the different levels of income – and poverty thresholds – in each country. Only with increased benefits will these programmes lift a higher proportion of households over the poverty line.

Economic Security in a Decentralized Welfare State

As stated above, the general risk of poverty is alleviated only by regional schemes. In the second half of the 1980s, a controversial debate took place over the best design for these programmes. The crucial question was how to reconcile the need to fill a historic gap in a late-developing welfare state with the increasing territorial decentralization of social protection. It was finally decided that the regional governments – to which the Constitution granted the social protection function – should be solely responsible for the development of programmes of this type in their respective territories. Unlike other government programmes, such as social services, the design lacked inter-territorial coordination mechanisms. This process provoked great controversy and heated debates about the potential of the Autonomous Communities to combat poverty.

Since their beginning, regional initiatives have been handicapped by serious problems of coordination and financing. This shortcoming, over and above natural regional differences, has produced a mosaic of highly varied schemes, with a striking disparity of regulations and results, and above all a certain widening of the differences the poorest citizens experience with regard to rights and resources. However, there have been important achievements as well. The number of people incorporated into welfare programmes testifies to their growing scope and their contribution to regional social action (Figure 13.8). Not only does a wide range of experience exist, but the development of 'insertion programmes' has been an important advance in social intervention and above all in innovative strategies providing an alternative to the traditional methods of the social services.[5]

Whatever the lessons this extreme model of fiscal federalism may hold, the key question is whether differences in regional levels of wealth or income explain the notable inequality existing in the coverage offered. In other words, regions with lower poverty rates could be those offering wider coverage as a result of their greater budgetary endowment. There are different ways to analyse the coverage of these programmes. The standard approach pays attention to differences in benefits, and the prototypical model focuses on the possibility of a strong relationship between benefit levels and the average income in each region (Moffitt 2003; Baicker 2005).

---

5   'Insertion' is the general term used to summarize the different types of activities aimed at improving life and labour skills of participants. In general terms, it means higher levels of social participation.

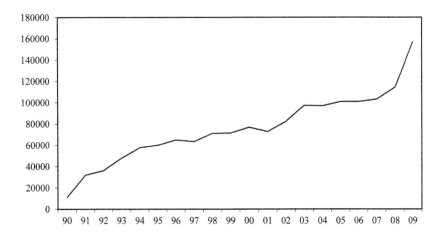

Figure 13.8 Number of recipients of regional minimum income benefits, 1990–2009

This approach paints only half the picture. Some regions can offer high benefits but the proportion of poor households within the programme can be very small. Two measures of adequacy and population coverage can be identified. The more closely the value of the benefit corresponds to the poverty threshold, the more adequate the programme will be. The population coverage will be greater the more recipients there are as a proportion of poor individuals in each region (pseudo take-up). Poverty thresholds can be estimated using the Living Conditions Survey. Potential recipients can be estimated using as a reference the proportion of households in each region with no earnings and not receiving unemployment or welfare benefits (Labour Force Survey).

The examination of both adequacy and population coverage confirms the hypothesis of significant regional inequalities. Whether one considers economic sufficiency or the population at risk covered by the programmes, there is a linear relationship with regional income. In general terms, the regions with greatest financial resources have the highest rates of population and economic coverage, whereas regions with lower levels of income have lower rates. Furthermore, these inequalities, far from decreasing with the development of the programmes, have instead become greater since 2000.

Inequality in the social entitlements of poor people in various regions and the lack of budget resources in other regions make coordination necessary. This is a complex matter, given the clash of rights that characterizes Spain's constitutional laws on this topic. Although these laws clearly prescribe that social assistance is the sole responsibility of the Autonomous Communities, they equally clearly prescribe that central government must guarantee sufficient social assistance and benefits if there is a need to do so.

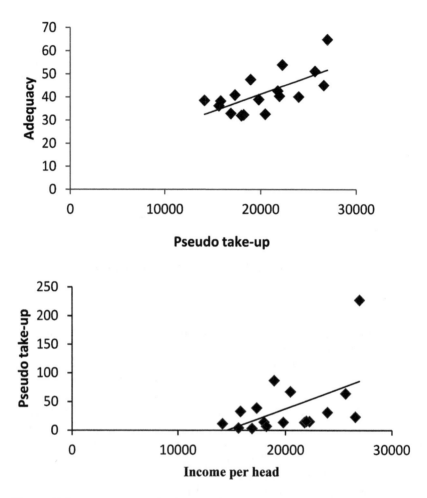

Figure 13.9   **Adequacy and take-up of minimum income programmes by regional per capita income, 2008**

Moreover, most means-tested benefits are currently the responsibility of the central government. Above all, the Constitution itself clearly establishes the need to regulate the basic conditions that guarantee the equality of all Spaniards when exercising their rights. An example here is in the field of social services, for which an agreement was reached at the three levels of government – central, regional and local – to promote the homogenization of basic features of the various regulations and to guarantee at least some common minimum levels of protection for all citizens.

Reconciling Employment and Social Protection

One of the strongest pressures on the design of these policies in Spain has been the conviction that the programmes might encourage behaviour leading to dependency on public social assistance. This assumption contrasts with a general lack of knowledge about the factors that determine the dynamics of social assistance and the extent of chronic poverty in Spain. The pattern revealed by the available studies analysing transitory and chronic poverty in Spain is one of much mobility – most of it short-range – and not too much chronicity (Barcena and Cowell 2006; Cantó, Gradín and del Río 2009).[6]

Regardless of the real extent of chronicity and dependency, some of the current means-tested benefits were designed to include specific, targeted welfare-to-work initiatives. Among the different benefits, regional minimum incomes are those that have been more directly tailored to improve the recipients' self-sufficiency through the individualized design of 'insertion' measures adjusted to both individual and household characteristics. Participation in these activities is mandatory while recipients are receiving benefits.

From the outset, the intention was that minimum income benefits should differ from other cash benefits through the incorporation of typical proactive labour-market policy features. Just as the administration takes responsibility for making the monetary payment, the beneficiary is in turn to make a commitment to take an active role in activities promoting his or her individual social autonomy. It could even be said that the establishment of these programmes was legitimized through the development of such measures. Nevertheless, it must be noted that while some regions run enhanced large-scale programmes others merely provide cash benefits.

The attempt to make the idea of achieving higher levels of social and labour participation compatible with the more specific goal of providing a guaranteed income has been put into question by policymakers and analysts. From the very beginning, controversy emerged over whether the combined strategy of cash benefits and in-kind services could yield better results than separate policies (Pérez Eransus 2005). In practice, the limited available evidence does not appear to achieve any consensus on whether these programmes are effective. In most regions, few people benefit from those actions. Nevertheless, the programmes yield better results than experiences prior to the implementation of minimum income systems in the various regions. On the one hand, they have favoured processes of social mobilization, channeling the demand for a more mixed way of welfare production. On the other hand, some estimates have found that these programmes produce better results in labour market participation and economic well-being.

---

6 Other studies have examined some features of social benefits duration in Spain (Ahn and Ugidos 1995; García Serrano and Jenkins 2000; Arranz and Muro 2002; Bover, Arellano and Bentolila 2004). Most of these studies focus on the effects of benefits on unemployment duration, and find these effects to be relatively limited.

Our own estimates based on administrative data from some of these programmes and other evaluations carried out in certain regions (Casado and Blasco 2009) seem to confirm these positive effects in terms of both self-sufficiency (Ayala and Rodriguez 2006) and employment and income poverty (Ayala and Rodriguez 2010). Employment effects are substantially greater for those sub-programmes aimed at improving labour opportunities. By increasing employment levels, work-related measures seem successful in moving low-income families away from dependence on welfare policies. However, higher labour participation rates do not seem enough to enable low-income families to achieve better results in terms of material well-being. If the overriding goal of social policy is to reduce material deprivation and social hardship, there is no doubt that work-related policies are not entirely appropriate. A positive result is that participation in work-related activities reduces the probability of re-entering the programmes and increases the off-programme spells. Recidivism is considerably lower in households taking part in these activities, which gives general support to the notion that 'insertion' measures contribute to promoting participants' self-sufficiency.

Empirical evidence suggesting that these public instruments have made low-income households less dependent on government and more self-sufficient does not mean that the programmes are cost-effective. The number of participants in work-related activities is small in many regions; and given the high levels of heterogeneity among recipients, possible inferences should be restricted to certain households. In practice, these strategies can be a solution only for a segment of the recipient population. For the unemployable, an upgrading of life skills through specific non-labour-related interventions may be more efficient.

Conclusions

One of the outstanding characteristics of the Spanish social structure is the persistence of higher levels of poverty than in other European countries. Low levels of social benefits also stand out in the European context; and they are far below the levels needed to achieve adequacy standards. The direction of the causal relationship between these two features is not completely clear. Empirical evidence, however, suggests that the current system of means-tested benefits is clearly inefficient in addressing the problems arising from the high incidence of poverty in Spain.

Available micro-data show a break in poverty trends in Spanish households since the mid-1990s. After some decades of poverty reduction, the rate of poverty stopped falling. It is especially noticeable that strong employment growth was not translated into lower levels of poverty. A non-negligible proportion of employment growth was based on low-wage jobs providing insufficient earnings to avoid income poverty. It must also be noted that, although poverty rates were rather stable from the mid-1990s to the beginning of the economic crisis in 2008, the vulnerability of certain population groups increased. This was the case with the elderly, families with children and single-parent households. Indirect indicators of the effects of the economic downturn also show higher future poverty rates associated with unemployment and joblessness in many households.

An extended system of means-tested benefits has been implemented in an attempt to address some of the social problems associated with the spread of poverty in Spain. The development of new schemes has helped to broaden the social safety net; their benefits are better targeted and involve less public expenditure. However, the expansion of the system has not been enough to provide complete coverage for all households at risk of poverty. The two dominant traits in the evolution of the system over recent decades have been its sharp expansion and its growing complexity. This expansion has not produced a last-resort safety net for disadvantaged households similar to those in most European countries.

Furthermore, the system seems inefficient in substantially reducing the incidence of poverty. While means-tested benefits have helped to alleviate the crudest circumstances of economic insecurity, the results have not been so good for more moderate forms of poverty. In practice, non-contributory benefits evince a much more limited capacity to reduce poverty rates than contributory benefits. Long-term series of per capita income and levels of social benefits also show a widening gap.

In order to achieve better results and increase effectiveness, the current system of means-tested benefits needs to be reformed in three ways. First, it is necessary to harmonize the current mosaic of welfare schemes in order to establish a universal income guarantee; furthermore, benefits should be upgraded to adequacy levels that approximate European standards. Second, there is an urgent need to coordinate the regional programmes of minimum income benefits. The radical model of fiscal federalism in this field causes series problems of horizontal inequity and remarkable inequalities in the social entitlements of poor households. Third, further advances should also be achieved in the design of new strategies that address the problems of jointly improving economic security and work incentives. Some of the current programmes have yielded positive outcomes in terms of higher self-sufficiency; but considerable margins exist for improvement. These changes are not sufficient conditions for substantially reducing poverty but they might at least help public policy to improve the living standards of vulnerable households.

References

Ahn, N. and Ugidos, A. 1995. Duration of Unemployment in Spain: Relative Effects of Unemployment Benefit and Family Characteristics. *Oxford Bulletin of Economics and Statistics*, 57(2), 249–65.

Arranz, J.M. and Muro, J. 2004. An Extra Time Duration Model with Application to Unemployment Duration Under Benefits in Spain. *Hacienda Pública Española*, 171(4), 133–56.

Arriba, A. and Guinea, D. 2009. Protección social, pobreza y exclusión social: el papel de los mecanismos de protección de rentas, in *Políticas y Bienes Sociales*, edited by A. Arriba. Madrid: Fundación FOESSA.

Ayala, L. and Martínez, R. 2005. Las políticas contra la pobreza: factores de cambio y efectos sobre la igualdad, in *Políticas Públicas y Distribución de la Renta*, edited by J. Ruiz-Huerta. Madrid: Fundación BBVA.

Ayala, L., Martínez, R. and Ruiz-Huerta, J. 1993. La distribución de la renta en España en los años ochenta: una perspectiva comparada, in *I Simposio sobre Igualdad y Distribución de la Renta y la Riqueza*, various authors. Madrid: Fundación Argentaria.

Ayala, L. and Palacio, L. 2000. Hogares de baja renta en España: caracterización y determinantes. *Revista de Economía Aplicada*, 8(23), 35–70.

Ayala, L. and Pérez, C. 2005. Macroeconomic Conditions, Institutional Factors and Demographic Structure: What Causes Welfare Caseloads? *Journal of Population Economics*, 18(3), 563–81.

Ayala, L. and Rodríguez, M. 2006. The Latin Model of Welfare: Do 'Insertion Contracts' Reduce Long-term Dependence? *Labour Economics*, 13(6), 799–822.

Ayala, L. and Rodriguez, M. 2010. *Evaluating Welfare Reform under Program Heterogeneity and Alternative Measures of Success*. Instituto de Estudios Fiscales (mimeo).

Baicker, K. 2005. Extensive or Intensive Generosity? The Price and Income Effects of Federal Grants. *Review of Economics and Statistics*, 87(2), 371–84.

Bandrés, E. 1993. La eficacia redistributiva de las prestaciones sociales. Una aproximación al caso español (1980–90). *I Simposio sobre Igualdad y Distribución de la Renta y la Riqueza*, 7. Madrid: Fundación Argentaria.

Bárcena, E. and Cowell, F. 2006. Static and Dynamic Poverty in Spain, 1993–2000. *Hacienda Pública Española*, 179(4), 51–77.

Blank, R. and Haskins, R. (eds) 2001. *The New World of Welfare*. Washington, DC: Brookings Institution Press.

Bosch, A., Escribano, C. and Sánchez, I. 1989. *Evolución de la Pobreza y la Desigualdad en España: Estudio Basado en las Encuestas de Presupuestos Familiares 1973–74 y 1980–81*. Madrid: Instituto Nacional de Estadística.

Bover, O., Arellano, M. and Bentolila, S. 2002. Unemployment Duration, Benefit Duration and the Business Cycle. *Economic Journal*, 112(479), 223–65.

Cantó, O. 1997. Desempleo y Pobreza en la España de los 90. *Papeles de Economía Española*, 78, 88–108.

Cantó, O., Del Río, C. and Gradín, C. 2003. La evolución de la pobreza estática y dinámica en España en el período 1985–1995. *Hacienda Pública Española* 167(4), 87–119.

Cantó, O., Gradín, C. and del Río, C. 2009. La Dinámica de la Pobreza en España: Cronicidad, Transitoriedad y Recurrencia, in *Desigualdad, pobreza y privación*, edited by L. Ayala. Madrid: Fundación FOESSA, 291–342.

Casado, D. and Blasco, J. 2009. *Programa de la Renta Mínima de Inserción. Informe final de evaluación*. Barcelona: Departament de Treball de la Generalitat.

García Lizana, A. and Martín Reyes, G. 1994. La pobreza y su distribución territorial, in *V Informe Sociológico sobre la Situación Social en España*, edited by M. Juárez. Madrid: Fundación FOESSA.

García Serrano, C. and Jenkins, S.P. 2000. *Re-employment Probabilities for Spanish Men: What Role Does the Unemployment Benefit System Play?* ESRC Working Paper No. 2000–17. University of Essex: Institute for Social and Economic Research.

Gimeno, J. 1993. Incidencia del gasto público por niveles de renta (España 1990 vs. 1980). *I Simposio sobre Igualdad y Distribución de la Renta y la Riqueza*, 7. Madrid: Fundación Argentaria.

Laparra, M. 2009. El sistema de garantía de ingresos mínimos en España: un 'sistema' poco sistemático, in *Actuar ante la exclusión: análisis, políticas y herramientas para la inclusión social*, edited by G. Jaraiz. Madrid: Fundación FOESSA, 173–95.

Martínez, R., Ruiz-Huerta, J. and Ayala, L. 1998. Desigualdad y pobreza en la OCDE: una comparación de diez países. *Economiaz*, 40, 42–67.

Martín-Guzmán, P. 1996. *Pobreza y Desigualdad en España*. Madrid: Instituto Nacional de Estadística.

Martín-Guzmán, P., Bellido, N. and Jano, D. 1995. Prestaciones sociales y redistribución en los hogares españoles. *Economistas*, 68, 20–28.

Moffitt, R. 2003. *Means-tested Transfer Programs in the United States*. Washington, DC: National Bureau of Economic Research Conference Report.

Moreno, L. 2007. Europa social, bienestar en España y la 'malla de seguridad', in *Estado de Bienestar y competitividad. La experiencia Europea*, edited by A. Espina. Madrid: Fundación Carolina/Siglo XXI, 445–511.

Oliver, J., Ramos, X. and Raymond, J.L. 2001. Anatomía de la distribución de la renta en España, 1985–1996: La continuidad de la mejora. *Papeles de Economía Española*, 88, 67–88.

Pazos, M. and Salas, R. 1996. Descomposición de la progresividad y redistribución de las transferencias públicas, in *Las políticas redistributivas*, various authors. Madrid: Fundación Argentaria-Visor.

Pérez Eransus, B. 2005. *Políticas de Activación y Rentas Mínimas*. Madrid: Fundación FOESSA.

Rodríguez Cabrero, G. 2004. *El Estado del Bienestar en España: Debates, Desarrollo y Retos.* Madrid: Fundamentos.

Ruiz-Castillo, J. 1987. *La Medición de La Pobreza y la Desigualdad en España.* Estudios Económicos, 42. Madrid. Banco de España.

Ruiz-Huerta, J. and Martínez, R. 1994. La pobreza en España: ¿Qué nos muestran las EPF? *Documentación Social*, 96, 15–110.

Chapter 14

Consolidation and Reluctant Reform of the Pension System

Elisa Chuliá

Introduction[1]

The Social Security pension system, which amounted to 9 per cent of Spain's GDP in 2010, represents the largest social expenditure programme in Spain. Population forecasts of an intense ageing process combined with the institutional maturation of the pension system and the recent deterioration of the system's revenues explain the current saliency of pensions in the Spanish welfare reform debate.

Despite recurrent warnings from experts as well as from national and international financial organizations about the worsening financial prospects of the pension system, Spanish governments and political parties have for at least two decades avoided policies that could be interpreted as benefit cuts or reductions of pension entitlements. They have instead opted to consolidate and reinforce the structure and performance of the pension system through an incremental reform agenda based on an all-party parliamentary agreement. In fact, from the mid-1990s and until the end of the first decade of the twenty-first century different economic, demographic and institutional factors have converged to create the illusion of long-term pension sustainability and to discourage reform. As a consequence, public policy choices during this period have had mixed effects. Thus, a significant increase in minimum pensions has gone hand in hand with efforts to stimulate late retirement and strengthen the link between contributions and pension benefits.

Only in 2010 did the government resolutely champion substantial reform. In the context of deep economic recession and growing fears about Spain's ability to service its sovereign debt, the minority Socialist government of Rodríguez Zapatero managed to gather the support of trade unions and employers' organizations as well as, more or less reluctantly, opposition parties to raise the statutory retirement age to 67 and to expand the contributory period for calculating benefits as well as the benefit accrual rate.

The Spanish case is unique in that, although Spain faces a more worrying demographic evolution than other European countries and has abundant robust

1   The author acknowledges with thanks the support of the Spanish Ministry of Science and Innovation (Project CSO2010-21881).

and consistent information about the financial difficulties of its pension system, until 2010 Spanish governments implemented only very modest reforms to curb pension costs. Following a strategy of blame avoidance that neither opposition parties nor social agents or civil society overtly questioned, governments led by the centre-right People's Party or the centre-left Socialist Party have repudiated these politically and electorally costly decisions. In this respect, Spain has clearly deviated from the pension reform path walked by other European governments since the 1990s.

In this chapter I first present the main features of the Spanish pension system as of 2010. After providing some evidence of the consensus of experts on the growing financial problems of the system, I set out the landmarks of Spanish pensions policy since the 1980s and try to explain their rationale. I then concentrate on the recent parametric reform of 2011, identifying continuities and discontinuities with previous reforms. Finally I sum up the main arguments and briefly reflect on the challenges the Spanish pension system faces in coming years.

An Overview of the Spanish Pension System: Structure and Main Data

The Spanish pension system rests on a public pillar and a private pillar. The former is mandatory and provides extensive coverage while the latter is voluntary and, in comparative terms, scarcely developed. The public pillar (Social Security pension system) includes two subsystems: the contributory scheme offers pay-as-you-go financed and earnings-related retirement, permanent disability and survivors' (widow[er]s, orphans and dependent kin) benefits, whereas the non-contributory scheme pays means-tested flat-rate benefits for elderly and disabled people who do not fulfil the eligibility conditions for a contributory public pension. For its part, the private pension pillar includes privately funded and managed occupational and personal pensions aimed at voluntarily supplementing public pensions.

The Social Security contributory pension scheme, whose origins can be traced back to the 1960s, in 2010 provided more than 8.5 million defined-benefit pensions (the Spanish population by then was 46 million) and allocated 95.6 billion euros to them (9 per cent of Spanish GDP). Contributory pensions, divided into the general regime and five special regimes (for the self-employed, coal miners, fishermen, agricultural workers and domestic employees), are exclusively paid by current contributions by workers.[2] Workers integrated into the general regime (about three-quarters of all workers) pay 28.3 per cent of their contributory base (which is linked to the salary): 23.6 per cent is paid by the employer and 4.7 per cent by the employee.

---

2   Civil servants working in municipalities, autonomous regions and specific public institutions are integrated into the Social Security general regime, while the rest have been allocated to different public mutualities.

Retirement pensions and widow[er]s' pensions represent the bulk of contributory pensions (60 per cent and 27 per cent respectively). The former make up about 67 per cent of contributory pension expenditure, while the latter add 20 percentage points. Since more than three-quarters of all widow[er]s' pensions are paid to women aged 65 years or older, it can be stated that the contributory public pension system covers predominantly elderly people. According to the OECD (2011), Spain's poverty rate for older people, after the lower dwelling costs due to the high percentage of owner-occupied housing are taken into account, is around 19 per cent, about 6 percentage points above the poverty rate for the whole population.

The government establishes every year the minimum and maximum contributory pensions as well as the minimum and maximum contributory bases for each of the eleven professional categories in which workers are classified.[3] For 2011 the minimum contributory retirement pension for a person aged 65 or older ranges from 7,883 to 10,255 euros per year depending on her family situation. The yearly amount of the maximum contributory pension for this same year is 34,527 euros, about four times higher than the minimum pension.

Non-contributory pensions, established in 1991 and financed through general revenues, are exclusively granted to people aged 65 or older. The amount of a non-contributory pension (4,803 euros per year in 2011) is well below the minimum contributory pension while the number of beneficiaries is rather low (453,000) and in recent years decreasing. Expenditure on non-contributory pensions represented in 2010 slightly less than 0.2 per cent of GDP.

Both contributory and non-contributory public pensions are managed by Social Security, integrated into the Ministry of Labour and Immigration. While public health care and social services are competences of the 17 Autonomous Communities that form the political-administrative structure of the highly decentralized Spanish state, Social Security is a central government institution.

Social Security revenues (nearly 90 per cent of which consist of contributions) have regularly exceeded its expenditure. The surplus (after the payment of some non-contributory pension outlays, particularly the supplement to reach the minimum pension) has been deposited in a reserve fund established in 2000, which at the end of 2010 had accumulated 64 billion euros (about 6.1 per cent of GDP), and invested in domestic and foreign public debt.

If non-contributory pensions are modest in number and amount, so also are private pensions. At the end of 2010 their beneficiaries amounted to 206,000. This figure will certainly increase in future years since around 8.5 million individuals have joined private pension schemes.[4] Nevertheless, the proportion of pension

---

3   The figures cited in the next paragraphs stem from official statistics published in the *Boletín de Estadísticas Laborales* (BEL). They can be retrieved at the website of the Ministry of Labour and Immigration (www.mtin.es).

4   In fact, at the end of 2010 the Spanish Association of Institutions for Collective Investment and Pension Funds (Inverco) registered nearly 10,850,000 private pension

income derived from private pensions will probably remain low. Occupational pension schemes are scarcely developed, with slightly fewer than two million members; the number of personal pension plans is four times higher, but investments in them are much smaller. In fact, compared with other European countries (particularly the United Kingdom, Netherlands, Germany or Denmark), the assets accumulated by participants in private pension funds are rather low (roughly 85,000 million euros, or about 8 per cent of Spanish GDP), though higher than those in other south European countries.

Neither non-contributory pensions nor private pensions are at the centre of the Spanish pension policy debate, which revolves around the financial sustainability of the contributory scheme. It is therefore important to be acquainted with its main rules.

The qualifying period for a contributory pension benefit is 15 full years. Since its establishment in the late 1960s (and until 2013, the first year in which the 2011 reform will go into effect) the statutory retirement age has been 65 years for both men and women. Workers entering retirement at this age and having contributed for at least 35 years receive 100 per cent of their pension base (which for pensioners entering retirement before 2013 is calculated by taking into consideration the contributory base of the last 15 years previous to retirement, whereby contributory bases are at best proxies of effective salaries).[5] Access to retirement with only 15 contribution years grants 50 per cent of the pension base (for those retiring at age 65).[6]

Workers having paid contributions for at least 31 years have the right to early or partial retirement from age 61 onwards provided they entered the system after 1967 (and one year earlier if they entered the system before 1967). Early retirees nonetheless suffer comparatively high penalties, ranging from 6 per cent to 8 per cent of the pension base for each year before 65. Partial pensioners may receive a pension benefit and work part-time if they have worked for at least six years with the last employer. Since 2005 the percentage of workers retiring before 65 has fluctuated yearly between 40 per cent and 46 per cent of all new pensioners (MTIN 2011b: 133).

As already stated, the Social Security contributory pension system grants minimum pensions. Thus, when the contributory benefit calculated for the individual beneficiary according to the pension rules falls below the legally established minimum, the system pays a supplement to reach the minimum after checking that the pensioner does not receive additional income. Figure 14.1 summarizes the main data of the Spanish pension system as of 2010.

---

contracts. This organization nonetheless estimates a smaller number of participants since some of them have taken out more than one pension plan.

5   The contributory bases of the first 13 years (within the last 15 years prior to retirement) are indexed for prices when the individual pension base is calculated.

6   For each contribution year between ages 16 and 25 the pensioner accrues 3 per cent of the pension base, and for each contribution year between ages 26 and 35, 2 per cent.

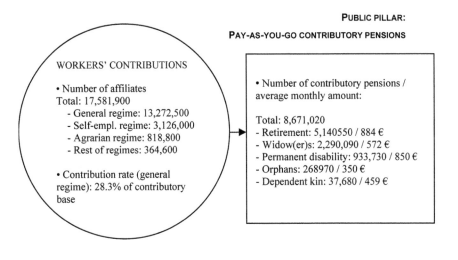

PUBLIC PILLAR:

PAY-AS-YOU-GO CONTRIBUTORY PENSIONS

WORKERS' CONTRIBUTIONS

• Number of affiliates
Total: 17,581,900
   - General regime: 13,272,500
   - Self-empl. regime: 3,126,000
   - Agrarian regime: 818,800
   - Rest of regimes: 364,600

• Contribution rate (general
regime): 28.3% of contributory
base

• Number of contributory pensions /
average monthly amount:

Total: 8,671,020
- Retirement: 5,140550 / 884 €
- Widow(er)s: 2,290,090 / 572 €
- Permanent disability: 933,730 / 850 €
- Orphans: 268970 / 350 €
- Dependent kin: 37,680 / 459 €

PUBLIC PILLAR:

MEANS-TESTED NON-CONTRIBUTORY PENSIONS

GENERAL REVENUES

• Number of non-contributory Social
Security pensions/ monthly amount:

Total: 453,295
   - Old age: 257,136 / 336 €
   - Disability: 196,159 / 336 €

PRIVATE PILLAR:

VOLUNTARY FUNDED PENSIONS

• Number of contracts / total assets
(in € billion):

- Individual system: 8,596,336 / 52.55€
- Employment system: 2,171,021 / 31.24€
- Associations: 80,127 / 0.97€

• Private pensions beneficiaries: 206,000

Figure 14.1   Main data of the Spanish pension system (2010)

Even though the average retirement pension is not very high (884 euros monthly in 2010), the Spanish contributory pension system stands out for its relative generosity. The net replacement rate (the ratio of the pension benefit to individual net earnings of a full-career worker entering the labour market in 2008) amounts to 84.9 per cent (OECD 2011). Furthermore, yearly pension indexation established by law in 1997 has maintained pensions' purchasing power. Benefits are indexed for expected inflation. Deviations have been compensated when real inflation has exceeded expected inflation, while in the opposite case governments have refrained from recouping excess payment. The year 2011 has been the only one in which benefits have not been revalued, one of the extraordinary measures adopted by the government in May 2010 to rein in the mounting public deficit.

Disturbing Prospects for Financial Pension Sustainability

In light of the information provided in the previous paragraph, the Spanish public pension system nowadays enjoys financial health: although pension expenditure in real terms has not ceased to grow following the clear and conspicuous tendency of recent decades, contributory revenues still match contributory outlays, and the Social Security has a reserve fund amounting to about nine months of total contributory pension expenditure (MTIN 2011a). But the flow of investments into this reserve fund has been diminishing since the beginning of the financial and economic crisis in 2007/2008, as a consequence of the rapid increase of the unemployment rate (20 per cent of the labour force in 2010) and the decreasing number of affiliates to Social Security.[7] Meanwhile, the demographic respite of recent years (in which the small cohorts born during the Spanish Civil War of 1936–39 entered the system) is over, and the growth rate of retirement pensions is again showing a significant increase (Figure 14.2).

However, what is more cumbersome is the projected acceleration of the number of people aged 65 and over in future decades. Demographers have long warned of a rapid and very substantial increase of dependency ratios.

---

7   Unemployed workers receiving contributory unemployment benefits also contribute to the Social Security: the government pays the share corresponding to the employer's contributions and about a third of the employee's contribution. Unemployed workers who receive non-contributory subsidies or who are not covered at all do not make contributions to the Social Security.

Figure 14.2   New retirement pensions and lost retirement pensions, 1980–2010

For the sake of simplicity I will cite only the data provided by the European Commission and the Economic Policy Committee, which in their *2009 Ageing Report* assumed that the old age dependency ratio (the population aged 65 and over divided by the population aged between 15 and 64) would increase in Spain from 24 per cent in 2007 to 59 per cent in 2050 (the corresponding data for the EU-27 are 25 per cent and 50 per cent), while the total dependency ratio (the population aged under 15 and aged over 64 divided by the population aged between 15 and 64) would rise from 45 per cent to 83 per cent (49 per cent and 75 per cent for the EU-27) (EC and EPC 2009: 280–81). According to the same source, the number of pensioners, around eight million in 2007, would more than double by 2050 (17 million), while the number of contributors would rise by only slightly more than one million, under macroeconomic and employment assumptions that at this point seem sensible.

As for the financial prospects, economists have in recent years projected increases in pension expenditure ranging from five to eight additional percentage points of GDP by 2050 (MTAS 2005; Jimeno et al. 2008; Doménech and Melguizo 2009; AFI 2009). The *2009 Ageing Report* estimates a rise in Social security pension expenditure from 8.4 per cent of GDP in 2007 to 15.5 per cent in 2050 (10.1 per cent and 12.3 per cent for the EU-27) (EC and EPC 2009: 282). Such an increase could not be absorbed by contributions at their current level.

These demographic and financial estimates are not new. In fact, since the mid-1990s the national and international literature on Spanish pensions has consistently produced similar data and warned about the risks of maintaining the current institutional design and rules for pensions. One may think that the projections have apparently not been taken seriously because of the failure of the earliest of them (published in the mid-1990s) to predict the massive expansion in employment from 1997 to 2007, which raised the number of Social Security affiliates from less than 13 million to 19 million contributors in 2007 and 2008.[8] The critics asked how experts who were unable to forecast accurately the near future could do so for the distant future. These reservations, linked to suspicions about a campaign by financial institutions to stimulate private pension savings by casting doubts on the financial sustainability of the public pension system, contributed to discrediting such projections and strengthening the arguments against pension reform. However, the main reasons for the reluctance to reform pensions since the 1990s lie in Spanish pension politics, as I try to show in the succeeding sections.

From the Socialist Pension Reforms of the 1980s to the All-party Toledo Pact of 1995

The Spanish contributory public pension pillar was designed and established in the last phase of the Francoist regime as the backbone of the new Social Security, which also included health care, family benefits and social services. The Social Security Law of 1963, enacted in 1967, laid the foundations for the unification and coordination by the central government of social insurance provision, which hitherto had been unsuccessfully managed by state-corporatist associations on a funded basis.

Under the initial legislation, the contributory pension system would provide defined-benefit pensions to workers who had contributed for at least ten years. The pension base was to be calculated on the basis of the highest earnings registered during two contribution years (within the seven years prior to reaching the age of 65), whereas the percentage applied to the pension base in order to determine the pension amount lay on a scale with an upper limit of 100 per cent corresponding to 35 years of contributions. The scale favoured those who had contributed for fewer years: with only 10 (instead of 17.5) contribution years, the pensioner accrued 50 per cent of the pension base. Furthermore, benefits were not directly linked to the amount of contributions paid, but to the contribution base (theoretically equivalent to the real salary, but often in fact below it), whereby contribution rates were initially set at 14 per cent (10 per cent paid by the employer and 4 per cent by the employee). The 1974 Social Security Law recognized, apart from the 'general regime' encompassing the lion's share of employed workers, 11 special regimes,

---

    8   See for example Herce and Pérez-Díaz (1995); Piñera (1996) and Herce et al. (1996).

thus fragmenting the system with regard to the rights and obligations of Social Security affiliates.

In 1978 the Social Security system paid 4 million pensions, half of them to retirees. The democratic Constitution promulgated in that year opted for continuity by establishing the duty of the state to maintain 'a public Social Security system for all citizens guaranteeing adequate social assistance and benefits in situations of hardship, especially in case of unemployment', adding that 'supplementary assistance and benefits shall be optional'. In the second half of the 1970s, during the transition to democracy, the centre-right governments of the Unión de Centro Democrático (UCD) implemented a fiscal reform to increase state revenues, which made possible the expansion of social expenditure,[9] but neither the structure of the pension system nor the rules to calculate benefits experienced significant changes.

When the Socialist Workers' Party won an absolute majority in the 1982 general elections and formed the government led by Felipe González, the Spanish pension system was mono-pillar, included approximately 11 million affiliates, and paid out nearly 5 million pensions. The majority of pensioners received a minimum pension that represented about 70 per cent of the minimum salary and was not periodically indexed. Furthermore, the design of the system produced unfair results: some pensioners (particularly those covered by the special regimes) could obtain higher pension benefits for paying the same or even less in the way of contributions.[10] The short period for calculating the pension base (two years) also encouraged strategic behaviour ('pension buying') by allowing workers to negotiate with employers an increase in the contributory base a few years before entering retirement.

The first Socialist government decided to put an end to these loopholes. It soon hardened the means test for receiving a minimum pension and then adopted measures to increase the contribution rates of self-employed workers and to prevent them to increasing their contributions immediately preceding retirement so as to qualify for higher pension benefits. After unsuccessfully trying to come to an agreement with trade unions and employers' organizations on pension reform, the government proposed increasing the minimum contribution period for eligibility for a contributory pension from 10 to 15 years (more concretely, 180 monthly salaries, whereby the inclusion of extra payments at Christmas and in the summer shortened the period from 15 to less than 13 years) and to extend the contribution period taken into consideration for calculating the pension base from two to eight years prior to the claim. As a sort of compensation for the changes in the pension formula (which implied an average cut of 13 per cent to all new pensions, as calculated by Herce and

---

9   According to data elaborated by Comín (1988: 96), expenditure on social benefits in terms of GDP doubled between 1977 and 1982: from 6.8 per cent to 13.8 per cent. During these years Social Security expenditure increased by 8 per cent in real terms (Mota 2002: 316).

10   For example, about 50 per cent of pensioners covered by the special regime for the self-employed had contributed for only 10 or 11 years, whereas this was true for fewer than 5% of the pensioners belonging to the general regime (Mota 2002: 281).

Alonso 1998: 12), the government made a commitment to automatically index new pensions at the beginning of each year for the expected inflation rate. This meant a move towards a stable indexing policy, which hitherto had enjoyed only very fragile legal backing.[11]

The bill was approved by the absolute Socialist majority in the parliament. But the government had to confront not only parliamentary opposition and the first general strike against its policy, but also the rupture of its historical unity and common political strategy with the Unión General de Trabajadores (UGT), the socialist trade union.

Party and trade union hostility was the response also to the bill regulating supplementary private pension schemes. The 1987 Private Pensions Law defined pension plans as 'free and voluntary' and 'in any case' an alternative to the mandatory Social Security pension system. The law established a threefold distinction among pension funds: the employment system that included pension plans set up by firms and enterprises for their employees, the associate system that included plans promoted by associations and trade unions, and the individual system that embraced pension plans directly contracted by individuals.

Despite the conflicts with the trade unions during the final phase of his second mandate, González again won general elections in October 1989, but with a reduced majority. In the context of economic recovery, at the end of 1990 the parliament passed the third significant pension bill: the Law on Non-contributory Pensions for old and disabled persons ineligible for a contributory pension and lacking other income sources.[12] The first non-contributory pension benefits were paid out in the summer 1991 and represented approximately 57 per cent of the minimum retirement contributory pension for a 65-year-old beneficiary with a dependent spouse.

---

11 In fact, Article 92 of the General Law of Social Security, inherited from the Francoist regime, prescribed that pensions 'would be periodically revalued by the government ... taking into account, among other indicative factors, the growth of the average wages, the CPI and the general evolution of the economy, as well as the economic capacities of the Social Security System'.

12 Before the enactment of that law the central administration, together with the autonomous regions and the city councils, offered means-tested economic aid to different groups, among them old and handicapped people. But in fact the provision of these benefits was discretionary inasmuch as it depended on the availability of public resources. Moreover, since these benefits were not based on entitlements, citizens could not appeal against their refusal.

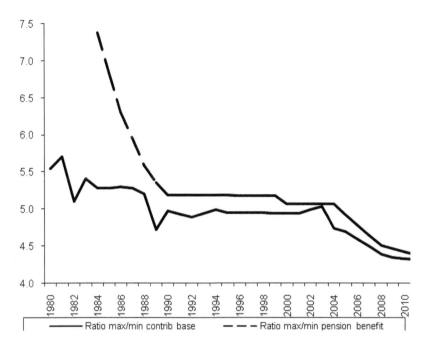

Figure 14.3   Relationship between maximum and minimum pension amount and maximum and minimum contribution base, 1980–2011

At the beginning of the 1990s González could congratulate himself for having substantially changed the pension system. First, his government had modified the contributory pension rules, removing the clauses that encouraged fraudulent behaviour and enhancing the match between contributions and benefits, while in fact furthering the system's redistributive character by reducing the ratio between minimum and maximum benefits while also approximating the ratio between minimum and maximum contributory bases (Figure 14.3). Second, the González government had created from scratch the private pension pillar, thus allowing well-off workers to supplement their future public benefits by means of private and tax deductible pensions contributions to pension funds. And, third it had completed the public pillar with non-contributory pensions based on the idea of solidarity. This threefold success was due to the absolute majority that the González governments enjoyed between 1982 and 1993.

In fact, the 1980s showed that pensions were a very conflictual political issue, as also became manifest during the 1993 election campaign.[13] By 1995 the political

13   In the eyes of some People's Party members, one important reason for their electoral defeat in the 1993 general elections was a television debate between González and

parties had closed ranks in face of the mounting financial strain on the pension system (given a practically stagnant number of workers of around 12 million since 1989) and the publication of many reports and analyses identifying the system's sustainability problems and the advisability of reinforcing private savings. The parties agreed on a document titled the 'Toledo Pact', which explicitly excluded either substituting 'the present system of pay-as-you-go and inter-generational solidarity for another based on the capitalization of the public pension system and on individual provision' or limiting the Spanish public pension system 'to the simple provision of minimum pensions'. The Pact was designed for the definite purpose of 'consolidating' Social Security and furthering its convergence with European Member States in terms of expenditure as percentage of GDP. It included 15 recommendations, most of them aimed at rationalizing the system, enhancing equity and improving the quality of benefits.[14]

Rationalization was to be mainly achieved through the separation of the financing sources so that contributions would exclusively finance contributory benefits (whereby the supplements for reaching the minimum contributory pension were considered as non-contributory expenditure). Equity was to be enhanced through greater parity between real wages and contributory bases, the removal of the privileges of certain special regimes that paid lower contributions for equal benefits and the achievement of greater proportionality between contributions and benefits. The Pact also called for maintaining the purchasing power of pensions and strengthening the rights of survivors' pensioners. Besides these recommendations, the agreement included proposals to stimulate job creation, the voluntary delay of retirement age as well as voluntary participation in supplementary private pension schemes.

The Toledo Pact, approved by all parliamentary parties and backed by the unions and the employers' associations, became in fact a point of agreement between those who gave priority to the maintenance and, if possible, extension of the current level of social expenditure, and those who were more worried about the growing financial burden of the welfare state and its implications for employment and economic growth. The Pact marked a critical juncture in Spanish pensions policy. As I have argued elsewhere (Chuliá 2007), as a result of the Pact all parties became partisan veto players as regards pension reform. The risk of being accused of breaking such a broad political and corporatist consensus made the exit costs from the Pact extremely high for an individual party. In addition, the Pact displaced pensions from the political debate and the electoral arena. Likewise, this 'non-aggression pact' benefited the People's Party, which in 1996 won elections and formed a minority government under the presidency of José María Aznar.

José María Aznar during which the Socialist candidate and incumbent accused the People's Party candidate of planning not to revalue pensions. See Aznar (2004: 125).

14   The text of the Pact is published in *Boletín Oficial de las Cortes Generales*, E, 134, 12 April 1995.

Consensual and Incremental Reforms in the Context of the System's Recovery (1996–2007)

The Toledo Pact has not only framed but also locked in pensions policy since 1995 and for most of the first decade of the twenty-first century. The first People's Party government (1996–2000) refused to introduce some of the pension reforms that experts were strongly advocating, and decided to negotiate changes in the pension rules with the trade unions, thus refuting the claims that it was hostile towards the unions and intended to cut welfare benefits. In the autumn of 1996, only six months after its formation, Aznar's government signed an agreement on the reform of the pension system with the leading trade unions, consisting of 12 points that fleshed out certain recommendations included in the Toledo Pact.

One of the most important decisions agreed on by the government and the trade unions was the separation of the financing sources of contributory and non-contributory benefits by the year 2000, so that the surplus of contributory revenues could be invested in a reserve fund. Another important aspect of reform was the extension of the period for calculating the pension base from the last 8 years prior to retirement to the last 15 years, together with changes in the accrual rate in order to reduce privileges for workers with short contributory careers.[15] The trade unions were satisfied with achieving a reduction of the penalty for early retirement under certain circumstances (like job loss after long working careers), the automatic indexation of pensions for anticipated inflation (with compensation with a deferred extra payment if expected inflation was undervalued), the rise in the maximum age for entitlement to an orphan's pension from 18 to 21 and the increase in minimum pensions for widows and widowers younger than age 60 (MTIN 2011b: 81).

The 1996 agreement and the subsequent 1997 law demonstrated the ability of the centre-right government to bargain with social partners. In the context of a positive turn in the economic cycle and an unprecedented labour market expansion absorbing millions of new workers (particularly women and immigrants), Aznar's first government took pension policy decisions that calmed and pleased trade unions as well as elderly voters. It even decided to significantly revalue all minimum pensions in 2000; retirement pensions as well as disability pensions were raised by over 6.5 per cent, while pensions for survivors experienced higher increases. The People's Party government behaved as predicted by Pierson and Weaver (1993): electoral motivations clearly overrode the influence of ideology.

But in fact ideology had an impact on policy choices regarding private pensions. Simultaneously, although less visibly, the government improved incentives to save privately for retirement. In 1998 and 1999 it increased the limit of tax-deductible contributions to pension plans, especially for people aged 53 and over, promoted the opening of pension plans in favour of handicapped relations and made easier

---

15   The first 15 years would give the right to 50 per cent of the base (instead of 60 per cent), and each year of additional contributions would add 3 per cent (from years 16 to 25) or 2.5 per cent (from years 26 to 35).

the withdrawal of pension assets in circumstances of severe illness and long-term unemployment.

In May 2000, just a few weeks after the People's Party obtained an absolute majority in the general elections, all parties agreed on the creation of the non-permanent parliamentary commission to assess the results of the Toledo Pact. In parallel with the constitution of this commission the government began to negotiate a new pension reform with the trade unions. The core of the agreement signed in April 2001 (this time backed only by one of the two big trade unions and the employers' associations) was the encouragement of late retirement. The agreement was given force in a decree published few days before the end of 2001 and later in a law approved in July 2002 in which the government established a new system of gradual and flexible retirement. To incentivize retirement beyond age 65, the new legislation established an increase in the pension benefit of two percentage points of the pension base per year (with at least 35 contribution years). Moreover, employers providing jobs to old people would be exempted from the bulk of contributions to Social Security. Partial retirement was also regulated with the aim of easing the exit of older workers from the labour market while simultaneously furthering new working contracts for young people.

At the beginning of 2003 the European Council warned the Spanish government of 'the risk of unsustainable public finances' and of 'budgetary imbalances in the long run' based on 'the large projected increase in age-related spending on public pensions', and regretted that 'no major review of the public pension system has yet been undertaken'.[16] Nevertheless, a few months later the parliamentary commission on the Toledo Pact presented its report to the parliament. The report included five new recommendations, none of them stressing the advisability of reducing future pension costs. These recommendations referred to social problems perceived as challenges to the well-being of workers and pensioners, such as the extension of new forms of work (part-time, temporary), the equal protection of women and immigration.[17] Eight years after its parliamentary approval, the Toledo Pact in its renewed version seemed as solid as ever. Optimism was the prevailing mood among the commissioners and the government. The latter again revalued minimum pensions a few months before the general elections of 2004, especially favouring pensioners younger than 65.

In sum, Aznar's governments engaged in a pensions policy that continued firm support for the Toledo Pact and discreetly encouraged private pensions. Institutional factors, together with economic expansion and labour market growth as well as a slowing down of new retirement pensions for demographic reasons, significantly alleviated the pressure from experts and financial international organizations to reform the public pension system in order to ensure its long-term sustainability.

---

16   See *Bulletin EU* 1/2, 2003, as well as press coverage in *El País*, 30-01-2003.

17   The report was published in *Boletín Oficial de las Cortes Generales*, D, 596, 2 October 2003.

This was the situation in 2004 when the Socialist Party won the general elections. The new government of Rodríguez Zapatero followed the path of pensions policymaking. It first subscribed in 2006 to an agreement on Social Security measures with the trade unions, which was then embodied in a new law at the end of 2007. Changes in the pension rules were again very modest: the eligibility period for a contributory pension was extended to 15 full contribution years (i.e. 180 monthly salaries, excluding extra payments) while further incentives to postpone retirement were introduced. The law exemplified once again the strength of social dialogue in pensions policymaking: the government, the social partners and the parliamentary commission of the Toledo Pact formed the consensus triangle within which pension reform cautiously advanced (Ramos and Del Pino 2009: 97). Outside this triangle debate continued among the experts; different proposals based on reforms adopted in other European countries were explored and their impact analysed.

Meanwhile, the government manifested its ideological preferences through the periodic revaluation of minimum pensions: between 2004 and 2008 the value of minimum pensions increased by between 12 per cent and 19 per cent in real terms (OECD 2011), further reducing the gap between maximum and minimum pensions and thus enhancing redistribution within the pension system (see Figure 14.3).

Deep Economic Crisis as a Catalyst of Substantial Reform (2008–2011)

Study of Spanish pensions policy during the last decade of the twentieth century and the first years of the twenty-first century shows that, at a time when many European countries were implementing substantial parametric or structural pension reforms in response to the increasing financial problems of their pensions systems, centre-right and centre-left governments in Spain were putting forward 'adaptations' with moderate financial impact while at the same time increasing pension expenditure through the generous (and electorally biased) revaluation of minimum pensions. Meanwhile private pension assets were slowly increasing. At the end of 2007 fund assets approached 86 billion euros, but the average investment per participant was around 6,000 euros. In 2009, for the first time in the history of Spain's private pensions, the number of participants in pension funds decreased.[18] Assets had already experienced a decrease in 2008, but they recovered in 2009 in line with evidence of an increasing savings rate on the part of Spanish families.[19]

---

18   Pension funds of the individual system lost more than 120,000 participants in 2009 probably because unemployed workers opted to withdraw their investments.

19   The reasons for the weak development of private pensions are many. According to the findings of Fernández and Bermejo (2009) pension funds' returns performed rather poorly between 1991 and 2008. Indeed, those returns were in general lower than the rate of inflation and less profitable than bonds and shares. The authors explain this disappointing result from an economic point of view by stressing three factors: high commissions,

Despite its reluctance first to admit the seriousness of the crisis and then to adopt unpopular reforms in the labour market and the social protection system, in January 2010 the Spanish government surprised political parties, interest groups and the public in general with an announcement of substantial pension reform consisting of an increase in the retirement age from 65 to 67 and the extension of the working life period on which pension benefits were calculated. With this announcement the government tried to signal its resolve to undertake a substantial retrenchment reform and to reinforce Spain's financial credibility among international investors. All parties represented on the parliamentary commission assessing the evolution of the Toledo Pact, except the Socialists, complained that the commissioners had been neither consulted nor informed about this initiative. Although the government manifested its intention to explain and negotiate the new measures with the commission and to try to obtain the support of the social partners, the trade unions called a strike against this reform, which took place in February.

In face of renewed doubts about Spain's financial solvency, in May 2010 the government departed once again from the pensions policy path by decreeing the freezing of pensions in 2011. Without giving up the goal of recovering the lost policy consensus in the parliamentary commission and of persuading the commissioners and the social partners of the urgent need for substantial pension reform, the government made a public commitment to approve pension reform by January 2011 at the latest. Only a few hours before the deadline, the government managed to sign with trade unions and employers' organizations an agreement on pensions policy and other measures to promote economic growth and employment as well as reaffirming confidence in the welfare state. The agreement implied some concessions to the trade unions, but included the highly symbolic reference to 67 as the standard age of eligibility for a full pension with 37 contribution years (even if workers aged 65 with 38.5 contribution years are also entitled to a full pension). Besides restricting access conditions to anticipated retirement, reinforcing incentives for later retirement and increasing the contribution in case of partial retirement, the agreement also established the extension of the period for calculating the pension base from 15 to 25 years while maintaining 15 contribution years as the eligibility period. All these changes will be progressively phased in from 2013. In addition, the agreement refers to the introduction of an automatic review mechanism to adjust pension parameters to demographic evolution from 2027 onwards.

This highly celebrated social pact has put pressure on the other parties to back the reform, thus avoiding the 'electoral isolation' of the Socialist Party on this issue. Still, other parties are reluctant to adhere to the agreement since they are aware of the very ample support that the pension system enjoys among the Spanish

---

portfolio composition (first and foremost the predominance of fixed-interest investments) and active management (i.e. the ample room for manoeuvre enjoyed by pension fund managers to allocate assets).

population regardless of political persuasion and of the public's opposition to reducing its coverage (León and Orriols 2011).

After so many years of sluggish pension reform, the hasty circumstances in which the 2011 reform was negotiated have hindered a suitable provision of data about the likely impact of the proposed changes on pension benefits. Neither before nor immediately after the publication of the agreement have the government or the social agents provided any indication of this impact. Also lacking is any precise information about the type of adjustment which will be applied every five years after 2027. These flaws notwithstanding, many experts and financial institutions have praised the reform as an important step in the right direction and a significant contribution to strengthening the credibility of the Spanish economy.

De la Fuente and Doménech (2011) have calculated that the recent reform will reduce pension outlays by two GDP percentage points in 2027, but they have recommended to bring forward the implementation of the projected review mechanism by introducing already in 2013 a clearly defined sustainability factor (as established by pension reforms in Germany or Portugal). In the same vein, the OECD (2011) has emphasized that this reform will significantly improve the long-term sustainability of the pension system, cutting pension expenditure by around 3.5 per cent of GDP in 2050. It furthermore estimates a decrease of more than seven percentage points in the pension gross replacement rate, from 81.2 per cent to 74.9 per cent. However, it has pointed out that the new pension rules are less strict than those established in other European pension systems that have undergone reform in recent years (like those of France, Italy, Luxembourg and Germany). In sum, policy change has promoted policy convergence, but without erasing distinctiveness (Weaver 2003).

Conclusion and Final Remarks

Demography poses an extraordinary challenge to Europe's retirement-income systems. But the impact of population ageing on the financial sustainability of pension systems depends on the intensity of this process, on the capacity of the economy and the labour market to expand job supply as well as on the institutional adaptation of these systems to the demographic challenge. So far the discussion of Spanish pensions has included at least three solid consensus points: first, population ageing during the central decades of this century will be very intense; second, the labour market shows structural difficulties in absorbing supply, especially during periods of slowdown in economic activity; and third, the pension system will need further adjustments to contain expenditure growth.

Loss of political support and electoral punishment have deterred Spanish centre-right and centre-left governments from advancing pension reforms in response to the warnings of experts and national and international economic institutions. Instead of fostering public debate on these issues and trying to demonstrate the need to reform the pension system in order to assure its long-term viability, Spanish governments have confined the discussion to a parliamentary commission and the realm of dialogue with the social partners. As many experts stress, this tendency of decision-making elites can be counteracted by only providing quality information to the general public (Doménech and Melguizo 2009; Afi 2009). Survey data show that Spanish workers' knowledge about their contributions and their pension rights is very limited. To improve this knowledge so as to help people to take responsible decisions about when and how to retire and to show them that the survival of a fair pension system requires reforms is one of the main responsibilities of Spanish governments, political parties, social partners and experts.

References

Afi (Analistas Financieros Internacionales) 2009. *Los Retos Socioeconómicos del Envejecimiento de la Población*, report sponsored by UNESPA and edited by J.A. Herce and J.L. Fernández. [Online] Available at: http://www.unespa.es/ adjuntos/fichero_3009_20100125.pdf [Accessed: March 2011].

Aznar, J.M. 2004. *Ocho Años de Gobierno*. Barcelona: Planeta.

Chuliá, E. 2007. Spain: Between Majority Rule and Incrementalism, in *The Handbook of West European Pension Politics*, edited by E. Immergut, K.M. Anderson and I. Schulze. New York: Oxford University Press, 499–554.

Comín, F. 1988. Evolución histórica del gasto público. *Papeles de Economía Española*, 37, 174–83.

De la Fuente, Á. and Doménech, R. 2011. *El Impacto sobre el Gasto de la Reforma de las Pensiones: Una Primera Estimación*. BBVA Research. Documentos de trabajo n° 11/09. [Online] Available at: http://serviciodeestudios.bbva. com/KETD/fbin/mult/WP_1109_tcm346250828.pdf?ts=2732011 [Accessed: March 2011].

Doménech, R. and Melguizo, Á. 2009. *Projecting Pension Expenditures in Spain: On Uncertainty, Communication and Transparency*. BBVA Bank Working Papers, Economic Research Department n° 0911. [Online] Available at: http:// serviciodeestudios.bbva.com/KETD/fbin/mult/WP_0911_tcm346-212793. pdf?ts=2732011 [Accessed: March 2011].

EC and EPC (European Commission and Economic Policy Committee) 2009. *The 2009 Ageing Report: Economic and budgetary projections for the EU-27 Member States (2008–2060)*. Luxembourg: Office for Official Publications of the European Communities.

Fernández, P. and Bermejo, V. 2009. Rentabilidad de los fondos de pensiones en España. 1991–2008, IESE (Universidad de Navarra). [Online] Available at: http://ssrn.com/abstract=1353103 [Accessed: March 2011].

Herce, J.A. and Alonso, J. 1998. *Los Efectos Económicos de la Ley de Consolidación de la Seguridad Social. Perspectivas Financieras del Sistema de Pensiones tras su Entrada en Vigor*. Documento de Trabajo 98–16. Madrid: FEDEA.

Herce, J.A. and Pérez-Díaz, V. (eds) 1995. *La Reforma del Sistema Público de Pensiones en España*. Barcelona: La Caixa.

Herce, J.A., Sosvilla, S., Castillo, S. and Duce, R. 1996. *El Futuro de las Pensiones en España: Hacia un Sistema Mixto*. Barcelona: La Caixa.

Jimeno, J.F., Rojas, J.A. and Puente, S. 2008. Modelling the Impact of Aging on Social Security Expenditures, *Economic Modelling*, 25, 201–24.

León, S. and Orriols, L. 2011. ¿Nos cambia la crisis? Gasto público, impuestos e ideología en la opinión pública española 2004–2010. *Zoom Político 1*, Laboratorio de Alternativas.

Mota, R. 2002. *Regímenes, Partidos y Políticas de Suficiencia en Pensiones de Jubilación. La Experiencia Española*. Madrid: Instituto Juan March de Estudios e Investigaciones/Centro de Estudios Avanzados en Ciencias Sociales.

MTAS (Ministerio de Trabajo y Asuntos Sociales) 2005. *Report on the Spanish Strategy for the Future of the Pension System*. Madrid.

MTIN (Ministerio de Trabajo e Inmigración) 2011a. *Seguridad Social, Presupuestos, Ejercicio 2011*. Madrid.

MTIN 2011b. *Seguridad Social, Presupuestos, Ejercicio 2011. Informe Económico Financiero*. Madrid.

OECD 2011. *Spain. Country Note: Pensions at a Glance 2011*. Paris: OECD.

Piñera, J. 1996. *Una propuesta de Reforma del Sistema de Pensiones en España*. Madrid: Círculo de Empresarios.

Ramos, J.A. and Del Pino, E. 2009. Un análisis político del cambio en el sistema de pensiones en España, in *Reformas de las Políticas del Bienestar en España*, edited by L. Moreno. Madrid: Siglo XXI, 67–100.

Pierson, P. and Weaver, R.K. 1993. Imposing Losses in Pension Policy, in R. Kent Weaver and B. Rockman (eds), *Do Institutions Matter? Government Capabilities in the US and Abroad*. Washington, DC: Brookings Institution, 110–50.

Weaver, R.K. 2003. The Politics of Public Pension Reform. *Center for Retirement Research Working Papers, Boston* College. [Online] Available at: http://escholarship.bc.edu/retirement_papers/82 [Accessed: March 2011].

Chapter 15

Conclusions

Margarita León and Ana M. Guillén

Describing and critically analysing the characteristics of the Spanish welfare state since the transition to contemporary democracy has been the core aim of this book. As explained in the Introduction, although this project was not designed to use a comparative methodology, it includes a comparative dimension, in two main respects. First, we have systematically taken into account the impact of Europeanization on the construction and development of the Spanish welfare state. Second, we have comprehensively questioned and discussed patterns of convergence with, and divergence from, more mature European welfare states as well as those of other southern European countries. Again, although the project was not intended to systematically include Spain within the analytical framework of the regime-type literature, many contributors have chosen to highlight similarities with, and differences from, the broad welfare-regime typologies as a way of better understanding the evolution of the national Spanish case.

This concluding chapter is structured as follows. The first section looks at the evolution and consolidation of the Spanish welfare state, highlighting its most important achievements since the mid-1970s until today throughout the main phases of development and political change. Findings from several chapters of this volume are used to stress main points. Referring to the chapters in Part II of the volume, the second section depicts the broad architecture of the Spanish welfare state in terms of the importance of devolution, the role of social concertation, the changing nature of the welfare mix and the levels of support from public opinion. The third section summarizes evidence from several chapters in order to understand the influence of Europeanization processes on the construction and consolidation of different social policy domains. The fourth and final section highlights the main challenges that the Spanish welfare state faces today, with special reference to the impact that the current economic downturn might have on its future sustainability.

Evolution of the Spanish Welfare State: What Model of Welfare?

Chapter 2 by Rodríguez Cabrero shows how the interaction of national and international dynamics have produced a hybrid, mixed Spanish welfare state, where the realities of extremely high cyclical unemployment and a dual labour market have made it very difficult to surmount the mismatch between, on the one hand, the significant efforts towards a progressive expansion and universalization of social protection and welfare, and, on the other, the persistence of high relative poverty and growing social inequalities across occupations, age, gender and, increasingly, national origin.

The mix of Bismarckian (social security), social-democratic (health, education) and liberal (minimum income) features has in a sense offered a wide repertoire of strategies with which to face traditional unmet demands and new needs such as the long-term care of an ageing population and measures for the reconciliation of work and family life following the massive entrance of women into the labour market. However, as Rodríguez Cabrero argues, the combination of features of different models has also generated inconsistencies between the policies followed in the different areas. For example, the strong Bismarckian link between employment performance and social protection in a strongly dualized labour market produces more unequal outcomes than could have been the case with a more universal social-democratic approach or the social assistance logic of a liberal one.

Most definitely, as is shown throughout this book, the intensity of institutional change has been phenomenal since the transition to democracy in the mid-1970s, especially in relation to the modernization of the Social Security system and the expansion of social rights (universal education and health). Nonetheless, the consolidation and the effectiveness of welfare programmes have been constrained by the weaknesses of the labour market (high unemployment and precarious employment), which is aggravated by an economic structure where employment suffers a traditionally high dependency on unstable and seasonal activities (building, intensive agriculture, hotels and catering); with domestic service being one of the occupational categories with the most recent and fastest growth.

Following Rodríguez Cabrero, the fact that the origins of Spanish welfare can be traced back to pre-democratic efforts to accompany the modernization of the economy in 1960–75 with some forms of a Bismarckian-type authoritarian welfare state (mainly in social security), and that these 'Bismarckian' measures shaped the expansion of social expenditure in the first democratic governments of the decade 1975–85, contributed to the consolidation of a conservative model of welfare state. These origins, together with the fact that the main expansions were often the results of urgent attempts to alleviate the impact of severe crises, supports Rodríguez Cabrero's view that a Bismarckian model of the welfare state came into being 'more by chance than design'. At the same time, key industrial sectors almost indissolubly linked to the Bismarckian model, such as shipbuilding, iron and steel, were losing their weight in the economy just when the consolidation of the Spanish welfare state was starting to get into full swing. The difficulties in reforming the labour market also limited the room for manoeuvre in other areas.

As explained by Molina (Chapter 5), in this context of industrial restructuring and high inflation, the trade unions' need for institutional and organizational consolidation as socio-political actors led to comprehensive social pacts which strengthened trade unions' institutional role in exchange for wage moderation, and with little concern for social protection. As a consequence, while the increasing prominence of collective bargaining was decisive in buttressing Spanish democracy, it came at the cost of a substantial fall in the wage share in the economy, moderate increases in social spending, and the beginning of a progressive segmentation of the labour market which will burden the welfare state in the future.

As explained by León (Chapter 4), this initial Bismarckian rationale and the difficult socio-economic situation of the country during this first phase of welfare development also largely conditioned the capacity of the Spanish welfare state to address inequalities based on gender. And yet this conservative imprint coexisted with the extension of social rights, thanks to the social-democratic rationale of the first Socialist governments, especially from the mid-1980s until the mid-1990s, which Rodríguez Cabrero and Molina respectively term the 'consolidation' and 'universalization despite conflict' phase of the Spanish welfare state. This period of Socialist governments became the high point in the expansion of a social-democratic model mainly through the univeralization of the national public systems of health and education. Significant progress was also made in the application of anti-discrimination legislation. However, the period was not free of tensions and conflicts. The trade unions' view that the sacrifices of wage moderation outweighed the social benefits started a period of conflict with the Socialist government, including three general strikes (1988, 1992, 1994) and the absence of social pacts, since trade unions considered it was more advantageous for them to negotiate different issues separately. A particularly dramatic moment was that of the 1985 pension reform, as explained by Chuliá (Chapter 14). In an effort to improve relations with the trade unions after the first strike, and within a context of economic recovery, the government undertook the '*giro social*' (social turn), which resulted in a large expansion in social spending and an increase in the coverage rate of the social protection system through non-contributory means-tested programmes. Conflict among social and political actors continued to be present especially during the 1992–4 economic crisis, with dramatic consequences for unemployment and the implementation of liberal labour market reforms. In the welfare state arena the period culminated with the approval in 1995 of the so-called Toledo Pact, which aimed at consolidating social security and furthering convergence with other EU Member States. As Chuliá reports, the Toledo Pact removed pensions from political debate and the electoral arena.

The victory of the conservative Popular Party in 1996 marked the beginning of a new phase in the development of the Spanish welfare state, characterized by the consolidation of the Europeanization process of economic and social policies, the increasing rationalization and selective privatization of welfare programmes and the restoration of social dialogue. The Maastricht Treaty, entry into the eurozone and the Lisbon Strategy of 2000 were landmark events for Spanish social and economic policymaking. The more recent practice of flexible, area-specific forms of social dialogue, instead of the pre-1988 catch-all social pacts, favoured important agreements in several areas: consolidation and rationalization of Social Security in 1996, the pension agreement and the reform of collective bargaining in 2001. Perhaps one of the most significant policy innovations of this period, directly imported from Europe, was the introduction of 'new' policy domains such as activation and policies for the reconciliation of work and family life. Through the framing of the latter, and as León and Salido point out in their respective chapters, the conservative government managed to reintroduce 'the family' as a key element in the political debate.

Finally, the fourth period (2004–2009) in the consolidation of the Spanish welfare state, labelled as 'recalibration' by Rodríguez Cabrero, swings between expansion and contraction. Expansion is best exemplified in the volume of new legislation on social issues of a progressive character, especially significant in the area of gender equality, as described in Chapter 4. Contraction reflects the severe constraints imposed by the imperatives of cost containment. The challenges that these tensions present are explored in greater detail in the final section of this chapter.

Policy Concertation, Political Devolution and Public Support: Main Traits of the Spanish Welfare State

The characteristics and circumstances affecting political exchange between the consecutive governments and their social partners, as described in the previous section, help to explain the weight given to welfare policy in the social dialogue over the decades. Since the 1995 Toledo Pact, which reconfigured welfare programmes and especially the pension system, social partners have become more involved in social policy, giving policy concertation a more central role in the consolidation and rationalization phases of the Spanish welfare state. The trade unions' shift in preferences since the 1990s, from wide social pacts to more narrow and specific bipartite or tripartite negotiations, so that a complete disagreement on one topic did not block initiatives in others, allowed a consensual rather than a distributional approach to policymaking, and helped to move welfare issues to the top of their agenda. The downside of this tapered concertation is a diminished capacity to set up synergies across policy areas, one of the serious problems of the Spanish welfare state, as is the case with the 'activation' ingredient of social policies to make welfare work. Besides, social dialogue in Spain is often instrumentalized as a legitimizing device, which makes policy concertation highly dependent on the political needs of incumbent governments. According to Molina, in the Spanish case the political exchange is the crucial dimension in the negotiation processes, which presents a different angle to the importance given by neocorporatist theory to factors like the strength of a social-democratic party, the presence of channels for concertation or the organizational characteristics of the trade unions. Although Spanish trade-unions suffer from low rates of membership, they have enjoyed a strong mobilization capacity and control over wage policy, which, given the institutionalization of collective bargaining, have been significant resources in the political exchange leading to concertation. Together with that, the growing presence of social policy issues in collective bargaining offers good prospects for trade unions' continuity.

As for the impact of political devolution on welfare, undoubtedly the intense Spanish political and administrative decentralization since the transition to democracy has transformed a previously unitary state into one of the most decentralized states in Europe. Against the widespread perception of growing disparities among the 17 autonomous regions of Spain due to increasing decentralization, Gallego and Subirats (Chapter 6) emphasize that some of the territorial differences in terms of provision and services are not the product of the devolution process as such, but rather inherited territorial inequality from the past. Moreover, the authors signal significant evidence of policy learning and lines of convergence whether in economic development in some cases or in public coverage of services in others – although without a positive correlation between the two. Gallego and Subirats' positive assessment of decentralization might be crucially influenced by their focus on two areas of the welfare state, namely education and health, which prior to being subjected to devolution to regional authorities were fully the competence of the central state. A very different picture is painted by Ayala (Chapter 13) in his analysis of minimum income policies, or Sarasa (Chapter 12) in his account of long-term care services. Both of these policy fields have developed in a more decentralized context where, in the absence of national minimum standards, disparities across all Autonomous Communities are noticeable with serious problems of coordination among the different territorial administrations. The subject of political devolution is also considered by Montagut in Chapter 7 when dealing with the mixed system of private and public provision of social services. She argues that the multi-level coordination needs of social services adds to the complexities of reaching a consensus on the different roles of the different administrations, as well as of the non-profit and for-profit private sector. Montagut, however, also concedes, as indeed do Gallego and Subirats, that the potential of decentralization lies in the less explored areas of the welfare state, such as social services and minimum income programmes, in the sense that it allows for some regions to be at the forefront of policy innovation, performing well above the national average.

In future studies of the effects of devolution on policymaking, the concluding question posed by Gallego and Subirats reminds us of an enduring issue in decentralization/convergence debates: that is, how to couple the values of equality and diversity. Two outstanding questions are *what* the desired balances are between hierarchical decision-making and learning dynamics among the different levels of government, and *why* they are so.

As shown by Calzada and Del Pino (Chapter 8), public support for the welfare state reflects to considerable extent diversity among the Autonomous Communities, with varying degrees of satisfaction/dissatisfaction with the welfare services offered in each region. All in all, however, Spaniards' evaluation of the performance of welfare services seems to be similar to average levels in other European welfare states.

Europeanization

All contributors to this volume agree that Spain's membership to the EU has had a big impact on the development and consolidation of its welfare state. EU integration has involved the development of common institutions and modes of governance at a supranational level, and the diffusion of procedures and policy paradigms with shared aims and objectives, including the use of benchmarks around which social outcomes can converge. Moreno and Serrano (Chapter 3) highlight three dimensions of the Europeanization process: first, the cognitive one that refers to how EU institutions provide different national actors with key concepts and their articulation in political discourses, which offers additional symbolic hegemony and politic legitimacy; second, the definition of procedures of policy implementation within a model of multi-level governance; and third, the dissemination of a series of indicators and comparative statistics. In the authors' view, this European frame of reference favoured a significant consensus among Spanish political parties and social partners to promote the expansion of the Spanish welfare state. Moreno and Serrano stress how the European influence in Spain was further strengthened by Spain's historical background, which made most national actors conflate the ideas of Europe and modernity, making strategic use of Europe to support their agendas. Moreover, both main political parties have often referred to Europe in difficult moments, such as unpopular labour market and public pension reforms, as a 'blame-avoidance' device.

The 'deep and intense' effects, in Moreno and Serrano's terms, of the Europeanization processes on Spain's model of social protection are illustrated in a number of chapters. Calzada and Del Pino (Chapter 8) point towards a process of European convergence in citizens' opinion of the welfare state. Ibáñez (Chapter 9) argues that the origin, method and content of the national agreement on stable part-time employment signed in 1998 were significantly influenced by the European Directive on part-time employment. Likewise, Salido (Chapter 10) concludes that the introduction of policies for the reconciliation of work and family life in Spain have been crucially inspired by EU hard law (especially EU Directives on maternity and parental allowances) and soft law (to meet targets and benchmarks set up under the Lisbon Agenda). Even the process of devolution that seems so specific to the Spanish case has been implemented following the European principle of subsidiarity.

Present and Future Challenges of the Spanish Welfare State

The links between social protection and a dualized labour market with recurrent high rates of unemployment and a permanently high number of precarious jobs is arguably the main present and future challenge facing Spanish society. No other reality shows this better than the persistence since the 1990s of chronically high levels of poverty and inequality, among the highest in the EU. Chapter 13 by

Ayala reveals how, despite substantial development of the main redistributive policies of social protection, Spanish levels of social benefit remain inadequate. The implementation of an extended system of means-tested benefits has had a significant impact in alleviating the crudest forms of hardship, but so far has proved clearly inefficient in changing the structural patterns of poverty in Spain. The fact that the economic expansion of 1997–2008, which led to a spectacular increase in employment levels, did not translate into lower levels of poverty is perhaps the most unsettling reality.

The very high levels of unemployment that the Spanish labour market has to endure at the moment of writing is to a large extent a consequence of a model of economic growth that was highly successful in job creation (and praised by the European Commission) but at the cost of increasing inequalities in the labour market. Several authors in this volume concur on the need for labour market reforms to facilitate access to employment by the most vulnerable groups and at the same time to reduce the number of working poor. Ibáñez (Chapter 9) sheds some light on the difficulties to consolidate flexible forms of employment that do not lead to vulnerable situations. Low Spanish part-time is a revealing example of the troubles of Spanish labour market institutions to come up with new solutions and learn from other experiences, given that part-time is the most extended form of working-time flexibility across Europe. Here, we find another case of 'institutional inertias' difficult to challenge. The eight-hour working day is still the main normative reference since it was first imposed by regulation in 1919, and the average working week for the core group of male full-timers has remained almost unchanged since 1977, which contributes to make Spain the EU country with the third-longest working hours, after Portugal and Greece. The high levels of temporary contracts, an unintended consequence of Spanish labour market regulatory decisions in the 1980s and 1990s, together with low salaries, do not help to make part-time attractive to the trade unions and many employees. More striking, however, as it is more clearly linked to public policies' capacities, is the even lower levels of stable part-time in the public sector. Significant institutional constraints have to be taken into account to understand the problems in replacing severe labour segmentation with flexi cure alternatives.

Certainly, the Spanish welfare state has not found it easy to adopt a consistent and coherent approach to its different challenges, as it has had to cope at the same time with two main kinds of demands. On the one hand is the urge to converge with its European neighbours in a very short period of time in the provision of key services such as education or health, in a context where the social consensus that was at the origin of leading European welfare states has started to dwindle in those same countries. On the other hand is the unavoidable need to respond to new and explosive (because of their magnitude and speed) changes, mainly the massive entrance since the 1990s of young cohorts of women into the labour market – a process that in other European nations took decades; but also the huge influx of economic immigrants, around five million in just ten years – over 10 per cent of the total population – one of the most intense immigration processes of the industrialized countries, which has transformed a highly uniform society into one that is distinctly multicultural. Here, too, what in other countries took generations has happened in Spain within the short time span of a decade. The new role of women, despite revealing important gaps in care-giving, was a change that was pursued socially and politically, and in a sense was significantly foreshadowed in the 1970s and the 1980s by the massive entrance of women into higher education and the growing female presence in skilled and male-dominated occupations. By contrast, high immigration has been a more surprising, less anticipated phenomenon, and the capacities of the different welfare dimensions to juggle with its effects are being put to test.

Laparra (Chapter 11) highlights significant issues arising from this recent episode of mass international migration. First, the economic dynamism of the 1997–2008 demanded, and hugely benefited from, foreign labour, and the informal and irregular parts of important sectors of the Spanish economy contributed to easing the flow. Second, the largely successful institutional embrace of rapid immigration before the recession is not easily continued in times of economic difficulty. The challenge in this case is the extent to which Spanish social policies, in a context of a dualized labour market with, as Ayala points out, at best a mixed achievement in terms of equality and cohesion, will be able to deal with the still limited social integration of migrant workers.

Last but not least, the ageing of the Spanish population due to the combined effects of rising life expectancy and a falling birth rate (among the highest and the lowest respectively in Europe) requires a revision of an allegedly predominant feature of the Spanish welfare state: that of familism in welfare provision. As Sarasa points out in Chapter 12, the unequal distribution of burdens among social classes and genders has limited women's opportunities in the labour market. Although the 2006 law on long-term care (*Ley de Dependencia*) can be read as a big step towards 'defamilization', in reality reliance on informal family provision continues to be the norm.

To conclude, in the near future the Spanish welfare state will have to cope with two kinds of demands: those arising from its present shortcomings and lagging developments; and, no less important, those originating in the successes in which the welfare state has already played a crucial part, such as the new role of women, an ageing population and the 'cohesion puzzles' of post-industrial societies. In the future, the demands posed by an ageing population and female integration in the labour market, and the need to adapt to international circumstances (especially Europeanization and neo-liberal globalization) within a national context characterized by decentralization and political conflicts between the main actors, will test the resilience of the coordinative and consensus-building capacities of the Spanish welfare state.

Index